D1379714

The Evolving Role of
Statistical Assessments as
Evidence in the Courts

Stephen E. Fienberg
Editor

The Evolving Role of Statistical Assessments as Evidence in the Courts

Panel on Statistical Assessments as Evidence in the Courts

Committee on National Statistics and Committee on Research on Law Enforcement and the Administration of Justice

Commission on Behavioral and Social Sciences and Education

National Research Council

Springer-Verlag
New York Berlin Heidelberg
London Paris Tokyo

1989

Stephen E. Fienberg, Department of Statistics, Carnegie Mellon University, Pittsburgh, PA 15213, USA

NOTICE: The project that is the subject of this report was approved by the Governing Board of the National Research Council, whose members are drawn from the councils of the National Academy of Sciences, the National Academy of Engineering, and the Institute of Medicine. The members of the committee responsible for the report were chosen for their special competences and with regard for appropriate balance.

This report has been reviewed by a group other than the authors according to procedures approved by a Report Review Committee consisting of members of the National Academy of Sciences, the National Academy of Engineering, and the Institute of Medicine.

The National Research Council was organized by the National Academy of Sciences in 1916 to associate the broad community of science and technology with the Academy's purposes of furthering knowledge and advising the federal government. Functioning in accordance with general policies determined by the Academy, the Council has become the principal operating agency of both the National Academy of Sciences and the National Academy of Engineering in providing services to the government, the public, and the scientific and engineering communities. The Council is administered jointly by both Academies and the Institute of Medicine.

Library of Congress Cataloging-in-Publication Data
The Evolving role of statistical assessments as evidence in the courts
    / Stephen E. Fienberg, editor.
        p.   cm.
    Bibliography: p.
    Includes indexes.
    1. Forensic statistics—United States.   I. Fienberg, Stephen E.
    KF8968.75.E96   1988
    349.73′021—dc19
    [347.30021]   88-31207

Printed on acid-free paper

Camera-ready copy prepared by the editor using T$_E$X.
Printed and bound by R.R. Donnelley and Sons, Harrisonburg, Virginia.
Printed in the United States of America.

9 8 7 6 5 4 3 2 1

ISBN 0-387-96914-4 Springer-Verlag New York Berlin Heidelberg
ISBN 3-540-96914-4 Springer-Verlag Berlin Heidelberg New York

Preface

With increasing frequency, the proof of facts in legal proceedings entails the use of quantitative methods. Judges, lawyers, statisticians, social scientists, and many others involved in judicial processes must address issues such as the evaluation and interpretation of quantitative evidence, the ethical and professional obligations of expert witnesses, and the roles of court-appointed witnesses. The Panel on Statistical Assessments as Evidence in the Courts was convened to help clarify these issues and provide some guidance in addressing the difficulties encountered in the use of quantitative assessments in legal proceedings.

This report is the culmination of more than three years of research and deliberation. In it, we address a variety of issues that arise in federal and state court proceedings when statistical assessments such as quantitative descriptions, causal inferences, and predictions of events based on earlier occurrences are presented as evidence. We appraise the forms in which such assessments are presented, aspects of their admission into evidence, and the response to and evaluation of them by judges and juries.

Our recommendations include several innovations to improve the comprehension of statistical evidence by judges and juries. In addition to jurists, who must evaluate statistical testimony, our report is addressed to lawyers, who may have occasion to draw on statistical testimony or to present factual arguments that incorporate statistical assessments; to statisticians, social scientists, and others who may serve as expert witnesses presenting statistical arguments; and to the research communities in law, statistics, and the social sciences that seek to understand how courts cope with unfamiliar and technically complex information. Our ultimate goal is to improve the legal process.

Our study was a joint effort of the Committee on National Statistics and the Committee on Research on Law Enforcement and the Administration of Justice. We benefited greatly from the suggestions and advice provided by the members of these committees, especially from their diverse areas of expertise and experiences, which they also ensured was well represented on the panel.

Some who have read drafts of this report have asked why the scope of the report is limited to statistical assessments as evidence when many of the same issues arise when courts in general are faced with complex scientific testimony. The sponsoring committees debated this point in developing the study and agreed that statistical evidence was sufficiently rich to cover the important issues in a variety of applications, especially in the social sciences, without being so broad a topic as to be intractable of study by a small panel. We acknowledge, however, that, had the members of the sponsoring committees not been jurists, social scientists, and statisticians, another focus for the study might have been chosen. We have attempted to indicate some of the points where the results of our study extend to scientific or complex evidence in general, but the reader may still justifiably feel that other topics discussed primarily in the context of statistics and statistical evidence are applicable more broadly to science and scientific evidence.

The study was funded by the National Science Foundation. We are grateful to Felice Levine, head of the NSF Law and Society Program, and Jerome Sacks and the NSF Division of Mathematics for their valuable advice. The West Publishing Company graciously donated use of WESTLAW for computer-assisted searching of legal research. A special leasing arrangement was made by direct aid for us to have software to access WESTLAW. The Federal Judicial Center, especially through Joseph Cecil, provided valuable advice and access to legal resources. The Center for Advanced Study in the Behavioral Sciences hosted the panel for one of its meetings and also provided resources that aided the preparation of this report, while one of us was a Center fellow.

We also benefited greatly from the thoughtful and scholarly work of several consultants: Thomas J. Campbell, John H. Langbein, Daniel L. Rubinfeld, and Neil Vidmar. Appendix H, which reviews the impact of statistical evidence in the legal system, was prepared for the panel by Neil Vidmar after the main text was completed in order to supplement the report's discussion of relevant social science literature on the topic. While the panel had previously reviewed some of the materials cited in this appendix and had chosen not to discuss or reference them, the alternative perspective provided by this supplemental material should prove valuable to many readers. Gordon J. Apple, National Research Council fellow and Albyn C. Jones, research associate—both with the Committee on National Statistics—served as staff on the study and made important contributions to the preparation of this report. A number of other Committee on National Statistics staff, including Edwin D. Goldfield, Roberta R. Pirosko, Anne M. Sprague, Kristine L. Smith, Eleanor M. Bateman, and Michele Zinn, provided highly competent administrative and secretarial assistance. Jeffrey A. Roth, study director of the Committee on Research on Law Enforcement and the Administration of Justice, provided valuable input at several stages in the panel's deliberations. Christine L. McShane, in the Commission on Behavioral and Social Sciences and Education, through careful editing of our report, made many improvements. Eugenia Grohman of the Commission provided valuable assistance in the review of the report, as well as in its editing and production. To all we are very grateful.

Our special appreciation goes to Margaret L. Smykla of the Department of Statistics, Carnegie Mellon University, and to Lee R. Paulson and Miron L. Straf of the Committee on National Statistics. Margaret Smykla typed innumerable drafts of the panel report and supervised the computer-based photo-typesetting of the final version on equipment at Carnegie Mellon University. Lee Paulson helped in the editing of the report and provided research and library assistance that was crucial in the completion of our work. Finally, we thank Miron Straf, who, as research director of the Committee on National Statistics, guided the development of the study from its inception as an idea, through the preparation of a proposal and appointment of the panel, to the development of this report. By serving as study director for this project, he participated in and guided our work. In addition to planning our meetings and coordinating our investigations, deliberations, and drafts, he also organized presentations at professional societies and even the development and production of a mock trial, which illustrated many of the issues discussed in this report.

May 30, 1988   Stephen E. Fienberg
                                Samuel Krislov
                                Cochairs, Panel on Statistical Assessments
                                as Evidence in the Courts

Contents

Contents

1

Introduction

1.1 Overview

This report addresses a variety of issues arising from the use of statistical evidence and analysis in federal and state court proceedings in the United States. The panel has examined these issues from the perspectives of statistics, of law, and of the behavioral and social sciences. This report states the assumptions and limitations of the inquiry, specifies the methods and findings, and makes recommendations aimed at improving the use of statistical knowledge in court settings.

In addressing the law-statistics nexus, the panel has assumed that statistical knowledge will continue to be needed and used in litigation. This use will include quantitative descriptions, causal inferences, and predictions of future events based on earlier occurrences.

The effectiveness with which statistical knowledge can address issues in litigation depends on the type of statistical usage. In general, statistical analysis is most widely accepted when the question is confined to descriptive statistics. Greater uncertainty emerges in causal inference, since real-world conditions rarely provide the equivalent of experimental control. Finally, projections of future outcomes based on earlier events compound the uncertainties of causal inference with the additional problems of changing conditions and factors over time.

In recent years statisticians and others who use statistical methods have participated in the legal process with increasing frequency, both as consultants and as expert witnesses. This trend can be attributed in part to the increasing amount of information relevant to legal cases that requires statistical interpretation. Use of statistical experts also rests on the belief, among legal decision makers and others in the society, that both statistical knowledge and its applicability to real problems involving inferences have increased. This belief reflects the evolution of statistics as a body of knowledge and as a professional activity, especially over the past 85 years.

The increasing use of statistics in legal proceedings creates the need for a critical appraisal of how this body of information and expertise is in fact used. Are good statistical demonstrations being rejected by courts because they are not properly understood? Are defective demonstrations given credence because their defects have not been noticed or understood? Are these problems with the use of statistical testimony more severe than in other areas of specialized knowledge used in the law? This report addresses these questions and, through a series of case studies and reviews of areas of litigation, suggests ways in which settled statistical knowledge and methodological issues can be more accurately and effectively used by the courts.

One of the special features of statistics as a field of knowledge is its use by those in a broad spectrum of fields, e.g., in biology, in medicine, and in the behavioral and social sciences. As a language for analyzing data and drawing inferences, statistics is used by professionals in a variety of disciplines, and experts from these disciplines often use statistical methods as part of their presentations to the court. The use of statistical arguments in the legal setting thus allows for introduction of inter- as well as intradisciplinary disputes between statistical experts.

Moreover, experts employing statistical analyses for causal inferences frequently reach different conclusions depending on the method employed to handle aspects of sampling variability, model specification, the choice of explanatory variables, and so on. Legitimate bases of disagreement cannot be banished by judicial fiat, nor can a panel such as this one attempt to resolve them. But knowledge of the origins of these expert differences can and should be available to triers of fact and to appellate judges to help explain the opposing views of the experts. This report suggests ways in which the courts can be more effectively informed on the bases of these differences and how they can best be handled.

This report is intended to serve several audiences: (1) jurists who must evaluate statistical testimony and occasionally preside over a battle of expert witnesses, (2) lawyers who may have occasion to draw on expert statistical testimony in a case or to present statistical evidence in a form understandable to courts, (3) statisticians who are called on to serve as expert witnesses or to prepare expert testimony, (4) the researchers in law, social science, and related fields who seek to understand how courts do and can cope with unfamiliar and technically complex information. In particular, many of the issues examined in this report have implications for basic research in statistics and in law and social science, in which the concern is with understanding the legal process and its broader relationship to society. Our ultimate goal is improvement of the legal process.

All members of the panel concur in the formal recommendations presented in the report. The material incorporated in it, however, is the product of compromise. The report is intended for a wide spectrum of readers—sophisticated lawyers who know little about statistics, sophisticated statisticians who know little about law, both well-informed and little-informed laypersons, as well as a few who are familiar with both law and statistics. As a consequence, there is wide variation in the depth and the width of the discussions. Nevertheless, much of the information and analysis embodied in this report will, we believe, be useful to all of these audiences and provide a basis for helpful work in the future as well as a better understanding of where we stand now.

1.2 The Field of Statistics and Statistical Assessments

The term *statistics* is often used to mean data or information. Here we use statistics in a more specific sense. Statistics as a professional discipline is concerned with the systematic and efficient collection and accurate analysis of data and with the development of methods to make inferences from data. The collection of data may involve observational studies (studies in which the selection of data or conditions under which observations are made are not under the control of the investigator), sample surveys, censuses, or randomized controlled experiments. The analysis of data is the attempt to extract useful information from a set of data. Statistics is concerned both with the logic of scientific method and with how we learn from data.

For the purposes of this report a *statistical assessment* is an interpretation of statistical data—a reasoned judgment—informed by knowledge of and experience in statistics. Since a statistical assessment is based on data and statistical analyses of them, it must inevitably take into account how the data were collected. Statistical assessments may take a variety of forms including:

(1) The presentation, analysis, and interpretation of descriptive statistics relating to the social, demographic, or economic characteristics of a population.

(2) Statistical inferences, in particular those relating to cause and effect, from analyses of special sample surveys, censuses, controlled experiments, or observational studies.

(3) Projections of future events or outcomes based on analyses of earlier events.

(4) Theories, hypotheses, and opinions that are advanced and developed by experts based on personal inferences, interviews, observations, reviews of research, and other limited studies that provide support for opinions but that do not necessarily generalize to a population relevant to the case at hand.

Inferences regarding cause and effect in virtually all legal cases depend heavily on subject matter assumptions. Only when randomized controlled experiments have been done directly on the cause and effect of interest does statistical inference provide a vehicle for avoiding such substantive assumptions.

Most statistical evidence does not fall neatly into one or another of these four categories, but one can see general patterns of how statistical evidence is used. For example, in school desegregation cases, the first type of evidence, the interpretation of statistics describing a population, is primary;

for the most part, this form of evidence helps to describe (or to decide) the degree of racial segregation in residential neighborhoods and schools. In employment discrimination cases, the second type of evidence, involving statistical inference from observational studies, has generally been used in attempts to infer discriminatory practices in employee selection, promotion or remuneration, frequently through elaborate regression studies that seek to control for the effects of other factors on which hiring, promoting, and wage setting can be based. Description and inference are often combined with prediction, as in school desegregation cases in which experts project the impact of new policies. Finally, many assessments involve implicitly—or occasionally explicitly—expert opinions about the quality of the data collected, the measurement of nonresponse, the choice of a level of significance, and potential sources and effects of bias.

One school of statistical thought defines statistics as the science of decision making under uncertainty and, since courts deal with uncertainty in reaching decisions, this school argues formal statistical theory can provide a proper framework for improving judical decision making. Indeed, terms and phrases such as "beyond a reasonable doubt," "preponderance of evidence," "more likely than not," and "substantial probability of cause" are arguably subject to statistical representation and analysis. While the use of statistics has burgeoned in court cases, this use has almost never extended to quantifying and analyzing the uncertainty reflected in legal terms. Some courts have, in fact, resisted such application. For example, some judges in their instructions to juries still discourage them from referring to probabilities (*U.S.* v. *Clay*, 476 F.2d 1211 (9th Cir. 1973)), and equate "beyond a reasonable doubt" with moral certainty rather than with any probability value.

This report does not focus on the use of statistics and probabilistic thinking for judicial decision making, even though some of the panel members are advocates of such an approach. Appendix A contains a brief summary of the controversy surrounding suggestions for the formal use of probability for judicial decision making, and a description of attempts to quantify standards of proof in civil and criminal litigation. Although there are occasional references in the report to these issues, the primary focus remains on statistical experts and their more limited role in the legal process as expert witnesses presenting statistical assessments of data or as consultants preparing analyses for counsel but not actually testifying.

Throughout this volume we use the term *statistician* to refer to those with formal training in the field of statistics, and who in some form identify themselves as such, e.g., via membership in professional associations. Many professionals in other fields do statistical work and testify as *statistical experts* in courts on issues such as data collection, analysis, and inference. Such professionals often have considerable background in statistics and some belong to umbrella statistical organizations such as the American Statistical Association.

The panel recognizes the difficulty in measuring expertise in statistics, and in separating statistical and substantive expertise, especially when the statistical issues in actual litigation are almost always embedded in subject matter such as economic determinants of labor markets. The courts exercise considerable discretion in deciding what qualifications are appropriate for experts testifying on statistical issues, and the panel concluded that it would be inappropriate for it to recommend formal standards for the identification of statistical experts.

Many of the issues surrounding the role of statistical experts are similar to those related to the role of scientific experts in other fields (e.g. see Saks and Van Duizend, 1983, and Black, 1988). The panel would have liked to broaden the scope of its inquiry to explore whether it is possible to distinguish between those problems confronting most technical experts and those that appear to be distinctly statistical in nature. Unfortunately, this was too extensive a task given the limited funds available. Nonetheless, there are some points in the report where the panel tried to indicate that the issues or concerns raised in the context of statistical evidence are applicable more broadly to scientific evidence.

1.3 Methodology

In developing this report we, as panel members,

(a) pooled our collective experiences,

(b) searched for cases or opinions using statistical materials,

(c) solicited information on cases through announcements in professional newsletters,

(d) listened to presentations from invited experts,

(e) commissioned background papers, and

(f) engaged in discussions, often heated, of the ethical and professional obligations of statistical experts and lawyers working in this area.

The panel examined cases in which statistical evidence was introduced, but we did not attempt by interviews with decision makers to determine what influence such evidence had on the resolution of the case beyond that expressed in the formal opinion or decision.

The panel also attempted a systematic review of selected areas of litigation and, in the process, took note of the legal and statistical commentaries that have been published on actual and potential uses of statistical assessments in the legal process. In particular, the panel has examined treatises on the uses of statistical assessments in the law (e.g., see Baldus and Cole, 1980; Barnes, 1983; Eggleston, 1983; and Finkelstein, 1978) as well as articles published in legal, statistical, and social science journals.

1.4   Early Uses of Probability and Statistics in the Law

Reference is often made to the prediction of Oliver Wendell Holmes, Jr. (1897), that in law "the man of the future is the man of statistics and the master of economics." When Holmes wrote those words statistics had yet to emerge as an organized discipline, and the bulk of the statistical methods that have formed the tools of expert witnesses in recent years— e.g., confidence intervals, multiple regression analysis, and even probability sampling—had not been developed. Since the time of Holmes, there have also been major changes in the law, especially with regard to expert testimony, and more specifically to expert statistical testimony.

The recognition of the probabilistic nature of legal inference goes back at least to antiquity, and the informal use of statistical decision rules pervades much of Talmudic law. In modern times, however, prior to Holmes, attempts to apply probability and statistics to the law rarely reached the courtroom. There are the writings of the early probabilists, such as Leibniz, Jacob Bernoulli, Nicholas Bernoulli, Cordorcet, Laplace, and Poisson, on the topic, as well as texts on evidence by lawyers, such as Starkie, addressing matters of quantification. But, with a few exceptions, these early discussions had little impact on legal practice. Some of this early history is described in more detail in Appendix B, along with vignettes illustrating the actual use of statistics as evidence or in legal opinions in selected cases through approximately 1960. Few of the cases described there, however, actually involved presentations by expert witnesses using statistical methods.

It was only in the 1950s that a more accepting attitude toward statistics began to emerge, primarily due to the increasing acceptance of sampling evidence, especially in administrative settings. There is one early instance of a sample survey being received into evidence (*U.S.* v. *Aluminium Co. of America*, 35 F.Supp. 823 (S.D.N.Y. 1940)), but surveys were rarely given any substantial weight until nearly 20 years later, in the case of *U.S.* v. *E.I. du Pont*, 177 F.Supp. 1 (N.Ill. 1959). A sample of stockholders was used to determine the potential tax implications of a particular event.

Given the burgeoning judicial resort to statistics now taking place, it is easy to overlook the limited, fragmentary, and suspicious attitude of much of the law to statistical forms of proof prior to 1960. But it is useful to remember that the science of statistics has itself undergone a tremendous expansion during the twentieth century, especially in the years after World War II. The increasingly pervasive legal use of statistics in accounting, employment discrimination, environmental protection, antitrust, product liability, and other types of cases may merely reflect the increasingly pervasive acceptance of statistics throughout society generally.

1.5   The Increasing Volume of Statistical Argument

A search of published opinions in federal courts with a computer-based legal information retrieval system reveals the dramatic growth since 1960 in cases involving some form of statistical evidence. Between January 1960 and September 1979 the terms *statistic(s)* or *statistical* appeared in about 3,000 or 4 percent of the 83,769 reported district court opinions. In the courts of appeals, the same terms appeared in 1,671 reported opinions.

Table 1-1 gives the frequencies of use in reported opinions of some specific statistical terms as aggregated over several classes of federal cases for various time periods through February or March 1982. For terms with nonstatistical meanings as well, the cases were reviewed to ensure that the terms searched on were used in their statistical meaning.

Additional sorting of cases by periods of time indicate that most of the references to more complex statistical techniques are quite recent. For example, of the 46 references to regression, only 3 occurred prior to 1972, and most appeared in 1977 or later, with 20 references in the 2-1/2 years between September 1979 and February 1982. Thus courts are being faced with increasingly more complex forms of statistical material.

The preceding exploration of court workloads counts only cases for which there are published opinions and makes no attempt to assess the burden to courts from them. Cases involving statistical arguments often take more court time and more hours of reflection by the judges involved than do nonstatistical cases. In addition, published opinions reveal only some of what actually occurs in the courtroom, and they rarely provide information about unappealed jury trials. Moreover, even when statistical witnesses play a substantial role at trial, the reported opinion may not contain any key statistical terms that allow computerized information retrieval of the kind we used in our search. A judge, for example, might not use the testimony of statistical experts in the preparation of the opinion, perhaps because the testimony was difficult to understand. Finally, a large proportion of civil cases involving statistical experts are settled either before or during trial, and no published reference is made to the statistical component of these cases, even though they use substantial court resources, including the time of judges, magistrates, and clerks. Thus the actual burden that statistical evidence imposes on courts is difficult to assess.

There are several explanations for the growing use of statistical argument. First, expanding government regulation has brought before the courts and regulatory agencies factual issues that invite its use, and many of the resulting court cases are inherently statistical in nature. Second, statisti-

TABLE 1–1: Numbers of Reported Opinions in Which
Selected Statistical Terms Were Used*

Statistical Terms	No. of Opinions
type I and type II error	3
scatter diagram, scattergram	5
significance level	10
analysis of variance	10
sample survey	14
least squares	16
correlation coefficient	19
chi-square(d)	40
regression	46
degrees of freedom	47
sample size	94
statistical inference, statistical significance	151

*Opinions searched using the LEXIS
retrieval system:

U.S. Supreme Court	1/25–3/82
Courts of appeals	1/60–2/82
District courts	1/70–2/82
Courts of claims	1/77–2/82

cal expertise and methodology are now regularly utilized by advocates to reduce large masses of data to manageable and interpretable dimensions, and increasing numbers of social scientists and statisticians are interested in applying experimental and statistical techniques to legal questions, both as scholars and as expert witnesses. Third, access to computers is easier and cheaper than ever before, thus making statistical data easily manipulable and highly accessible. Fourth, more younger lawyers feel at ease with statistical arguments because of graduate and undergraduate training in statistics and the social sciences. Several law schools have added courses on statistical methods to their curricula. Fifth, the Supreme Court's apparent reliance on statistical approaches in recent years has generally legitimized and in some situations virtually mandated the use of statistical arguments. Sixth, the financial stakes in many areas of litigation have become substantially higher, making many parties and their lawyers more willing to invest in statistical expertise. Finally, the enactment of the Federal Rules of Evidence in the mid–1970s eased restrictions on the use of expert witnesses, including those who focus on statistical issues.

1.6 Costs and Benefits Associated With Increased Use of Statistics

The benefits associated with the increased use of statistics in the courts are relatively easy to state. Statistical methods and forms of analysis can be invaluable in presenting succinct summaries of complex data, in providing a reliable basis for inference and predictions, in providing quantitative estimates of damages, and in clarifying loose verbal formulations of complex relations. Properly used, statistical approaches can benefit the court in much the same fashion that statistics has assisted those who work in other disciplines. For example, Adams et al. (1982) documents the important role played by statistical planning and analysis in major advances in behavioral and social science research.

Some of the costs to the legal system of increased statistical usage can, in principle, be measured in dollar terms. For example, there are the direct costs incurred by the parties in hiring and preparing expert witnesses. There will also be additional court hours for the presentation of statistical assessments as evidence and greater time spent by the fact finder to evaluate such evidence. These costs increase with the increased complexity and volume of the data analyzed and the complexity of the statistical analysis employed.

Other costs are more difficult to quantify. Limited familiarity with statistical forms of argument sometimes leads judges to make technical errors when evaluating statistical evidence, and such errors can lead to erroneous legal judgments. Moreover, as trials come increasingly to depend on nonintuitive statistical procedures, there is a danger that the perception that justice has been done in a case will become obscured. Finally, there are potential costs to the statistical profession when lawyers and judges view statisticians as partisan actors in the legal process. As we see in what follows, there are ways to reduce some of these costs for both the legal process and the legal and statistical professions.

1.7 Outline of Report and Summary of Principal Recommendations

1.7.1 Outline

Chapter 2 of the report contains six case studies—three involving employment discrimination, one an environmental matter, one antitrust damages, and one identification evidence in a criminal proceeding. The case studies illustrate what happens when statistical assessments are introduced as evidence and the reactions of the courts to such evidence. The cases were chosen to illustrate issues and problems that the panel believes are of broader interest and concern. These issues and problems are discussed in an integrated form at the end of the chapter, with specific references to the case studies, and then in greater detail and generality in Chapters 4 and 5.

Chapter 3 provides in-depth reviews of the use of statistics in three areas of litigation: antitrust, employment discrimination, environmental issues. These areas reflect the growth in the use of statistical assessments described above. Each review discusses several important or landmark cases and the commentaries on them, indicates the statistical techniques used, notes how and by whom they are introduced into evidence, and provides references for the reader to other reviews and relevant commentary. Five of the six case studies in Chapter 2 fit into the broader pictures presented in these reviews.

The cases and area reviews reflect problems posed for the courts in the use of statistical assessments. Chapter 4 gives a more general treatment of these issues, setting them in the context of the differences between and commonalities in legal and statistical thinking. Chapter 5 explores some possible solutions to the problems that statistical assessments pose for the legal process. Below we summarize the key issues on which the panel focused and present the panel's principal recommendations. For a more detailed justification of these recommendations the reader must turn to Chapter 5.

1.7.2 Summary of Conclusions and Principal Recommendations

Role of the Expert Witness

Many practical considerations underlie the use of statistical assessments within the justice system. An expert is almost always hired by attorneys for a particular side, and, although an attorney's job is to act as an advocate for a client, this is not necessarily the role of a statistician. Because the U.S. judicial system is an adversarial one, however, an expert may identify and be identified with the side for which testimony is presented. The panel believes that the ethical obligation of an expert witness encompasses certain principles.

- Experts should not present opinions they do not believe, unless they make clear that the opinions are not their own.

- An expert ordinarily is under no legal stricture to volunteer information; nonetheless, professional ethics may compel such disclosure.

- Experts should not allow themselves to be used by an attorney for behavior that would be considered, for the attorney, unethical.

- Statistical experts must meet certain professional standards in preparing work products despite the lack of a legal obligation to undertake studies that might yield unwelcome results.

Preparation of formal statements of standards has not been given sufficient attention.

> Recommendation 1. *The panel recommends that professional organizations develop standards for expert witnesses in legal proceedings who use statistical assessments with respect to (1) procedures required to ensure reliability in connection with frequently used statistical techniques, (2) disclosure of methodology, and (3) disclosure of aspects of their work that may raise ethical considerations.*

Whether experts should work under contingency fee arrangements is a particularly difficult area of ethical responsibility. Several panel members believe that ethical standards should prohibit statisticians from accepting contingency fees and note the importance of avoiding both unethical conduct and the *appearance* of impropriety. Other panel members believe that experts who accept contingency fees should be allowed to testify if the court rules do not prohibit such arrangements. Panel members agreed that contingency fee arrangements should be made part of court records to permit the trier of fact to take account of that information when assessing expert testimony.

There are various means by which the testimony of an expert witness is held accountable by the legal system. The expert's qualifications may be examined and challenged. The expert's reports and testimony are subject to scrutiny and cross-examination. The evidence the expert presents is subject to rebuttal by other experts. And, of course, the law imposes a stricture on perjury. But courts look even beyond these means to hold the expert ultimately responsible to professional standards.

Regardless of whether an expert exhibits an allegiance to one party or an inclination to a particular point of view, the court may accept the credibility of testimony because the expert's knowledge and research methods devolve from a professional scientific community. Rather than being looked on by the court to present a view that is a consensus of statisticians or other scientists, experts are looked on to present their own views based on the principles and standards of their professional community. It is important that experts be cognizant that they represent their profession in this manner and that they conduct their research accordingly.

> Recommendation 2. *The panel recommends that statistical experts who consult or testify in litigation maintain a degree of professional autonomy similar to that associated with independent scientific research.*

Examples of such independence may include the following practices:

- If the expert testifies, or if his results are used in testimony by others, he be free to do whatever analysis and have access to whatever data are required to address the problems the litigation poses in a professionally respectable fashion.

- The expert be free to consult with colleagues who have not been retained by any party to the litigation.

- The expert receive an engagement letter that expressly provides for the above and other appropriate safeguards for independence that the expert deems necessary given the context of the case.

Statistics and Pretrial Discovery

Pretrial discovery of evidence in civil cases is frequently extensive and directly involves experts. Because the collection of acceptable statistical data is often expensive and agreement on the accuracy and scope of appropriate data, if not the analysis, is desirable, statistical issues may mandate greater pretrial judicial control than other issues involving experts.

The Manual of Complex Litigation, 2d (1985) recommends that pretrial procedures be adopted to facilitate the presentation of statistical evidence at trial and to reduce disputes over the accuracy of the underlying data and compilations derived from such data. It does not, however, suggest what procedures to use. To the panel's knowledge, only a special committee of the New York Bar has prepared detailed protocols for handling large-scale data bases. The panel found these protocols statistically sound and consistent with both the recommendations in the *Manual* and the goals of the panel.

Recommendation 3. *The panel recommends that, to facilitate understanding of statistical procedures and analyses, the legal profession should adopt procedures designed to (1) narrow statistical disputes prior to trial, particularly with respect to the accuracy and scope of the data and (2) disclose to the maximum extent feasible the methods of analysis to be used by the testifying experts. To foster these aims, the panel supports the development and use of protocols such as those recommended by the Special Committee on Empirical Data in Legal Decision Making of the Association of the Bar of the City of New York (see Appendix F).*

An attorney has an independent ethical obligation not to intentionally mislead the courts on the facts or the law. Although rules of professional legal conduct do not require an attorney to reveal adverse facts, the panel's view is that attorneys deliberately mislead courts if they reveal only the favorable portions of statistical analyses that have been done. It is inappropriate for an attorney to seek to hide unwelcome results of statistical analyses by consulting a series of experts, commissioning different analyses until favorable results are achieved, and presenting favorable results as if they were the only analyses conducted. It is also improper to retain an expert to testify without disclosing the history of the involvement of other similar experts in the litigation.

Recommendation 4. *In furtherance of the aim of full disclosure for experts, the panel recommends that, if a party gives statistical data to different experts for competing analyses, that fact be disclosed to the testifying expert, if any.*

Although the opinions of experts retained for litigation but not expected to be called as witnesses need not ordinarily be revealed to an opponent under Rule 26(b)(3)(B) of the Federal Rules of Civil Procedure, many members of the panel believe that the names of such nontestifying experts who have conducted statistical analyses should be revealed to opposing parties prior to trial.

Provision of Statistical Resources

The issue of unequal or inadequate resources to pay for expert assistance has been addressed recently in the context of criminal cases. Similar issues arise in civil litigation. If resources for gathering data are unequal, they are also likely to be unequal for the statistical analysis of the data. Part of this problem may be resolved through the discovery process.

Recommendation 5. *The panel recommends that a group be organized to supply expert statistical advice and assistance in selected cases in which the absence of such expertise might result in a denial of justice.*

The panel expects that experts working under the auspices of such a group would serve for modest fees or on a pro bono basis with reimbursement for expenses.

Role of Court-Appointed Experts

In reviewing the use of court-appointed experts in the U.S. system, the panel tentatively concluded that European judicial systems gain strength from their reliance on the use of neutral experts. The closest parallel in the U.S. system is the use of court-appointed experts. The Federal Rules of Evidence provide for the appointment of experts who can be used to assist the trier of fact in understanding statistical testimony and resolving conflicting statistical testimony.

> Recommendation 6. *The panel believes that judges have been unduly reluctant to appoint statistical experts to assist the court and it recommends the increased use of court-appointment procedures such as those provided by Rule 706 of the Federal Rules of Evidence.*

Enhancing the Capability of the Fact Finder

There are various methods by which lawyers and expert witnesses can enhance the capability of the fact finder to understand the issues and facts. The court also can be of assistance in focusing the issues. This may be done through judicial questions, comments, or instructions, by the appointment of experts, and by referring complicated issues to a master who can assimilate complex material and present it at trial (provisions for which are contained in Rule 53 of the Federal Rules of Civil Procedure and elsewhere).

Presenting statistical evidence so that it is both accurate and easily understood is a difficult task. In standard courtroom practice witnesses are presented sequentially with one party presenting all of its witnesses before the other party presents its witnesses. This traditional sequence of evidence and arguments is not necessarily the the most effective method, nor is it required by formal court rules. F.R.E. Rule 611 allows the trial judge to modify standard procedures for the presentation in the interests of intelligibility and efficiency and gives judges the authority to adjust trial procedures in ways that might make statistical evidence more understandable.

An additional problem with statistical presentations in the court is the role played by the judge in interpreting evaluations and assessments. Judges may use their background, training, and experience to evaluate and understand evidence that has been introduced. Furthermore, many judges discuss problems they confront with their law clerks and fellow judges. This type of informal discussion, particularly between judges, is generally viewed as legitimate. But judges may also conduct their own research to obtain information about the utility and validity of statistical evidence. In seeking to develop general understanding, they may review textbooks and other literature, whether or not it is introduced by a party. In certain situations, they may also reanalyze data provided to them. The latter, however, is seldom wise because the modes of self-education available to judges are unlikely to give them full appreciation of various factors that must be considered in performing and interpreting statistical analyses.

> Recommendation 7. *The panel recommends that, in general, judges should not conduct analytical statistical studies on their own. If a court is not satisfied with the statistical evidence before it, alternative means should be used to clarify matters, such as a request for additional submissions from the parties or even, in exceptional circumstances, a reopening of the case to receive additional evidence.*

Statistical Education

Judges and jurors are likely to be unfamiliar with the language of statistics and statistical concepts. Persons without special training often have difficulty evaluating statistical data and the inferences drawn from the data. One possible approach to this problem is to educate judges and jurors about statistics prior to or as part of the presentation of statistical evidence. A second possibility is for judges and jurors to examine witnesses when confused by testimony.

Most panel members strongly support the development of courses in statistics for law students; however, they also recognize that law school curricula already are overcrowded. An alternative method is to include statistical instruction in substantive courses treating areas in which statistical assessments are frequently involved. This use of this method would depend in part on the students' background and knowledge and would require instructors with some training in statistical methods.

> Recommendation 8. *The panel recommends that efforts be made to integrate instruction on basic statistical concepts into the law school curriculum and to provide instruction for practicing lawyers and judges on such matters. In law schools this can be done by allowing students to take for-credit courses outside the law school, by developing courses on statistics for lawyers, and, by discussing statistical issues and concepts in specific courses such as those dealing with antitrust law, discrimination, environmental law, evidence, and torts. For practicing attorneys and judges, such instruction may be provided by existing professional organizations, the Federal Judicial Center, programs for continuing legal education, and the like.*

A final aspect of education involves the preparation of critiques of the statistical approaches adopted in actual cases.

·   Recommendation 9. *The panel recommends that legal, statistical, and scientific journals publish, on a regular basis, critical statistical reviews of expert presentations and judicial opinions in cases involving important uses of statistics.*

Implications for Statistical Studies to Assist the Courts

There are situations in which one can foresee that litigation of important disputes affecting many people is likely to require statistical studies that transcend the capability of individual experts in particular cases. Examples include studies relating to the causes or effects of Agent Orange, asbestos, chemical dumps, DES, formaldehyde, thalidomide, and toxic shock syndrome.

> Recommendation 10. *The panel recommends that a mechanism be created whereby impartial bodies, such as the Centers for Disease Control, can consider conducting relevant studies in advance of, or during, particular litigation to assist the courts, other public bodies, and the public in evaluating the issues.*

Without neutral, well-financed, and timely studies of this kind, serious mistakes can be made such as those that authorize public access to unacceptably dangerous drugs and other substances or deny the public access to useful drugs and other substances when benefits outweigh risks.

2

Case Studies

2.1 Introduction

The panel uses a series of case studies to illustrate many of the points and issues in the use of statistical assessments as evidence. The choice of cases was strongly influenced by the knowledge about them possessed by individual panel staff and members, the interests of individuals in specific areas of litigation, and a variety of other factors.

These case studies are not a random sample from any universe of cases. They are intended to illustrate what happens when statistical assessments are introduced as evidence and the different ways in which courts react. The cases reflect issues and problems. At least one case illustrates a possible solution. Since the case studies were developed by different individuals and in different circumstances, there is substantial unevenness in the depth of discussion and detail. In some instances, only court opinions were examined. In others, relevant parties (judges, lawyers, and expert witnesses) were interviewed, and all documents pertaining to the statistical evidence in the court's possession were examined. In one instance, a separate case study had been carried out by Saks and Van Duizend (1983), and some information collected in interviews by them has been incorporated into the presentation here.

Three of the case studies are in the area of employment discrimination, which has been the primary area of litigation involving growth in the use of statistical assessments over the past decade.

1. *Vuyanich* v. *Republic National Bank* is a much-cited case that involved allegations of race and sex discrimination in a Texas bank. The case study examines aspects of the statistical presentations by nine different expert witnesses and the court's response to the conflicting statistical testimony, especially in connection with the principal statistical method used by these witnesses, multiple regression analysis. This case is notable for the extensive treatment of the statistical issues by the judge in his 127–page opinion.

2. *Carter et al.* v. *Newsday* also involved allegations of employment discrimination on the basis of sex by a newspaper publishing company. Many of the statistical issues raised in *Vuyanich* also were of concern in this case, but in *Carter* the judge chose to appoint a court expert to help resolve factual disputes over the data base, to reduce the differences between the parties, and to educate the judge about the statistical issues the case presented. The case was settled prior to trial.

3. *E.E.O.C.* v. *Federal Reserve Bank of Richmond* involved allegations

of race discrimination, and experts testified for both parties on statistical issues in connection with hiring, promotions, training, and wages. The primary statistical disputes revolved around the appropriateness of various methods for group comparisons and the choice of level of aggregation for the analysis of employment data. Questions about the statistical methodology used by the experts were also an important part of the appellate review and played a prominent role in the appellate decision.

A fourth case was chosen in the environmental area to illustrate the role of federal appellate courts in the review of decisions made by regulatory agencies.

4. In *Gulf South Insulation* v. *U.S. Consumer Product Safety Commission*, a federal appellate court overturned an order of the Consumer Product Safety Commission banning the use of urea-formaldehyde foam insulation in residences and schools. The major statistical issues that arose in this case involved (a) the choice of a risk assessment model to calculate the risk of increased incidence of cancer resulting from formaldehyde exposure and (b) the selection of quality of the data that were used in the model. Statistical experts and their reports were used by the commission in reaching its decision, and the written record was available for review by the court. The oral arguments in the case, however, involved attorneys for the parties and the three-judge panel but not the experts.

The use of probabilistic arguments and statistical information about identification in criminal cases has been the focus of considerable legal commentary. One of the panel's case studies focuses on a trio of cases involving the same form of probabilistic identification evidence.

5. *U.S. ex rel. DiGiacomo* v. *Franzen* was the third of a series of criminal cases involving the use of a probabilistic description of hair identification. The defendant was accused of rape and other offenses, and a criminologist compared hair found at the scene of the crime with hair taken from the defendant. Her testimony included the statement: "the chances of another person belonging to that hair would be 1 in 4,500." This case study reviews the scientific studies relied on by forensic experts testifying on matters of hair identification, explores how expert witnesses misinterpreted the results of these studies, and includes comments by various courts on probabilistic identification evidence.

The sixth case study reviews the analyses introduced by econometricians in the assessment of damages as part of an antitrust case.

6. *Corrugated Container Antitrust Litigation* involved two trials in class action litigation brought by purchasers of cardboard containers and corregated sheets against the manufacturers of these products. In the first trial, the plaintiffs' expert presented multiple regression analyses to estimate the overcharge during a 16–year "conspiracy period." The defendants challenged the expert's estimates but did not produce their own expert. The jury found for the plaintiffs. The second trial involved certain plaintiffs who had opted out of the original class. The same expert presented

similar evidence for the plaintiffs in this second trial, but this time his testimony was countered by that of another economist testifying for the defendants. The jury in this second trial found that, although a conspiracy had existed, it had not affected the prices paid by the plaintiffs, and thus it awarded no damages. The case study reviews the expert's testimony and the appellate review of the second trial.

The final section of this chapter attempts to draw some lessons from these case studies and examines issues and problems raised by the presentation of statistical assessments as evidence in the courts.

2.2 Case Study: Vuyanich v. Republic National Bank, 24 FEP Cases 128 (N.D. Texas 1980), vac. and rem'd. 723 F.2d 1195 (1984)

Introduction

The area of litigation that has generated the greatest demand for witnesses with expertise in statistics has surely been class action employment discrimination suits brought under Title VII of the Civil Rights Act of 1964. What follows is a review of one such case that has received considerable attention, *Vuyanich* v. *Republic National Bank.*

This case involves the liability phase of a class action claiming race and sex discrimination, under Title VII of the Civil Rights Act that at one point or another was assigned to five different judges of the Northern District Court of Texas. The plaintiff, Joan Vuyanich, is a black woman who worked for the Republic National Bank for three months in 1969 as an agent contact clerk in the money order department. On August 13, 1969, shortly after being discharged, Vuyanich filed a charge with the Equal Employment Opportunity Commission (EEOC) against the bank for discharging her because of her race and sex, in violation of Title VII. On November 6, 1972, the EEOC issued a determination of "reasonable cause to believe a violation" had occurred, which was followed shortly by the issuing of a "statutory right-to-sue letter." Vuyanich filed suit in district court and was subsequently joined by a second plaintiff, who filed separate charges with the EEOC, and three other plaintiffs ("intervenors"), who did not file such charges with the EEOC. These plaintiffs not only brought individual charges against the bank, but, following a complex procedural path through the court, they also were certified in early 1978 as "class representatives" for a class consisting of all women of all races and all blacks of either sex who (a) are or have been employed by the Republic National Bank on or after February 16, 1969, and (b) applied for employment but were not hired at the Republic National Bank on or after February 16, 1969, to date.

The trial took place over 24 days in October and November 1979, and Judge Patrick E. Higginbotham issued his opinion in October 1980, almost one year later.

The Expert Witnesses: Conflicting Statistical Evidence

The judge's opinion is notable both for its size, 127 printed pages, and for its treatment of the statistical issues. Almost 80 pages of the opinion are devoted to a review of "the mathematics of regression analysis" and its relevance to the case and to a detailed examination of the conflicting statistical evidence presented by the experts for the two parties. The opinion has been widely cited and studied by those interested in the use of statistics as evidence (e.g., see Fienberg and Straf, 1982; Saks and Van Duizend, 1983: 32–36; and Barnes, 1983, who devotes over 20 pages to excerpts from the opinion).

The plaintiffs, in presenting their case, used five expert witnesses whose evidence consisted of statistical assessments: two professors of economics, a professor of sociology and political economy, a professor of business, and a professor of geography and political science. None of these experts had a doctoral degree in statistics. The defendants countered with four statistical expert witnesses who presented alternative analyses and rebutted the testimony of the plaintiffs' experts: an economist, a professor of mathematical sciences, and two other social science professors. Only one of these experts possessed a doctoral degree in statistics; he and one of the other defendant's experts were the only expert witnesses who are listed as members of the American Statistical Association, the primary professional statistical association in the United States.

The experts in this case were found by the attorneys through word of mouth (Saks and Van Duizend, 1983:33):

> The EEOC recommended an expert whom they had been pleased with and that expert referred plaintiffs' lawyers to other competent experts. If the experts in this case were of especially high competence—and the consensus is that they were—that was because an especially well informed grapevine had been tapped. One attorney said that more experts were interviewed than hired and that the ability of the expert to communicate was the deciding factor.

With some exceptions, such as the use of Census Bureau data and a survey of bank employees, all data used by parties in the case were ultimately derived from records maintained by the bank as its permanent business records. The judge pressed the parties early to agree on and use a common data base, ordered production of that data base, and required that statistical briefs be filed before trial.

Each set of experts divided "the issues" in the case, and neither side attempted to present evidence that dealt with all of the issues through a single expert. The conflicting statistical testimony involved (a) somewhat

different versions of the data bases; (b) critiques of the opponents' choice
of variables and their treatment of measurement problems; (c) alternative summary statistics of the bank's hiring and employment practices; (d)
regression analyses involving different variables and different model specifications; and (e) critiques of the appropriateness of the specifications used
in the other side's regression analyses.

The reports prepared by the experts and submitted prior to trial were not
unusually voluminous, nor did they contain esoteric or even nonstandard
forms of statistical analyses. Saks and Van Duizend (1983:35) note that the
participants characterized the trial as lucid, yet hard to follow because it
was complex and dull:

> At the end of each day of trial the judge dictated notes and im-
> pressions of what had been learned during the day's testimony.
> He felt the lawyers were well prepared. The lawyers and experts
> commented that the best questions were those put to the ex-
> perts by the judge. The lawyers' questions were more likely to
> search for weaknesses or inconsistencies, while the judge's were
> more likely to go to the substantive heart of the evidence. That
> is not to say, however, that the lawyers did not also deal with
> substantive evidence. The judge employed flexible procedures
> in managing the trial. On several occasions he allowed experts
> to conduct what in essence was an in-court seminar through
> which they were invited to explain in more detail their underly-
> ing conceptualizations or mathematical procedures. Although
> the attorneys objected to this departure from the traditional
> procedures for eliciting testimony, they were overruled.

In and of themselves, neither the reports nor the testimony of the experts
at trial can account for the surprisingly detailed opinion. The judge subsequently revealed that he and his clerks took a full month off from their other
duties to devote themselves to understanding the evidence presented by the
experts and arguing about the findings to be reported. Indeed, perhaps it
was the paucity of evaluative technical details that may have convinced the
judge that he needed to provide appropriate background himself for others
to follow his evaluation. The judge also wanted to facilitate the consideration of his decision and his basis for it by the court of appeals. While
the opinion contains several statements regarding statistical analyses with
which many members of this panel would take issue, on balance it remains
a remarkable description of some basic statistical issues in a legal context,
something that even the most diligent and able judges can rarely take the
time to do.

The defendant appealed the original 1978 class certification, and the Fifth
Circuit Court of Appeals vacated the judgment in 1984 and remanded the
case to district court with directions to reconsider the determination of the
classes to be maintained. The appeals court discussed only briefly, at the

end of the opinion, the statistical analyses used at the trial itself, and it declined to reach judgment on their appropriateness. The appeals court did state that disparate treatment not disparate impact [1] should be the "model for the statistical measurement of discriminatory hiring claims" on remand. Despite this turn of events, the role of the expert statistical witnesses at the original trial and Judge Higginbotham's opinion are worthy of considerable study.

Extracts from the Judge's Opinion

Some quotes from the judge's opinion provide us with insights into the manner in which he approached the resolution of the conflicting statistical assessments and their importance for the legal issues under consideration (p.152):

> In light of ... the fact that the parties' approaches to the data assembly problem are facially reasonable and the fact that the parties' respective data bases are at their core quite similar, a heavy burden must be met before a party can justify the rejection *in toto* of any statistical analyses on grounds of errors or omissions in the data. Identification of flaws is helpful for later use in evaluating the results, but identification is not alone sufficient to warrant rejection. Instead, the challenging party bears the burden of showing that errors or omissions bias the data, i.e., that erroneous or omitted items are not distributed in the same way as items which are present and correct.

On the role of statistical evidence, and its meshing with the individual testimony, the judge noted (p.155):

> The anecdotal evidence ... lends support to the idea that any discrimination found in the statistical analyses is due to discriminatory behavior rather than to chance.

On the court's need to adjudicate between and extend the arguments of witnesses by performing its own analysis, the judge expressed great caution in remarking (p.154):

> Only where the expert has justified the use of an approach for a particular problem, evaluating the risks and limitations—ought the court to apply the technique in performing calculations not

---

[1]Disparate treatment occurs when an employer simply treats some employees less favorably than others because of their race, color, religion, sex, or national origin; Disparate impact occurs if the employer's practices are facially neutral in their treatment of different groups but nonetheless fall more harshly on one group than on another and cannot be justified by business necessity.

performed in the evidentiary presentation. ... An overwilling-
ness to undertake computational efforts also creates the risk of
decisional disparity. Courts with varying degrees of inclination
and ability in the application of complex technical approaches
to the solution of social problems will reach varying results, and
the outcome of cases requiring such application will turn more
on the plaintiffs' choice of forum and the luck of the draw in
the District Clerk's office than on the merits of the cases. Indeed, absent some neutral and consistently applied approach
to computation by the court, a court must risk the accusation
that it has picked and chosen among the data, performing or
not performing additional computations to suit a preconceived
result.

Finally, on a specific aspect of the testimony of two of the expert witnesses, the judge favored the impressions of one expert rather than another,
because of his assessment of their qualifications (p.203):

Dr. [X] quite properly asked why the "dummy coefficient" mode
of determining inequality of treatment of twins was used, rather
than the more general method wherein it would not be necessary to assume that all the coefficients for the explanatory variables are exactly the same for the two groups being compared.
... Dr. [Y] has testified that she had a "very strong guess" that
running separate regressions for males and females would not
affect her results. ... No evidence contradicted this empirical
judgment by an expert with a background in labor economics
who was familiar with the relevant empirical work. Dr. [X] is
an impressive expert as to statistical issues, but not as to labor
economics issues.

Given the large amount of space devoted in this opinion to issues of model
misspecification, it is surprising to see this aspect of model selection treated
so blithely. Many statisticians would take strong objection to the judge's
conclusions and would argue that the issue is indeed statistical and that
"guesses" of substantive experts are far from reliable in such circumstances.
The substantive theory of labor economics offers few clues as to how to proceed in such situations, but analyses in other Title VII cases have shown
that regression models for male and female employees have markedly different regression coefficients—differences that are also statistically significant
(see also the related discussion in McCabe, 1980).

The judge's findings in this case included the following on the issue of
compensation:

1. The plaintiffs established a prima facie case of race discrimination by the bank in compensation as to blacks, but only from

1973 on, by presenting regression analyses that compared jobs in terms of the bank's evaluation system. The dummy variable for race in the regressions had large, negative, and statistically significant coefficients.

2. The defendants presented regression analyses that they claimed show that sex and race are not statistically significant influences on pay. The judge found the defendants' model to be not probative because it did not control at all for work performed. "In the absence of more finely-tuned controls for work, the regressions tell too little about whether wage discrimination is occurring," the judge concluded, and thus these results "cannot rebut the plaintiff's regressions."

3. The plaintiffs used age as a proxy variable for experience. The judge viewed this as a serious error, especially as it affects women. The judge commented (p.201):

> Given the seriousness of this proxy error, the plaintiffs should have used actual measures of general experi-ence, or the plaintiffs should have met the burden of showing that such a serious proxy error did not sufficiently affect their assertions of discrimination. Plaintiffs did neither.

His ultimate conclusion was that the plaintiffs failed to establish a prima facie case of compensation discrimination for women.

4. The judge noted that he did not rely on the cohort analysis presented by the plaintiffs for his finding of discrimination, be-cause the analysis did "not control in any way for job level and so cannot be used in support of a wage discrimination claim."

On the other major issues of hiring, initial placement, and promotion, the judge ruled that the plaintiffs' statistical evidence established a prima facie case that the bank discriminated against black and female "nonexempt" (low-skill and moderate-skill) employees, and against black "exempt" (more highly skilled) employees. Moreover, he concluded that the defendant had failed to rebut this evidence. The plaintiffs' statistical evidence for female "exempt" employees was faulty or inadequate and failed to establish a prima facie case.

Implications

The opinion in *Vuyanich* highlights several of the issues regarding the evaluation of statistical assessments described elsewhere in this report. On each issue, the judge examined the data and the analyses and attempted to "apply the law to the data," first expounding the relevant legal principles and then asking how these principles apply in an examination of the statistical results. The give and take of the adversarial process and a consideration of the qualifications of the experts are presented in the opinion as a partial means of sorting out the evidence. While this case should not necessarily be thought of as a model for the evaluation of statistical assessments, it does suggest some standards that courts and other participants of the legal process may wish to ponder. These are best put in the judge's own concluding comments (p.254):

> This opinion has been written and rewritten, or equally accurate, has been calculated and recalculated, over the past year. It is modular in structure but hopefully possessed of sufficient internal consistency to squeeze as a whole into a traditional suit of judicial opinion. Even if that effort was successful, it has to judicial eyes a surrealistic cast, mirroring the techniques used in its trial. Excursions into the new and sometimes arcane corners of different disciplines is a familiar task of American trial lawyers and its generalist judges. But more is afoot here, and this court is uncomfortable with its implications. This concern has grown with the realization that the esoterics of econometrics and statistics which both parties have required this court to judge have a centripetal dynamic of their own. They push from the outside role of tools for "judicial" decisions toward the core of decision making itself. Stated more concretely: the precision-like mesh of numbers tends to make fits of social problems when I intuitively doubt such fits. I remain wary of the siren call of the numerical display and hope that here the resistance was adequate; that the ultimate findings are the product of judgment, not calculation.

The publication of the opinion in *Vuyanich* had a dramatic impact on those who were then engaged in Title VII litigation. It was widely read, not only by lawyers, but also by statistical experts who were preparing material for trial. Many parties who had retained a single statistical expert hurried to hire additional experts, especially economists. Moreover, the opinion was cited by other judges who often deferred to *Vuyanich* both on issues of law and on technical statistical issues. Despite the praise that was lavished on the opinion in print and the standards it seemed to set, there was disquiet expressed about the opinion in several quarters. Some attorneys felt that the opinion was leading to more elaborate presentations than were necessary and to an escalation in the costs of Title VII litigation. Others wondered how many judges would have the expertise to confront the issues that Judge Higginbotham described in his opinion. Their reservations were shared by some statistical experts who noted that the statistical assessments presented as evidence in *Vuyanich* were at best undistinguished and did not merit the lengthy disquisition provided by the opinion. For example, there was little attention paid by the experts of either side to the adequacy of the statistical models used, and none of the usual residual plots or regression diagnostics was presented. A briefer and more critical commentary by the judge may have been more to the point.

These criticisms notwithstanding, the *Vuyanich* opinion has had an important impact on Title VII litigation and has pointed the way toward improved use of statistical evidence.

2.3   Case Study: Carter et al. v. Newsday

Introduction

One of the issues explored in depth by the panel has been whether it is possible to enhance a judge's or jury's ability to resolve conflicting statistical evidence prepared by two sides in a legal setting. The problem of conflicting statistical testimony has become especially severe in complex civil litigation, and several authors have proposed the use of court-appointed experts as one means of facilitating resolution in such contexts (see, e.g., an early suggestion in a nonstatistical context by Learned Hand, 1902, or much more recently Fienberg, 1982). The adoption in 1975 of the Federal Rules of Evidence provided an explicit procedure, described in Rule 706 (see Appendix C), for the court to appoint expert witnesses of its own in civil cases. There are, however, few examples of the use of court-appointed statistical experts to date, and the effectiveness of this procedure remains in doubt in the minds of many. This case study, based on Coulam and Fienberg (1986), provides a description of a case settled before trial with no published opinion. For a detailed discussion of Rule 706 and its use, see Chapter 5.

Carter et al. v. *Newsday* involves a class action lawsuit brought in federal district court under Title VII of the Civil Rights Act of 1964. Plaintiffs were the female employees of (and applicants to) a medium-sized company, the defendant. The company's operations included management and professional positions (specifically in writing and editing), as well as sales, clerical, and basic production positions. The suit claimed that women faced discrimination by the company in hiring and initial job placement, promotions, wages, quality of work assignments, and personal treatment by male colleagues and superiors.

Outline of the Case

The lawsuit lasted approximately 8–1/2 years, from late 1973 to mid–1982. But it never reached trial—it was settled by the parties just before trial was scheduled to begin. The essence of the plaintiffs' complaint was that the defendant had engaged in patterns and practices of sex discrimination across its entire work force. These alleged discriminatory acts affected hiring, placement, promotions, wages, work assignments, and other practices of the defendant. These claims affected both applicants to and employees of the defendant, and the class certified by the court in 1976 included both applicants and employees.

During the course of the litigation, there was input from at least four statistical experts: one who prepared reports for the plaintiffs, two employed by the defendant, and a court-appointed expert. The plaintiffs' expert was a statistician who taught at a large eastern state university and had been employed as a statistical expert in many Title VII class action discrimination cases, working both for plaintiffs and for defendants. The defendant's experts were distinguished university professors, one with expertise in mathematical statistics and the other in economics, more specifically labor markets. Both of the defendant's experts had appeared as witnesses in several lawsuits, including Title VII class action cases. The court-appointed expert was a professor of economics, with strong expertise in statistical methodology. He had appeared as a witness in one previous case, not involving Title VII litigation. It is in exactly such situations, with strong statistical experts on both sides of the case, that the adversarial nature of court proceedings often makes it difficult for a judge to reconcile conflicting statistical evidence.

In 1978, the defendant moved for partial summary judgment and modification of the class. The motion was denied, with leave to renew at trial. In 1981, when the motion was renewed, the character of the evidentiary record had changed. Discovery was complete, and the experts for both sides had issued reports and had been deposed. The court-appointed expert had worked with the parties, performed his own critical analyses, and answered certain statistical questions posed by the judge. Finally, a thousand-page pretrial order had been negotiated by the parties. In other words, unlike in 1978 when the motion was first made, the factual record was essentially complete; data relating to the factual record had been subjected to elaborate statistical analyses; there were many outstanding disagreements on statistical issues, but these had been to some degree moderated by the pretrial negotiations of the parties and by the efforts of the court-appointed expert; and the parties were on record (in the pretrial order) as to the proofs they proposed to offer at trial.

For one key group—applicants for editorial positions—the defendant could make a strong empirical case that its hiring had been nondiscriminatory over the pertinent period. Since the question was presented as a motion for summary judgment, the burden was entirely on the defendant to show that there was no issue of material fact between the parties concerning the defendant's claim. The judge ultimately agreed that the defendant met that burden—he agreed with the defendant's argument that none of the plaintiffs' data: (1) demonstrated a statistically significant disparity between the percentage of women hired versus the percentage of women in the defendant's applicant pool or (2) otherwise demonstrated a pattern and practice of discrimination in editorial hiring. As to the statistical data, the disparities between hires and applicants that the judge found were less than a single standard deviation for the female editorial applicants. The judge found these deviations statistically "insignificant," especially with reference to the "two or three standard deviation" measure proposed by the Supreme Court in *Castaneda* v. *Partida*, 430 U.S. 482, 496 n.17 (1977). Meanwhile the judge found other, nonstatistical evidence advanced by the plaintiffs (e.g., anecdotal evidence) insufficient to support an inference of sex-biased hiring of editorial applicants by the defendant.

The judge therefore concluded that the plaintiffs could not demonstrate a "pattern and practice" of discrimination by the defendant against these applicants. He accordingly found for the defendant on this part of the motion.

This ruling eliminated an important group of applicants from the plaintiffs' class. The judge's ruling in other respects (concerning class action requirements) complicated the plaintiffs' pursuit of the lawsuit but left the defendant still exposed to liability for discrimination against noneditorial applicants and all female employees. A tentative settlement of the case was reached by the parties shortly thereafter and definitively negotiated over the next few months.

Questions of discrimination with respect to other groups of female *applicants*—and with respect to promotions, wages, and other practices concerning female *employees*—were at issue throughout the lawsuit and would have been the main factual issues in contention at trial. These issues were the objects of extended discovery by the lawyers and of analysis by the statistical experts. They were never authoritatively judged, as the settlement by the parties preempted any formal judgment on them. Each party, however, sought in the course of the lawsuit to strengthen its case on these issues. Much, though by no means all, of the evidence adduced on these issues was statistical. For the statistical evidence, the plaintiffs attempted to demonstrate patterns of statistically significant differences in the treatment of men and women, while the defendant attempted to show that there was no such statistically significant pattern.

Major Statistical Issues

In an interview long after the settlement, one of the experts provided a succinct summary of the major statistical issues:

> It was a typical Title VII situation. The two sides had somewhat different but overlapping data bases. The Plaintiffs' expert made a selection from his data base and used certain variables in a series of regression analyses. The defendant's experts made a different data selection and used an overlapping but different

set of variables in their regressions. As a consequence, the two sides disagreed.

Some of the details regarding these disagreements is given below, with special attention given to the regression analyses.

Plaintiffs' Case

The plaintiffs' expert carried out a variety of statistical analyses on issues relating to hiring, initial placement, promotion, and compensation as they differentially affected female applicants and employees. His basic data base included (1) the defendant's employment master payroll tapes for 1973–1977, (2) census labor market data, (3) employees' educational attainment data as coded from company personnel files, and (4) manually generated employment statistics for 1965–1973.

On the issue of hiring and initial placement, the plaintiffs' expert analyzed hires by sex and position (for nonproduction jobs excluding clericals) and found that women "are hired at a disproportionately low rate into the more desirable positions," when compared with labor market sex ratios. He focused specific attention on disparities in writing and editorial jobs and noted that, while the rate of female hires in other professional jobs was "not statistically significantly less than expected," women were hired into the lowest-paying of these jobs. On the issue of promotions, he attempted to show that for 1975–1977 the promotions to the higher-paying jobs in sales and in writing and editorial job groups went disproportionately to men, but he presented no formal statistical inferences to support this contention.

Finally, on the issue of compensation, the plaintiffs' expert used regression analyses to control for differences in seniority, age (used as a proxy for prior experience), educational attainment, and Equal Employment Opportunity (EEO) category of current job, while assessing the effect of sex on salary. The regression analyses used all full-time employees as of December 31, 1977, and led the expert to conclude: "The effect of the sex variable was highly statistically significant at well below the 0.00001 level. ... Females with the same seniority, educational attainment, age, and EEO category as males would earn $61 a week or $3,172 a year less than the similarly situated males." In addition, he reported on separate regressions for each EEO group, for the editorial department, for the writing staff, and for all employees hired since 1971. For each, the variable used to indicate the difference between the sexes (henceforth referred to as the sex variable) had a statistically significant regression coefficient, with the estimated coefficient varying from a low of $14 per week for the clerical group to a high of $112 per week for the managerial group.

Defendant's Response

As noted above, the defendant's response to the statistical issues raised by the plaintiffs came in two parts, prepared by two different experts.

The defendant's economics expert attacked the way in which the plaintiffs' expert structured the company's data, citing errors in classifying job groups and gross errors in tabulating data extracted from the payroll tapes. Working with company staff, he prepared an alternative data base of hires and promotions for 1974–1978, especially those associated with editorial positions, and he claimed that the application and hiring processes for these editorial positions were handled by the editorial department, outside the application and hiring processes for essentially all other parts of the company (a point not contested by the plaintiffs). For the editorial staff, he noted that the data "show no statistical evidence of discrimination of [sic] hiring" relative to the applications, the latter being data not included in the plaintiffs' expert's report. He then went on to provide what he labeled as a "more refined" comparison with census data, using an approximation of the relevant labor pool for a highly select group such as the company's editorial staff, again finding no evidence of discrimination. He also carried out a detailed analysis for noneditorial positions, again reaching a conclusion that there was no evidence of discrimination.

The defendant's statistical expert took on the issue of discrimination in compensation, reviewing the use of regression analysis by the plaintiffs' expert and presenting his own alternative regressions. The discussion at the beginning of his report adopted a stance similar to that used by defendants in other Title VII cases, e.g., that salary differentials by sex are attributable to differences in labor market pay rates for, and the differences in female representation in, various job categories, and this paved the way for the use of different explanatory variables in his regression analyses. His basic criticism of the plaintiffs' regression analyses was that they "cut across different occupations with differing pay scales and in which there are widely varying female representations." His own analyses focused on six job groups that are much more narrowly defined than the EEO groupings used by the plaintiffs' expert and were based on payroll data as of December 31, 1978 (a year later than the data used by the plaintiffs). The total number of employees covered by these analyses was about 660, with almost 500 of these in two of the six groups. The resulting multiple regressions showed estimated regression coefficients for the sex variable that were not statistically significant at the .05 level, although two of the groups show substantially large coefficients interpretable as sex-related pay differentials of in excess of $30 per week.

A major factor in the regressions for several of the groups was the inclusion of special explanatory variables. For example, for the editorial job group, the added variables were (a) whether the employee received a promotion since January 1975, (b) whether the employee received any merit increase since January 1975, and (c) whether the employee had previously served as a manager but was returned to the nonmanagerial group without a reduction in pay. The inclusion of these variables have a very substantial effect on the sex coefficient, reducing it in magnitude. (The use of these additional variables was challenged by the plaintiffs' expert in his rebuttal report.)

The defendant's expert concluded from his regression analyses "that no valid statistical inference can be drawn to substantiate the assertion of a pattern and practice of sex discrimination in compensation."

The Report of the Court's Expert

The report of the court's expert was prepared in two parts, the first (chronologically) of which addressed the compensation analyses, and the second addressed issues of hiring, placement, and promotion. In response to these reports, the judge prepared a series of questions about technical statistical terminology and outlined the conclusions of the court's expert regarding the conflicting claims of the party experts. The answers to these questions were presented by the expert in an addendum to his report.

From a procedural perspective the report on compensation issues may be of greatest interest. In it, the court-appointed expert described a series of additional regression analyses that he directed the experts for the two parties to perform—these were intended to supplement the analyses described in their reports and to allow him to assess the validity of the specifications used for the various regression equations. For example, the plaintiffs' expert was asked to perform analyses to elucidate the impact of missing information for the education variable (594 missing values out of 1,701 individuals), and various additional regressions to examine the impact of pooling across job groupings, i.e., a possible bias due to aggregation. These analyses led the court's expert to conclude that the impact of the missing data on the plaintiff's regressions was minimal, that aggregation bias does exist in some of the analyses, but that there remained "strong evidence of statistically significant results," in connection with the coefficient of the sex variable in the regressions, for several large groupings of employees. The major exception to these findings was for editorial department employees.

The defendant's statistical expert was also asked to carry out additional regression analyses, e.g., to exclude various "employer controlled variables," such as seniority. For the editorial employees, the court's expert found these analyses convincing, but he raised a series of questions about the remaining regression models and the related conclusions regarding the lack of statistically significant, sex-related wage differentials. His first report concluded with an attempt to examine the overall disparity in wages by sex in the defendant's results, using first a sign test and then Fisher's technique for combining p-values. For the sales groups, in particular, the court's expert found "quite striking evidence of overall wage differentials by sex."

The judge in his questions on this part of the report focused directly on the conclusions of his expert regarding the editorial department and sales department employees. The court-appointed expert responded in his addendum that, for the editorial workers in particular, he remained "unconvinced by results [of the plaintiffs' expert] in the narrow sense of a finding of a statistically significant wage disparity." Despite a marginally significant result for editorial staff workers in these analyses, he did not find the results with respect to sex "strong enough to make a conclusive inference of wage discrimination"—that is, while the differences are marginally statistically significant, they are not as large as the plaintiffs' expert originally suggested, and the specification of the defendant's expert's analysis for this group is quite reasonable.

The second report of the court-appointed expert analyzed the remaining statistical issues. In it he reported, not on requested reanalyses done at his direction by the experts for the two sides, but rather on his own statistical tests. He also attempted to weigh the conflicting arguments and data. Without reviewing all of the details in his 34–page report, we note that he appeared to be reaching conclusions that reflect a middle road between the claims of the experts for the two parties. On some issues, such as those relating to editorial employees, he affirmed most (but not all) of the analyses and conclusions of the defendant's economics expert. On others, he accepted the results of the plaintiffs' expert. On yet others, he argued that neither expert has quite carried out convincing analyses.

The judge once again focused several of his questions specifically on issues regarding the editorial department. In his responses, the court's expert again appeared to suggest that evidence of discrimination in hiring, placement, and promotions for editorial employees was weak and that the analyses for the defendant were, in general, convincing.

The Use of the Court-Appointed Expert

While the court's expert did not by himself resolve the major factual disagreements in this case, he did help to reduce the differences between the parties and to educate the judge about the statistical issues the case presented. What follows is a brief summary of how the court expert was actually used, focusing on how he was able to work with the parties and the judge amidst the intense adversarial environment of this case. Rule 706 itself provides only the outlines of how a court-appointed expert is to be used, leaving much to the discretion of the judge and the accommodations of the parties.

The judge had appointed an expert in one prior case: a patent case, involving complex chemical data. He knew of other cases in which a Rule 706 expert had been used to sort out medical testimony of party experts. His reason for appointing his own expert in this case was straightforward. The parties were far apart in their statistical arguments. He felt that having his own expert would enable him and his law clerks to sort out the contending statistical arguments, with a confidence they could not easily obtain from the piecemeal education that party experts would provide. In late 1980, the judge on his own motion (and to the apparent surprise of the parties) issued an order to show cause why he should not appoint an expert (Rule 706 establishes this procedure). A hearing to show cause was held, and no objections were entered. The judge directed the parties to submit names for the position, an optional procedure under Rule 706. Each of the parties submitted different names. The judge also asked others not involved in the case for names of possible experts for his use. The judge then picked as his statistical expert an econometrician who was on neither the plaintiffs' nor the defendant's list and issued a written order appointing the expert and defining the expert's duties in January 1981. The expert was authorized to consult with the employees, representatives, and experts of the plaintiffs and the defendant as he might deem necessary, and the order provided that costs for the expert's services would be fixed by court order when appropriate.

The judge began his use of the court's expert by holding a meeting with him and the attorneys. The judge made it clear to the attorneys that they were to provide his expert with whatever materials he requested. The judge's general approach was to dramatize his impartiality and that of the court's expert by doing as many as possible of his dealings with him in the open. Thus, while the judge held informal conversations with his expert, he had the attorneys present whenever substantive matters were discussed. When the expert submitted his written analyses of the parties' experts' reports, the judge responded with a set of written questions to his expert, who then answered in writing. In these ways, both sides were kept informed about what the judge was doing with the court-appointed expert, and suspicions about the expert's power were allayed.

One main function of the court-appointed expert was to educate the judge on statistical matters. Indeed, the expert feared that the judge might listen to him too much, taking his word as definitive. (There is no evidence that this in fact happened.) As a check on abuses, the parties did have the right to depose the court's expert and to cross-examine him at trial, under Rule 706.

One important issue created by the presence of a court-appointed expert was expense. To do his work, the court's expert required the parties to do reanalyses of certain data. These reanalyses were expensive. But there was no practical way for a party to object to them, if the party was to win critical statistical arguments. For the plaintiffs, the costs were particularly important. The plaintiffs had not only to buy the time of their expert and other personnel, but also to pay for computer services. None of these costs were budgeted by the plaintiffs, since they had no idea that the court would appoint an expert. The defendant, however, had its own computer and was probably in a better position to absorb this and other unexpected expenses. In addition, the court-appointed expert himself had to be paid by the parties. There was a short but intense dispute between the parties as to who should pay the expert, as part of the overall settlement of the case. The parties could not agree on an allocation of these costs, but they ultimately agreed to leave their detailed settlement agreement silent on the issue—in effect, to leave the matter to the judge. At the defendant's request, the expert was required to submit a detailed breakdown of the time he had worked on the case. In the end, the judge allocated these expenses 90 percent and 10 percent between the defendant and the plaintiffs, respectively.

The court-appointed expert helped to resolve a key statistical issue in the case: whether the data could support the plaintiffs' claim that the defendant had engaged in discriminatory hiring of editorial applicants. The judge ruled on this issue in response to the defendant's motion for partial summary judgment. The judge found for the defendant, thus eliminating this claim and excluding these applicants from the plaintiff class. He expressly emphasized in his ruling that his judgment was not affected by the court-appointed expert's views. Nonetheless, as we note above, statistical issues surrounding the appropriateness of the claims for the editorial applicants were a focus of the judge's official exchange with his expert and paved the way for the judge's ruling. At the same time, given the commitment of attorneys and judges to the traditional adversary process, and given possible questions that might be raised on appeal, a judge might be cautious in explicitly acknowledging the contributions of a court-appointed expert.

Implications

This case, and the account of the judge's use of a court-appointed statistical expert, raises many issues and settles few. What the actual impact of the court's expert was must remain a matter of speculation. Although his existence and activities appeared to hasten the settlement of the case, matters of cost and convenience may have been the true determinants.

Even within the context of this individual case, some broader questions arise. For example, would all court-appointed experts with the same "neutrality" and same goals as the court's expert in this case have proceeded in the same way? Would all experts have wanted a common data set created? Would they all have ordered the same additional tests? Would they all have done the same additional tests on their own? Given the diversity of experts available, it is highly unlikely that any two would have proceeded in an identical fashion, and one is left wondering what difference the particular choice of expert made in this case.

Nonetheless, the case did reach settlement prior to trial, and the court was not required to deal directly with demands that the statistical evidence may have placed on its resources. Moveover, none of the experts involved expressed any substantial misgivings about the procedural aspects of the use of a court-appointed expert. The result might thus be described as a reasonable one, and the procedure as one worthy of further use.

2.4   Case Study: E.E.O.C. v. Federal Reserve Bank of Richmond, 698 F.2d 633 (4th Cir. 1983)

Introduction

E.E.O.C. v. *Federal Reserve Bank of Richmond* involves a Title VII class action lawsuit brought originally in the Federal District Court for the Western District of North Carolina. The plaintiffs were black employees of the bank who alleged that the bank discriminated against them and others on account of race in matters of pay, promotion, training, discipline, and discharge. There was extensive testimony on statistical evidence, primarily relating to the existence of a pattern of discrimination in promotions but also addressing hiring, training, and wages. Questions of statistical methodology were also an important part of the appellate review and played a prominent role in the appellate opinion.

Case History

The EEOC initiated the case on March 22, 1977, charging the bank with discriminatory practices in promotions. Five months later, four current and former employees were granted intervenor status and were certified as representatives of the class of black employees hired after January 3, 1974. Originally the class was to include all blacks and women hired after 1965, but the parties agreed in 1978 to limit the case to blacks hired after January 3, 1974.

Two expert witnesses figured prominently in the district court proceedings, testifying on statistical analyses relevant to the various issues of the case. While neither was specifically trained as a statistician, both had a good deal of experience in statistical analysis. The defendant's expert has a Ph.D. in psychology, with a specialty in employment research, and the plaintiffs' expert has a Ph.D. in economics and professional experience in labor force analysis. Both experts had testified in other Title VII cases prior to this one, and both operate small consulting firms that deal with similar cases and issues. The defendant's expert was hired on the basis of his performance and demeanor on the stand in a previous case that the defendant's counsel had observed. The plaintiffs' expert had worked for the lawyer representing the intervenors on several previous occasions.

Early in the discovery period the plaintiffs had acquired a payroll data base, which their expert analyzed extensively even though it was lacking sufficient detail on personal histories to allow an appropriate analysis. As pretrial discovery drew to a close, the plaintiffs accepted the defendant's offer of its data base, thereby avoiding the disagreements about data base accuracy that often crop up in Title VII cases.

The plaintiffs' expert had problems with his contract with the EEOC and found himself working under a time constraint, with no firm guarantee from the EEOC of reimbursement for expenses. In fact, he claims that he was never completely reimbursed. Since the expert worked on the case under the assumption that he might never get paid, he gave the case a lower priority than his other projects. In retrospect, he believes the distractions of time and money significantly interfered with his ability to do good work.

Due in part to lack of preparation, the trial testimony of the plaintiffs' expert was often confusing. (This is apparent from the trial transcript and was used in connection with the appellate decision.) The expert completed his analysis the night before he was due to testify. He provided counsel with an outline to be followed during the questioning, but they never discussed the testimony in detail prior to the actual testimony. Furthermore, the expert reports that he and the attorney engaged in a heated argument over an unrelated matter shortly before the testimony was given. The expert felt that his anger interfered with his performance on the witness stand. In addition, he believes that it is common in discrimination cases for the defendants to have rehearsed their testimony more carefully than the plaintiffs: the defendants typically have more resources to devote to the trial.

The statistical issues in the case involved analyses relating to hiring, promotion, and employment training opportunities (further details are given below). In his opinion, the judge ruled that the bank had discriminated against its black employees, but only in promotions from pay grades 4 and 5.

In January 1983, a three-judge panel of the Fourth Circuit of the U.S. Court of Appeals issued its opinion overturning the case on the grounds that both the anecdotal evidence and the statistical evidence were insufficient to show a pattern or practice of discrimination. Specifically, the circuit court found that the trial court had "incorrectly" accepted the hypergeometric model in testing for differences in promotion rates and had further biased the issue by the use of one-tailed hypothesis tests instead of the more common two-tailed test. After reanalyzing the data using the binomial model and two-tailed tests, the circuit court found that no disparity had been shown. The plaintiffs filed a petition for a rehearing that included several amicus curiae (friend of the court) briefs from well-known statisticians who argued the applicability of the hypergeometric model as opposed to the binomial model and discussed the one-tail versus two-tail issue. The appeals court, in a 4–4 vote, decided not to rehear the case.

The Fourth Circuit Court also ruled that, under the doctrine of res judicata, the class members could not press individual claims against the bank. The res judicata doctrine states that once a dispute has been tried and decided by the courts, that judgment precludes further action by either side on the same issue. The Supreme Court handed down its decision on the appeal of several class members to this ruling in *Cooper et al.* v. *Federal Reserve Bank of Richmond* 104 S.Ct. 2794 on June 25, 1984. The Court ruled that a judgment that the employer did not engage in a class-wide pattern or practice of discrimination does not preclude subsequent individual claims by class members and remanded the case to the lower courts. The

Court seems to be saying that a class claim of discrimination is a distinct issue from an individual claim:

> Claims of two types were adjudicated in the Cooper litigation. First, the individual claims of each of the four intervening plaintiffs have been finally decided in the Bank's favor. Those individual decisions do not, of course, foreclose any other individual claims. Second, the class claim that the Bank followed "policies and practices" of discriminating against its employees has also been decided. It is that decision on which the Court of Appeals based its res judicata analysis. ... Given the burden of establishing a prima facie case of a pattern or practice of discrimination, it was entirely consistent for the District Court simultaneously to conclude that Cooper and Russell had valid individual claims even though it had expressly found no proof of any classwide discrimination above grade 5. It could not be more plain that the rejection of a claim of classwide discrimination does not warrant the conclusion that no member of the class could have a valid individual claim.

In other words, the class action was adjudicated, but not all of the individual claims.

Statistical Issues and Their Treatment

The plaintiffs argued that the case involved both disparate impact and disparate treatment. The basis for their claim of disparate impact was the difference in outcomes of the promotion process. This is not a typical disparate impact claim; typically some "objective" test or criterion is involved. The advantage to the plaintiff of a disparate impact standard is that the plaintiff need not show intent to discriminate: different outcomes are sufficient. The trial court accepted the plaintiffs' argument without extensive comment. After finding that the plaintiffs had demonstrated disparate treatment in promotions from grades 4 and 5, the judge's only statement about disparate impact was: "Plaintiffs' statistics also demonstrate statistically significant disparate impact of defendant's promotion practices [on promotion] of black employees from grades 4 and 5."

On appeal, the circuit court rejected the disparate impact claim:

> As is now well recognized, the class action commonality criteria are, in general, more easily met when a disparate impact rather than a disparate treatment theory underlies a class claim. The disparate impact "pattern or practice" is typically based upon an objective standard applied evenly and automatically to affected employees: an intelligence or aptitude test, e.g., *Griggs* v. *Duke Power Co.*, 401 U.S. 424, 91 S.Ct. 849, 28 L. Ed. 2d

158 (1971); an educational requirement, id.; a physical requirement, e.g., *Weeks* v. *Southern Bell Telephone & Telegraph Co.*,
408 F.2d 228 (5th Cir. 1969). The existence of such objectively
applied patterns or practices are likely to be indisputable from
the outset, so that no real commonality problems for class action maintenance ever arise in this regard. On the other hand,
the disparate treatment pattern or practice must be one based
on a specific intent to discriminate against an entire group, to
treat it as a group less favorably simply because of its sex (or
other impermissable reason). The greater intrinsic difficulty in
establishing the existence and common reach of such a subjec-
tively based practice is obvious. In the instant case, it is clear
that the plaintiff's ultimate reliance would of necessity have
been upon showing a pattern of disparate treatment. There is
no suggestion in the record of a Griggs-type objectively imposed
practice having discriminatory impact.

The circuit court noted, however, that its decision would have been the
same even had the issue been disparate impact, presumably because it
found no statistically significant differences in promotions by race.

The main issue in the trial was the possible difference in promotion
rates between blacks and whites. The plaintiffs' expert presented three
major analyses: (1) comparisons of promotion rates by year and grade
with hypothesis tests based on the hypergeometric distribution; (2) a life-
table analysis of promotions from 1973 to 1977 with associated tests for
differing time-in-grade means; (3) a "matched pairs" analysis, presented to
show that the disparities found in the other studies were not explained by
training, experience, education, etc.

The comparisons of promotion rates presented by the plaintiffs' expert
were in the form of a series of hypothesis tests for the years 1974 to 1977
within grades 4, 5, 6, and 7. For each grade and year the expected number of
black promotions was based on a reference population intended to represent
the pool of workers eligible for promotion. The plaintiffs' expert presented
two sets of tables, one using the population in grade at the beginning of
the year; in the second set of tables, he excluded from the pool of eligibles
all who were promoted, fired, or left during the year. He also excluded from
the counts of promotees those who were fired or left within a short period
after promotion. He calculated t-statistics using the normal approximation
to the hypergeometric model and calculated p-values based on a one-tailed
test of hypothesis.

The plaintiffs' expert testified that his use of the one-tailed test was based
on a prior expectation that the defendant was discriminating. When asked
if a particular result was statistically significant, he responded: "This is a
significant difference if one makes the assumption that it's reasonable to
believe that blacks have been discriminated against." The Fourth Circuit

Court accepted this statement uncritically but then argued that it found no evidence to justify the use of a one-tailed test on this basis.

The general argument in support of one-tailed tests was not discussed in the trial. As several of the affidavits attached to the petition for a rehearing point out, one can argue for a one-tailed test without any presumption of guilt. The null hypothesis is that promotions are random with respect to race: blacks and whites are treated the same. There are three possible alternative hypotheses: (1) blacks are treated differently than whites (either better or worse); (2) blacks are treated worse than whites; (3) blacks are treated better than whites. The first yields a two-tailed test, the last two yield one-tailed tests. Some would argue that, so long as the issue before the court is whether there is discrimination against blacks, especially in light of anecdotal evidence of individual discrimination, the second is the appropriate alternative hypothesis, and the one-tailed test is the correct test, which yields a greater probability of detecting a disparity when there really is one. A more comprehensive discussion of this idea may be found in one of the amicus briefs filed in support of the plaintiffs' petition for rehearing:

> The resolution of this controversy turns on the reasons for selecting the critical level of significance. The particular level selected should represent a balancing of the error of finding discrimination when there was none (Type I error) against the error of failing to detect discrimination when it is present (Type II error). A 5% critical significance level means that the rate of Type I errors will be 5%.
>
> In the present case it must be assumed that a finding of discrimination against the employer would only be made if blacks received less than their expected number of promotions, i.e. the point representing their number of promotions lies in the left tail. No finding of discrimination would be made if blacks received more than their expected number of promotions, so that the point representing their number of promotions lies in the right tail.
>
> That being so, the rate of erroneous findings of discrimination is determined by looking only at the probability in the left tail. The possibility that an innocent employer might by chance promote a disproportionately large number of blacks (the right tail) does not add to the error rate because no finding of discrimination would be made in that case. If both blacks and whites had sued, the probabilities in both tails would have to be added to determine the total Type I error rate because wrongful findings of discrimination could be made in either direction. But except in that unlikely situation, a two-tailed test will overstate by a

factor of two the risk that an innocent employer will nonetheless
be found guilty of discrimination.

The defendant's expert presented a similar tabulation covering all grades
and all promotions from 1967 to 1978, using the population in a given grade
the previous year as the reference population for that grade. He calculated
t-statistics using the normal approximation to the binomial model and a
two-tailed test of significance across all grades. The result of this analysis is
a classic example of what statisticians refer to as Simpson's paradox (e.g.,
see Simpson, 1951, Fienberg, 1980, or Meier, Sacks, and Zabell, 1984):
blacks are "underpromoted" in virtually every grade, yet, because of the
differing numbers of blacks and whites in the various grades, blacks appear
to be "overpromoted" in the aggregate.

To illustrate Simpson's paradox and a related problem, consider the data
in Table 2–1, taken from the defendant's Exhibit 111. The defendant's expert used the previous year's employees and promotions to compute expected numbers of promotions for blacks. This analysis understated the
difference in promotion rates since the proportion of blacks in the firm was
increasing over time. For example, consider grade 13. Since no one was promoted in the previous year, the "expected" number of blacks promoted in
the current year is 0. But 1 black was actually promoted. We illustrate the
calculation for the other grades using grade 14. There were 3 promotions
out of 63 the previous year, for a rate of 4.8 percent. This is applied to the
number of blacks in that grade the previous year to yield $18 \times (3/63) = 18 \times 4.8\% = 0.9$. Across grades the numbers of black promotions are less than
the expected numbers. The total number of expected black promotions is
351, considerably in excess of the actual number of 306. But when we do
the calculation using numbers aggregated over grades, the expected number
of blacks promoted is $1,048 \times (1,114/3,953) = 295.3$, less than the 306—
thus the erroneous aggregate view that blacks are overpromoted. Much was
made of this apparent overpromotion by the defense; the plaintiffs' expert
and counsel did not argue the point.

Promotion decisions may be correlated across grades, since a person promoted in one year may be less likely to be promoted a second time the
following year; it is not clear how to combine tests. There is, however, a
clear tendency across the board for blacks to be promoted at a lower rate
than whites. Neither side commented on this pattern.

The life-table analysis presented by the plaintiffs' expert reveals a similar
pattern across years and grades. Neither the trial court nor the appellate
court mentioned the life-table analysis or the associated tests of mean time-
in-grade differences.

It remains a substantive issue whether the pattern displayed is indica-
tive of sufficient disparity to support a legal finding of discrimination. There
are other possible explanations that might account for this disparity: (a)
differences in qualifications correlated with race; (b) differences in job per-

TABLE 2–1: Defendant's Exhibit 111

Grade	Number in grade in previous year	Promotions (%)	Blacks in grade in previous year	Number of black promotions	
				Actual (%)	Expected
0	9	0 (0)	3	0 (0)	0.0
16	46	0 (0)	1	0 (0)	0.0
15	62	3 (4.8)	4	0 (0)	0.2
14	102	2 (2.0)	10	1 (10)	0.2
13	72	0 (0)	20	1 (5)	0.0
12	63	3 (4.8)	18	0 (0)	0.9
11	183	17 (9.3)	24	2 (8.5)	2.2
10	137	9 (6.6)	54	2 (3.7)	3.5
9	490	92(18.8)	52	6 (11.5)	9.8
8	515	102(19.8)	115	22 (19.1)	22.8
7	878	250(28.5)	172	52 (30.2)	49.0
6	752	286(38.0)	300	101 (33.7)	114.1
5	501	268(53.5)	187	74 (40.0)	100.0
4	114	60(52.6)	78	37 (47.4)	41.0
3	21	16(76.2)	8	8 (100)	6.1
	8	6(75.0)	2	0 (0)	1.5
	3,953	1,114	1,048	306	351.3

formance correlated with race; (c) differing promotion rates in different jobs (blacks were more likely to be in jobs, such as janitorial or food services, in which promotions were less likely). The appellate court was clearly aware of these arguments and noted: "In a bank where the opportunities for promotion were in the clerical office fields, it is to be expected that those whose work and experience were in those fields would have an advantage in promotions over employees in service and cafeteria jobs" (698 F.2d at 659).

The matched pairs or "buddy" analysis was presented by the plaintiffs in order to preempt the argument that the above analyses do not control for other factors. However, the plaintiffs' expert managed to match up only about a third of the promotions, even with fairly liberal tolerances for the matches. In the eyes of the appellate court, this weakened the value of this type of analysis as evidence. Again, the result of the hypothesis test used in the buddy analysis was significant at the 5% level only when using a one-tailed test. The trial court seemed to accept this analysis as evidence that the only explanation for the disparity in promotions was race.

The issue of the appropriate level of aggregation is not easy to resolve. At one extreme lies complete disaggregation: a breakdown of the data by year, grade, and department. One possible argument for this treatment is that promotion decisions are heavily influenced by these categories, e.g., clerks are more likely to be promoted than janitors, and race (or sex) is associated with these categories. Disaggregation, however, decreases the numbers in each category and increases the number of parameters to estimate, increasing the likelihood that no category will exhibit a statistically significant departure from the null hypothesis even in the presence of discrimination, unless there are substantial gains in power, as there often are in matched-pair studies. The appellate court took an interesting position in this issue, arguing both for and against disaggregation. In the passage quoted above they argue against the analysis of the plaintiffs' expert for his failure to disaggregate, but they accepted complete aggregation when presented by the defendant's expert: "This data showed the percentage of black employees in the entire workforce of the bank in the 1974–1978 period was 33%, during this period black employees received 35% of all promotions" (698 F.2d at 662).

Both the trial and the appellate courts followed a procedure something like the following in their reasoning as they tried to put together the evidence from the various tests of hypotheses: examine each grade individually, testing for significance at the 5% level. If the grade in question fails to pass the test, declare there is no evidence of discrimination in that grade and proceed to examine the next one. Both courts' reliance on the multiple use of hypothesis testing without an overall test of significance was in accord with the experts' approaches, but it leaves much to be desired. While this approach may not have led to an incorrect result in this case, expert witnesses and lawyers study the decisions of the courts before which they will appear and are influenced by them. If the court makes it clear that it expects or endorses a certain type of presentation, then some lawyers and experts are bound to toe the line, whether or not it makes sense in the next case. For example, the plaintiffs' expert said that his presentation was designed not to exceed the trial judge's perceived level of tolerance for statistical evidence. In addition, he felt pressured to do a regression analysis because the Fourth Circuit Court was thought to be attentive to it. The defendant's expert also indicated that he was sensitive to such issues.

Another major issue was the possible existence of a disparity in pay rates. The plaintiffs' expert presented several regression analyses of pay rate and pay grade, again relying on one-tailed tests of significance for the race coefficients. The defendant's expert presented no similar analysis but instead relied on attacking the opposing expert's analysis. He noted that the analysis did not include job category as an independent variable and thus did not control for the variation from that source. For example, computer programmers of a given grade have higher salaries than clerks of the same grade. The circuit court further criticized the regression analysis of pay rates for its failure to include pay grade and length of employment as predictors. It is not altogether clear what should have been done in this case. If blacks were discriminated against in promotion, then pay grade would be a tainted variable (i.e., an explanatory variable that itself may have been influenced by discrimination) and perhaps should not have been included. The variables that were included in the regression study may predict job category quite well, making the inclusion of the tainted variable unnecessary. For example, in the regression for 1975 the independent variables included bachelor's degree, secretarial experience, months of craft experience, months of service experience, training in management, and training in computer programming. The defendant's expert also presented a labor market analysis showing that the bank hired blacks in greater proportion than their availability in the local region. This analysis was not a subject of controversy during the trial.

The Reaction to the Expert Witnesses

While there were various factors that may have contributed to the outcome of the case, as its opinion makes clear, the circuit court viewed with great skepticism the evidence presented by the plaintiffs' expert. This reaction was due, at least in part, to a perception of bias in his presentation. He entered two sets of promotion tables into the record, one based on occupants of the grade at the start of the year, the other based on occupants at the end of the year with some subgroups excluded from the analysis. In the court's words (698 F.2d 648, 649):

> There are a number of significant facts to be observed about the numbers used in these two Tables which are crucial in any examination of the District Court's findings derived therefrom.

First, the number of employees in each pay grade for any one
of the four years in issue, as listed in these Tables, is neither
"Total Incumbents at Beginning of Interval" (that is, at the beginning of the year in question) nor, as the Tables themselves
state, "Total Incumbents at End of Interval" (that is, after the
end of the year in question). The number of employees in the
pay grade for any year, as used in the Tables, is the number
of employees who were employed in the pay grade at the beginning of that year and who remained in the pay grade at the
end of that year. In other words, any employee who quit, was
promoted out, or was fired, or was replaced during the year is
not counted in this calculation. This method of calculating the
employee numbers out of which promotions were to be made
in any stated year increased, particularly in pay grade 4, the
percentage of black employees over what it would have been
had the Tables used the actual number of employees in the pay
grade at the beginning of the stated year, or the actual number
at the end of the year, or any average of the two. More important for meaningful analysis than this method of calculating the
employee mass for determination of the sample is the manner
in which the expert calculated the number of black promotions
made in the grades for each of the years in question. It was
undisputed that the actual number of black promotions in pay
grade 4 for the years 1974–77, for instance, was 39 but the Tables used by the District Court gave the number as 35. The
reason for the difference is that any employee, whether black or
white, who, after promotion might have terminated voluntarily
or involuntarily, was simply eliminated from the calculations of
black promotees during that year, as set forth in these Tables.
Plaintiffs' witness admitted that such a procedure where only
the number of black promotees who, after promotions, continued to be employed and not the actual, correct number of black
promotions was used in the calculations, "change[d] the statistics dramatically in the case of grade 4." The reasons assigned
by the expert witness for the use of such artificial numbers on
promotions of blacks during the relevant years in his tables were
that, to quote the expert, "there may be promotions that are
given to individuals which are not permanent in nature, which
the incumbent leaves quickly after he is promoted and for a
variety of reasons—either he's going back to school or he's dissatisfied with his work or he's dissatisfied with the promotion or
he fails at the promotion and wishes to leave employment." All
of these promotees should be eliminated in the calculations of
annual black promotions in the expert's judgment. The District
Court did not inquire into the reasonableness of this justifica-

tion for the omission of such promotions for a fair and impartial analysis in the critical years, nor are we able to find any basis in the record for such a justification. It seems difficult to assume that when an employee, whether white or black, has requested a promotion to a particular job vacancy (that is the way the evidence shows promotions were generally made) he would be "dissatisfied with the promotion" he had sought and would quit because he got it. Similarly, it is a little odd that, when it is the plaintiffs' contention (which, incidentally, is somewhat specious, as we see later) that it took an average of almost four years for a black to be promoted out of grade 4 the defendant would be promoting a black schoolboy, whose work life would normally be no more than the three school vacation months and who would quit at the end of his school vacation. Moreover, if the question is whether the defendant intentionally failed to promote blacks in pay grades 4 and 5 in a particular year, it would seem that the correct test figure should be the actual promotions made in that particular year out of those pay grades. We are unable to perceive any rational basis for using an inaccurate figure for promotions during the pertinent years for black promotions in exhibits 34a and 35a unless it was "to obtain a desired result" of a standard deviation in excess of 2.

The circuit court opinion also expresses distrust of the methodology of the plaintiffs' expert. He used the hypergeometric model instead of the binomial model, with which the judges were familiar due to the Hazelwood case, and they note that this was in the plaintiffs' favor. (The confusion here was over the appropriateness of a sampling model without replacement.) Finally, the plaintiff's expert used one-tailed tests instead of two-tailed tests, making it easier to achieve the 5% significance level.

When interviewed after the trial, the experts for the two sides differed in their assessment of the utility of court-appointed experts. The plaintiffs were in favor of the idea, and the defendant was opposed. The plaintiffs' expert thought that a court-appointed expert would have helped in this case and proposed it as a quality control measure. He was not opposed to adversarial proceedings but thought that a court-appointed expert could play a role similar to peer review in academic journals. The defendant's expert thought that the legal system had worked well in this case and that a court-appointed expert would not have helped much. He also thought that, although making minor errors in its attempt to analyze the data, the circuit court had done a good job of evaluating the strength of the evidence overall.

Conclusions

The most interesting statistical feature of this case for the panel is not the debate over the appropriateness of the hypergeometric model versus the binomial model, or that of one-tailed tests versus two-tailed tests. Rather it is the extent to which those debates and the associated attention given to hypothesis testing in general may have interfered with the interpretation of the data.

Both the district court and the circuit court seem to have examined each piece of evidence separately. If a particular hypothesis test was not significant at the 5% level, then that segment of the evidence was discarded, or worse, considered to be proof of the null hypothesis. The courts never stood back to look at the overall picture, which included anecdotal as well as statistical evidence. In fact, the appellate court argued that anecdotal evidence of discrimination should be ignored when the person delivering that anecdotal testimony was an employee in a grade in which the observed differences between the blacks and whites failed to be significant at the 5% level.

2.5 Case Study: Gulf South Insulation v. U.S. Consumer Product Safety Commission, 701 F.2d 1137 (5th Cir. 1983)

Introduction

The appeal to the federal courts of administrative law decisions raises many issues about the appropriate standard of judicial review of scientific issues and, in particular, statistical assessments. In *Gulf South Insulation* v. *U.S. Consumer Product Safety Commission*, a three-judge panel of the United States Court of Appeals for the Fifth Circuit overturned an order of the Consumer Product Safety Commission (CPSC) banning the use of urea-formaldehyde foam insulation (UFFI) in residences and schools. This case study examines some of the legal and statistical issues that were raised by the parties to the case and explores how the court confronted and resolved them in the process of reaching its decision.

The major statistical issues that arose in the *Gulf South* case involved (a) the CPSC's choice of a risk assessment model to calculate the risk of increased incidence of cancer resulting from formaldehyde exposure and (b) the selection and quality of the data that were used in the model. How these issues were raised and addressed by the parties and how the court ruled on the importance of these issues provides some useful insights into the role of statistical assessments as evidence.

Administrative Case History

The court's decision in *Gulf South* came 6–1/2 years after the Metropolitan Denver District Attorney's Consumer Office filed a petition with the CPSC requesting development of a safety standard for certain home insulation products, including UFFI. The petition claimed that there was an unreasonable risk of injury from irritation and poisoning associated with such insulation. On March 5, 1979, 2–1/2 years after receiving the petition and reviewing the available information, the CPSC deferred a decision relating to UFFI and instructed its staff to gather additional information.

The CPSC staff gathered data and performed analyses on the levels of formaldehyde gas in UFFI and non-UFFI homes and on the health hazards associated with these exposures. UFFI products were tested by the CPSC and private laboratories to measure the levels of formaldehyde emitted under simulated in situ conditions. In addition, the CPSC contracted with the National Academy of Sciences (NAS) to investigate whether, for long-term continuous exposure in the household environment, there was a threshold below which there is no irritant effect of formaldehyde on the population. While examining the evidence of the acute effects of formaldehyde exposure, the CPSC was presented with data from an animal bioassay by the Chemical Industry Institute for Toxicology (CIIT), which showed formaldehyde to be an animal carcinogen. A subsequent animal study by scientists at New York University was viewed by the CPSC as confirmation of the CIIT results. During this period, a federal panel on formaldehyde studied the available data and concluded that formaldehyde should be presumed to pose a carcinogenic risk to humans.

On the basis of these studies, the CPSC concluded that formaldehyde posed a cancer risk to humans. After deciding that there was a risk, the CPSC sought to quantify it. Using Global 79, a well-known quantitative risk assessment model, the CPSC calculated that, based on actual exposure measurements, there would be as many as 1.8 additional cases of cancer from every 10,000 residences insulated with UFFI. In an alternative analysis using test data in place of actual exposure measurements, the CPSC estimated that there would be as many as 1.3 additional cases of cancer for every 10,000 homes insulated with UFFI.

The CPSC investigated the possibility of product standards to reduce the risk, but it concluded that such standards would be inadequate. The only alternative was a ban on the use of UFFI. Therefore, on February 5, 1981, the CPSC issued a proposed ban of UFFI from residences, schools, and other public and commercial buildings. Almost 300 interested parties submitted written comments on the proposed ban, and more than 20 parties presented oral comments in a public hearing. The CPSC, by a 4–1 vote, found that UFFI posed an unreasonable risk of injury that could be prevented only by banning its use. The final rule, published in the *Federal Register* on April 2, 1982, banned the use of UFFI in residences and schools after August 10, 1982.

Petitions for review of the CPSC ban were filed by numerous parties in the Circuit Court of Appeals in the District of Columbia and the Fifth Circuit. Four petitioners sought to vacate the ban; one sought to have its product exempted, and one complained that the ban was too narrow. In addition, three amicus curiae briefs were filed—two urging the court to vacate the ban and one seeking its affirmance. The petitioners attacked both of the CPSC's conclusions supporting the ban: (1) the finding that UFFI poses an unreasonable risk of cancer and (2) the finding that UFFI presents an unreasonable risk of acute irritant effects. In challenging these findings, the petitioners and the two amicus briefs argued that the administrative record did not contain the necessary substantial evidence to support CPSC's conclusions.

The major challenge to the ban was concentrated on CPSC's finding that UFFI poses an unreasonable risk of injury from cancer. As stated in the opinion, the petitioners argued that: (1) neither the formaldehyde levels found in the 1,164 test homes nor the test results from the Franklin Institute Research Laboratory of the Oak Ridge National Laboratory are accurate indicators of the formaldehyde levels in average UFFI homes; (2) the CPSC erred in relying exclusively on the Chemical Institute's rate data in its risk assessment model and ignored numerous epidemiologic studies indicating that formaldehyde is not a human carcinogen; (3) the CPSC ignored the explanation for the incidence of tumors at the high levels of formaldehyde exposure involved in the Chemical Institute's study; (4) no substantial evidence supports the CPSC's assumption that the effective formaldehyde dose for humans is the same as that for rats; (5) Global 79 incorporates several assumptions about formaldehyde carcinogenicity that are not supported by substantial evidence; (6) Global 79 predicts only an upper limit of risk and does not constitute substantial evidence that "it is at least more likely than not the [UFFI] presents a signficant risk of [cancer]," *Industrial Union Dept. AFL-CIO* v. *American Petroleum Inst.*, 448 U.S. 607, 653, 100 S.Ct. 2844, 2869, 65 L.Ed.2d 1010 (1980); and (7) other federal agencies have determined that formaldehyde does not pose a substantial health risk to humans.

Standard of Review

In the *Gulf South* case, the court reviewed the CPSC's decision under the congressionally mandated "substantial evidence" standard of review, which requires that the agency's regulatory actions must be supported by substantial evidence on the record taken as a whole.

In general, when a court reviews the decision-making process of an agency, it reviews the agency action under either the "arbitrary and capricious" standard or the substantial evidence standard. Judicial review under either standard requires the reviewing court to make three distinct judgments. First, the court must make the determination of whether the agency acted within the scope of its powers delegated by Congress. Second, the court must decide if necessary procedural requirements were followed in the agency decision-making process. Finally, in the most difficult task, the court must look at the substantive basis for the agency decision and judge its sufficiency under the appropriate standard of review.

Under the arbitrary and capricious standard, the level of review is limited. As Supreme Court Justice Marshall stated in *Citizens to Preserve Overton Park, Inc.* v. *Volpe*, 401 U.S. 402 (1971): "the Court must consider whether the decision was based on a consideration of the relevant factors and whether there has been a clear error." Although this inquiry into the facts is to be searching and careful, the ultimate standard of review is a narrow one. The court is not empowered to substitute its judgment for that of the agency. The issue before the court under the arbitrary and capricious standard is whether the agency had a rational basis for its decision; if so, the court must defer and approve the action.

The substantial evidence standard of review, by contrast, requires a more probing inquiry by the court. In the words of the *Gulf South* opinion (footnotes and citations deleted):

> The leading decision in this circuit on the meaning of the substantial evidence test in the context of this Act is *Aqua Slide 'N' Div* v. *CPSC*, 569 F.2d 831 (5th Cir. 1978), which involved the first product standard the Commission promulgated. There we found that "Congress put the substantial evidence test in the statute because it wanted the courts to scrutinize the Commission's actions more closely than an 'arbitrary and capricious' standard would allow." The facts that detract from the agency as well as those that support it are to be considered. "The ultimate question is whether the record contains 'such relevant evidence as a reasonable mind might accept as adequate to support a conclusion.' " If it does, the Commission has sustained its burden of adducing "substantial evidence on the record as a whole" and the rule must be affirmed. If not, the rule must be vacated.

The Global 79 Risk Assessment Model

To calculate the risk to humans of increased incidence of cancer from exposure to formaldehyde emitted by UFFI, the CPSC chose a risk assessment model. The data the commission had to work with included the results of the CIIT bioassay and empirical as well as test exposure data.

To project anticipated human cancer risk from experimental animal data, it is necessary to use some procedure for extrapolation to low doses. Long-term animal bioassays are generally focused on the detection of carcinogenic potential, and this potential is most quickly observed when the test animals are exposed at near-lethal levels. Since human exposure is generally at orders of magnitude lower than these test levels, an extrapolation procedure is required to estimate expected human responses. In addition, a species extrapolation "scaling factor" must be used. Together, the low-dose extrapolation and the scaling factor are incorporated into a statistical risk assessment model.

Different classes of statistical models incorporate different assumptions as to the unknown dose-response relationship between exposure to a carcinogen and a carcinogenic response. For example, tolerance distribution models are based on the assumptions that every member of a population has a threshold or tolerance level below which the individual will not respond to the exposure in question and that the variability among individual threshold levels can be described in terms of a probability distribution. A second class of models is mechanistic in nature, e.g., the one-hit, multistage, and multihit models. These models derive their names from the presumed mechanism of carcinogenesis and they are based on the assumption that a tumor originates from a single cell that has been damaged by either the chemical or one of its metabolites. The multistage model is perhaps the most commonly employed of all current low-dose extrapolation procedures and was proposed 30 years ago by Armitage and Doll. It reflects the observation that a developing tumor goes through several different stages, which can be affected by the carcinogen in question before it is clinically detectable (see Armitage, 1985, for a review of these models). A third class of models builds on the multistage approach and attempts to describe the complex relationship between dose, tumor latency, and cancer risk. This class includes the Cornfield-Van Ryzin and the Hartley-Sieken models. These models differ primarily in their assumptions as to the nature of the dose-response curve at very low doses. No single low-dose extrapolation procedure has yet gained universal acceptance within the scientific community, and the standard approaches of assessing goodness-of-fit do not prove to be useful in discriminating among models.

After reviewing the available information on carcinogenicity, the CPSC chose the multistage model that had been incorporated into a computer program known as Global 79. Petitioners presented numerous arguments why the CPSC's choice of the Global 79 risk assessment model was wrong, including that it incorporated the multistage theory assumption of a linear dose-response curve at low doses and the risk of increased incidence of cancer was projected at the 95% upper confidence limit. Petitioners contended that the selection of Global 79 and the use of the 95% upper confidence interval was in error because it was based on the assumption that formaldehyde would interact with other carcinogens in a synergistic way. In assuming this interaction, the CPSC rejected other models that provided a reasonable fit to the available data but did not incorporate the multistage dose-response model of carcinogenicity with its assumption of linearity at low exposure levels. Petitioners contended that if the CPSC had used any of the other models, the projected risk of cancer from formaldehyde exposure would be insignificant.

The petitioners attempted to show that there was a threshold below which formaldehyde has no carcinogenic effect and, therefore, the CPSC was wrong in accepting the multistage model with its assumption of low-dose linearity. As evidence for their threshold hypothesis, petitioners noted the steep dose-response curve of the CIIT study and the opinions of numerous scientists as to the mechanisms of carcinogenesis from formaldehyde exposure.

The petitioners also challenged CPSC's use of the 95% upper confidence limit, arguing that the maximum likelihood estimate (MLE) provided the best estimate of risk. Using Global 79, the CPSC had calculated that up to 51 cases of cancers could occur per 1 million people exposed to formaldehyde gas emitted by UFFI, whereas the MLE showed zero risk.

In explaining that the 95% upper confidence limit represents only the upper limit of a range of possible cases of cancer, the petitioners claimed that the CPSC should have used the MLE as the best estimate. To support their claim, the petitioners cited the Supreme Court's 1980 benzene decision, in which the Court found that before the Occupational Safety and Health Administration (OSHA) could regulate benzene, it had to "show on the basis of substantial evidence, that it is at least more likely than not that long term exposure to 10 ppm [parts per million] of benzene presents a significant risk of material health impairment." Since the 95% lower confidence limit as well as the maximum likelihood estimate of risk of cancer are at zero, petitioners contended that the CPSC had violated the "more likely than not" standard of the benzene decision. In addition, the Formaldehyde Institute made an attempt to discredit the use of the 95% upper confidence limit by stating:

> The only information which can be validly derived from the 95% confidence limits (assuming, arguendo, that CPSC's methodology were otherwise correct) is that there is a 95% probability that the risk of cancer to humans from UFFI is between zero and 51:1,000,000. This is like saying there is a 95% certainty that the New Orleans Saints will in a regular season of 16 games win between zero and fifteen games; that may be true, but it does not indicate the number of actual wins.

The CPSC's brief responded by asserting that the petitioners' attacks on the Global 79 risk assessment model showed a misunderstanding of the facts, presented an explanation of what it claimed to be the current general theory of carcinogenicity, and noted that there was extensive support in the scientific community for the multistage model: "The multistage model has been selected for use by Dr. David Gaylor of the National Center for Toxicological Research and the carcinogen assessment group at EPA, among others. The current scientific literature contains extensive support for the selection of this model."

After pointing to evidence in the record that formaldehyde is an initiator and promoter of the carcinogenic process, the CPSC attempted to explain why the dose-response curve derived from Global 79's analysis of the CIIT data could be nonlinear at high doses (supported by the data) and linear at low doses (not supported by the data). This explanation was necessary to counter the petitioners' contention that there was a threshold level below which formaldehyde did not act as a carcinogen.

First, the CPSC provided an "oversimplified but easily understood example" of how the multistage theory could explain the rising nonlinear dose-response curve observed in the CIIT tests:

> [A]ssume a three-stage progression to cancer and that, at a particular exposure level, formaldehyde has a one in 100 chance of causing any one of the stages. Thus, at that exposure level, the chance that all three stages will occur as the result of the formaldehyde exposure is one in a million ($1/100 \times 1/100 \times 1/100$). If the exposure level is doubled and thus the chance that each stage will occur doubles, the likelihood that all three stages will occur would rise to 8 in a million ($2/100 \times 2/100 \times 2/100$). Thus, the risk of cancer developing rises in a disprotionate relationship to an increase in the dose.

Second, the CPSC explained the need to view formaldehyde in connection with other carcinogens to estimate the possible effects from exposure at low doses:

> [A] cell that has had the progression to cancer initiated by exposure to other carcinogens could be transformed to a cancerous state by an additional stage caused by exposure to formaldehyde. ...We are concerned not just with what levels of formaldehyde, viewed in isolation, can cause cancer, but with lower levels of the substance that might have a significant additive effect (a linear dose-response relationship) on cancer progression in humans.

The CPSC concluded that because the dose-response curve for formaldehyde would be linear at low exposure levels and nonlinear at higher concentrations, the multistage theory and the Global 79 model were rational choices for analyzing the CIIT data.

The CPSC also responded to the petitioners' assertion that use of the 95% upper confidence level in Global 79 overestimated the risk of cancer and that the maximum likelihood estimate was the better estimate, noting that, given the assumed interactive nature of formaldehyde, the actual tendency for formaldehyde to induce cancer would probably be closer to the upper confidence limit generated by Global 79 (which incorporates low-dose linearity at the upper confidence limit) than to other estimates, which do not account for interaction (citations omitted):

> Petitioners contend that the risk at low dose should instead be estimated by extending the curve shown in the CIIT study to zero (i.e., the "maximum likelihood estimate" or "MLE"), thus ignoring the likelihood of interaction with other carcinogens and ignoring the fact that the CIIT study is inherently insensitive to the response at these low doses. This methodology was considered by the Commission but, as explained above, the "linear at low dose" estimate obtained by the upper 95 percent confidence limit methodology was determined to be a better estimate of the likely effects of formaldehyde exposure.

Selection and Quality of the Data

The second group of statistical issues that arose in the *Gulf South* case involved the selection and quality of the data that were the basis for the CPSC's risk assessment, which were challenged by the petitioners. These data consisted of the CIIT animal bioassay, measurements of formaldehyde gas levels in UFFI and non-UFFI homes, and laboratory measurement of formaldehyde gas levels emitted under simulated in situ conditions. The petitioners' main arguments against use of the CIIT data on rats were that the mechanism by which formaldehyde induces cancer in rats precludes its inducing cancer in humans, and that the exposure data were incorrect. Because the first argument is purely biological, only the issue of exposure data is discussed below.

The petitioners, in attempting to discredit the rat data, noted that the maximum concentrations to which the rats were exposed were more than double the "mean" concentrations. For example, rats exposed to an average of 14.3 ppm were at times exposed to levels as high as 32.4 ppm. In a footnote, the petitioners also stated that "the foregoing maximum exposures only refer to maximum daily average exposures. ... (It did not provide information concerning the absolute maximum exposure.)" Given these high exposures, the petitioners made three arguments against the use of the CIIT data. First, they claimed that the significance of the CIIT cancer bioassay should be called into question, since the rats had been exposed to near-lethal doses. Second, they cited the high exposures as support for "the argument made by commenters that the cancers found likely were induced by the severe damage the high concentrations inflicted upon the noses of the rats." Third, the petitioners stated that "the striking disparity between 'average' and true maximum exposure levels calls into question the quality of the study itself."

The CPSC dismissed the petitioners' arguments, claiming that the high exposures were not of particular significance, given the limited duration of the exposure. The Commission's brief stated:

> Although rats may have been exposed on a given day to values higher than those targeted, such "maximum" doses were for an exceedingly short period of time. Since CIIT made (on most days) 12 measurements a day during the 6-hour exposure period (i.e., approximately every half hour), and since the daily averages were always close to the targeted values ... such a maximum would have been present on the day it occurred for no more than about a half hour (and could have been for much less). Therefore, the CPSC risk assessment properly used CIIT's average exposure levels, since any disproportionate dose-response caused by the maximum exposure levels would have been negligible when compared to the entire 24 month exposure period.

In a further rebuttal of petitioners' arguments, the CPSC noted that the petitioners had misread the CIIT data regarding maximum exposures, mistakenly claiming that the maximum exposures were daily averages when they were not.

The petitioners also challenged the accuracy of the formaldehyde exposure data that the CPSC used to estimate cancer risks for residents of UFFI homes. The CPSC had collected both observational and test data on the levels of formaldehyde gas emitted from UFFI products. The observational data consisted of the results of formaldehyde measurements in 1,164 homes with UFFI over 9 years. The test data came from measurements of formaldehyde gas from simulated UFFI wall segments in tests performed by the Franklin Institute Research Laboratory of the Oak Ridge National Laboratory (ORNL) and by the CPSC. Using the Global 79 risk assessment model with the CIIT rat data, the empirical exposure data generated a 51/1,000,000 increased risk of cancer, whereas the test data generated a 37/1,000,000 increased risk.

The petitioners attempted to raise numerous doubts about the accuracy of the empirical data. They claimed that the CPSC had used exposure estimates that were nonrandom and biased upward, resulting in an overestimate of risk. In particular, they pointed out that, of the 1,164 UFFI homes that were measured, 827 of them were from complaint homes—homes in which someone suspected that adverse health effects were attributable to UFFI. Many of the complaint homes had high formaldehyde gas levels as the result of faulty installation. These homes were not "average" UFFI homes and therefore could not be used in the risk assessment model. The petitioners believed proper industry standards, not a ban, could control such errors. The petitioners further claimed that there were no significant differences between the levels of formaldehyde in homes without UFFI and in homes where UFFI had been installed properly, citing several studies and a recent Massachusetts Superior Court opinion, *Borden* v. *Commissioner of Public Health*, which struck down a Massachusetts Department of Public Health ban on UFFI. In *Borden*, the court stated that "there has been no showing that the ambient level of formaldehyde concentration in housing in which UFFI has been properly installed is significantly more appreciable or different than the level of formaldehyde in similar houses without UFFI." (On appeal, the *Borden* case was reversed and the ban was reinstated (*Borden* v. *Commissioner of Public Health*, 448 N.E. 2d 367 (1983))). Finally, petitioners contended that the CPSC had improperly used a level of 0.12 ppm as the exposure level for its risk assessment, when the real level of formaldehyde in UFFI homes is much lower; thus, the risk was overstated.

The petitioners also claimed the laboratory test data failed to indicate the formaldehyde levels that would be found in UFFI homes. Among the petitioners' claims were that the tests were not representative of the conditions prevalent in homes, that the tests did not take into account the capacity of dry wall to absorb formaldehyde gas, that installation errors were made, that there was an unexplained wide variance in emissions from test panels, and that pretesting storage of the panels rendered them unfit for testing.

In its brief, the CPSC replied to most of the petitioners' concerns regarding formaldehyde levels in UFFI homes but failed to explain why homes to be measured were not randomized. The CPSC labeled as incorrect the petitioners' contention that a level of 0.12 ppm was the basis of its risk assessment. The CPSC stated that the value of 0.12 ppm was:

> ... the average of the levels in a sample of UFFI homes actually measured for formaldehyde—without regard to the age of the foam. ... What was used in the risk assessment was the declining curve of formaldehyde levels in UFFI homes taking into account the age of the foam.

The CPSC disagreed with the petitioners' position that there is no difference between the levels of formaldehyde in homes in which UFFI has been installed properly and non-UFFI homes. The CPSC stated that the studies cited by petitioners did demonstrate a significant difference in formaldehyde levels—a difference that would have been magnified had new UFFI homes been included, because emission rates decrease with the age of the foam.

The CPSC also defended the use of the laboratory test data. Concerning the argument that the foam was not installed properly and, therefore, emission rates were higher, the CPSC noted that the panels were foamed by industry installers who were aware of the reasons for the test and were expected to be "as careful as possible" to ensure that the panels were properly foamed. The CPSC also rejected the idea that the test data were inaccurate because of the wide variance in results, noting that the varied results were comparable to actual home measurements. Finally, the CPSC answered the charge that improper storage of test panels had invalidated the results. The CPSC noted (citations omitted):

FI (Formaldehyde Institute) contends that the ORNL and CPSC test results are not reliable because the panels were stored in a carport and covered by a plastic tarpaulin. As the Commission found however, these storage conditions would not exceed in severity the situation where a house is left unairconditioned and unheated. In fact, as far as the exterior of an actual house is concerned, the storage conditions were less severe.

Oral Argument and the Decision

The statistical issues that were raised by the parties in their briefs provoked a variety of responses from the court during oral argument and in the final opinion.

The Low-Dose Linearity Concept

The issue of the CPSC's assumption of linearity in the dose-response curve surfaced at oral argument and in the court's final opinion. The apparent difficulty of the judges in understanding the low-dose linearity concept could be viewed as providing support for the position that substantive review of mathematical and scientific evidence by technically untrained judges is dangerously unreliable.

During the oral argument, an industry attorney argued that, given the assumption of low-dose linearity, the CPSC would next attempt to regulate the air we breathe, since ambient levels of formaldehyde would be carcinogenic. One of the judges, in an exchange with the attorney on this point, confused the ranges of formaldehyde levels with the issue of linearity for low dosage, two issues that are conceptually independent.

At the oral argument, a second judge raised a question regarding the assumption of low-dose linearity built into the Global 79 model. Noting that the dose-response curve from the Global 79 model differed from the actual data in that it showed a dose-response below 5.6 ppm, the judge asked what the government had done. The attorney responded:

> Well, I'm not sure that I can answer the question in your terms. There is a model that the Commission used to assess the risk. And what this model assumes is that you take the data from the study and, you know, you feed it into a computer program, and we feed in the data. We know it exists at 14 and at 5.6. And I might add that there were tumors produced below five, at two parts per million, but those were not even part of the Commission's risk assessment. Okay? So we do not feed that information into the computer program. And in this sense the Commission was being conservative in underestimating risk, if anything, because those other tumors were not part of its risk assessment. And the computer program that's used and the model that was selected by the Commission does not simply

chart the data from the study, and this is the model that petitioners would like the Commission to have used, because then
if you do that, you will get to what they say is an essentially
zero risk.

The judge then remarked:

Well I don't blame them so much. You may be right. All I'm
saying is I don't blame them. If I see somebody starting out
to do something to me and they start a curve here and wanted
to decide when I'm going to go broke and start out here at a
hundred and go over here to 50 and come over to 25 and say,
"well, we're going to cut that in half. We'll go just straight down
to zero," I could understand why they would object, and that's
what you've done.

The court did not address the assumption of low-dose linearity in reaching its decision, but it did observe in a footnote that the assumption was
of questionable validity:

Probably the most controversial assumption incorporated into
Global 79 is that the risk of cancer from formaldehyde is linear
at low dose—in other words that there is no threshold below
which formaldehyde poses no risk of cancer. As the Commission
acknowledges, this assumption leads inescapably to the conclusion that ambient air is carcinogenic, albeit to a lesser extent
than UFFI.

Measurement Error

At the oral argument, the issue of possible measurement error in the CIIT
study was raised by a third judge. In questioning the CPSC's attorney
regarding rat exposure levels, he asked: "Was that not a mean average?
Were they not exposed to as much as 32 parts per million?" The government
attorney replied:

There may have been brief periods when the animals were
exposed to higher doses. But as we point out, these doses
were measured regularly at about half-hour intervals a day and
... they were approaching the level intended by the study. And
if there was an occasional time when doses were higher, in fact
that was for very brief periods, and the overall average was the
targeted dose.

The judge had no further questions regarding the exposure levels.

In the opinion, however, the court showed that it was directly influenced
by the petitioners' argument concerning the exposure levels. In rejecting

the CPSC's reliance on its Global 79 risk assessment using the CIIT rat data, the court stated:

> This problem [reliance on a single study] is exacerbated by con-
> cerns about the Chemical Institute study raised by the industry.
> Although the average level of formaldehyde exposure was 14.3
> ppm, the rats in fact were exposed regularly to much higher
> doses. Measurements of between 17 and 20 ppm were not un-
> common. The highest recorded level was a near-lethal 32.4 ppm.
> We do not have to agree with the industry that this disparity
> renders the study invalid for all purposes to conclude that the
> Commission could not properly use the study as it did. To make
> precise estimates, precise data are required.

In stating that precise data are required to make precise estimates, the court both misunderstood the nature of the animal studies involved in such evaluations and the way in which such data are incorporated in risk assessments that attempt to account for uncertainties.

The Opinion—Rejecting the Data

In its opinion, the court ruled that the CPSC failed to produce sub-stantial evidence of unreasonable risk of injury (cancer) from exposure to formaldehyde. Although it raised several questions about the use of the Global 79 risk assessment, it did not find that it was an unacceptable means for calculating risk. Instead, the court rested its findings on what it perceived to be inadequate data for the model: the exposure assessments and the CIIT study. The court delved deeply into the substantive scien-tific basis for the CPSC's ban and found it lacking. In engaging in this "hard-look" judicial review, the court demonstrated that it correctly un-derstood several technical issues, but it also revealed confusion with regard to complex scientific arguments.

The court rejected as imprecise both the empirical and test data on formaldehyde exposure levels. The court found that the studies, although adequate as generalized findings, were inadequate to serve as a data base for the Global 79 risk assessment model, which the court described as "ex-acting, precise, and extremely complicated." The court stated:

> The goal of the model was to determine the risk of cancer
> to a consumer living in an average UFFI home. The diffi-
> culty in reaching this goal is that neither the in-home nor the
> Franklin/Oak Ridge Labs studies were consistent with this aim.
> The in-home study focused on complaint residences, not average
> residences, not randomly selected residences. The Franklin/Oak
> Ridge Labs studies reflected conditions similar to an unheated,

unair-conditioned home, not an average home. The similar results achieved by the two studies validate neither.

The court also found the CPSC's exclusive reliance on the CIIT study as unsupportable. The court noted that the CIIT study was the only "empirical datum with respect to formaldehyde carcinogenicity that was incorporated into the Global 79 model." The court discussed three areas that raised doubts about the utility of the results of the CIIT study, doubts that were substantial enough to discredit the risk assessment. First, it concluded that the size of the animal bioassay was too small, thus presenting room for a large margin of error. The court made the generalized statement that "had 20 fewer rats, or 20 more developed carcinomas, the risk predicted by Global 79 would be altered drastically." Second, the court held that, even though the CIIT results were approved by the Federal Panel on Formaldehyde, the panel's findings did "not authenticate the use of the study's results and only those results, to predict exactly the cancer risk UFFI poses to man." Finally, the court cited the variance in actual exposure levels in finding that "the Commission could not properly use the study as it did. To make precise estimates, precise data are required."

When the court repeatedly emphasized the precision and exactness that it believed were incorporated into the risk assessment model, it outlined the improper context in which it reviewed both the formaldehyde level data and the CIIT bioassay data. Although admitting that both the exposure data and the bioassay data were adequate as generalized findings, the court rejected both as being too imprecise for use in Global 79. In so doing, the court misrepresented the process of assessing the risks of carcinogens on the basis of animal data. Although precision in the assessment of risk is an ideal, no scientist familiar with the process of risk assessment modeling would describe it as either exacting or precise.

Conclusion

In the *Gulf South* case, the Fifth Circuit was confronted with a massive amount of scientific evidence, which is stated that it did not review fully. The briefs of the opposing parties shaped the issues before the court, and their presentations at oral argument were supposed to clarify them. The court was able to review part of the voluminous record, but a reading of the briefs, the transcript of the oral argument, and the decision itself shows that the court basically confined itself to the limited set of facts presented in the briefs and at oral argument. As indicated by the various questions asked at oral argument and statements in the decision, there was a mixture of comprehension and confusion of exceedingly complex evidence.

In reviewing administrative decisions under the substantial evidence standard, "[t]he ultimate question is whether the record contains 'such relevant evidence as a reasonable mind might accept as adequate to support a conclusion' " [citations omitted]. There is no easy solution to the problem of having the judiciary, trained in the intricacies of law and not science, decide what scientific evidence is or is not adequate to support an agency conclusion.

2.6   Case Study: U.S. ex rel. DiGiacomo v. Franzen, 680 F.2d 515 (7th Cir. 1982)

Introduction

The use of probabilistic arguments and statistical information in identification, especially in the context of criminal cases, has long fascinated both statisticians and legal commentators. Perhaps the most widely cited case in this regard is *People* v. *Collins*, 68 Cal. 2d 319, 438 P. 2d 33, 66 Cal. Rptr. 497 (1968), in which the State of California Supreme Court held that the admission at trial of the testimony of a college mathematics instructor, regarding the probability that another couple possessed the distinctive characteristics of the defendants, constituted prejudicial error and reversed the case. The witness had, among other things, assumed without proof the independence of characteristics that to most people would seem intuitively dependent. (It is interesting to note that, several years prior to this testimony, Chernoff and Moses (1959) included in their introductory statistics text a discussion of exactly this problem in an example dealing with a hypothetical murder trial.)

The use of identification evidence since the *Collins* case has flourished, primarily in connection with the use of blood tests in paternity cases, but some empirical work relating to identification of hair samples by Gaudette and Keeping (1974) has been used in several recent cases and has triggered many of the old arguments surrounding *Collins* as well as some new ones. This case study focuses on one of these cases, *U.S. ex rel. DiGiacomo* v. *Franzen*, but also includes a review of the Gaudette-Keeping work and some related cases.

Two Earlier Cases

In *State* v. *Carlson*, 267 N.W. 2d 170 (Minn. 1978) the defendant was accused of brutally murdering a 12-year-old girl, who had last been seen in his company. The investigating officers found two foreign pubic hairs stuck to the skin of the deceased in the groin area and head hairs clutched in her hand. When questioning the defendant, the police noticed a bloodstain on his jacket. At trial, the prosecution called on two expert witnesses to describe tests they carried out on this physical evidence and statistical interpretations of them. A third expert was called to testify on the statistical validity of the methodological studies relied on by the other experts.

The first of these witnesses, a local forensic laboratory analyst, testified that the blood on the defendant's jacket possessed ABO, PGM, and EAP characteristics identical to those of the victim and that only 1 percent of the population would have the same blood characteristics. She further testified that, based on a microscopic comparison, the two pubic hairs and head hair found on the victim matched hairs taken from the defendant. Finally, she testified that head hair found in the defendant's room on a shoe rag was similar to the victim's hair.

The second witness, a forensic expert working for the Royal Canadian Mounted Police, testified in connection with the same microscopic hair comparisons as did the first witness. He used a somewhat more elaborate comparison system but reached the same conclusions regarding the matches. He further testified that, on the basis of his own studies, there was a probability of 1/800 that each of the pubic hairs stuck to the victim were not the defendant's and a probability of 1/4,500 that each of the head hairs found on the victim were not the defendant's.

The following exchange between counsel for the prosecution and the second witness shows how these probabilities were presented to the court:

> Counsel: Now, based on your comparisons in this case, your specific studies in the area, and your years of experience in hair comparison, can you give a statement as to the likelihood that the pubic hairs found in the vaginal area of [the victim's] body did not come from David Carlson?
>
> Witness: Yes, I would estimate that the chances that those hairs did not come from David Carlson would be on the order of 1 chance in 800 for each hair.
>
> Counsel: One chance in 800 for each hair that those pubic hairs are not David Carlson's?
>
> Witness: That is correct.
>
> Counsel: Now, based on your hair comparisons in this case, your specific research in this area, and your years of experience in hair comparison, can you give an estimate as to the likelihood that the head hairs found on the victim's clothing, on her boots, and on the sheet that carried her to the hospital, did not come from David Carlson?
>
> Witness: I would estimate that the chances that the hairs which you have just referred to did not come from David Carlson would be of the order of 1 chance in 4,500 for each hair.
>
> Counsel: One chance in 4,500 for each of the nine hairs?
>
> Witness: That's correct.
>
> Counsel: Now, regarding the head hair that was found in the rug in the defendant's room, based on your hair comparison in this case, your specific research into the area, and your years of experience in hair comparison, can you give an estimate as to

the likelihood that the hair found on the rug in the defendant's
bedroom did not come from the victim?

Witness: An estimate of the likelihood that the hair found on
the rug in ... Carlson's bedroom ... did not come from the victim would be on the order of 1 chance in 4,500.

The jury returned a verdict of guilty of murder in the first degree, and
the court sentenced Carlson to life imprisonment. On appeal, the defendant
presented several arguments, including one regarding the expert witnesses'
expressing their findings in terms of mathematical probabilities. In the
brief, he cited several cases in support of the proposition that evidence at a
criminal trial may not be expressed in the form of probabilities, including
People v. *Collins.*

The Minnesota Supreme Court noted that, despite the defendant's contentions, a proper foundation for the evidence and statistical probabilities
had been laid "based upon empirical scientific data of unquestioned validity." It went on to state that the evidence in the second forensic expert's
testimony was improperly received because of "its potentially exaggerated
impact on the trier of fact." The court concluded, however, that the first
expert's testimony concerning microscopic hair comparison was properly
admitted and that it regarded the second expert's "statement as cumulative, and thus nonprejudicial on the facts of the case." The court made no
comment on whether the first expert's use of probability to describe the
blood analysis was proper.

In *U.S.* v. *Massey*, 594 F.2d 676 (8th Cir. 1979), an FBI agent testified
at the trial that 3 of the 5 hairs found in a ski mask used in a bank rob-
bery exactly matched the defendant's hair. He then cited the probability of
1/4,500 from that referred to in *Carlson*. In reviewing the case, the Eighth
Circuit Court, following the lead of *Carlson*, held that the use of the statistical evidence was prejudicial error because of its potentially exaggerated
impact on the trier of fact. In addition, the court noted that an insufficient
foundation had been laid for the introduction of the evidence, because the
witness did not know the nature and extent of the comparisons made to
derive the probability of 1/4,500. Finally, the prosecutor, in his summation,
confused the issue of identity of hair and identity of the perpetrator (for a
discussion of related issues, see Finkelstein and Fairley, 1970).

U.S. ex rel. DiGiacomo v. Franzen

In 1977, the defendant James DiGiacomo was tried in an Illinois state
court on charges of rape, deviate sexual assault, aggravated kidnapping,
and battery. As part of the information presented, the prosecution introduced a number of hairs recovered from the victim's automobile, used during the commission of the crime. A criminologist at the Illinois Bureau of
Identification then testified that she compared these hairs with a sample
of DiGiacomo's hair and found them to be microscopically similar. Asked

whether she could testify as to the statistical probability that the hair found belonged to someone other than the defendant, she responded that, on the basis of a recent study she had read, "the chances of another person belonging to that hair would be one in 4,500."

After several hours of deliberation, the jury submitted the following question to the court in writing: "Has it been established by sampling of hair specimens that the defendant was positively proven to have been in the automobile?" The trial judge consulted the parties and then instructed the jury in writing that it was their duty to determine the facts from the evidence presented at trial and that he therefore could not provide an answer to their question. The jury later returned a verdict of guilty.

The defendant appealed, claiming that the judge had erred in permitting the state to use mathematical odds to identify him as the perpetrator of the crime. The Illinois Appellate Court held that the testimony was properly admissible and affirmed the conviction. After leave to further appeal was denied by the Illinois Supreme Court, the defendant filed a petition for habeas corpus in the U.S. District Court, claiming that the admission of the statistical evidence constituted a denial of due process. The district court denied the petition, and an appeal to the Circuit Court of Appeals followed.

The Opinion of the Court of Appeals

The appellate court decided that the defendant's rights were not violated by the expert testimony as to the mathematical likelihood that the hairs found in the car belonged to the defendant and refused to grant habeas corpus premised on the theory that the jury was confused by the mathematical probability testimony. In doing so, it distinguished the circumstances involved from those in the earlier decisions in *Carlson* and in *Massey*, by noting that: (1) in *DiGiacomo* the prosecutor did not emphasize the statistical evidence in the closing argument and did not confuse the issue of identifying the hair with identifying the perpetrator and (2) DiGiacomo had been free to cross-examine or call his own witness to change or clarify the testimony of the prosecution's expert.

The court also noted that in *U.S.* v. *Cyphers*, 553 F.2d 1064, 1071–72 (7th Cir. 1977), it had already rejected a claim that expert testimony based on microscopic analysis of hair samples was not based on reasonable scientific certainty. The court further stated (p.519):

> Even now, DiGiacomo does not claim that [the expert witness] was wrong in her conclusion as to the likelihood of the hair found in [the victim's] car belonging to someone other than him. His contention is only that she should not have been allowed to express the conclusion in terms of mathematical probability. Instead, he contends she should have stated only whether or not the hairs were similar. But to limit her testimony in this way

would have robbed the state of the full probative value of its evidence. To say that the defendant's hair is merely similar to the hair found in the victim's automobile is significantly different than saying that there's a one in 4,500 chance of it belonging to someone else. If the expert's testimony is the latter, we know of no constitutional principle by which its admission could be held improper. While the better practice may be for the court specifically to instruct the jury on the limitations of mathematical probability whenever such evidence is admitted, we have no authority to impose such a rule on the Illinois courts.

Many statistical and legal issues are swept up in the debris of this ruling. Unlike *Carlson*, the witnesses in both *Massey* and *DiGiacomo* did not understand the studies from which the probability of 1/4,500 came, but neither the courts nor the opposing parties in all three cases seemed to want to explore the basis for the number.

The Gaudette-Keeping Study

The witnesses in *Carlson, Massey,* and *DiGiacomo* all referred directly or indirectly to a Gaudette and Keeping (1974) paper on human hair comparisons. This paper was followed by a second paper by Gaudette (1976) on pubic hair comparisons and, in part as a result of the court cases in which they have been cited, the papers have provoked considerable criticism in the forensic literature (e.g., see Barnett and Ogle, 1982). At the time the studies were carried out, Gaudette was a forensic scientist working for the Royal Canadian Mounted Police, and Keeping was a retired professor of mathematical statistics.

The 1974 Gaudette-Keeping study of human hair comparisons had the following methodology. Samples of 80 to 100 "randomly selected" hairs were taken from various regions of the scalps of 100 subjects. For each subject 6 to 11 mutually dissimilar hairs were selected to represent the full range present in the sample of 80 to 100. An elaborate macroscopic examination based on 26 characteristics and a microscopic examination led to the pairwise comparison of 861 hairs from the 100 individuals—i.e., $\binom{861}{2} = 370,230$ comparisons. Of these, all comparisons within the same person were excluded—approximately 3,600—leaving 366,630 comparisons. Only 9 pairs of hairs were found to be indistinguishable. Gaudette and Keeping concluded that:

> The probability, then, that a hair taken at random from Individual A is indistinguishable from a hair taken at random from Individual B in the population studied may be estimated at 9/366,630 or 1 in 40,737. If nine dissimilar hairs are independently chosen to represent the hairs on the scalp of Individual B, the chance that the single hair from A is distinguishable

from all nine of B's may be taken as $[1 - (1/40,737)]^9$, which is approximately $1 - (1/4500)$. This means that the probability that in *at least one* of the nine cases the two hairs examined would be indistinguishable is about 1/4500. If the number of hairs chosen for comparison is 6, 7, 8, 10 or 11, this probability would be somewhat different, but still small (less than 1/3700).

The independence of the 9 hairs in the calculation above is not an important assumption since the use of the Bonferonni inequality yields an upper bound for the probability in question of 1/4,526 (Gaudette, 1982). Other aspects of human hair comparisons are described in Gaudette (1978).

In a follow-up to the study with Keeping, Gaudette (1976), used the same kind of methodology to produce an estimate from pubic hair samples of 1/800 for the probability that a pubic hair taken at random from Individual A will be indistinguishable from at least one of a sample of 6 to 11 hairs taken at random from Individual B.

Barnett and Ogle (1982) have criticized these studies on a variety of grounds, including the fact that those carrying out the comparisons were aware that the individuals were not the same. Gaudette (1982) has prepared a detailed response. Other subsequent critiques include those by Aitken and Robertson (1987), Miller (1987), and Moellenberg (1984).

What the courts and the lawyers in the three cases were clearly interested in learning was the probability that the hair found belonged to the defendant. Instead they received an estimate of the probability that the hairs "selected at random" from two individuals are indistinguishable. What is the relevance of this estimated probability for the kind of identification situation described in *Carlson, Massey,* and *DiGiacomo*? To begin with, we examine the evidence of the Gaudette-Keeping and Gaudette studies. It cannot be used by itself to make the probability statements described about the event: "the hair found belonged to an individual other than the defendant." Even if we interpret 1/4,500 or 1/800 as the probability of a match given a comparison of a suspected hair with a sample from a different individual, we would still need the probability of a match given a sample from the same individual as well as a priori probabilities of "same" and "different." Tawshunsky (1983) comes close to this observation but then veers away along a somewhat irrelevant and erroneous Bayesian tangent. Moellenberg (1984) comes closer but her comments are embedded in a lengthy criticism, not all of which seems relevant. Aitken and Robertson (1987) address these probability issues in a clear and direct fashion.

Taken at face value, the 1/4,500 and 1/800 figures can be interpreted as p-values for the null hypothesis that the suspected hair and the sample come from different individuals. In this case, we have the classic misinterpretation of a p-value as the probability that the null hypothesis is false (for further details, see Appendix A). No one involved in the three cases described above seemed to have recognized this error.

Relating the Gaudette-Keeping Study to the Issue in the Case

There appear to be several steps required to justify the use of the Gaudette-Keeping study as supportive statistical information in connection with hair identification evidence of a forensic expert such as in the DiGiacomo case. First, we must ask if the expert actually understands the methodology and the details of the study producing the probability of 1/4,500. In *Carlson* one of the experts clearly did have this understanding, whereas in *Massey* and in *DiGiacomo* the expert witnesses erroneously cited the conclusions of the study, i.e., the probability of 1/4,500, while expressing confusion about the details of the Gaudette-Keeping study. The same numbers with similar confusions have subsequently been cited in other cases (e.g., see *Huff* v. *State of Alaska*, 675 P.2d 268 (Alaska App. 1984)).

Next, we need to ask whether the hair identification methodology used by the forensic expert was the same as that used in the Gaudette-Keeping study. Was a random sample of 80 to 100 hairs taken from various regions of the defendant's scalp, and then 6 to 11 mutually distinct hairs selected from the sample? Did the expert examine the hair found at the scene of the crime before taking the sample from the defendant? How were the comparisons actually made? Even holding the methodology constant does not imply that the probability of a match would be the same for different experts doing a specific set of comparisons. Gaudette (1978) himself notes that hair comparisons are somewhat subjective "since everyone's observation powers are different." In fact, when "common featureless hairs" were involved in experimental comparisons, specially trained assistants of Gaudette found indistinguishable a much higher proportion of hairs from different individuals than in the original study. The opinions in the three cases make no explicit mention of the methodology used by the expert witness to decide whether or not a match had occurred.

Finally, there is the question of how to relate all the information on hair identification to the question of interest to the courts. One needs to ask whether probabilities should be calculated conditional on the age, race, and sex of the perpetrator (when these are known to coincide with those of the defendant). If so, what should be done about the fact that the Gaudette-Keeping study used a sample primarily in the 20–35 years age category, over 90 percent of whom were Caucasian? The expert in *Carlson* addressed this question and attempted to explain the relevance of this reference population. What about external information on hair color? Only then could a witness begin to consider the ultimate question: What is the probability that the hair found at the scene of the crime belongs to the defendant? To date, as in the *Carlson*, *Massey*, and *DiGiacomo* cases, the courts have not understood that the leap from the collection of statistical information on hair identification to the calculation of such a probability is not a simple task, nor is it a task that the expert witnesses in *Massey* and *DiGiacomo* were equipped to carry out.

Gaudette (1978, 1982) attempts to make the analogy between hair identification in criminal cases and blood group comparisons and other forms
of associative evidence, suggesting that the hair comparisons are superior
scientifically. Aspects of the use of probabilistic assessments of hair identification as evidence in the courts resemble the worst features of the use of
blood group testing in paternity cases (e.g., see Aickin and Kaye, 1983, or
Berry and Geisser, 1986), but the basic methodology rests on far weaker scientific information. In *Massey* and *DiGiacomo* the witnesses gave the court
misinformation, albeit unknowingly. This is especially distressing since the
misinformation was about evidence that had the potential for careful statistical assessment and presentation. Fortunately, the statistical aspects of
hair identification, in the cases considered here, were only a small part of
the evidence presented.

2.7 Case Study: Corrugated Container Antitrust Litigation, J.P.M. D.L. 310 (S.D. Tex. 1977)

Introduction

In 1977, following the Supreme's Court's decision in *U.S.* v. *Container
Corporation of America*, 393 U.S. 333 (1969) that an exchange of price
information may not be exempt from coverage by antitrust laws, purchasers
of cardboard containers and corrugated sheets brought treble-damage class
actions against the manufacturers of these products. The charge was price
fixing between 1960 and 1976. A group of defendants settled by putting
up a fund of some $300 million. However, three defendants—Alton, Mead,
and Westvaco—did not settle and stood trial before a jury. During the trial,
Alton and Westvaco settled for some $6.4 million, leaving Mead as the sole
remaining defendant. This account of the statistical aspects of this case is
adapted in part from the discussion in Finkelstein and Levenbach (1983).

Estimates of Damage at the First Trial

The key statistical component of this case revolved around the determination of damages. The plaintiffs' expert, an economist, presented two
similar multiple regression analyses. In one study, the monthly average price
per square foot of corrugated containers and sheets shipped by members of
the Fiber Box Association (FBA) was regressed on (1) price the previous
month; (2) change in the cost of production from the previous month; (3)
level of manufacturing output in industries using corrugated containers (a
demand factor); (4) the wholesale price index (WPI) for all commodities
(justified as another demand factor, although the reason is unclear); (5)
the productive capacity of paperboard plants (a supply factor); and (6) a
dummy variable to reflect the period of price controls (a factor that was
given the value 1 in the period of price controls March 1971–March 1974

and 0 otherwise). The data were all expressed in the form of index numbers. The period covered by the regression was January 1963 through December 1975 (156 monthly observations); it is during this period that price fixing was determined to have occurred. The estimated regression equation was thus computed solely from data during the conspiracy period. The fit appears to be very good: the square of the multiple correlation coefficient, R^2, being greater than 0.99. A second model was of the same form and used the same variables, except that the price of containers was drawn from a Bureau of Labor Statistics (BLS) price series (which uses the price of a representative container rather than an average price as in the FBA price series). The plaintiffs' expert subsequently dropped variables 5 and 6 from the BLS model because they were not statistically significant in that model.

The plaintiffs' expert then used the estimated regression equation for the conspiracy period ending December 1975 to predict prices in the 1978–1979 post-conspiracy period. These predicted prices were higher than the actual prices, the average of the difference between the projected and actual prices as a percentage of the projected prices being 7.8 percent for the BLS price study and 19.1 percent for the FBA price study. From this, the plaintiffs argued that the overcharge in the conspiracy period was at least 7.8 percent.

The defendants challenged these estimates on various grounds but did not introduce a competing model. The jury found that the overcharge was 5 percent. The case was then sent to a special master to compute damages by applying a 5 percent overcharge figure to the purchases by the plaintiffs in the conspiracy period. While the case was pending before the special master, the parties settled, with Mead agreeing to pay $45 million over a 10-year period.

Second Trial: Plaintiffs' Expert

A second trial followed for certain plaintiffs who had opted out of the class. Most defendants settled by putting up a fund of some $60 million. However, five defendants stood trial before a jury in late 1982 and early 1983. The regression model analyses used at the first trial were introduced again by the same expert witness, this time with certain technical revisions in the explanatory variables. Among other changes, the variables for the level of manufacturing output and for the WPI were refined; a variable for inventory of liner board was added; and costs were used instead of changes in costs. Perhaps more important, the period of collusion was viewed as having ended a year earlier, this time in December 1974. Thus, the period of transition to a fully competitive market was 1975–1978 (for which the plaintiffs also claimed damages) and the period of full competition was 1979 through August 1981 (the latest period for which data were available). Using the same technique and relying solely on the FBA price series, the plaintiffs' expert found a remarkable 26 percent industry-wide overcharge. The damages estimated from the BLS price series were about half those estimated from the FBA price series. The expert translated this by a complex method into an overcharge for each plaintiff.

Second Trial: Criticisms by the Defendants' Expert

For the second trial the defendants had their own expert, a distinguished econometrician from a large private university in the Northeast, who appeared as a witness at trial and leveled a barrage of criticism at the regression models and analyses of the plaintiffs' expert. He contended that the models and the estimates of damages they yielded were "worthless." In particular he noted that if the defendants had charged prices based on the predictions of the plaintiffs' regression model, they would have operated in the red. A synopsis of some of the more salient aspects of the statistical criticisms of the defendants' expert follows. This discussion is based on the transcript of the testimony of the defendants' expert.

The Choice of Explanatory Variables. The fitted regression models displayed high correlation between projected and actual prices over the period used to fit the equation. This goodness-of-fit was cited by the plaintiffs' expert as evidence that the models were correct. However, it has been demonstrated repeatedly that a high correlation in the fit period does not prove that the explanatory factors are in fact good predictors. Sometimes defects in the explanatory variables are fairly obvious. One such case occurs when coefficients have the wrong signs. Such misspecification is not uncommon. A costs variable with a negative sign indicates a misspecified equation because it implies that prices would go down as costs go up.

But even when all coefficients have the correct sign, the equation cannot be assumed to be correct; its reliability must be tested by using it to make projections on another sample of data. The defendants' expert performed such a test by reversing the procedure of the plaintiffs' expert. He estimated the plaintiffs' model from data for the competitive period and then used the model to project what the competitive price would have been in the collusive period. In any event, the projected competitive prices were far above the actual collusive prices—a result suggestive that the explanatory factors were not in fact good predictors of price movement.

Lagged Dependent Variables. One type of explanatory variable deserves separate discussion because its use raises special problems. In an econometric model it is not uncommon to find that the dependent variable itself, lagged by a time period, has been included as an explanatory factor. The justification is that (1) the lagged variable picks up other influences on price not specified by the regression equation or (2) the lagged variable reflects price "stickiness," that is, the slowness with which price responds to changes in explanatory factors. The plaintiffs' expert justified the use of price in the previous month as an explanatory variable by the fact that some prices were determined by annual contracts and thus could not respond immediately to changes in costs and other explanatory factors. He did not explain how this would justify the one-month lag that he used.

One difficulty with a lagged dependent variable is that, if the lag is short, that variable will tend to dominate the equation if its coefficient is estimated from smoothly trending data, so that the equation becomes a poor predictor of changes in trend. These problems were evident in the models used by the plaintiffs' experts in both trials. In those models the dominant explanatory factor was lagged price; no other factor approached it in importance or statistical significance. The result was that the model tended simply to project smooth trends from wherever the fit period was ended. The defendants' expert demonstrated this by showing that the model would have projected collusive prices below the competitive prices in the post-conspiracy period if the fit period had simply stopped at the end of 1971 instead of the end of 1974.

Collusive and Competitive Periods. The results of a multiple regression study will generally be significantly influenced by the choice of the collusive and competitive periods. The principal issues have centered on the length of the collusive period and the existence of a transition to full competition. The regression coefficients of the explanatory variables represent averages over the period used to fit the equation. When this period is long, the estimate of the conspiracy coefficient is open to the objection that, being an average, it does not fairly represent the period immediately adjacent to the competitive period used for comparison. The plaintiffs' regression equations in both *Corrugated Container* trials were fitted over a long period, which raised a question whether the result would have been different if the regression had been calculated using a shorter period adjacent to the competitive period. The defendants' expert computed regressions for subperiods within the collusive period and concluded (not surprisingly) that, on the basis of the results of a standard statistical test, the regressions had significantly different coefficients, thus indicating that the relationships did change over time.

As part of his calculations the plaintiffs' expert argued that there was a post-conspiracy transition period in which prices were still affected by the residue of the conspiratorial activities. Whether there was such a transition was a sensitive issue because the allowance of such a period changes substantially the estimated effects of the collusion considerably and increases greatly the uncertainty of the econometric statistical projections. One technique for determining whether there is a transition period is to compute separate regressions for successive time periods (for example, successive years) after the termination of the conspiracy. A shift in the coefficients of the regressions as the period of collusion recedes is evidence of a transition, which comes to an end when the coefficients stabilize in the post-conspiracy period. The defendants' expert tested the alleged transition period 1975–1978 and found no statistically significant difference between the regression coefficients in this period and in the later period; he relied on this finding to reject the assertion by the plaintiff's expert that there was a transition.

Second Trial: Judgment and Appellate Review

The arguments of the defendants' expert in the second trial were apparently effective in that the jury found that, although a conspiracy had existed, it had not affected the prices paid by the opt-out plaintiffs. Hence there was no recovery in the case. The jury's decision may also have been affected by the evidence that the plaintiffs, who were high-volume, sophisticated purchasers, were less likely to have been overcharged than other purchasers.

On appeal, the jury's verdict was affirmed, 756 F.2d 411 (1985). In its opinion the Fifth Circuit Court discussed one of the plaintiffs' complaints regarding the testimony of the defendants' expert (p.416):

> Plaintiffs offered expert testimony built around an economic model which resulted in an estimate of the amount by which the plaintiffs had been overcharged for corrugated boxes during the conspiracy. Defendants rebutted with expert testimony to the effect that if defendants had charged prices which qualified as fair under plaintiffs' economic model they would have operated in the red. Plaintiffs argue that defendants' expert testimony should have been excluded because a conspiracy tends to inflate costs as well as prices charged and that in an untainted competitive market reduced prices would not have resulted in a loss posture. Plaintiffs' challenge to this testimony goes to its weight, exclusively a jury function, and not to its admissibility. The evidence was relevant and admissible on the issue of the credibility and accuracy of plaintiffs' expert testimony and the question presented was for the jury. This claim of error lacks merit.

Conclusions

The two trials in the corregated container antitrust litigation present an interesting contrast. In the first trial there was only one expert witness, and the jury apparently believed his testimony, finding on behalf of the plaintiffs. In the second trial, this same expert was countered by an articulate expert who testified as a witness for the defendants. He made a strong attack on the statistical analyses of the plaintiffs' expert and successfully challenged many of the assumptions on which the plaintiffs' regression models were based. As a consequence of this testimony the jury found the plaintiffs' arguments far less compelling and did not allow them to recover damages. The battle of the experts in this instance appeared to have a clear winner, although the jurors may have been swayed less by the technical merits of the arguments presented by the defendants' witness than by the effectiveness of the presentation of the evidence.

2.8   Some Lessons: The Institutional Competence of Courts

Looking at the case studies collectively, we see that statistical evidence poses problems for courts and that courts respond to these problems in diverse ways. Sometimes courts seem to be overwhelmed by the statistical evidence and are unable to comprehend its likely import. In the *Gulf South* insulation case, for example, the confusion of the appellate court is obvious, as is the inappropriateness of the shorthand rules that the court used to make sense of the evidence before them. In saying that "to make precise rules, precise data are required," the court is both misunderstanding the potential contribution of statistical models and misinterpreting its own responsibility in reviewing an agency decision.

In *U.S. ex rel DiGiacomo*, the court misunderstands both statistics and the underlying research in hair identification to allow testimony that is impossibly and misleadingly precise. In *Federal Reserve Bank of Richmond*, the trial court faced grave difficulties in evaluating the claim of discrimination because the two sides brought different skills and resources to bear on the case. Moreover, not only was the plaintiffs' expert less than fully prepared for trial, in that his research was not complete until shortly before he testified, but also relations between the expert and the plaintiffs' attorney were such that little attention was paid to the question of how to present the statistical evidence in a clear and effective manner. Confusion was confounded because at trial the plaintiffs' lawyer was unprepared to deal with the implications of the well-known Simpson's paradox, and evidence was presented in forms (i.e. regression analysis) that responded more to perceptions of the court's expectations than to the expert's view of appropriate methods. Nor did matters improve on appeal. The court appeared more concerned with statistical rules about how to evaluate evidence (one-tailed versus two-tailed tests and binomial versus hypergeometric models) than with understanding the evidentiary implications of the data before them.

Even in those cases in which courts performed better, problems exist. In *Vuyanich*, an able judge and his two clerks spent a year to produce an opinion, devoting a full month to just this case. The subsidy of the court system to civil litigants in the resolution of their disputes and the implications for already crammed court calendars of making such intense considerations routine is obvious, and, even with such effort, the resulting opinion is not, from a statistical point of view, error free. Moreover, the justice or injustice of the final verdict is unclear, and, as it turns out, the case will have to be retried in any event because the appellate court, without fully addressing the implications of the statistical evidence, reversed. In many cases, to fully understand statistical evidence a judge will need to learn specialized subject matter knowledge as well as statistics, i.e., statistical analyses are used within the context of the subject matter, such as labor market economics or analytical chemistry.

Carter et al. v. *Newsday*, which from a statistical point of view is perhaps the most successfully handled of the cases we studied, is also not an un-alloyed success. The final settlement came after 8-1/2 years of what must have been expensive and perhaps disruptive litigation. Moreover, the appointment of a statistical expert by the court, a rare and costly procedure, was required. It appears likely that the procedure more than paid for itself by promoting settlement, but it is impossible to say what the implications of this process would have been had the case gone to trial. Interestingly, the expert conceded something to both parties, a familiar technique in success-ful mediation. What would have happened had the evidence in the expert's eyes consistently favored one side is also unclear, but, with the sunk costs of 8-1/2 years of litigation already paid, it would not have been surprising had the disfavored litigant pursued the matter to trial. Similarly, it is diffi-cult for us to disentangle, on the basis of this study, the importance of the choice of the particular "neutral" expert from the institutional implications that the role of "neutral expert" has for statistically complex litigation.

We did not examine the statistical evidence and procedures in the *Cor-rugated Container* case in sufficient depth to reach a judgment about how well the case was handled or about the processes used. It appears on the surface that the first trial illustrates the potential of statistics to mislead when one side does not attempt to mount an expected response to argu-ments made by experts for the other side. The second case suggests that, at least in some settings, a jury can understand conflicting statistical ar-guments and can reach a reasoned judgment as to which is stronger. It is not clear, however, that strength in the minds of the jurors is the same as technical strength.

It is tempting, and perhaps correct, to conclude from these case studies that courts do not ordinarily handle cases well when a significant portion of the evidence, or crucial evidence, is statistical in nature. It is also tempting, and again perhaps correct, to conclude that this is due to a lack of fit between judicial dispute resolution procedures and the quality of statistical procedures and evidence.

In what follows we assume the truth of these conclusions and seek to explicate and explain them. Since we are only assuming a truth, several caveats are in order. First, if we are judging the performance of courts, one may always ask, "good or bad compared to what?" The mandate for the panel did not include an examination of the performance of courts gen-erally or even their performance when confronted with esoteric scientific evidence other than that involving statistics. It is possible that a close look at how courts deal with evidence generally would reveal considerable con-fusion and flawed judgments of the kind we identified in courts confronted with unfamiliar statistical evidence. Even more likely is the possibility that if we examined how courts deal with specialized scientific evidence of a nonstatistical nature we would find cases involving other forms of scientific expertise with problems similar to those we have identified. Thus, it may be the esoteric and unfamiliar nature of statistical evidence rather than anything about statistics per se that poses problems for courts confronted with it. Finally, our look at these cases tells us nothing about the ultimate decision rendered. We have not attempted to nor could we say whether, based on all the evidence, the decisions in these cases are defensible or just. We are similarly unable to say how effectively, relative to cases that do not involve statistics, the courts resolved the disputes before them or established valuable precedent. Thus, to theorize about the institutional obstacles that courts confront when dealing with statistics and to speculate on the resources that courts have to surmount them is not to judge absolutely the court's performance in statistical cases, nor is it to suggest that judicial tribunals are necessarily inferior to other methods that might be used to resolve disputes that turn on statistical evidence.

Points of Tension: Understanding Evidence

The case studies reveal that in dealing with statistical evidence courts can face substantial problems of institutional competence. Here we discuss such competence as it relates to expertise and understanding.

The range of expert witnesses admitted to testify in American jurisprudence is deliberately kept very broad. An expert is defined, by Rule 702 of the Federal Rules of Evidence, as someone qualified by knowledge, skill, experience, training, or education whose expertise will assist the trier of fact to understand the evidence or to determine a fact in issue. When it comes to statistical expertise, courts seem to be willing to accept claims that individuals with training in such diverse areas as economics (e.g., in *Vuyanich*), forensic medicine (e.g., in *DiGiacomo*), and psychology (e.g., in *Federal Reserve Bank of Richmond*) all have sufficient background in statistical methodology to qualify as experts who present statistical testimony.

The diversity of experts permitted to testify in the courts lends itself to the use of terminology that has no precise meaning but sounds precise and therefore carries weight. The opposing counsel and experts may assume such empty terms are terms of art in other fields. Similarly, the judge may assume the existence of expertise that a field simply does not confer (e.g., generalizing from studies on animal populations to human populations). Compare the explicit recognition of this point by the judge in *Vuyanich* with the highly garbled and erroneous discussions in *Gulf South*.

Another problem in most of the case studies is the lack of clarity of exposition by the experts presenting the statistical assessments. Many of the experts made confusing statements in oral testimony, and these were repeated by the judges in their opinions (e.g., in *Federal Reserve Bank of Richmond*). In their written reports (especially in *Vuyanich*, *Carter*, and *Federal Reserve Bank of Richmond*) the statistical experts failed to present a careful description of what statistical approaches they were applying and why. Such clarity may be crucial to the understanding of judges and jurors.

Demeanor is probably overvalued in such a system, and judges may have an obligation to understand where expertise is precise and definitive and where it merely betokens familiarity. Some would argue that this is primarily the task of the lawyers, but their partisanship prevents their assertiveness from being too helpful. The standard tactics of discrediting experts have little to do with ascertaining genuine qualifications. See especially the judicial commentary in *Vuyanich* on the issues of expert communication, in *Gulf South* on expert judgments, and in *DiGiacomo* on what constitutes "expertise."

Later in this report we address the complexity and unfamiliarity of statistical evidence and the "two expert" problem. Both problems surface in the cases we examined. In *Federal Reserve Bank of Richmond*, for example, the Court of Appeals for the Fourth Circuit reversed because in its eyes the lower court had applied an incorrect statistical model and biased its conclusions by applying a one-tailed test of significance. The error of the lower court's decisions is by no means clear, and the appellate court obviously does not understand the relation between the binomial and hypergeometric models. In *Gulf South*, the appellate judges did not grasp the concept of low-dose linearity.

The two-expert problem surfaces in *Vuyanich* in an interesting way. When the plaintiffs' model specification was challenged by the defendant's expert, the judge accepted the plaintiff's decision not to run separate regressions for male and female employees but instead to use a single equation with sex effects measured by a dummy variable because, in the court's view, the plaintiffs' expert combined knowledge of labor economics and statistics while the expertise of the defendant's witness was confined to statistical issues. In doing this the court, despite its relatively substantial competence in dealing with statistical evidence, was responding in a rather typical way to a conflict of experts. It was deciding which witness's expertise was more on target and accepting that witness's judgment without a further probing of the issue. The effect was to accept an intuitive guess that male and female salaries are affected in much the same way by variables other than sex when, with the data that had been collected, the issue easily could have been put to an empirical test. By the same token, however, there is no apparent reason why the defense could not have run the tests in question had they thought it crucial. Thus, the criticism by the defendant's expert of the plaintiffs' statistical approach may have simply been a variant of criticisms commonly made of evidence entered by parties bearing the burden of proof: "It is suspect because it could have been better." Yet such a complaint is commonly and properly dismissed when access to the supposedly better evidence is readily available to the opposing party but is not offered.

In this respect the *Vuyanich* case stands in striking contrast to *Carter*. In *Carter* the court's expert forced the parties to do additional statistical analyses prior to trial in order to resolve issues that might otherwise have led to speculative criticisms similar to those made in *Vuyanich*. Had this occurred at trial, the judge might have felt compelled to look closely at the experts' credentials rather than at the data to decide which expert to believe.

Carter, of course, did not reach trial, and it is doubtful if the court's expert could have continued to perform as he did had things advanced that far. At trial the parties are allowed—within the rules of evidence—to present their case as they see fit, and the rapidity with which most trials proceed largely precludes statistical refinement of the data base or of the statistical analyses employed such as occurred before trial in *Carter*. Nor does the role accorded the court-appointed expert under the rules of evidence allow him to demand that the parties conduct further analyses once the trial has commenced. Instead he testifies as an ordinary witness on the basis of his expertise and observations. The appointed expert's persuasive power stems from his expert credentials and his facial neutrality.

The tendency of courts to judge statistical analyses in large measure by the witnesses who present them is in marked contrast to the tendency in science and statistics to judge scholars by the quality of the statistical analyses they present. This contrast occurs for other fields as well, and it is just one way in which a court is institutionally distant from the scientific speculation that will inform it.

The Extensiveness of Investigation

A second point of distinction that tends to estrange law from statistics lies in the criteria each uses to decide when an investigation has been extensive enough to be terminated. In the sciences that use statistics, research ideally proceeds until sufficient information has been generated so that all plausible rival hypotheses can be evaluated, if not disposed of. This procedure often involves the scientist in a "conversation" with the data in which the patterns revealed in one analysis suggest further possibilities that can then be examined. It also requires a good sense for the strengths and weaknesses of various statistical procedures and ways of compensating for them. In *Vuyanich*, for example, the defendant's expert suggested the possibility that the variable of sex interacts with other factors that are used to predict salary (e.g., experience, education, supervisory responsibility). The reasonableness of this possibility might have been assessed by running separate regression analyses using men and women and examining the coefficients on the variables predicting salary in the two equations for statistically significant differences. Had the plaintiffs' study in this case been submitted as an article to a refereed scholarly journal, a referee might well have suggested further analysis of the kind described, and an editor might have agreed to publish the study with a single equation model using sex as a dummy variable only if separate regression analyses supported the author's contention.

This is not to say that statistical investigations proceed indefinitely until all plausible alternatives to the favored hypothesis have been discarded.

There are limitations of time and money in the sciences as well as in law. An investigator with the money and time would not eschew a further, perhaps crucial, analysis because the hypothesis being investigated is not important enough to justify the expense of additional statistical work that would either dispose of a salient rival hypothesis or call the validity of the tested hypothesis into question. If, however, the crucial analysis was not done because the scientist allocated his limited resources to other activities, other researchers might be counted on to examine the viability of the plausible rival hypotheses in future work.

This attitude is understandably different from what one sees in law. A court, when faced with research by the parties that ignores untested plausible rival hypotheses or models, does not leave the matter open for future research. Nor does it typically hold the adjudication open while the parties conduct further analyses. Instead it tends—for the good institutional reason that it must decide the case—to reach an all-or-none decision. Either it accepts the preferred hypothesis despite unexamined plausible rival hypotheses, as in *Vuyanich*, or it rejects the preferred hypothesis, as in *Gulf South*, because plausible rival hypotheses have not been adequately disposed.

In addition to a judicial unwillingness to leave matters open for further research, courts may confront substantial ambiguity in the data presented because the appropriate extensiveness of the investigation largely depends on what is at stake. In the typical traffic case, for example, the investigation begins and ends with the patrol officer's decision to ticket the driver. At the other extreme, in a billion-dollar antitrust suit, the investigative proceedings may take years and millions of dollars may be expended. There is almost necessarily a close relationship between what is at stake and the amount spent litigating over it. Thus, even when substantial dollar amounts or important policies are at stake, it may make perfect sense for neither party to spend an additional $100,000 to collect and analyze the data needed for a statistical analysis that might definitively resolve a matter in litigation. If the results are inconclusive or favor the opponent, the cost of additional research might for each party exceed the expected return. This is one reason why the routine appointment of a neutral statistical expert with the authority to require further data analysis, as was done in *Carter*, may be problematic. It may take away from the parties the decision as to what level of investment the case merits.

On other occasions, the parties do not decide the extensiveness of the investigation because the party that is interested in a more extensive investigation lacks the resources to carry it out. This will almost always be the case in criminal litigation. In *DiGiacomo*, for example, the defendant might have wished to invest in further statistical studies of the possibilities of matching hair, but he lacked the resources to conduct such a study. Thus, the defense counsel is reduced to pointing out flaws in the studies the state cites, and even this way of coping is rare because it presupposes a defense attorney who is familiar with and understands the statistical evidence on which the state's expert relies.

When, on occasion, the normal processes of science call into question the theories and research that underlie novel or popular kinds of scientific evidence, lawyers can challenge such evidence without having to construct challenges to particular studies. The courts typically react by rejecting the evidence in the same all-or-nothing way they once accepted it. This most recently happened with voice identification testimony after a National Research Council (1979) review of the theories and techniques used by forensic experts in this area called the enterprise into question.

The Court's Quest for Certainty

Perhaps the most interesting and fundamental disjunction between law and statistics lies in the attitude each takes toward uncertainty. Statisticians are comfortable with uncertainty, for statistical science is often in the business of placing bounds on uncertainty and extracting information from situations in which uncertainty exists. Courts, by contrast, are made uneasy by uncertainty and often act as though uncertainty does not exist. This attitude may seen inconsistent with legal standards of judgment, such as the "preponderance of the evidence" or "beyond a reasonable doubt" burdens of proof that by their very language acknowledge that certainty in litigation is unlikely. Yet the behavior of courts constantly reveals the unease that uncertainty entails, despite the apparent reflection of uncertainty in plea bargaining and in pretrial settlements. For example, when judgments are reached in accord with some burden of proof, the sanction does not reflect the uncertainty that may figure in the judgment but instead will award the prevailing party everything to which it is entitled or will punish a guilty party as if the validity of the verdict were ensured. The law's attitudes toward witnesses provides another example. The law focuses considerable attention on credibility but often acts as if credibility is an all-or-nothing characteristic, with the testimony of credible witnesses to be believed in all particulars and that of incredible ones dismissed. Indeed, in accord with the maxim *"falsa in uno; falsa in ominibus,"* courts have instructed juries that if they find a witness has lied about one thing, they may on that ground disbelieve everything the witness has said.

The law's apparent preference for direct testimony also reflects the stress of uncertainty. The testimony of a witness who has seen the crucial event can, if believed, dispose of all issues beyond a doubt. Circumstantial evidence, however, is inherently probabilistic. Thus, there is always the possibility that a verdict in a case built on circumstantial evidence, which accords with the weight of the evidence, will be wrong. This may explain, in part, the law's view on hearsay evidence.

With this attitude toward uncertainty, it is not surprising that courts are uneasy with statistical testimony and try to impose on it rules of thumb that will give the appearance of certainty to information whose value may lie largely in the specification of degrees of uncertainty. Thus, in *Federal Reserve Bank of Richmond*, the appellate court appears to be acutely concerned with whether a one-tailed or two-tailed test is appropriate. The magnitude and direction of the differences between the salaries at issue will be the same regardless of the rejection range employed, but the court writes as if discrimination surely exists if one test is employed and surely does not exist if the other is appropriate. Moreover, the appellate court seemed to believe that, if discrimination against the plaintiff class could not be inferred from a regression in which the crucial coefficient was significant at the 5% level, then no member of the plaintiff class could through anecdotal evidence maintain a claim of discrimination—it simply did not exist. Not only does this view ignore the difference between aggregate and individual discrimination, but it also implicitly views the statistical test used in the litigation as ideal, guaranteed to spot discrimination using the .05 level if it does exist.

The all-or-nothing character of witness credibility judgments may become transformed into an all-or-nothing judgment of statistical models and procedure. If they pass muster, all their implications are to be fully credited; if they do not, all are to be dismissed. Similarly, in *Vuyanich*, the judge writes as if he must choose between statistical models on the various points at issue so that the choice of model determines the ultimate conclusion and not the information content of the research on both sides.

This quest for certainty sometimes leads courts to accept research that should be suspect because it is too precise. The expert's testimony in *DiGiacomo* that there was only a one in 4,500 chance that the hairs he examined belonged to someone other than *DiGiacomo* provides an example of such false precision.

At the other extreme, a court may reject testimony in its entirety and the information contained therein because it is admittedly and inescapably imprecise. The appellate court's concern with the implications of measurement error in *Gulf South* is an instructive example. In writing "to make precise estimates, precise data are required," the court reveals an intolerance for uncertainty and a failure to appreciate how information may be gleaned from imprecise data. They also take a "witness credibility" attitude toward the statistical study. Since there are admitted flaws in the way the design was carried out, the study was totally rejected. Unlike the statistician or the scientist, the *Gulf South* court did not inquire into the information content of what remains.

Adversary Procedures

A fourth point of tension between law and statistics lies in the adversary system. It is common in discussions of science and the law to note that the latter uses the adversary system and the former does not, and that science can be easily corrupted when scientists are enlisted to promote the interests of one side or the other in adversarial proceedings. Statistics may be particularly prone to being used by parties in litigation to generate desired answers because the choice of methods and data can easily influence the results. Moreover, when statistical analysis is conducted in private, an expert need not commit himself to an approach until finding one that yields favorable results. Of course, in actual practice, scientists often proceed as if they know what the results of analyses and experiments will show.

The case studies strongly suggest the ability of competing sides in litigation to acquire statistical experts who can generate analyses that the side that employs them will find felicitous. *Vuyanich, Federal Reserve Bank of Richmond, Carter,* and the second *Corrugated Container* case all involve experts who reached diametrically opposed statistical conclusions from essentially the same data. In each case there may be legitimate reasons to explain the ability of the experts to reach different conclusions based on different models and methods. Nonetheless, we are left with an impression that the adversarial nature of the legal process has contributed substantially to this battle of experts. This situation raises ethical issues that we explore at length in the following chapters.

On one hand, the ability to prove one's case may well hinge on such matters as the proper level of aggregation, issues that are mixed questions of reality and statistical analysis and may not have a right answer in any real sense. Here it is most appropriate for each side to urge its case with vigor and expertise. A neutral expert might side with one side or the other, depending on both technical and practical arguments (e.g., the particular cutoff point chosen for a variable may tend to exaggerate the facts or possible evidence of employment discrimination; or the work units being analyzed separately have neither the authority to hire nor homogeneity of skills). On the other hand, a clash of experts may obscure the commonality that is hidden in their analyses. Here a neutral expert might be of great help, noting what the experts agree on and exactly where they differ and why. See especially *Carter* and *Federal Reserve Bank of Richmond* for such instances.

The State of the Art

A final source of tension between law and statistics is not highlighted by the case studies but is implicit in them. It is that, with the possible exception of the risk assessment model used in *Gulf South,* the statistical techniques used in the litigation studies are relatively simple—often standard statistical tests or multiple linear regression analyses. It is difficult to say whether the data in these cases might have been better analyzed, but the techniques used were not state of the art; that is, they were not the techniques that would be employed by a statistician exploring the issue in question with an eye to publication in a leading research journal. But the most appropriate techniques of data analysis may be intuitively less understandable than less appropriate methods.

As statistics becomes yet more firmly entrenched as a way of presenting evidence and as more sophisticated statisticians become involved as experts in litigation, the results of research may take forms that are increasingly difficult to comprehend and judges may find themselves yet more frequently in the business of evaluating experts rather than the evidence the experts offer. There is a danger that trials involving extensive statistical evidence will leave judges and jurors with the sense that they are being increasingly alienated from both the basic evidence in the case and the judgmental task they are sworn to perform. For this reason, the courts and statisticians should probably be content with tried and true methods unless innovative approaches are essential.

Judicial Flexibility

We have discussed some of the darker implications that may be drawn from the case studies. Clearly there are tensions between law and statistics that are not mere misunderstandings but are rooted in the institutional structures and values of the two professions. But the case studies reveal a bright side as well. First, a crucial value is shared by law and statistics. Both seek to make sense of data and to understand the world as it is. Courts and statisticians are each in their own way committed to finding truth. The case studies show that courts wish to use statistics when it promises to aid them in reaching that end and that institutional customs do not necessarily bind the courts in their search for truth and justice. When courts perceive that statistics can aid them in reaching a just decision, they can be remarkably flexible in accommodating statistical evidence. Some courts—or, to be more precise, some judges—are willing to learn and to innovate in order to better understand and deal with statistical evidence when it is relevant.

Among the cases we have examined, *Vuyanich* and *Carter* stand out for the special efforts that the judges made to cope with the evidence before them. In *Vuyanich* the judge in tandem with his law clerks undertook a program of self-education in statistics sufficient to acquire far more than lay knowledge of the evidence in the case. As the work of one judge in one case, the effort is commendable, but individual self-education of this sort is unlikely to be a systemic solution. Many judges would not find the self-study of statistics easy, and the costs of self-education in both judicial and law clerk time are considerable, even if the investment pays off further for society when the judge encounters other cases raising statistical issues. The efforts of the judge in *Vuyanich* does suggest a judicial interest in statistics that, if widespread, may mean that a more formal program in understanding statistics would find a ready audience. If so, it would be possible to raise the bench's statistical knowledge considerably. Some programs already attempt to educate federal judges about statistics, but these are limited in form and depth.

In *Carter*, the judge did not try to evaluate the statistical evidence himself but instead appointed an expert to help the court understand and refine the statistical aspects of the case. The expert's effort appears from the case study to have contributed to a settlement that at least at this remove seems fair to both parties. Later in this report we discuss some of the arguments for and against the appointment of neutral experts to aid the court in difficult cases. Here we simply note the device as an example of the kind of institutional flexibility available to creative courts that seek to cope with the unfamiliarity and complexity of statistical evidence.

Significantly, in our case studies the district courts that try cases and listen to the presentation of statistical testimony appear to do better with statistical evidence than the appellate courts that pass on the proceedings below. *Vuyanich, Carter,* and the second *Corrugated Container* case all seem to be examples of courts coping relatively successfully with complicated statistical evidence. In *Federal Reserve Bank of Richmond, Gulf South,* and *DiGiacomo,* in which the appellate courts looked closely at statistical issues, fundamental misunderstandings of statistical analyses abounded. This may seem strange, for the general view of appellate courts is that, by virtue of being removed from the fray of trial, they can better educate themselves and be more thoughtful in their understanding of complicated issues.

It may be that this pattern of trial court success and appellate court difficulty in dealing adequately with statistical evidence is a mere coincidence, a function of the small number of cases we examined in detail, but we think not. When it comes to understanding and coping with statistical evidence, the institutional advantage appears to be with the trial court. In dealing directly with the expert witnesses and acquiring an intimate knowledge of the facts of the case, the trial judge has an opportunity that the appellate judge lacks for instruction on the role of statistical evidence in the case in question. The latter is aided only by the parties' briefs and a short oral argument by a lawyer who must deal with legal issues as well as statistical ones and may not fully understand the statistical issues in the case, a situation that provides little opportunity to probe deeply the statistical issues that divide the parties. Thus, the appellate judge cannot seek the aid of the parties' experts in understanding the statistical evidence, but is limited to what he can learn on his own. This limited opportunity to be educated on the statistical aspects of the case plus the general tendency of appellate judges to pronounce rules of law may account for the efforts of the judges in *Federal Reserve Bank of Richmond* and *Gulf South* to resolve statistical issues through law-like pronouncements of what is good and bad statistical technique without either a full understanding of the issues raised or an appreciation of what good statistical methodology implies given the specific facts of the case.

Thus, our case studies tell us something interesting about the institutional potential of differently located judges to come to grips with statistical information. In this statistics may differ from other forms of scientific evidence, in which an understanding of context may be less important in evaluating what has been presented. This is because understanding what is good applied statistical methodology requires an understanding not only of general statistical principles but also of what these principles imply given the data available in the case.

Conclusion

We see in our case studies definite points of tension between law and statistics that are reflected in the difficulties courts sometimes have in dealing with statistical evidence. These difficulties are not only a result of the fact that statistics may be complex and difficult for anyone without specialized training to understand. In addition, institutionalized ways of proceeding and habits of judicial thought interfere with the ability of the legal system to generate the most probative statistical evidence given the tasks the system confronts and with its ability extract the full probative value (and no more) from the statistical evidence that is presented. Yet if courts have institutionalized ways of thinking and proceeding, they are not locked into them. Both the rules of pretrial discovery and the rules of evidence leave much to judicial discretion. Moreover, the case studies reveal that at least some judges will educate themselves and adapt their procedures to better deal with statistical evidence when they are convinced that such changes will enable them to better do their mission, which is to achieve justice in accordance with the law. This flexibility tells us something important about courts in modern society, and we see in it considerable promise for improving the way that courts deal with statistical evidence.

3

Review of the Use of Statistics in Selected Areas of Litigation

3.1 Introduction

The growth in the use of statistical assessments as evidence has varied by area of litigation. As we noted in Chapter 1, however, the growth has been more dramatic in areas in which the financial stakes have become higher. Three such areas are employment discrimination, antitrust, and environmental law. This chapter reviews the uses of statistical evidence in these areas, drawing on the experience, knowledge, and interest of the panel members, staff, and consultants.

While the selected areas illustrate the use of statistical assessments in complex litigation, they also involve the use of statistical arguments to show cause and effect. But there are also important differences across the areas. Impetus for the use of statistics in employment discrimination litigation, in connection with Title VII of the Civil Rights Act of 1964, came in large part from the use of statistical arguments by the Supreme Court in three landmark cases in 1977. The growth was subsequently fueled by the close examination of statistical evidence in judicial opinions, in part because many class action employment discrimination cases are inherently statistical in nature. In antitrust cases, by contrast, the use of statistics has been more closely tied to economic arguments and testimony, and new law focusing on the statistical aspects of antitrust disputes has not emerged as rapidly, in part because of the prevalence of jury as opposed to bench trials. Finally, statistical evidence in environmental litigation is often tied to biological and epidemiological modeling and is typically introduced in administrative hearings. Only when administrative agency rulings are appealed does the statistical evidence come before federal court judges for review.

Each of the area reviews discusses several important or landmark cases and the commentaries on them, indicates the statistical techniques used, notes how and by whom they are introduced into evidence, and provides references for the reader to other reviews and relevant commentary. Each review ends with a general evaluation of the apparent impact of the use of statistical assessments and the appropriateness of the methodology being used.

3.2 Title VII Employment Discrimination Litigation

Of all the areas of civil litigation, employment discrimination cases have made the greatest use of witnesses with statistical expertise. Expert witnesses have been used especially in connection with class action suits brought under Title VII of the Civil Rights Act of 1964. This section reviews the evolution of statistical expertise in this area and draws heavily on the writings on this topic by members of the panel, its staff, and its consultants (see e.g., Campbell, 1984; Fienberg, 1982; Fienberg and Straf, 1982; Finkelstein, 1980; Meier, Sacks, and Zabell, 1984), as well as on their collective experience. Other basic sources in this area include Baldus and Cole (1980) and Morris (1977, 1978).

3.2.1 Title VII and Class Action Suits: The Beginning

The Civil Rights Act of 1964 forbids discrimination because of race, color, religion, sex, or national origin by employers, labor unions, programs receiving federal assistance, and places of public accommodation. In particular, Title VII of the act states that it is an unlawful employment practice for an employer to "fail or refuse to hire or to discharge any individual, or otherwise to discriminate against any individual with respect to his compensation, terms, conditions, or privileges of employment, because of such individual's race, color, religion, sex, or national origin" (§703(a)(1)). An elaborate procedure was established to adjudicate alleged violations of the act and includes a review by the Equal Employment Opportunity Commission (EEOC), after which individuals may file suit in federal district court on their own behalf, and often also on behalf of the class of individuals "similarly situated," against the employer (and sometimes others). Such class action suits lend themselves to statistical examination under the legal theories of "disparate treatment" and "disparate impact" (see the related discussion in Baldus and Cole, 1980). The law stipulates that Title VII cases be tried before a judge and not a jury.

The present use of statistical evidence in employment discrimination cases stems in large part from *Griggs* v. *Duke Power Company*, 401 U.S. 424 (1971), in which the Supreme Court established "disparate impact" as a basis for challenging employment selection procedures. Black employees contended that the Duke Power Company violated the act by requiring that new employees hold a high school diploma and to register scores at the level of the national median for high school graduates on certain tests if they wished to be placed in the desirable departments of "Operations," "Maintenance," and "Laboratory" at the Dan River Steam Station in North Carolina. Other new employees and previously hired employees who lacked a high school education or adequate test scores were assigned to "Labor" or "Coal Handling." The adverse impact of these requirements was shown on the basis of 1960 census statistics (which revealed that 34 percent of the white males in North Carolina had completed high school, while only 12 percent of the black males had done so) and on the basis of an EEOC finding that the company's use of a set of tests resulted in a pass rate of 58 percent for whites compared with 6 percent for blacks. The company made no attempt to validate the tests or the education requirement, but it denied discriminatory intent. The Supreme Court held that the selection procedure discriminated against blacks, in violation of the Civil Rights Act, because the company did not show that the use of the test was a business necessity.

In *Washington* v. *Davis*, 426 U.S. 229 (1976), two black men had been denied positions as police officers in the District of Columbia when they did not achieve a passing score on a written examination developed by the U.S. Civil Service Commission to measure verbal ability. The two applicants claimed that the hiring practice had a disparate impact on blacks. They showed that between 1968 and 1971, 57 percent of the black applicants for positions with the police department failed the examination, but only 13 percent of all other applicants failed. They also alleged that the examination bore no relation to job performance. The police department introduced evidence of its efforts to recruit black candidates. The Supreme Court held that the plaintiffs' case was insufficient.

The following year, the Supreme Court attempted to clarify the two notions of disparate treatment and disparate impact in *International Brotherhood of Teamsters* v. *U.S.*, 431 U.S. 334, 335, n.15 (1977) as follows:

> "Disparate treatment" [occurs when] ... the employer simply treats some people less favorably than others because of their race, color, religion, or national origin. ... Claims of disparate treatment may be distinguished from claims that stress "disparate impact." The latter involve employment practices that are facially neutral in their treatment of different groups but that in fact fall more harshly in one group than another and cannot be justified by business necessity.

But, as Kaye (1982) notes, some Supreme Court opinions have blurred the distinction between these two types of Title VII cases, and most cases that involve any serious statistical analysis are likely to be brought under both theories. An exception is the *Vuyanich* case described in Chapter 2, in which the appeals court vacated the original judgment because it deemed that disparate treatment and not disparate impact should be the approach for assessing hiring claims. That opinion, however, declined to reach a judgment of the appropriateness of the statistical analyses.

The *Teamsters* decision also provided two memorable quotes regarding the use of statistical evidence:

> Our cases make it unmistakably clear that "statistical analyses have served and will continue to serve an important role" in

cases in which the existence of discrimination is a disputed issue. (p.339)

We caution only that statistics are not irrefutable; they come in infinite variety and, like any other kind of evidence, they may be rebutted. In short, their usefulness depends on all of the surrounding facts and circumstances. (p.340)

The court was probably not prepared for the number of cases that followed. In 1978, for example, nearly 6,000 discrimination cases were filed in federal district courts, and the expected proof in many of these cases was to be statistical in nature.

3.2.2　Castaneda v. Partida, 430 U.S. 482 (1977)

The watershed for the acceptability of statistical analyses and formal inference for Title VII cases came, not in a Title VII case, but in one involving jury discrimination. In *Castaneda* v. *Partida*, which involved the jury selection system in a Texas jurisdiction, the Supreme Court gave a form of official sanction to the use of the binomial model for proportions, and the normal approximation to it, by buttressing its opinion with the following footnote (430 U.S. 496, n.17, citations omitted):

> If the jurors were drawn randomly from the general population, then the number of Mexican-Americans in the sample could be modeled by a binomial distribution. ... Given that 79.1% of the population is Mexican-American, the expected number of Mexican-Americans among the 870 persons summoned to serve as grand jurors over the 11-year period is approximately 688. The observed number is 339. Of course, in any given drawing some fluctuation from the expected number is predicted. The important point, however, is that the statistical model shows that the results of a random drawing are likely to fall in the vicinity of the expected value. ... The measure of the predicted fluctuations from the expected value is the standard deviation, defined for the binomial distribution as the square root of the product of the total number in the sample (here 870) times the probability of selecting a Mexican-American (0.791) times the probability of selecting a non-Mexican-American (0.209). ... Thus, in this case the standard deviation is approximately 12. As a general rule for such large samples, if the difference between the expected value and the observed number is greater than two or three standard deviations, then the hypothesis that the jury drawing was random would be suspect to a social scientist. The 11-year data here reflect a difference between the expected and observed number of Mexican-Americans of approximately 29 standard deviations.

Meier, Sacks, and Zabell (1984:142) note:

> In systems where jury selection is purportedly carried out by a random process, such statistical tests are appropriate. The key man system, whose constitutionality was not at issue in *Castaneda*, is not a random process, but the Court might well require as a matter of public policy that its operation closely approximate a random process.

3.2.3 Hazelwood School District v. U.S., 433 U.S. 301 (1977)

In *Hazelwood*, the plaintiffs alleged that blacks had been discriminated against in hiring teachers in the Hazelwood school district in a suburban area of St. Louis, Missouri. Part of the proof involved a showing that the proportion of blacks hired was less than their representation among qualified public schoolteachers in the relevant labor market. Two different sets of availability figures were presented, but no formal statistical techniques were used to analyze the data. The district court found for the plaintiffs, and, when the case reached the Supreme Court under appeal, the Court adopted the statistical rule it had just put forth in *Castaneda* to employment discrimination with little argument or justification (433 U.S. 301, n.17, citations omitted):

> Under the statistical methodology explained in *Castaneda* v. *Partida*, ... involving the calculation of the standard deviation as a measure of predicted fluctuations, the difference between using 15.4% and 5.7% as the area wide [availability] figure would be significant. If the 15.4% figure is taken as a basis for comparison, the expected number of Negro teachers hired by Hazelwood in 1972–1973 would be 43 (rather than the actual figure of 10) of a total of 282, a difference of more than five standard deviations; the expected number of 1973–1974 would be 19 (rather than the actual figure 5) of a total of 123, a difference of more than three standard deviations. For the two years combined, the difference between the observed number of 15 Negro teachers hired (of a total of 405) would vary from the expected number of 62 by more than six standard deviations. Because a fluctuation of more than two or three standard deviations would undercut the hypothesis that decisions were being made randomly with respect to race, ibid., each of these statistical comparisons would reinforce rather than rebut the government's other proof. If, however, the 5.7% area wide figure is used, the expected number of Negro teachers hired ... would be ... less than two standard deviations from the observed number of 10.

Note that a 2-standard-deviation criterion in effect implies a two-tailed test, using in excess of a 5% significance level. In a dissenting opinion Justice Stevens questioned this criterion and, in a footnote that attributed the calculation to his clerk, argued that the 5.7 percent availability figure is still significant at the 5% level. A careful review of the calculations makes clear that Justice Stevens' clerk used a one-tailed test. This was rather a subtle argument that Justice Stevens and the rest of the Court seemed not to have understood.

Critiques of this decision and its use of formal tools of statistical inference have been published in many places (see, e.g., Smith and Abram, 1981; Sugrue and Fairley, 1983; and Meier, Sacks, and Zabell, 1984). Meier, Sacks, and Zabell comment as follows (p.145):

> The random sampling model for nondiscriminatory hiring used by the Court rests on two implicit assumptions: (a) the chance that any particular teacher hired will be black is the same as the overall percentage of black teachers—5.7%, and (b) the racial outcomes of the 405 hires are "statistically independent." With these two assumptions it can be shown mathematically that the sample proportion (i.e., the proportion of blacks hired) should be near the population proportion of 5.7% and will deviate from it only to an extent described by the binomial probability distribution. Such a distribution permits one to calculate the probability that a sample proportion in a properly drawn random sample will deviate from the population proportion to as great an extent as actually found in the observed sample. The greater the observed deviation, the smaller this probability will be. If the probability is found to be very small, one might then reasonably conclude that the random selection model is not credible.
>
> ... The Court is correct in its assertion that the recommended statistical procedure tests "randomness" in hiring to the extent that "randomness" is read to mean random selection from a specified pool of teachers. However, the Court then appears to equate "randomness" with "fairness" or "nondiscrimination" in employment. The latter concepts are relevant to the legal issue, but only the former is tested statistically; since hiring will seldom be truly "random" even if it *is* fair or racially nondiscriminatory, the nexus between the two sets of concepts is more problematic than is usually recognized.
>
> ... In summary: (a) The standard statistical models are based on the assumption of random sampling, an assumption that is unjustified in hiring processes, at least in part, because of clustering or stratification. (b) Even when there is only a minor departure from the random sampling model, the sole use of statistical significance tests would be inappropriate because it can

lead (especially in large samples) to the detection of disparities even when discrimination is absent, because of correlations
between individual characteristics and applicant self-selection.

This view—that the employment process is necessarily highly nonrandom
and as a consequence the statistical analysis of employment patterns is
often highly questionable and of limited utility—is supported by many
within the statistical community. Nonetheless, statistical testing continues
to be used by expert statistical witnesses and by the courts, and judicial
opinions have shed little further light on the need for a quantitative criterion
of substantiality. Those who support the use of tests of significance in the
discrimination context argue that they serve as a valuable benchmark, and
this argument has substantial support among statisticians.

The following subsections describe the use of statistical methods, primarily by expert witnesses, in various employment discrimination cases from
1975 to 1984. The methodologies of the experts show increasing complexity,
but the comprehension of the judges has clearly not kept apace.

3.2.4 The 80 Percent Rule

Faced with the prospect of thousands of Title VII complaints and the need
to monitor compliance with the Civil Rights Act, several federal government agencies worked together to draft guidelines that would represent a
uniform federal government position on matters of employment discrimination. This effort resulted in the *Uniform Guidelines on Employee Selection
Procedures*, 43 F.R., No. 166, 38290–38296 (1978), issued not long after
the *Castaneda* and *Hazelwood* decisions and adopted by the EEOC, the
Departments of Labor and Justice, and the Civil Service Commission.

The section of the *Uniform Guidelines* most widely referred to presents
a criterion for substantiality of adverse or disparate impact:

> Sec. 6D. *Adverse impact and the "four–fifths rule."* A selection
> rate for any race, sex or ethnic group which is less than four–
> fifths (or eighty percent) of the rate for the group with the
> highest rate will generally be regarded by the Federal enforce-
> ment agencies as evidence of adverse impact, while a greater
> than four–fifths rate will generally not be regarded by Federal
> enforcement agencies as evidence of adverse impact. Smaller
> differences in selection rate may nevertheless constitute adverse
> impact, where they are significant in both statistical and practi-
> cal terms or where a user's actions have discouraged applicants
> disproportionately on grounds of race, sex, or ethnic group.
> Greater differences in selection rate may not constitute adverse
> impact where the differences are based on small numbers and
> are not statistically significant, or where special recruiting or

other programs cause the pool of minority or female candidates
to be atypical of the normal pool of applicants from that group.

The key features of this "80 percent rule" or "four–fifths rule of thumb"
are that adverse or disparate impact can ordinarily be found only when (a)
the difference in selection rates is statistically significant and (b) the selection rate for a protected group is less than 80 percent of the rate for the
group with the highest rate. In contrast to the *sole* use of statistical tests
of significance exemplified by *Hazelwood*, the 80 percent rule also incorporates a precise quantitative criterion for when observed disparities are to
be adjudged "substantial." As Meier, Sacks, and Zabell (1984) note, a substantial literature of comment on the 80 percent rule has emerged, mostly
adverse (see e.g., Shoben, 1978). But critics often ignore the statistical significance component of the rule or point to a need for symmetry in the
treatment of pass rates and fail rates. Often overlooked in these discussions
are the exceptions provided in the rule and the fact that statistical significance is not defined. Thus, those applying the rule need to make decisions
on the choice of level of significance, as well as whether a one-sided or two-
sided criterion should be used. More important, users of the rule need to
consider whether to adjust the significance level for multiple comparisons
among several groups and across several employment categories (see e.g.,
Miller, 1981).

Meier, Sacks, and Zabell (1984) argue that the 80 percent rule is prefer-
able to the sole use of statistical tests of significance (with their questionable validity) as the criterion of substantiality to be met by plaintiffs in
establishing a prima facie case of adverse impact. They note that the use
of the 80 percent rule has been implicitly endorsed by the Supreme Court
in *Connecticut* v. *Teal*, 102 S.Ct. 2525, 2529 n.4 (1982), in which the Court
noted that the petitioners had not contested the district court's finding of
disparate impact under the rule.

In *Teal* a test used to determine eligibility for promotion was challenged
on the ground of adverse impact. Of 48 blacks who took the test, 26 passed
(54.2 percent), while of 259 whites who took the test, 206 passed (79.5 percent). In this case, there is no standard pass rate for comparison. Without
an external standard, the only question was whether the pass rate for black
applicants is different enough from the pass rate for white applicants to indicate a substantial disparity. The sampling model for the testing situation,
analogous to that used in *Hazelwood*, presumes that, absent discrimination,
applicants in both groups had the same chance of passing and that the outcomes, pass or fail, for the 307 candidates (48 blacks plus 259 whites) were
statistically independent. The difference in pass rates was 25.3 percent, or
3.76 standard errors, well above the "2 or 3 standard errors" benchmark
enunciated in *Hazelwood*. The minority pass rate was 68.2 percent of the
majority rate and thus, under the 80 percent rule, easily passed the substantiality criterion of adverse impact.

Since the *Uniform Guidelines* leave open the possibility of a finding of adverse impact when the 80 percent criterion is not met but differences are significant in both statistical and practical terms, the Supreme Court's decision in *Teal* gave little guidance to the courts on the application of the 80 percent rule.

3.2.5 The Floodgates Are Opened

Not only did the Supreme Court's decisions in *Castaneda* and *Hazelwood* endorse the appropriateness of statistical analysis and inference in discrimination litigation, but they also signaled the need for statistical expertise to the parties involved in pending Title VII litigation. The EEOC, which was partially supporting a large amount of class action litigation, moved swiftly to hire statistical and economics experts for most of the cases in which it was involved. Attorneys pressed their statistical experts to prepare analyses in accord with those in *Castaneda* and *Hazelwood*, but the experts often introduced variations in methodology and raised statistical issues on which the Supreme Court had not ruled. In addition, lawyers, quantitative social scientists, and statisticians wrote numerous articles on the use of statistical methods in Title VII cases. Many of these papers contained misinformation and misinterpretations of statistical procedures that served primarily to confuse the courts as they looked for guidance on the issues being presented at trial.

Three issues that quickly surfaced were: (1) what to do when sample sizes are small, (2) whether to adopt a "one-sided" or a "two-sided" approach to statistical significance, and (3) how to adjust for other variables that are acknowledged to affect the outcomes in question. The response to the third issue is taken up below following the discussion of regression analysis.

The decision in *Hazelwood* and its dissent by Justice Stevens left the courts' position in doubt on the issue of one-tailed versus two-tailed tests of significance. A cogent discussion of the issues appeared in the opinion in *Commonwealth of Pennsylvania* v. *Rizzo*, 20 FEP Cases 130 (E.D. Pa. 1979), but the general pattern that emerged was that statistical experts for the plaintiffs used one-tailed tests while those for the defendants used two-tailed tests that appeared to make exactly the same evidence somewhat weaker! The issue is entangled with courts' choice of significance levels, and the general confusion on the matter displayed by both witnesses and judges is well illustrated by an exchange between the judge and the plaintiffs' expert in *EEOC* v. *Federal Reserve Bank of Richmond* (see Chapter 2).

Confusion abounded on suitable approaches for situations involving small samples. Sometimes the view expressed was that no test of significance is possible, as in *Lee* v. *City of Richmond*, 456 F.Supp. 756, 766 (E.D. Va. 1978). Other times the issue was the appropriateness of the normal approximation to the binomial and the chi-squared test (which are equivalent), the appropriateness of the correction for continuity, and the two- or one-sample binomial approach versus the hypergeometric model and Fisher's exact test (see the extended discussion of this matter in *EEOC* v. *Federal Reserve Bank of Richmond* and in *Harless* v. *Duck*, 14 Fair Empl. Prac. Cas. (BNA) 1616 (N.D. Ohio 1977), *rev'd.* 619 F.2d 611 (6th Cir.), *cert. denied*, 449 U.S. 872 (1980)). The latter case referenced the "cell of five" rule, which is a common misstatement of Cochran's rule of thumb for the applicability of the chi-squared approximation. Yet other courts seemed to believe that statistical significance could not occur in small samples, as in *Williams* v. *City & County of San Francisco*, 483 F.Supp. 335, 341–342 (N.D. Cal. 1979), in which the court misread the *Uniform Guidelines* (and a large number of cases) as equating small sample sizes with lack of statistical significance (see also *Lee* v. *City of Richmond*, in which the court stated that "thirty is a generally accepted minimum of persons for a sample used in statistical testing" in 2 × 2 tables).

Finally, confusion over the technical meaning of statistical terms, understandable distrust of the random sampling model, and an intuitive (but often erroneous) assessment of statistical significance as well as the classic misinterpretation of p-values (see Appendix A) were expressed in many cases. Meier, Sacks, and Zabell (1984) have an elaborate discussion of most of these issues. They note that many lower court decisions, law review articles, and books have either failed to clarify or have actually misstated the relationships between the various statistical testing procedures (pp.147–148, citations omitted):

> Here again, there is a single exact test, commonly referred to as the "Fisher Exact Test" (F.E.T.), which is appropriate for determining whether a difference in hire or promotion rates is statistically significant, and a number of alternative tests and variant approximations. But *all* the other tests—two-sample binomial, or chi-squared with or without continuity correction, for example—may properly be considered as more or less adequate approximations to the F.E.T. The failure to note this has caused confusion in the literature and has led to the incorrect assertion that there are substantially different procedures available for the comparison of two samples and that these different procedures lead to different conclusions.

3.2.6   Multiple Regression and Related Methodology

The use of multiple regression models in employment discrimination cases was first suggested in a 1975 student note in the *Harvard Law Review*. In his review five years later, Finkelstein (1980) reported on 12 published opinions that mentioned the use of multiple regression in employment discrimination cases up through early 1979. In the first of these opinions, *Patterson* v. *Western Development Laboratories*, No. 74–2177 (N.D. Cal.

opinion filed – Sept. 14, 1976), the judge criticized the plaintiffs for not presenting a regression study. When the plaintiffs did introduce a regression analysis in *Wade* v. *Mississippi Cooperative Extension Serv.*, 528 F.2d 508 (5th Cir. 1976), the defendants produced an expert who testified that regression methods were inappropriate in a social science setting. Although the appeals court did say that regression was "difficult and sophisticated," it also upheld the district court's finding of discrimination.

In *James* v. *Stockam Valves & Fitting Co.* 559 F.2d 310 (5th Cir. 1977), the plaintiffs alleged that the company maintained racially segregated facilities, discriminated against black employees in job assignments, promotion, training, and transfer, and employed discriminatory testing, education, and age requirements. The plaintiffs presented statistical proof in support of their contention but did not present a regression analysis. To rebut this proof, the defendant produced an economist who presented a regression analysis in an attempt to explain the difference in pay by race using various productivity variables as explanatory variables. The appeals court found that some of these variables were "tainted," i.e., may have reflected the discrimination at issue in the case. In *Stasny* v. *Southern Bell Tel. & Tel. Co.*, 458 F.Supp. 314 (W.D.N.C. 1978), the same economics expert was used by defendants to rebut a regression analysis presented by the plaintiff's statistical expert. Again, the court ruled that some of the explanatory variables in the defendant's regression were tainted.

Two 1977 cases illustrated a conflict over whether to allow the use of academic rank as an explanatory variable in cases brought by female university teachers and, if allowed, how to use rank. Both cases involved statistical experts and multiple regression. In *Mecklenburg* v. *Montana Bd. of Regents of Higher Education*, 13 EPD ¶11,438 (D. Mont. 1977), the defendant's expert did separate regression analyses within rank. The court objected to this on the grounds that "it was impossible to 'catch' any discriminatory salary treatment resulting from inequities in promotions." In *Presseisen* v. *Swarthmore College*, 442 F.Supp. 596 (E.D. Pa. 1977), the court ruled that rank was not a "tainted" variable because it had previously found that the plaintiffs' claim of discrimination in promotions at Swarthmore had not been sustained (for further details on these cases, see Finkelstein, 1980). Two more recent cases in which courts have accepted the notion of holding faculty rank "constant" by doing separate regressions are *Sobel* v. *Yeshiva University*, 566 F.Supp. 1166 (S.D. N.Y. 1983) and *EEOC* v. *D. Justin McCarthy et al.*, 578 F.Supp. 45 (D. Ma. 1983).

When multiple regression analysis is used to adjust for explanatory factors, a major issue is the specification of the model—e.g., which explanatory variables should be used and in what form. The omission of crucial variables in the regression analysis of the plaintiffs' expert was the claim of the defendants' experts in *Commonwealth* v. *Local 542*, IUOE, 18 FEP Cases 1561 (E.D. Pa. 1978). The court rejected this argument because: (1) the defendants' experts had not actually done an analysis to show that the variable, skill, mattered, (2) it concurred with the plaintiffs' expert that the union data on skill were unreliable, and (3) the court erroneously viewed that the relationship between skill and experience (which was used in the regression) made it inappropriate to include skill as well. In *Agarwal* v. *McKee & Co.*, 16 EPD ¶8,301 (N.D. Cal. 1977), the court concluded that the plaintiffs failed to meet their burden of proof, in part because the regression analysis of the plaintiffs' expert omitted variables that the court deemed potentially important.

Early rulings on the omission of variables in cases such as *Agarwal* and *Presseisen* often led to misguided excess on the part of experts with dozens upon dozens of variables being included in an analysis in the event that they might be somewhat important as explanatory variables. One case, *Greenspan* v. *Automobile Club of Michigan*, 22 FEP Cases 184 (E.D. Mich. 1980), is especially illustrative of the extremes to which some experts went (see also Fienberg, 1982).

In *Greenspan* a group of women filed suit against their employer charging discrimination in hiring, placement, promotion, and compensation. The plaintiffs' expert used a variety of regression models to predict salary at year-end 1978, ranging from a basic model that contained 6 variables based on sex, age, and tenure to an elaborate model with 128 variables that were not chosen on sound substantive or statistical grounds. In these analyses and in related logistic regression analyses, the coefficient of the dummy variable for sex consistently was highly statistically significant. By way of contrast, the defendants' expert constructed a simple regression model to predict salary at year-end 1978 with six variables, including 1974 salary. Not surprisingly, he found that the coefficient of the dummy variable for sex was not statistically significant. Although the court failed to see the folly of using 128 explanatory variables, it did reconcile the two analyses in a reasonable fashion by noting:

> No inconsistency exists, I believe, if I accept both analyses on their own terms, not withstanding the efforts of the part of the parties to cast them in opposing lights. As I understand these positions, one model is useful for determining what an average salary will be given the personnel data available, the other is useful for determining whether a particular factor (in this case, sex) plays a significant role in the amount of that salary.

In ruling for the plaintiffs, the court in effect said that their regression analyses supported a finding that women were discriminated against with respect to wages while the defendants' regressions demonstrated that much of this difference was accounted for by the initial wages received by the employees. These initial wages were related, in turn, to initial placement, a matter addressed by other aspects of the statistical evidence presented by the plaintiffs' experts.

The decision in *Vuyanich* v. *Republic National Bank* (see Chapter 2) was reported in late 1980 and led to a further escalation in the use of regression analyses in Title VII cases.

A misconception that has arisen in several recently reported opinions referring to regression analyses is that the square of the multiple correlation coefficient, R^2, is a suitable indicator of the fit of a regression model. For example, in *Valentino* v. *U.S. Postal Service*, 511 F.Supp. 917, 944 (D.D.C. 1981), *aff'd.* 674 F.2d 56 (D.C. Cir. 1982), the court rejected the regression presented by the plaintiff's expert with the following comments:

> For example, plaintiff's Exhibit 61, which was a regression for employees at the 17 and above levels, USPS Headquarters, as of January 1979, had an "R square" of .284. Dr. [X] testified that this was a "very, very low R square." ... Dr. [Y, the plaintiff's expert] admitted that this figure meant that 71.6% of the salary of these employees was *not explained* by his regression model. In view of the many other explanatory variables which Dr. [Y] could have added to his regression equation, the Court cannot give any weight to a regression that is admittedly unable to describe so much of the salary of USPS employees.

Similarly in *Lewis* v. *Bloomsburg Mills*, 30 FEPC 1715, 31 EPD ¶33,343 (D.D.C. 1982), the court rejected a regression analysis for which R^2 was less than 10%, while in *Wilkins* v. *University of Houston*, 654 F.2d 388 (5th Cir. 1981), *pet.r'hrng. den.*, 662 F.2d 1156 (5th Cir. 1981), the court asked "whether the fact that the model explains only 52 to 53% of the total variation in average salaries means that the model as a whole is not very reliable." These opinions and some commentaries on them confuse the issues of causality and the goodness of fit of the regression model with issues of "substantiality," i.e., the magnitude of effects *and* the "explanatory power" of the predictor variables.

One particular administrative agency discrimination case provoked considerable interest in the legal and statistical communities. In *U.S. Dept. of Treasury* v. *Harris Savings & Trust*, Dept. of Labor Administrative Case 78-0FCCP-2, one of the plaintiff's experts performed a series of regression analyses—one for all full-time employees at each of several different points in time—using salary rate as a dependent variable and race, sex, a race-by-sex interaction, and various labor market variables as explanatory. Because the defendant had not turned over the studies of its experts, in violation of an order by the administrative law judge (ALJ), the ALJ ruled that the bank could not put on a statistical defense. In rebutting the evidence of the plaintiff's experts, however, the defendant's expert argued that the plaintiff's regressions, which were of the standard direct form, were inappropriate and that reverse regressions (in which the roles of salary and productivity, the dependent and explanatory variables, respectively, are reversed) were called for to properly take into account the measurement error in the explanatory variables, which were imperfect proxies for productivity variables. This reverse regression approach attempted to address in a novel fashion a statistical problem known as "attenuation," in which the regression coefficent of an imperfectly measured explanatory variable is inflated in magnitude when nothing is done to take the measurement error into account. Nonetheless, the ALJ rejected the defendant's criticisms and found for the plaintiff. The decision of the ALJ is, however, only a recommendation to the secretary of labor, who remanded the case back to the ALJ in 1983 (31 FEP Cases 1223) with instructions to allow an affirmative defense. This reopened case is pending.

Although the reverse regression approach was rejected by the ALJ in the *Harris Bank* case, both Conway and Roberts (1983) and Dempster (1984) have provided a careful technical accounting of the methodology. These papers have been followed by spirited critiques (see Ferber and Green, 1984; Goldberger, 1984a, 1984b; Greene, 1984; Michelson and Blattenberger, 1984; and Miller, 1984) with a rebuttal by Conway and Roberts (1984). A professional statistical consensus on the relevance and validity of reverse regression has not yet been achieved and thus courts should take cognizance of the lack of agreement if an expert chooses to use reverse regression as a primary statistical tool.

One problem rarely mentioned when regression analysis is used as proof of discrimination is that it is usually used for salaries or wages as they are at a given point in time. Such static or situational analyses are typically proffered as a form of bottom-line presentation. Michelson (1986) notes that, if men and women are "equally situated," conditional upon their qualifications, then the idea that they have been treated differently is difficult to accept. But what should one conclude if the analysis shows differences attributable to sex? Forms of dynamic or longitudinal statistical analysis are, to many, far more convincing forms of evidence because such analyses can be used to focus on events, e.g., decisions regarding promotions, that in turn influence the setting of wages. But most such analyses would probably not use standard regression techniques (Michelson, 1986). The form of cohort-based regression analysis suggested by Conway and Roberts (1983, 1986) is still a situational analysis and is one that the courts have rejected (often for the wrong reasons) in *Segar* v. *Civiletti*, 508 F.Supp. 690 (D.D.C. 1978), *af'd.* as *Segar* v. *Smith*, 35 FEP Cases 31 (D.C. Cir. 1984) and in *Trout* v. *Hidalgo*, 517 F.Supp. 873 A (D.D.C. 1981), *af'd.* as *Trout* v. *Lehman*, 702 F.2d 1094 (D.C. Cir. 1983), vac. and rem. in part, 104 S.Ct. 1404 (1984).

Despite the apparent willingness of courts to accept the use of regression and related techniques in Title VII litigation, some judges have resisted—especially when the attorneys and experts involved have not attempted to explain in detail the nature of the methodology and its applicability to the case at hand. For example in *Key* v. *Gillette*, 29 E.P.D. ¶32,909 (D. Mass. 1982), the court noted:

In his opening statement, counsel for the plaintiff stated (p.26, 310):

Now I would like to describe a regression analysis, having in mind we are in the '80s, your Honor, as a sort of black box. It's an equation. It's like a breathalyzer test that is given in drunk driving cases. You don't have to introduce evidence to your Honor in the '80s about what a black box is. And we don't believe, because the law supports that, we don't have to introduce evidence about regression analysis—how computers work, how you put the information in and how it comes out, the various equations and cosines and all of that. It's an accepted practice of statistical analysis.

Contrary to the assertion of counsel for the plaintiff, this Court does not know or understand what a "black box" of the type adverted to is. The Court is not aided by the comparison of a black box to a "breathalyzer," and the Court rules that contrary to counsel's assertion, a plaintiff does have to introduce evidence in the '80s about what a "black box" is.

I find no fact has been proven in this case by the use of a "black box," and I close by noting that this case concerns people, not black boxes, computers, or breathalyzers.

In particular the court rejected the use of the plaintiffs' regression analysis because of the use of age as a proxy for past experience:

I find that such a substitution is unreasonable, circular, and even a bit dishonest, in a case where the plaintiff is suing on the basis of a statute passed by Congress to correct a cultural situation which results more often than not in men being able to achieve far greater experience than women of equal age. ... Plaintiff produced no evidence which would support a finding that for the purpose of this suit, age at time of hire is a good and dependable substitute for past experience.

Unfortunately, the plaintiffs were unable to do analyses with variables representing experience because the defendant failed to maintain its personnel files, but the court did not appear to give this matter any weight.

3.2.7 Logistic Regression

After regression analysis was accepted as a standard statistical technique in the toolbag of expert witnesses in Title VII cases, statistical witnesses began to use logistic regression in analyses of hiring and promotion to adjust for explanatory variables other than sex or minority status. This form of analysis is designed to deal with categorical outcome variables (e.g., hire/reject or promote/not promote), whereas standard regression methods assume that the outcome variable is essentially continuous (e.g., salary). In many situations, logistic regression techniques were presented as the natural generalization of standard regression analysis for dichotomous dependent variables (see, e.g., the earlier discussion of *Greenspan* v. *Automobile Club of Michigan*). In this analogy, the logarithm of the odds of being hired or of being promoted (or the logit as it is more commonly called) is said to be regressed on various explanatory variables. The techniques are justifiable as extensions of the two-binomial model for comparisons used in *Castaneda* and *Hazelwood* and are tied to the statistical literature on loglinear models and categorical data analysis (e.g., see Fienberg, 1980). Logistic regression analysis, when used in connection with hiring and promotion, focuses on the events at issue and is responsive to the situational critique of standard multiple regression, mentioned earlier.

This form of logistic or loglinear analysis of categorical data is closely related to techniques used by statistical experts to aggregate results across a number of groupings of employment categories or ranks. For example, in *Hogan* v. *Pierce*, 31 FEP Cases 115 (D.C. 1983), the court noted with approval the use by the plaintiff's expert of the Mantel-Haenszel test for combining information in a set of 2×2 tables on promotions of blacks and whites in different time periods. This test can be interpreted as essentially equivalent to a statistical test for the effect of race on promotion controlling for grade in a loglinear or logistic regression model (e.g., see Bishop, Fienberg, and Holland, 1975, pp.147–148). This equivalence connection was clearly understood by the testifying statistical expert in this case, but it has not been noted in any court opinion to the panel's knowledge. The combined analysis in *Hogan* yielded a discrepancy in promotions between blacks and whites that was significant at the .007 level, whereas the results for any one time period did not yield statistical significance at the .05 level using a one-sided, two-binomial comparison.

In *Coser* v. *Moore*, 587 F.Supp. 572 (1983), the court directly addressed the specification of a logistic regression model. The plaintiffs' expert statistical witnesses introduced a multiple logistic regression analysis that purported to show that from 1972 to 1976 women faculty members at the State University of New York at Stony Brook, as compared with men with "comparable qualifications," were initially assigned to lower faculty ranks. Their model did not consider prior faculty rank or experience among the explanatory variables used to predict rank. The defendants' expert, using the same data, also did a logistic regression analysis that included as an explanatory variable "rank immediately prior to hire." The court, in addressing the conflicting conclusions reached by the parties' experts, noted that both the plaintiffs' and the defendants' analyses "are unrealistic because they seek to describe a condition that does not exist," in that they focused on "the aggregate results of a large number of separate, uncoordinated decisions in a number of different departments." Nonetheless, the court found the defendants' logistic regression approach to be a more accurate measure of the university's placement practices than the plaintiffs' approach and concluded that it provided a nondiscriminatory explanation for the apparent disparity shown by the plaintiffs' statistics.

More recently the use of logistic regression was disputed in *Craik* v. *Minnesota State University Bd.*, 731 F.2d 465 (8th Cir. 1984). This class action case was brought on behalf of female employees, and the plaintiffs' statistical expert performed a multiple regression analysis to test whether women at St. Cloud State University were discriminatorily assigned to lower ranks than similarly situated men. The dependent variable was rank, to which the expert witness assigned numerical values (1 = professor, 2 = associate professor, 3 = assistant professor, 4 = instructor). The analysis produced an estimated sex coefficient that was significant at the .01 level. The defendants' experts criticized this analysis on three grounds: (1) it included comparisons beyond the scope of the class, (2) it failed to include certain relevant independent variables, and (3) it improperly used a four-category dependent variable as if it were continuous. The defendants' experts presented their own analyses overcoming these deficiencies using a series of logistic regressions on the "continuation ratios" (see Fienberg, 1980), first comparing assistant professors to instructors, then associate professors to assistant professors and instructors, and finally professors to those in the other three ranks. In each of these analyses, the estimated sex coefficient was far from being significant at the .05 level. In rebuttal testimony, the plaintiffs' expert corrected the first two flaws noted by the defendants' experts and redid her regression analysis, finding that the sex coefficient was significant at the .05 level but not the .01 level. All these analyses, multiple regression and logistic regression, fall into the category of situational analyses.

The case was tried before a magistrate for the district court in Minnesota, who entered judgment in favor of the defendants but did not rely explicitly on the defendants' logistic regressions. The plaintiffs appealed and the Eighth Circuit of the Court of Appeals reversed in part, affirmed in part, and remanded for reconsideration of some of the individual claims for relief. In the majority opinion, two judges explicitly endorsed the plaintiffs' multiple regressions and said that the defendants' logistic regression "analyses did not rebut the plaintiffs' studies based on multiple linear regression. ... Moreover, the defendants did not show that the values which the plaintiffs assigned to the various ranks in their multiple linear regression analyses produced misleading results." In a lengthy, 39–page dissent (to a 28–page majority opinion), Chief Judge Swygert disagreed strongly with his colleagues with regard to the critical statistical analyses and concluded that the defendants' logistic regression analyses "which unlike the plaintiffs' used a proper methodology, showed that rank assignments at St. Cloud may be explained by neutral criteria. Although the magistrate despaired of understanding this powerful evidence, he did analyze the more particularized evidence offered by the parties, and after close reexamination of the evidence I cannot conclude that his finding of no discrimination was clearly erroneous."

Although logistic regression is a widely accepted statistical method that is more appropriate than standard multiple regression for the analysis of categorical outcome variables in Title VII settings, it has not yet been as widely used as multiple regression, nor have courts automatically accepted the use of logistic regression in place of multiple regression. Many of the cases involving the use of logistic regression and loglinear models of which panel members were aware have ended in settlement; thus there is no recorded opinion available to provide judicial reaction.

3.2.8   Critique, Overview, and Implications

The receptivity of the courts to the use of statistical methods in Title VII litigation opened courtroom doors to virtually all forms of data collection and all kinds of statistical methodology. As a consequence, the status of the acceptance of statistical methodology in 1985 is dramatically different from that of 25 years ago, when well-done sample surveys were still being rejected on hearsay grounds.

What lies behind the rapid growth of the use of statistical experts in Title VII litigation? First, interpretation of the law evolved rapidly in connection with Title VII litigation during the 1970s and early 1980s. Second, civil rights and affirmative action issues had high visibility in the late 1970s; thus, Title VII litigation attracted the attention of those who wanted the courts to fashion new law. Third, because a large proportion of Title VII litigation involved class action cases in which possible damages were extensive, the financial stakes were substantial and the parties were often more than willing to invest in expertise that might help win cases. Fourth, the EEOC provided funding for plaintiffs' experts in many cases. Finally, lawyers and judges turned to statistics with unrealistic expectations. They hoped that statistical methodology would provide simple and easily administerable rules to assist in the adjudication process, as was suggested in the Supreme Court rulings in *Castaneda* and in *Hazelwood*. Instead they found new problems in statistical methodology overlaid on the legal problems with which they began.

The costs associated with employment discrimination litigation, brought under Title VII of the Civil Rights Act of 1964, were enormous. Settlements and judgments in class action cases were typically in the millions of dollars. Because plaintiffs in Title VII litigation tended to have few resources in comparison with defendants, they would not have been able to bear the costs of data preparation and analysis without the financial support of the EEOC and other public and private agencies. Although attorneys often perform legal work on a contingency basis, it is a broadly held view in the statistical community that statisticians should "accept no contingency-fee arrangements" (Ad Hoc Committee on Professional Ethics, 1983). Because the EEOC supported the work of experts in Title VII litigation, it had great influence during the late 1970s; however, recent cutbacks in its resources and changes in administration philosophy toward Title VII litigation have led to a diminished support for litigation preparation, and plaintiffs have been pressured to accept settlements in lieu of going to trial. In fact, a large proportion of Title VII cases were settled even before such financial constraints, in part because pretrial disclosure practices lead to early notice to opposing parties of the nature and extent of statistical evidence amassed by the other side.

Although the use of statistics in employment discrimination litigation originated with a handful of cases in the mid-1970s, use increased sharply after the *Castaneda* and *Hazelwood* decisions. Methodology used by expert statistical witnesses has become increasingly complex, and some statisticians express serious reservations about the statistical appropriateness of the models and methods employed and the legal relevance of the information obtained. For example, the assumptions implicit in multiple regression models and their analysis are substantially more difficult to state and interpret than those for the simple statistical models used in the *Castaneda* and *Hazelwood* cases. Such problems as model specification, model fit, attenuation associated with the use of proxy variables, and the effects of the exclusion of tainted variables have already been mentioned. In addition, the focus of multiple regression on situations, e.g., salaries at a given point in time, instead of on the events in question, i.e. decisions on hiring and promotion, is a problem from the perspective of legal relevance.

These difficulties are compounded by a problem rarely addressed in Title VII litigation or in commentaries on it. Most statistical analyses in Title VII cases are performed on what can be viewed as population data, e.g., all persons who applied to or were employed by a company during a given period. Thus there is no source for the random variation normally used to justify statistical tests and formal methods of inference. Freedman and Lane (1983) and Levin and Robbins (1983) have recently attempted to develop randomization tests for regression models that might be of some use in this regard.

Meier, Sacks, and Zabell (1984) also raise the question of when to shift the burden of proof in an employment discrimination case if complex methods such as multiple regression and logistic regression are used:

> A substantial and statistically significant difference in simple pass rates for blacks and whites may indeed seem reasonable ground for shifting the burden of proof to an employer to justify the reason for such a disparity. But a difference in average salary for male and female academics resulting from a complex multiple regression adjustment, based on assumptions that are false on their face, is a very different matter.

In response to such criticisms, other statisticians continue to argue that despite the problems, both potential and real, statistical approaches may still offer the best hope for the analysis of evidence on adverse impact and adverse treatment in employment situations. They note that, without formal statistics, all that remains is pseudo statistical arguments and unverifiable accusations, true or not.

3.3 Statistical and Economic Assessment in Antitrust Litigation

3.3.1 Introduction

Antitrust violations can be pursued either privately or publicly and under both federal and state law in many cases. Federal suits can be brought under the Sherman Act, which prohibits "contracts, combinations and conspiracies in restraint of trade" (Section 1) and monopolization in interstate trade (Section 2). The Clayton Act, with the Robinson-Patman Amendments, cites certain firm practices as illegal. Its most important provisions include Section 7 (applying to mergers and acquisitions), Section 2 (limiting price discrimination), and Section 3 (regulating exclusive dealing and tying arrangements). Federal government cases are brought either by the Antitrust Division of the Department of Justice or by the Federal Trade Commission. Private suits and Department of Justice cases go to trial in federal district courts, while Federal Trade Commission cases are heard by the Federal Trade Commission itself. Both types of cases can be appealed to the appropriate circuit court of appeals.

The adversarial process in antitrust cases often involves assertions about (a) what occurred; (b) what caused what occurred; (c) what would have occurred "but for" some event. The validity of these assertions in turn depends on facts on which statistics and econometrics can shed light. As in other areas of the law, statistical analyses are not the only form of evidence available to resolve competing claims, but they are surely among the more useful.

Unlike in some other areas of litigation such as employment discrimination, there is no unified underlying theme that characterizes the application of statistics in antitrust. In Title VII cases, for example, one might argue that the question of whether wage rates vary by race or by sex is fundamental to the underlying legal issues, and that statistical methodology is the most direct means by which the hypothesis of no discriminatory effect can be evaluated. In antitrust litigation the law focuses its attention on issues ranging from standing and market definition to questions relating to liability and the calculation of damages.

A second comparison between antitrust and employment discrimination litigation comes in the availability of statistical materials for examination.

A large body of case law was built up in a relatively short time period on the Title VII employment discrimination area, and this was due primarily to the fact that such cases are, by law, tried by judges and not by juries.[1] As a consequence, after the use of statistical methods was sanctioned by the Supreme Court, district and circuit court published opinions have attempted to codify and explain the relevance of statistical methods of proof beyond the simple tests originally suggested. These opinions and the related trial reports and records allow for a form of systematic review. In antitrust litigation, cases are typically tried before juries, and many of the more elaborate uses of statistical methodology are suggested but not completely described in pretrial discovery. This leads to a relative paucity of source materials on statistical analyses and only a limited attempt, typically at the appellate level, to explain how the use of such analyses fits with the law. Therefore, the panel's brief review of the use of statistical methods in antitrust litigation must of necessity involve a hit-or-miss approach, and it relies heavily on the knowledge of the panel and its consultants.

A third difference between antitrust and employment discrimination litigation arises from the role of economic theory and economists in the former. Economic theories shape the form of much antitrust litigation and are reflected in the law and in our description of it. In addition, the Antitrust Division of the Department of Justice and the Federal Trade Commission, which is also involved in antitrust litigation, have economists on their staffs. Although economists such as Fisher, McGowan, and Greenwood (1983) are highly critical of the role of their fellow economists in such settings, describing them as handmaidens to the lawyers, the fact is that economists are present and economic advice is being proferred. It may be true that many cases brought by the government lack economic coherence, as Fisher et al. argue, but the role of economic theory in antitrust litigation appears to be substantial.

The growth of antitrust litigation over the past 30 years has been primarily due to large increases in the number of cases initiated by private parties. Geisel and Masson (1986) note that although only 1,092 private cases were initiated from 1900 through 1949, 2,146 new cases were brought in the period 1950–1959, 6,490 cases in 1960–1969 (including 2,233 electrical equipment cases), 13,162 cases in 1970–1979, and 4,978 in 1980–1983. This growth in numbers of cases has been paralleled by a growth in the use of statisticians and economists as expert witnesses.

The overview of the use of statistics in antitrust laws is organized around the major legal issues of standing, market definition, liability, and damages. The first legal issue is standing, since a case will not proceed if the plaintiff is found not to be in the class of those for whom antitrust laws intend relief. At

---

[1]Discrimination based on age, however, is tried under a different statute, and jury trials are used. The age discrimination legislation came six years after Title VII, and thus much case law had already been developed.

trial, a second preliminary issue underlying many cases is market definition, from which the calculation of market share and market power often follow. Third, statistical inference can be fruitful in establishing liability when more direct evidence is not available. Fourth, the damage issue involves statistical modeling to answer the question of what price and output would have been but for the legal violation. We begin with a brief discussion of the use of statistical assessments as evidence in each of these four areas and then continue with additional comments about statistical applications that might arise in the antitrust context. (For a broader discussion of the role of economics, and to a lesser extent statistics, in antitrust litigation, see Greenfield, 1984; for a discussion of the use of statistics to measure economic concentration in merger cases, see Finkelstein, 1978, Chapter 5.)

3.3.2   Standing

There may be situations in which probabilistic or statistical statements might be pertinent or probative with respect to the question of whether the plaintiff has standing to bring a lawsuit. The question of standing is a difficult one to address empirically because of a number of recent cases that have limited the ability of certain parties to bring suit for antitrust violation. For example, in *Brunswick* v. *Pueblo Bowl-o-Mat*, 429 U.S. 477 (1977), the Supreme Court excluded lawsuits brought by parties whose harm may have flowed from the activity complained of, but did not follow from the antitrust-violative nature of that activity. In *Brunswick*, the plaintiff was a competitor challenging Brunswick's acquistion of a failing firm. The plaintiff would have preferred the weakened competition from the eventual failure of the acquired firm to the stronger competition Brunswick would provide. Since this disadvantage to the plaintiff did not flow from the antitrust nature of the alleged violation, standing was denied.

Six years later, the court denied standing to a union that complained against an agreement among employers not to deal with subcontractors signed up by the union, *Associated General Contractors, Inc.* v. *California State Council of Carpenters*, 103 S.Ct. 897 (1983). The harm was directed to the business of the subcontractors, not directly to the employment of the union members, the court decided. Hence, the union lacked the direct harm required under the court's earlier decisions denying standing to indirect purchasers. In *Illinois Brick Co.* v. *Illinois*, 431 U.S. 720 (1977), the court also denied standing to indirect purchasers of products.

One statistical issue that arises in the context of standing cases is the practical prerequisite that is thrust on antitrust plaintiffs to show that "but for" the illegal nature of the alleged violation, they would have enjoyed some advantage now denied them. If there is an intervening event or actor in the chain of causation, standing is denied. Probability and statistics can be relevant for deciding the standing questions, although the applications are not easy to summarize.

For example, in a bid-rigging case, a disappointed bidder is not entitled by law to have won the bid, but is only entitled to a fair chance to compete. In that kind of situation it is necessary to estimate the probability of having been chosen the winner in a fair selection process or lottery. Statistical analyses can be used to compare similar situations of competitors or with this defendant in the past. If the probability of having been chosen a winner in a fair selection process is sufficiently low, the court will deny standing. If the probability is sufficiently high, standing is more likely to be granted. In *Bayou Bottling* v. *Doctor Pepper*, 543 F.Supp. 1255, *aff'd.* 725 F.2d 300 (5th Cir. 1984), the plaintiff charged the defendant with violations of the Sherman Act, Sections 1 and 2, on the sale of a bottling franchise to one of Bayou's competitors, following a rigged bidding process. The court held that the disappointed bidder had no certainty of having been selected and thus lacked cognizable antitrust injury. Summary judgment was granted to the defendant.

Statistical methods and, in particular, sampling procedures can be used to test class certification questions in private class action antitrust suits. In order for a private case to be brought, there must be a sustainable class of individuals who have been harmed in a similar fashion. A sample of potential class members, or alleged class members, can be used to characterize the population of all potential class members and to evaluate either (a) how an appropriate class ought to be formed or (b) whether a particular class that has been formed is sustainable under the antitrust laws.

For example, consider the case of *United States* v. *Nissan Motor Corporation in USA*, 1973–1 Trade Cases CCH 74, 333, Northern District of California, February 26, 1973 (Consent Decree). The government charged that Nissan, the Japanese maker of Datsun cars, was guilty of resale price maintenance (RPM) of sales in the United States. In addition to the case brought by the Justice Department, private plaintiffs also brought class actions on behalf of purchasers of Datsun cars (see *In re Nissan Antitrust Litigation*, 577 F.2d 910 (5th Cir. 1978), *cert. denied*, 439 U.S. 1072 (1972)). The issue was whether there was some impact of RPM on all purchasers who claimed to be members of the class. RPM was alleged to have had the effect of reducing discounts below what they would otherwise have been and to lead to overpayments and damages to all buyers of Datsuns within the class.

The focal point of the Nissan case was the certification of the class. If, for example, the proposed class consisted of all buyers of Datsun vehicles in the United States, it is conceivable that the violation led to uniformly higher prices in some states but not in others. In that event, a national class might not be sustainable, but class actions in individual states might survive. Within any individual state, a similar set of questions might be asked: Did all purchasers in the state suffer a reduction in discounts, or did discounts vary according to say, type of vehicle, so that the alleged resale price maintenance scheme led to overcharges in some cases and not in others?

The private civil suit in the *Nissan* case was fought on the class certification question. Defendants, seeking to prevent certification of the class
under Federal Rule 23, collected information from all invoices from selected
dealers in 14 states over 6 years. This collection of course represents a sample of dealers and not the entire population of all sales, but it was clear
that the inclination of the defendants was to obtain information about the
entire population. Over 40,000 individual transactions were studied, with
detailed tabulations made by a major accounting firm. Nissan won the case
in the end, in part because its data collection revealed sufficient heterogene-
ity in prices across states and across models of cars as to undermine the
notion of uniformity of impact that was vital to sustaining the class action.
Nonetheless, this case was a good example of how proper statistical sampling could have saved money and generated an effective analysis. After
the data were collected, defendants hired statistical experts to analyze the
data. The analysis of the actual data as well as more general information
about statistical sampling made it clear that defendants could have developed an effective case by taking a relatively small sample of the actual
sales that were examined, in the range of 12 percent (see Rubinfeld and
Steiner, 1983, for further details). Experts were able to show, in a way that
seems likely to have been convincing to the court, that an appropriately
designed sampling procedure could allow one to make inferences about the
population of all Datsun sales with sufficient accuracy so as to make it
unnecessary to expend the hundreds of thousands of dollars that went into
the defense analysis.

The methodological and conceptual questions are not fully answered in
cases such as this, however, since there remains some doubt as to whether
the sampling procedure would have satisfied lawyers, judges, or jurors. Yet
the acceptance of survey evidence has become commonplace, as is suggested
by the section describing its appropriateness in the newly revised *Manual
for Complex Litigation* 2d (1985). Statistical sampling plays an especially
important role in cases in which large sums of money cannot be expended
and the alternative is the use of inadequate anecdotal information.

3.3.3   Market Definition

Once the proof stage of an antitrust claim has been reached, the proper definition of market becomes fundamental, since it is directly tied to questions
of market share and market and monopoly power. The economic theory underlying market definition appears simple in concept, but it is quite complex
in application; a market is that collection of goods within a geographical
region whose producers could successfully, if acting together, raise prices
for a substantial period of time and achieve higher revenues (see *Department of Justice Merger Guidelines*, 1984). The key concepts are the ability
of consumers to switch between products and the ability of producers to

alter production decisions when the price of an item rises or falls. Statistical procedures can be used to get at the extent to which consumers are capable of substituting products in consumption and producers are capable of substituting inputs in production. The forms of statistical evidence, however, vary substantially by situation. For example, one might use statistical and econometric techniques to estimate price cross-elasticities of demand, or elasticities of substitution in production. Such elasticities have been measured in studies in areas such as energy economics, but they are frequently difficult if not impossible to calculate in the context of a particular piece of litigation. An interesting methodological question involves deciding the extent to which experts can rely or should rely on the statistical studies of others in order to build up their conclusions about market definition.

Another approach to market definition involves sampling, in which plaintiffs and defendants survey producer and consumer opinions about how they would respond to hypothetical price increases. The question asked might, for example, mimic the 1982 version of the Justice Department *Guidelines*, which focus on the extent to which firms and consumers respond to a nontransitory 5 percent price increase over a period of six months to two years depending on whether it relates to new plant construction or to a new product line from an existing plant. An early example of surveys in this connection occurred in *U.S.* v. *E.I. Dupont Demours & Co.*, 118 F.Supp. 41 (D.C. Delaware 1953), in which a sample survey was part of the evidence used in developing the market setting for the sale of cellophane. There are, of course, serious problems with surveys that ask hypothetical questions of the kind just described, since consumers and producers have strong incentives to respond in ways that are in their own self-interest. The courts ought to be skeptical about the results of such surveys unless it can be shown that the questions are likely to generate unbiased responses.

Statistical techniques can be used in a more direct although less elaborate approach to the market definition question. For example, assume that one is interested in the question of the geographic market for a wholesale or retail product. One can simply analyze a sample or the set of all invoices of a firm or firms in the business to see the extent to which the firm sales are geographically spread. A broad pattern of sales across a large region provides substantial evidence that the geographic market ought to be at least that broad. The difficulty with such studies is that evidence of sales that occur within the narrow geographic area is not likely to be dispositive about the market definition question. Suppose that all firms are pricing competitively and have narrow geographic ranges for their sales, and that a 5 or 10 percent price decrease by a group of colluding firms would lead to an influx of customers across a much broader geographic area. Then it would be appropriate to include in the geographic market the larger area, since the market ought to include not only actual but also potential competitors.

In addition to sample survey data, historical data are often of great use. For example, in determining the proper geographic market for crude petroleum, the influx of oil from the Caribbean in response to the Arab oil embargo of 1973 provided very useful information. But statistical techniques such as regression were necessary to attempt to segregate the effect of factors other than the price rise in the United States. King (1986) describes the two statistical uses common in defining a market: sampling techniques for opinion surveys and segregation of extraneous factors from historical data.

3.3.4   Liability

A. Proof of the Effect of Challenged Conduct

In the *non per se* or "rule of reason" area, liability hinges on the proven effect on competition of the conduct at issue. This involves analyses to focus on what would have happened "but for" the crucial activity. While it is difficult to discuss in a general fashion the kinds of statistical techniques that can be applied in such a context, it might be useful to distinguish between hypothesis-testing approaches on one hand and forecasting and simulation approaches on the other. In the hypothesis-testing approach, the statistician or econometrician would typically choose as a null hypothesis that there is no effect of the particular behavior on output or on price or both, and as the alternative hypothesis that there is some effect. Often, although not necessarily, a null hypothesis of this type can be tested using a t-test within a multiple regression framework.

There are a number of important conceptual as well as legal problems associated with the relevance and application of the hypothesis-testing approach. First, the conclusion of no effect is not legally equivalent to the conclusion of no violation. Certain pricing and other practices could be deemed to be a violation even if there is no effect. Second, the hypothesis test is built on the assumption that the model being used is correctly specified, an assumption that can and often will be attacked by the opposing party. Third, statisticians and econometricians might use a 5% or even 1% level of significance, but for purposes of litigation the appropriate level of significance might well be deemed to be different. (For a further discussion of this point, see Rubinfeld, 1985.) Finally, failure to reject the null hypothesis may show no effect, because violations that have occurred affect only a minority of the individuals involved and therefore show little or no *average* effect on the entire class of consumers or producers being studied. Here, as in Title VII employment discrimination litigation, difficult conceptual problems relating the relationship between statistical significance and practical significance remain.

Rubinfeld and Steiner (1983) have documented the statistical problems encountered in the hypothesis-testing approach in the context of two pieces of antitrust litigation. In *In re Ampicillin Antitrust Litigation* (88 F.R.D.

174 (D.D.C. 1983)), the experts involved were concerned with whether the decline in the price of the drug ampicillin in the market in which city, county, and state governments purchase ampicillin would have occurred earlier and to a larger extent had generic drug manufacturers not been excluded by patent from entering the market. In this case, the plaintiffs' hypothesis was that the presence of generic houses in the market resulted in a lower price; the defendants' hypothesis was that the presence of generic houses had no effect on price. The case was settled before the defense presented its statistical analyses; however, experts for the defense did apply a t-test in a multiple regression context to test whether the coefficient of the variable measuring the number of generic houses that had bid for the sale of ampicillin in the relevant market could be considered to be zero. Failure to reject the null hypothesis was used to support the view that there is no effect. Firm conclusions, however, would require a more thorough analysis that examined the question of specification of the multiple regression model and the practical significance of the coefficients involved in more detail.

One of the problems with the line of argument in the *Ampicillin* case is that it assumes that patent holders should not be allowed to charge higher prices than competitive generic drug manufacturers who did not have to bear the research and development costs. Thus, if the generic manufacturers had been allowed into the market earlier, the patent holder might still have charged a higher price than the generics but perhaps not as much higher as occurred in practice. It would be extremely difficult to do a former test of hypothesis and statistical analysis of this more complex formulation of the competition situation.

The forecasting and simulation approach builds a multiple regression model to identify the effect of the conduct under scrutiny and then follows one of two alternatives. First, it might compare the description of this model to another regression model based on data drawn from a different period of time or different practices of other firms in which the conduct alleged to violate the antitrust laws was not present. A second possibility is simply to estimate a single model for the entire period under scrutiny but to test whether there is a difference in mean price or output being studied, other things equal, between the period when the conduct was present and the period when it was not present. The forecasting approach can be particularly appealing when there are sufficient data to allow a quasi-experimental version of the "but for" experiment described previously to be carried out with sufficient accuracy. There is a dangerous tendency, however, for experts to avoid the presentation of statistical information that describes the accuracy of the "but for" forecasts involved. To the extent that this occurs, one is open to the possibility of (a) concluding that there is no violation when, as before, there was a poor model or insufficient data; (b) concluding that there was a violation when there was not, or (c) overlooking substantial uncertainty in the size of the effect, not to mention bias (noncomparability) in the "but for" model.

An example of the application of the forecasting approach is given in the *Plywood Antitrust Litigation*, 655 F.2d 627 (5th Cir. 1981); cert. granted 456 U.S. 971 (1982); cert. dismissed, 103 S.Ct. 3100 (1983). As described in Rubinfeld and Steiner (1983), one of the issues in the *Plywood* case was whether the growth and development of the southern plywood industry, in coordination with an allegedly conspiratorial method of quoting delivered prices, served to raise plywood prices in the South higher than they would have been had the market been competitive. The experts involved used multiple regression to explain the movement in plywood prices during a period in which the conspiracy was alleged to have been in effect. The regression model was then used to predict what hypothetical conspiratorial prices would have been in a period in which no conspiracy was alleged and therefore when prices were agreed by all parties to be competitive. A comparison of the predicted conspiratorial prices and the actual competitive prices can, in principle, provide a test for a violation as well as a measure of damages if a violation has occurred. If predicted prices are substantially higher during the nonconspiratorial period than actual prices after controlling for the relevant variables, the analysis provides support for the theory that the conspiracy raised prices. However, if there is little or no systematic excess of predicted prices over actual prices, the defense position is supported.

The experts' analysis in the *Plywood* case showed no systematic relationship between the levels of predicted and actual prices, supporting the inference that, if a conspiracy existed, it had no effect on price. The experts made clear, however, that the test is not a fully satisfactory one. Forecast reliability needs to be taken into account and, as shown by the experts, the limited nature of the data generates a reasonably large standard error of forecast and wide prediction intervals for forecasts that makes almost anything possible. The experts' conclusion was cast in a negative tone: while forecasting as a test adds no support to the conspiracy hypothesis, that one cannot say with certainty on the basis of such a test that a conspiracy could not have occurred.

B. Inference of Coordinated Conduct

A second statistical issue arises under Section 1 of the Sherman Act, which proscribes joint behavior. In contrast with the requirement for plaintiffs to demonstrate the market effect of challenged conduct, it is not necessary for plaintiffs to prove that market effects exist in order to win a case in this area, in which the joint behavior deals with price. The difficult factual point, rather, is to prove from observed conduct that an actual agreement exists (except in the rare case in which direct proof exists of competitors meeting and agreeing). The *Plywood* litigation just described was of this type.

Statistical methods are critical in establishing the inference that certain forms of conduct are unlikely to be arrived at short of agreement. A simple example would be when all the firms in an industry announce an identical increase in price at the identical time. That competitive firms will have similar prices is not inconsistent with individual decision making; that they would all reach an identical decision at the identical time strains credibility.

Statistics, therefore, must be employed to answer the question of how likely certain conduct is if there is, in fact, no collusion. The forms of conduct most often subjected to such analysis are similar pricing and marketing practices and similar reaction to a competitor or firm at another stage of a distribution scheme. See, for example, *Theatre Enterprises* v. *Paramount Film Distributing Corp.*, 346 U.S. 537 (1954), in which each of the major film distributors rebuffed the plaintiff theatre owner's request for first-run films.

Statistics are important to this analysis in other ways as well. A court's decision about the likelihood of collusion often turns on structural phenomena that suggest that collusion would be easy to achieve in an industry. Evidence for such conclusions often is drawn from facts and practices other than the precise conduct under scrutiny. A list of such factors appears in the Federal Trade Commission's 1982 *Statement Concerning Horizontal Mergers*:

> The most relevant factors appear to be: the homogeneity (or fungibility) of products in the market; the number of buyers (as well as sellers); the similarity of producers' costs; the history of interfirm behavior, including any evidence of previous price-fixing by the firms at issue; and the stability of market share over time.

It is clear that at least two of these factors directly call for statistical examination and possible inference: the similarity of producers' costs and the stability of market share over time.

In addition, enforcement agencies make decisions about which industries to investigate in part on the basis of profit level. No court has condemned an industry merely for being profitable, but the Department of Justice and the Federal Trade Commission, following economic theory, consider supranormal profits a fairly strong indicator of either oligopoly conduct (which may not be illegal) or cartel behavior (strictly illegal). Statistical inference is necessary to determine whether, factoring in risk, one industry's profit rate is greater than the overall average in the economy.

C. Countervailing Efficiencies as a Defense

The case law in antitrust has been very slow to recognize a defense that has long been urged by economists: countervailing efficiencies. Although this defense does not dispute the potential for some anticompetitive result from a proposed undertaking, it argues that the improved efficiency or other cost savings caused by the proposal will more than offset that potential.

It is in the area of vertical restraints that the use of an efficiencies defense is growing most quickly—the rule of reason has often been expressed as a weighing of the procompetitive *inter*brand competition aspects of such a restraint against the anticompetitive *intra*brand competition effects. See, for example, *Beltone Electronics Corp.*, [1979–83 Transfer Binder] Trade Reg. Rep. CCH ¶21,934 (FTC, 1982), announcing that vertical restraints would be allowed despite harm to competition within a brand, whenever there was benefit to competition between brands.

Mergers have also been proposed as candidates for countervailing efficiencies analysis. Both the Department of Justice and the Federal Trade Commission have expressed some limited willingness to consider such a defense in deciding whether to bring a lawsuit, but court approval is yet to come.

In both settings, there is a demand for statistical methodology to demonstrate that a particular practice leads to less output or higher price than would otherwise occur. Both need not be present; often, in the vertical restraints area, the only positive evidence is of less output. In *NCAA* v. *Regents*, 104 S.Ct. 2948 (1984), the Supreme Court condemned the advertising plan of the National Collegiate Athletic Association principally on this ground: the total amount of televised college football was less than otherwise.

A statistician or economist will often be asked in such a context to study other firms in an industry or other time periods for the firm in question when the practice at issue was absent. On the basis of these observations, the expert then builds a model to project what output would have been in the period in question, had the practice under scrutiny not been followed. This is essentially the same task as has been described before in yet another setting, and the most commonly used statistical approach is multiple regression analysis.

3.3.5 Damages

Standing, market definition, and liability tend to be yes-or-no questions as courts have approached them. When the discussion turns to damages, a totally different approach is typically adopted. Under the assumption that a violation has taken place, the expert's task is to provide a point estimate of the magnitude of loss suffered by the plaintiff or the class represented. It is critical for the expert to segregate the effects of the conduct in question from the influence of other factors in the economy during the same period. Experts typically provide confidence intervals to go along with the point estimates that they obtain. Such confidence intervals may be large, but, since the issue of violation has been settled, it seems reasonable to allow the courts with the expert's help to obtain the best point estimate possible, even if the zero damages estimate is within a reasonable confidence interval. The latter may happen when inclusion of additional variables and coefficients in a model increases the uncertainty or when the model used to estimate damages differs in other ways from the one used to test for violations.

As with other aspects of antitrust litigation, the model of choice among expert economic witnesses in this area is the multiple linear regression model. Rubinfeld and Steiner (1983) describe the use of regression modeling in the *Plywood* antitrust case, and Finkelstein and Levenbach (1983) provide a critical review of the use of multiple regression to assess damages in that case and in three others: *In re Corrugated Container Antitrust Litigation*, 441 F.Supp. 921 (S.D. Tex. 1977), *New Mexico v. American Pipe and Constr. Co.*, Civ. No. 7183 (D. N.M. 1970), and *In re Chicken Antitrust Litigation*, 1980–2 Trade Cas. (CCH) para 63, 485 (N.D. Ga. 1980). A description of the *Corrugated Container* case appears in Chapter 2.

The recent decision of the Supreme Court in *Monsanto v. Spray-Rite*, 104 S.Ct. 1464 (1984) is also of interest. The plaintiff had been terminated as a distributor of the defendant's product and claimed that the loss of that one product caused his entire operation to fail. He then projected total earnings from that operation over the next 10 years without discounting. The basis for the projection was a multiple linear regression tying his own sales to industry sales. Despite the obvious weakness in this evidence, the defendant chose not to introduce rebuttal evidence from its own economist/statistician, perhaps from concern that the jury would confuse discussion of damages with a concession of liability. The defendant's gamble failed; liability was found, and the full amount of the plaintiff's requested damages, trebled, was awarded.

There are particular problems associated with the use of multiple regression techniques in the estimation of damages that differ in the forecasting approach as compared with the hypothesis-testing approach. In general, the regression approach makes sense if there is a long enough previolation period to establish competitive impact of the usual supply/demand variables that an economist might include in the model or, if the other explanatory variables are known to be independent of the cartel or other activities involving violation. If such independence is not the case, a multiple regression analysis might reasonably account for price changes, but it would not tell us anything about the damages resulting from the violation. To see why, it is only necessary to realize that while a cartel can (1) raise price, restrict output, and gain profits in the context of given supply and demand, it can also (2) cause shifts in the demand and the supply that lead to price increases and (3) take advantage of shifts in the demand and supply outside the activities of the cartel. Such indirect effects of the cartel bias downward statistical estimates of prices but for the cartel. Such indirect effects are likely to occur if demand and/or supply are heavily affected by individual expectations, for the cartel deliberately influences those expectations by its actions.

The international uranium cartel that operated at least between 1971 and 1975 provides a case in point. As described in detail in Rubinfeld and Steiner (1983), a regression analysis of uranium prices that includes a number of important factors surrounding the energy shortage, information about Westinghouse's future contracts for uranium, and the occurrence of a formal decision by the Canadian government related to the cartel can do much to explain the rise in uranium prices without any reference to a producers' cartel. Because these events and the cartel meetings were occurring during approximately the same period, each was closely correlated with the price rise. Had the events been independent of one another, the relative importance of the cartel might have been sorted out by multiple regression. But many of the events were critically interdependent. For example, if the oil embargo created fear among nuclear plants of any energy shortage, cartel members were in a position to convert that fear into virtual panic by a moratorium on commitments to sell uranium. The uranium cartel could, and arguably did, affect price by restricting output. It could also, arguably, affect the level of demand at each price and decrease the elasticity of demand by actions that increased buyers' willingness to purchase uranium.

In such a complex environment, the use of statistical or at least multiple regression techniques to estimate damages is likely to be problematic at best. Changes in prices may be due to supply and demand, but it is difficult to tell whether a cartel is or is not responsible for the shifts in supply and demand themselves. The point of this discussion is that additive models of behavior, which are implicit in relatively simple regression models, can be dangerous if misapplied. When numerous events are occurring simultaneously and independently, the interaction of the individual variables may be more important than their individual effects. Correct specification of these interactions is necessary if damages are to be reasonably accurately measured. For many of these effects, the measure of damages by a simple "but-for" regression model may understate the true level of harm inflicted. This is different from the usual multiple regression situations in which the more variables one brings in, thereby removing proxy effects, the smaller the estimated effect of interest tends to be.

3.3.6 Further Use of Regression and Survey Sampling

In a consumer class action case, *In re Antibiotic Antitrust Actions*, 410 F.Supp. 669 (D. Minn. 1974), known as the *Antibiotic Drug* case (see detailed discussion in Bartsh et al., 1978, and a brief discussion in King, 1986), the plaintiffs' experts demonstrated substantial damages due to an alleged conspiracy to maintain prices using a relatively crude statistical argument, and a negotiated settlement was reached. Several problems remained regarding how to allocate the agreed-on damage amount of approximately $20 million to consumers in the six plaintiff states. Simple regression models were used at this stage based on data from the 1963 and 1967 *Censuses of Business* using information on state populations and sales of all prescription drugs.

After this allocation was made, a process was set up under the supervision of special masters with statistical expertise, in which claim forms were mailed to potential claimants who purchased tetracycline during the period of alleged damages. The returned forms were then processed for payment. It was necessary to audit the forms to screen out erroneous claims as well as those that were clearly fraudulent. Because there were nearly 1 million claims, the special masters used probability sampling methods with selection rates based on expected losses due to missed errors (King, 1977).

3.3.7 Summary

The most important issues that arise in antitrust law involving the use of statistical methods are (1) defining a market and establishing market shares, (2) determining liability, (3) assessing damages. Statistical sampling methods are widely used in connection with the first, econometric models (including multiple regression models and hypothesis testing) with the second, and multiple regression models with the third. As in other legal settings, the use of sampling methods rests on a firmer statistical foundation than the use of regression methods, which rely more heavily on economic theory and the proper specification of models. In the *per se* area, the calculation of damages takes on heightened importance, since proof of anticompetitive effects to the economy is not required. In the rule of reason area, all aspects of proof are open to the use of statistical methods. Instances of misuse of statistics by expert witnesses have come to light in each of these areas, especially through misspecified null hypotheses and "but-for" regression models in which major assumptions are made but not clearly identified. The statistical difficulties with and the lack of justification for multiple regression analysis in antitrust litigation are at least as grave as in Title VII litigation settings. They place heavy reliance on extrapolation and prediction, and depend on unjustified assumptions in as critical a fashion as is the case in the Title VII area. Nonetheless, there is often no better way available to approach the questions at issue in the litigation.

Because of the use of jury trials in antitrust cases, there is less in the way of legal opinions to guide the admission and evaluation of statistical and economic evidence than there is in other areas of litigation. As a consequence, economists and statisticians appearing as expert witnesses are given broad latitude in the economic theories they rely on and in the methodology they use to address the issues described above. The *Manual for Complex Litigation 2d* (1985) suggests ways to deal with the possibility of conflicting expert opinions in antitrust litigation:

Agreement on a common data base to be used by all experts

is highly desirable; and the court may require the parties to
seek accord on methodology and form before surveys or polls
are conducted. ... Major questions regarding the admissibility
of experts' opinions may be addressed in advance of trial ... and
conflicts between the parties' experts on matters of theory may
suggest the advisability of the court's appointing an expert under Rule 706.

In private antitrust cases, the costs associated with adequate preparation and testimony by expert witnesses are often a major concern. Unlike
plaintiffs in Title VII discrimination cases, who are assisted by agencies
such as the EEOC in paying for the expenses of experts, plaintiffs in private antitrust cases must bear the cost of such expertise. At least one case
speaks to this issue. In *Person* v. *Association of the Bar of the City of New
York*, 414 F.Supp. 144 (1976); reversed, 554 F.2d 534 (1977), the plaintiff
was the attorney representing 10 plaintiffs in an antitrust action in the
Southern District of New York. He alleged that he was unable to prosecute
their case because the plaintiffs could not afford adequate expert testimony
in the fields of accounting, franchising, financing, and economics, and the
practice of retaining experts on a contingency fee basis was not permitted by a rule adopted by the New York State Bar Association. The lower
court held that the bar association rule was in violation of the Fourteenth
Amendment, but when the case reached the court of appeals the decision
was reversed. The judge held that the rule prohibiting contingency fees had
a sufficient rational basis to withstand constitutional challenge.

Even a brief review of the use of statistical and economics expertise
in antitrust litigation would be deficient if it failed to at least mention the
statistical and economic preparations for litigation in two highly publicized,
government-initiated cases, against AT&T and IBM. In the AT&T case
there was a settlement and the IBM case was dropped before trial, but
some of the experts involved have described their preparations in book-
length treatments—Evans (1983) for the AT&T case and Fisher, McGowan
and Greenwood (1983) for the IBM case. The latter book is organized in
large part according to the major economic/statistical issues here. In it the
authors, who worked for IBM, present their analysis of what they deemed
to be the failure of the government's case, and they comment on the proper
role of economists as consultants and expert witnesses.

3.4   Statistical Assessments as Evidence in Environmental Law

3.4.1   General Background

Interaction between science and law has grown with the search for scientific answers to environmental problems. Scientific data form the basis on

which environmental policy is established, legislation enacted, regulations promulgated, rules enforced, and cases litigated. In particular, quantitative data often are involved in environmental law at three important junctures: (1) determining whether a particular substance or situation represents an unacceptable risk and, if so, (2) establishing appropriate regulatory policy that will deal satisfactorily with the problem, and (3) resolving disputes arising from such regulations or statutes. Unfortunately, data used for these purposes often are imprecise, sometimes even contradictory.

Statistical assessments are presented as evidence in environmental law in numerous contexts. The most common are (a) judicial review of administrative agency rules and regulations, (b) enforcement actions against polluters, and (c) common-law tort actions seeking to recover damages for injuries suffered as the result of exposure to harmful substances or seeking to enjoin polluters from continued polluting activities. The most prevalent types of assessments are (1) analyses of monitoring data and data collection methods to ensure compliance with pollution control standards, (2) epidemiologic studies, (3) risk assessments based on data derived from either animal bioassays or epidemiologic studies, (4) modeling pollution effects, and (5) forecasting of long-term environmental effects.

Many important environmental concerns that have received wide publicity involve statistical issues. They include the possible dangers of 2,4,5-T (an herbicide and plant growth regulator that is a constituent of Agent Orange), saccharin, cigarette smoke, benzene, nuclear radiation, water pollutants, air pollutants, formaldehyde, and other allegedly hazardous substances.

Participants in the legal process generally are unfamiliar with the formidable array of statistical problems in environmental data and the statistical tools available to cope with them. Some troublesome aspects of environmental data include complex and unknown cause-and-effect relationships, measurement and nonmeasurement error, serial correlation, and seasonal fluctuations. The implications for society may be severe if such data are handled improperly. If a decision is made incorrectly in administrative rule making, it is likely that technical errors will go unrectified, especially if the decision is reviewed by a judiciary that is untrained in science and bound to a minimally intrusive standard of review.

3.4.2 Administrative Law

The U.S. Environmental Protection Agency (EPA) has the statutory duty of implementing federal environmental laws. Data collection and analysis are important factors in how the EPA promulgates and enforces environmental standards, guidelines, and regulations. Because of their importance, statistical assessments relied on by the EPA in the decision-making process often are challenged in the courts.

Disagreements arise over the choice of statistical methodology to be used by an environmental agency. For example, an affected party might believe that the agency's choice of a particular extrapolation model to calculate the risk of increased incidence of cancer is an approach that is either too conservative or too cavalier. Since the selection of a statistical methodology may constitute a rule under the Administrative Procedures Act (APA), the agency's choice may be challenged in the courts (see *Batterton* v. *Marshall,* 648 F.2d 694,700 (D.C. Cir. 1980), in which the court found that the selection by the Department of Labor of a statistical methodology for analyzing unemployment data was a rule within the APA). Whether a particular statistical methodology constitutes a rule subject to judicial review depends on its purpose. If the choice of statistical methodology forecloses alternate courses of action or conclusively affects the rights of parties, then it is a legislative rule that must be promulgated under the procedures of the APA and is subject to judicial review (id. at 702). If, however, the choice of statistical methodology merely expresses an agency's interpretation, policy, or internal practice or procedure, then it is a nonbinding rule and not subject to the APA.

One fundamental problem faced in any challenge to the statistical methodology used by an agency is judicial deference to agency expertise. In *FMC Corp.* v. *Train,* 539 F.2d 973 (4th Cir. 1976), the court remanded EPA guidelines for the discharge of effluents from plastics and synthetics point sources. One of the petitioner's arguments was that the EPA's use of regression to determine factors influencing the effluent limitations was incorrect, because the data points were not normally distributed. The EPA defended its use of regression by asserting that the underlying data deviated only slightly from a normal distribution pattern. The court stated: "This court feels that the choice of statistical methods is a matter best left to the sound discretion of the administrator."

Other circuit courts have cited the court's statement in *FMC Corp.* v. *Train* in upholding an agency's choice or use of a particular form of statistical methodology (see *American Petroleum Institute* v. *EPA,* 540 F.2d 1023, 1035 (10th Cir. 1976); and *BASF Wyandotte Corp.* v. *Costle,* 598 F.2d 637, 655 (1st Cir. 1979)). More recently, the Third Circuit Court of Appeals upheld the EPA's use of regression analysis in calculating water pollution effluent standards (see *National Association of Metal Finishers* v. *Environmental Protection Agency,* 719 F.2d 624, 13 ELR 21042 (3rd Cir. 1983)).

The following cases are good examples of judicial deference in action, although they do not cite *FMC Corp.* v. *Train. Sierra Club* v. *Sigler,* 432 F.Supp. 1222 (S.D. Texas 1982) was an unsuccessful challenge to the issuance by the Army Corps of Engineers of permits authorizing private construction of a multipurpose deep-water port and crude oil distribution system. One of the plaintiff's complaints was that the final environmental impact statement (FEIS), prepared pursuant to the National Environmental Policy Act (NEPA), contained an inadequate and misleading discussion of the potential impacts and probabilities of a major oil spill associated with the proposed action.

The FEIS concluded that the probability and the likely environmental impacts of a major oil spill associated with the proposed action would not be significantly greater than at present. The FEIS found that there would be an overall reduction in tanker traffic that would reduce the overall probability of an oil spill in one area while creating a new risk elsewhere. The FEIS also considered statistical data concerning spill frequency: "Consideration of spill frequency data in conjunction with the projected decrease in overall tanker traffic led the FEIS to conclude that the proposed action would not increase the probability of a major oil spill."

The plaintiffs attempted to prove that the probability analysis was invalid with competing expert testimony. The court found that the plaintiffs merely presented an alternative method:

> The testimony of plaintiff's experts establishes that equally reliable means of assessing oil spill probabilities do exist. Arguably, other methods of assessing probabilities might be preferable, and different conclusions drawn. At most, plaintiffs have demonstrated only a divergence of views about experts. ... The standard of review under NEPA demands judicial deference to the expertise of the decision-making agency unless overborne by substantial and credible evidence of arbitrary and capricious action.

Of course, the judgment that the plaintiffs have *merely* presented an alternative method is itself a substantive judgment, albeit in disguise, not just a judgment involving the adequacy of administrative review.

A further elaboration of the courts' policy of deference is provided in *Lead Industries Association* v. *Environmental Protection Agency*, 647 F.2d 1130 (D.C. Cir. 1980), in which the court upheld EPA's ambient air quality standards for lead. In an opinion by Chief Judge Skelly Wright, the court discussed its role when confronted by expert opinion on both sides of a position (p.1160):

> Disagreement among the experts is inevitable when the issues involved are at the "very frontiers of scientific knowledge," and such disagreement does not preclude us from finding that the Administration's decisions are adequately supported by the evidence in the record. ... It is not our function to resolve disagreement among the experts or to judge the merits of competing expert views (*AFL-CIO* v. *Marshall*, 617 F.2d 636, 651 and n. 66 (D.C. Cir. 1979); cf. *Hercules, Inc.* v. *EPA*, 598 F.2d 91, 115 (D.C. Cir. 1978)) ([C]hoice among scientific test data is precisely the type of judgment that must be made by EPA, not this court.).

Both of the cases cited above indicate that parties who challenge agency statistical assessments and other expert evidence must convince the court that their evidence is not just an alternative view. Instead, it is necessary to show that their position is significantly better based, something that is often difficult to do even with compelling statistical evidence.

3.4.3   Proof of Harm and Causation

The concepts of harm and causation are fundamental in environmental law, and their proof is often dependent on statistical assessments. An environmental dispute involving possible threats to the public health is fundamentally a dispute over whether a harm is occurring (or did or even would occur), whether a given party is responsible, and, if the answer to both of these questions is yes, whether it should be compelled to cease or modify the activity or compensate the injured. These questions all revolve around the concepts of harm and causation.

Harm

The concept of harm in environmental regulation relates to identifiable damage and harm that can be foreseen based on experience and predictions of risk. For example, groundwater shown to have been contaminated by a hazardous water dump is an identifiable harm, while the risk of increased incidence of cancer from drinking the water is an intangible harm based on predictions of risk.

Identifying environmental harm is extremely difficult when there is a long latency period between exposure and harm. The threats posed by low levels of substances such as organochlorides, phenoxy herbicides, and polychlorinated bi-phenols are not apparent immediately. The problem of a long latency period may be compounded by several features of ecosystems that make identification of causal relationships more difficult (Gelpe and Tarlock, 1974:404–407). First, the immediate or near-term effect of an environmental change often differs appreciably from ultimate long-term effects. Second, intervening or multiple sources of causation are more likely to complicate the relationship when harm is temporally remote from exposure. Finally, in some cases, the harm may be geographically remote from the point of production or exposure.

To promulgate regulations, an agency must establish that there is a need to regulate. The question of what degree of certainty is required to justify an agency decision to regulate was addressed by the majority and the dissent in *Ethyl Corporation* v. *Environmental Protection Agency*, 541 F.2d 1 (D.C. Cir. 1976). In that case, several manufacturers of leaded anti-knock gas additives sought review of an order by the EPA requiring a phased reduction in the lead content of leaded gasoline. Regulation was undertaken by the EPA administrator on the basis of a standard that required that "a significant risk of harm" to the public health be demonstrated as a consequence of leaded fuel use. The EPA had promulgated lead phase-down regulations after concluding that environmental lead exposure was a major health problem in the United States (38 Fed. Reg. 33734, 1973). The EPA found that a small but significant portion of the urban adult population as well as 25 percent of children in urban areas were overexposed to lead. Although the EPA acknowledged that lead from gasoline was only one source of lead exposure in the environment and, therefore, only part of the problem, it regulated leaded gasoline because it was a source of air and dust lead that could be readily and significantly reduced in comparison with other sources.

The dissent in *Ethyl* v. *EPA* argued that a significant risk of harm could be established only by proof of actual harm:

> If there can be found potential harm from lead in exhaust emissions, the best (and only convincing) proof of such potential harm is what has occurred in the past ... from which the Administrator can logically deduce that the same factors will produce the same harm in the future.

The majority, however, concluded that the standard applied by the administrator did not require direct proof that lead emissions themselves had caused actual harm. Rather, the court recognized that the wording of the statute suggested that it was precautionary in nature and that regulatory action was justified to protect public health. The court found that:

> Sometimes, of course, relatively certain proof of danger or harm from [environmental] modifications can be readily found. But, more commonly, "reasonable medical concerns" and theory long precede certainty. Yet the statutes—and common sense— demand regulatory action to prevent harm, even if the regulator is less than certain that harm is otherwise inevitable.

Unfortunately, there is no numerical standard to indicate how much less than certain an administrator may be. It is a question that must be addressed case by case.

Causation

Before administrators can regulate, they also must have established that the thing to be regulated is or can be the cause of the actual or potential harm. Contemporary environmental problems typically pose extraordinary difficulties in establishing causation. In many areas of environmental regulation, especially in efforts to regulate carcinogens, there is no direct and simple connection between the harm and the suspected cause. For example, epidemiologic studies may indicate that workers exposed to an agent have an increased incidence of lung cancer. It may also be shown that, within the group of workers studied, those who smoke account for the majority of lung cancer victims. Questions arise whether the agent is the cause of the cancer, an initiator of carcinogenisis, a cancer promoter that acts in synergy with smoking, or not a human carcinogen at all. It may be difficult in such circumstances to obtain definitive answers, especially if there is a long latency period between exposure and harm. Deciding if a sufficient causal connection exists to justify regulatory action is a difficult task.

To justify its regulations of leaded gasoline, the EPA had to make an initial showing that there was a significant risk of harm to the population from elevated blood lead levels. The EPA did not need to prove it is more reasonable than not that harm would result to part of the population, but merely had to show that, based on available evidence, a reasonable person could agree that there was a risk of harm—without defining either the degree of harm or the probability.

Meeting this rational basis standard—even though it is low compared with that applied in civil and criminal litigation—can be difficult. When the risk is one of a remote harm, and when causation cannot be well established, the links in the chain of reasoning from known fact to alleged harm may be quite weak or even absent. The evidence necessary to shore up these weak links may not exist or be obtainable. If the courts required the agencies to have an ironclad case, few environmental regulations would be upheld.

The EPA's lead phase-down regulations addressed the issue of causation in two parts. First, the EPA found that lead from gasoline was the most ubiquitous source of lead found in air, dirt, and dust in urban areas. The EPA also noted that human exposure to the lead is by inhalation and by ingestion of dirt and dust contaminated by air lead fallout. Second, the EPA pointed to scientific studies that indicated that airborne lead contributed significantly to lead exposure in the general population, although other studies did not indicate a strong correlation between air lead levels and blood lead levels. The EPA then cited additional studies indicating that contaminated dust and dirt from motor vehicle exhaust were believed to be important sources of exposure contributing to lead poisoning in children. The EPA concluded that the evidence was sufficient to establish a causal link between lead in exhaust and lead in the human body, and therefore regulation of leaded gasoline was justified.

The issue of causation sharply divided the court. The dissent believed that a causal connection had to be established by a chain of scientifically probable assertions:

> The thought process by which an agency reaches its conclusion on informal rulemaking resembles a chain. If there is a link missing, then the agency, to reach the conclusion that it did, was required to take an arbitrary jump in its logic to reach that conclusion.

Judge Wright, writing for the majority, strongly disagreed with this position. The regulatory standard involved, he argued, was precautionary in nature:

> Where a statute is precautionary in nature, the evidence difficult to come by, uncertain, or conflicting because it is on the frontiers of scientific knowledge, the regulations designed to protect the public health, and the decision that of an expert administrator, we will not demand rigorous step-by-step proof of cause and effect. ... The Administrator may apply his expertise to draw inferences from suspected, but not completely substantiated, relationships between facts, from trends among facts, from theoretical projections from imperfect data, from probative preliminary data not yet certifiable as "fact," and the like.

The court deferred to the expertise of the agency in its determination that the data showed sufficient likelihood of causal connection to justify regulation. Of more significance, the court pointed to the legislative intent, which it claimed called for a "precautionary standard," and found that to provide the highest level of protection for public health, regulatory action could precede scientific proof.

3.4.4 Types of Statistical Evidence

The types of statistical assessments presented as evidence in environmental lawsuits vary from simple compilations of monitoring data to complex models of transport of pollutants and resultant health effects. The degree of controversy over statistical evidence is usually a function of its complexity.

Among the most controversial statistical assessments presented as evidence in administrative law are quantitative risk assessments that attempt to estimate the risk of increased incidence of health problems from exposure to various substances. Great scientific uncertainty is associated with almost all phases of the risk assessment process and with the assumptions that are made in light of that uncertainty.

A National Research Council report, *Risk Assessment in the Federal Government: Managing the Process* (1983), identifies areas of uncertainty in the risk assessment process and points out that how that uncertainty is handled is as much a question of public policy as it is one of science. In examining the elements of uncertainty in risk assessment, the report states (p.28):

> When scientific uncertainty is encountered in the risk assessment process, inferential bridges are needed to allow the process to continue. The Committee has defined the points in the risk assessment where such inferences must be made as *components*. The judgments made by the scientist/risk assessor for each component of risk assessment often entail a choice among several

scientifically plausible options; the Committee has designated these *inference options.*

The report lists 50 components for which inferential bridges are needed, many of which contain subcomponents.

In explaining how scientists address areas of uncertainty through inference, the report discloses numerous areas in which policy considerations intrude on the risk assessment process. It concludes that "policy considerations inevitably affect, and perhaps determine, some of the choices among the inference options."

Given these considerations, and the large number of "inferential bridges," it is not surprising that quantitative risk assessments are challenged in the courts. Recent cases that have addressed the issues surrounding the use and interpretation of quantitative risk assessments include *Public Citizen Health Research Group* v. *Auchter,* 702 F.2d 1150 (D.C. Cir. 1983)—Petition for an Emergency Standard Regulating Industrial Exposure to Ethylene Oxide— and *Gulf South Insulation* v. *Consumer Product Safety Commission,* 701 F.2d 1137 (5th Cir. 1983)—Petition for Review of a Ban on the Use of Urea-Formaldehyde Foam Insulation (see the case study in Chapter 2).

Another controversial issue in environmental law is the evidentiary value of negative epidemiological studies that are presented as proof that a particular environmental condition is safe. The use of negative epidemiological studies arises in the context of challenges to regulatory standards (usually occupational) that seek to limit exposure to a toxic or carcinogenic substance. The major strength of epidemiology in an environmental setting is that it studies humans, rather than animals. Risk assessments that use analyses of data from human populations invariably are given more credence than those based on extrapolations from animal data. There are, however, weaknesses in epidemiology that can undermine its strength: e.g., lurking variables or synergism among variables may lead to a false inference in moving from a positive association to a causal conclusion; the size of a study may be too small to detect an effect; the period of study may be too short to detect diseases with long latency periods (such as cancer). Different methods of analysis of retrospectively or even prospectively gathered epidemiological data may lead to different conclusions. This divergence of views, often along government, industry, and environmental lines, finds its way into the courtroom, where judges must balance the conflicting viewpoints.

Although negative epidemiological studies never can prove a null hypothesis, there is a growing consensus that well-constructed studies with sufficient statistical power but negative results should be considered by agencies in promulgating exposure standards. For the courts to make judgments regarding such studies can be a seemingly impossible task, especially when experts make confusing statements. Consider the following statement explaining the value of negative epidemiological studies (*UAW* v. *Donovan*

[#82–2401 D.D.C. Oct. 5, 1984]) from the affidavit of one of the experts:

> The point is that the power of epidemiological evidence is the power of the totality of the available studies, whether or not any single study does or does not have adequate power. I repeat that the power of the epidemiological evidence rests not on the results of any one study, but on the negative results of studies now in the literature.

The term *power* is used in both its technical, statistical sense and its nonstatistical, general sense; the expert makes no effort to distinguish between the two. Moreover, a sequence of negative results does not necessarily reinforce the negative conclusion. Given such misstatements by experts, however, courts are likely to repeat them.

The actual presentation of statistical assessments in cases involving judicial review of administrative decisions is limited. In general, a court reviewing an agency action can consider only evidence relied on by the agency—the administrative record (*Asbestos Information Assocation* v. *OSHA*, 727 F.2d 415, n. 12 (5th Cir. 1984)). This precludes the court from trying the case de novo and limits the parties to citing evidence already in the administrative record. However, in the rare instance in which new evidence will aid the court in examining the record, the court may use its discretion and allow the parties to introduce such evidence (see *Asbestos Information Assocation* v. *OSHA*, 727 F.2d 415, n. 12, citing *Amoco Oil Co.* v. *EPA*, 501 F.2d 722, 729, n. 10 (D.C. Cir. 1974), admitting evidence accumulated after rule promulgation to assess validity of prerule predictions).

How, then, do statistical assessments enter into the judicial review of administrative proceedings? The answer is through affidavits of experts. The standard technique used to establish the validity of a party's scientific data, methods, and assumptions is divided into two phases. First, experts prepare affidavits that bolster the position advocated. The content of an affidavit can vary from broad supportive statements to lengthy detailed analyses of the evidence in the record. Second, attorneys copiously cite the affidavits to prove that science is on their side.

Although not considered evidence in the sense of documents in the administrative record, experts' affidavits are important in the advocacy of a case. Take, for example, the affidavit of an expert in a suit currently before the District Court for the District of Columbia. In a petition to the court, the United Auto Workers (UAW) seeks to have the court find that the Occupational Safety and Health Administration unlawfully denied its petition for the issuance of an emergency temporary standard (ETS) to lower workplace exposure limits for formaldehyde (*UAW* v. *Donovan* [D.D.C. 82–2401, Oct. 5, 1984]). One of the central issues in the case was whether OSHA's methods for calculating the risk of increased incidence of cancer from exposure to formaldehyde are valid. A professor of statistics at a major university prepared an affidavit addressing OSHA's risk assessments on behalf of the Formaldehyde Institute, an intervenor in the case. His affidavit discusses the same methodology that was in dispute in the *Gulf South Insulation* case described earlier (see Chapter 2): (a) the use of mathematical risk assessments generally, (b) OSHA's risk assessments, (c) the choice of models, (d) the assumptions in OSHA's models, and (e) the use of upper confidence limits. This affidavit is cited repeatedly as support for the Formaldehyde Institute's argument that none of the quantitative risk assessments available to OSHA demonstrates grave danger (a necessary requirement for the issuance of an ETS) because the risk assessments fail to incorporate all available data and even the purely quantitative predictions are flawed because their underlying assumptions are unsupported (see the intervenor's brief, *UAW* v. *Donovan* [D.D.C. 82–2401, Oct. 5, 1984] at 24–37). Without the affidavit of an expert scrutinizing OSHA's risk assessments, it is doubtful that the Formaldehyde Institute could have made the technical arguments that it did.

3.4.5   Common Law

The problems associated with the proof of harm and causation in administrative law also exist in civil lawsuits in which a party has been injured and seeks compensation for the injury. Toxic torts constitute a new class of environmental lawsuits, for which statistical assessments provide important evidence of harm and causation.

A tort, as broadly defined by Prosser (1971), "is a civil wrong, other than breach of contract, for which the court will provide a remedy in the form of an action for damages." Toxic torts, however, recently have arisen from the fairly new phenomenon of exposure to toxic substances, usually chemicals.

Numerous situations give rise to toxic tort litigation. The most publicized lawsuits have involved workers who suffered chronic and terminal diseases from inhalation of asbestos, children who have suffered injuries because their mothers took synthetic estrogens (for example, diethylstilbestrol—DES), and people who have been injured from exposure to toxic substances leaching from landfills.

Under traditional tort doctrine, a plaintiff must prove that he or she suffered an injury and that it is "more likely than not that the conduct of the defendant was a substantial factor" in causing the injury (Prosser, 1971). The plaintiff's burden of providing these facts in a toxic tort is substantial.

At a recent conference on environmental law, Grad (1984) addressed the issue of proving the "causal nexus between injury or disease complained of and the environmental condition (such as the disposal of hazardous wastes) for which the defendant is allegedly responsible." He cited a 1982 congressionally authorized study that explored the dimensions of proof, which noted (Superfund Study Group, 1982:70–71):

> The issue of proof of causation is rendered more difficult by a number of recurring circumstances. In the case of exposure to a hazardous waste disposal site, the plaintiff may find it difficult to pinpoint responsibility because the site has usually received a variety of hazardous wastes from a variety of sources over an extended period of time. The problem will be rendered even more complicated because of the long latency periods. ... During a ten-to-forty year latency period, the site may have changed ownership several times—and the plaintiff, too, has probably moved about to different locations, thereby potentially exposing himself to a variety of other environmental influences or toxic exposures.
>
> Proof of causation will require large amounts of sophisticated medical and scientific testimony to demonstrate the epidemiologic or statistical correlation between certain diseases and certain environmental exposures. ... Medical testimony on the etiology of the disease is necessary to show how the particular substance caused the condition in issue. ... It is clear ... that proof of the causal connection between exposure and injury is an almost overwhelming barrier to recovery, particularly in smaller cases (regardless of their merit) because the cost of mounting the massive probative effort and the arrays of technical and scientific evidence will be prohibitive.

The use of statistical assesments is important in establishing the causal connection. In fact, it is the only way to do so. The same controversy that surrounds epidemiological studies and quantitative risk assessments in administrative law, of course, is also present in common law, toxic tort litigation.

Problems also arise in environmental law when novel concepts of harm run into established common law doctrines. In *Ayers* v. *Township of Jackson*, 13 ELR 20631 (1983), the New Jersey Superior Court ruled on a motion for partial summary judgment in a lawsuit concerning the contamination of drinking water by toxic and carcinogenic chemical leaching from a landfill. It is illustrative of the difficulties parties have in seeking compensation for the enhanced risk of disease from exposure to hazardous substances. In this case, expert witnesses were prepared to testify that all individuals exposed to well water contamination are at an increased risk of developing cancer and liver and kidney damage. To the lay person, it might seem unfair for these people to be denied compensation for this enhanced risk. However, under the law of torts, the court found that the inability of the experts to quantify the enhanced risk precluded the recovery of damages. The court stated: "As long as the risk exposure remains within the realm of speculation, it cannot be the basis of a claim of injury against the creator of that harm." In effect, the lack of statistical evidence in the form of a quantitative risk assessment defeated the plaintiffs' claim. Although the plaintiffs had been harmed, the harm was deemed to be without legal and scientific significance because of the absence of quantification.

In *Pierce* v. *Johns-Manville Sales Corporation*, 464 A.2d 1020 (C.A.M.D. 1983), the Court of Appeals of Maryland addressed the burden of proof that a party must meet for the recovery of damages based on the risk of future injury. The court noted that (p. 1026):

> In Maryland, recovery of damages based on future consequences of an injury may be had only if such consequences are reasonably possible or reasonably certain. Such damages cannot be recovered if future consequences are "mere possibilities." Probability exists when there is more evidence in favor of a proposition than against it (a greater than 50% chance that a future consequence will occur). Mere possibility exists when the evidence is anything less (citation omitted).

This statement is unhelpful because it attempts to associate specific probability values to vague descriptions of levels of uncertainty, but it offers no operational defintions of key terms. For example, it gives little indication of what types of evidence will satisfy the burden of proof placed on the plaintiff. It is clearly necessary for the plaintiff to look at prior cases to see what has satisfied the burden in the past. For instance, have triers of fact been persuaded by risk assessments based on animal bioassays? If a court wanted better evidence, did it say what kind? Assuming the plaintiff knows what types of evidence are persuasive as to future consequences, it is then necessary to discover its availability. It is quite possible that very little research has been done on the particular toxic substances involved and that limited data are available.

Legal concepts such as "reasonably possible," "reasonably certain," or even "preponderance of the evidence" often are equated with greater than 50 percent by commentators and courts. This was the case in *Pierce* v. *Johns-Manville*. Yet the meaning of such statements is unclear despite their seeming precision. While there is little consensus on such a standard of evidence or how it should be used, it is clear that the level of certainty expressed in the expert's testimony can often be determinative. As Obadal (1983) notes:

> At times science can only state that exposure "could" have caused the illness. In the same case, another scientist may answer that exposure "probably" caused the malady. The dividing line between the two is, in many cases, a thin one. However, the consequences are of major importance to the parties. In the case of "could" a court will hold that a plaintif has failed to carry

his burden of proof and reject the claim. No liability results. In
the case of "probably" the court allows a finding of liability.

He goes on to ask whether "such divergent results [are] fair when the scientific bases for the underlying opinions are so imprecise."

3.4.6 Mass Torts

One of the most troublesome parts of common law tort litigation is the area
of "mass torts." Mass torts can generally be classified into two categories.
The first category is composed of cases in which plaintiffs' injuries are fairly
easy to prove and the cause of the injuries is clear. An example of a case in
this class would be an airplane crash. The second category is composed of
cases in which plaintiffs allege injuries suffered as the result of the use of a
product or from exposure to a hazardous substance. In this second category,
plaintiffs' injuries may be linked to the actions of the defendants, but they
may also be linked to a number of other causes. Examples of these types
of injuries include lung cancer and birth defects. It is this second category
of cases that pushes the judiciary to the limits of its competence as it tries
to resolve issues of law, fact, and social policy. The following discussion
highlights some of the troublesome aspects of this second category of mass
torts.

Two recent cases illustrate some of the difficulties associated with legal
and public policy issues presented by cases in which large numbers of plaintiffs allege that their injuries are the result of the conduct of a few defendants. In the first case, *Allen* v. *United States*, 588 F.Supp. 247 (C.D. Utah
1984), *rev'd*. 816 F.2d 1417 (10th Cir. 1987), civilians living downwind from
the U.S. government's Nevada nuclear test range sued the United States,
claiming death and injury from exposure to radioactive fallout from nuclear
tests. On May 9, 1984, Judge Bruce S. Jenkins of the United States District
Court for the District of Utah filed a 489–page memorandum opinion in
the case. Judge Jenkins found that although the government was clearly
negligent in its conduct of the nuclear testing program and had violated its
duty of care to the plaintiffs, only a limited group of plaintiffs was entitled
to damages. (While the final version of this report was in production the
decision was reversed by the Court of Appeals for the Tenth Circuit.) In the
second case, *In re "Agent Orange"*, 597 F.Supp. 740 (E.D. N.Y. 1984), 611
F.Supp. 1223 (D.C. N.Y. 1985), *aff'd*. 818 F.2d 145 (2d Cir. 1987), veterans of the Vietnam War sued the U.S. government and a group of chemical
companies, claiming death and injury to themselves, their spouses, and
children from exposure to herbicides used in the Vietnam War. There were
more than 1,000 plaintiffs in this class action litigation. On May 7, 1984,
the day the trial was to begin, this litigation was tentatively settled by an
agreement between the plaintiffs and the defendant chemical companies.
The United States was not a party to the settlement. Final settlement was

approved in January 1985.

In the 1950s and the early 1960s the U.S. government engaged in an ambitious program of nuclear testing. Scores of tests were conducted in an isolated corner of Nevada, releasing clouds of radioactive fallout. Although the testing took place away from civilian population centers, thousands of civilians in a three–state area of the desert Southwest (Utah, Nevada, and Arizona) were exposed to high levels of radioactive fallout. It was some 20 years after the last above-ground nuclear test that Judge Jenkins issued his decision.

In the introduction to *Allen* v. *U.S.*, Judge Jenkins outlined the broad issues to be addressed before a finding could be made: (a) whether there was a causal connection between the tests and subsequent cases of cancer and leukemia in civilians exposed to fallout; (b) whether the federal government had a duty to inform its people of the dangers to them from above-ground testing; (c) whether the government was excused from liability because of political exigencies; (d) whether the plaintiffs were negligent in allowing themselves to be exposed to radioactive fallout; (e) who should bear the cost of injuries caused by the radioactive fallout; and (f) the question of what did the decision makers know about the effects of nuclear testing. The issue of causation is discussed below.

The 13–week trial involved 24 bellwether cases out of 1,192 individual claims. The case was not a class action, and, since it was tried under the Federal Torts Claims Act (28 U.S.C. 1346 et. seq.), it could not be tried before a jury. The bellwether cases were picked in an effort to try a selection of cases *typical* of the total to "provide a legal and factual pattern against which the remaining issues in the pending cases may be subsequently matched." As noted by Judge Jenkins:

> The trial was conducted as well so as to make a full and complete record concerning legal, historic, and scientific matters common to all of the 1,192 plaintiffs with the idea in mind of avoiding future duplication of effort.

Even with this judicial economy in mind, the court received into evidence the testimony of 98 witnesses and 1,692 documentary exhibits.

Judge Jenkins' opinion begins with a commentary on the problem of uncertainty. The judge cited the failure of most people to distinguish between empirical and inferential facts and warned that "we must be constantly aware of the nature of that which we say we 'know'." As an example he pointed out that many people believe they "know" of the existence of the atom even though they have never seen one. Even though the existence of the atom is based on the work and observations of many scientists, Judge Jenkins adopted the idea that "we remain uncertain still of our scientific certainties." In expressing the view that there are no absolutes, the court set the stage for dealing with the differences between the quest for justice in the judicial forum and the search for knowledge in the scientific arena. Just as uncertainty lingers in findings of scientific fact, so too it is an element in judicial fact finding. Nonetheless, the judiciary cannot delay decisions pending further investigations. The court explained its attempt to formulate a theory of decision as follows:

> While the effort lacks the mathematical purity of physical theory, it is the *judicial* resolution of the questions raised by the case with which the court is concerned. The theory of decision melds the method of science with principles of law and public policy [emphasis in the original].

After finding that the employees of the defendant had negligently and wrongfully breached their legal duty of care to the plaintiffs, the judge addressed the question of causation. Before any of the plaintiffs could recover for their injuries, they had to show that their injuries were connected to the defendant's conduct. Unlike the case of an automobile accident, in which there is a relatively clear relationship between cause and effect, proving the causal connection between radiation exposure and cancer or leukemia presented myriad problems for the plaintiffs. The judge outlined the difficulties in stating:

> In this case, the factual connection singling out the defendant as the source of the plaintiffs' injuries and deaths is very much in genuine dispute. Determination of the cause in fact, or factual connection, issue is complicated by the nature of the injuries suffered (various forms of cancer and leukemia), the nature of the causation mechanism alleged (ionizing radiation from nuclear fallout, as opposed to ionizing radiation from other sources, or other carcinogenic mechanisms), the extraordinary time factors and other variables involved in tracing any causal relationship between the two.

The judge identified two of the most difficult hurdles in establishing cause in fact as being the long latency period between exposure to radiation and the observed cancer or leukemia and the nonspecific nature of the alleged injury. The court found, however, that these obstacles could be overcome. After a detailed analysis of traditional tort law and of innovations in tort law that have arisen in answer to the problems presented in similar cases, the court held that:

> Where a defendant who negligently creates a radiological hazard which puts an identifiable population group at increased risk, and a member of that group at risk develops a biological condition which is consistent with having been caused by the hazard to which he has been negligently subjected, such consistency having been demonstrated by substantial, appropriate, persuasive and connecting factors, a fact-finder *may* reasonably

conclude that the hazard caused the condition absent persuasive proof to the contrary offered by the defendant [emphasis in
the original].

The key issue was identified as whether the defendant's conduct was a
"substantial factor" in the alleged injury. The burden on the plaintiff was
not to prove the case beyond a reasonable doubt, but rather:

It is enough that he introduces evidence from which reasonable
men may conclude that it is more probable that the event was
caused by the defendant than that it was not. *The fact of causation is incapable of mathematical proof,* since no man can say
with absolute certainty what would have occurred [emphasis in
the original].

After pointing out that causation is incapable of mathematical proof, the
judge proceeded to note that "the strongest evidence of the relationship
(between a cause and non-specific effect) is likely to be statistical in form."
He concluded:

If relied upon as a guide rather than as an answer, the statistical evidence offered in this case provides material assistance
in evaluating the factual connection betwen nuclear fallout and
plaintiffs' injuries.

Finally, after reviewing the evidence on the dose-response relationship
between radiation exposure and cancer and leukemia along with the incomplete data on dosimetry, the judge listed the determinations to be made in
the review of each of the bellwether cases:

In each of the 24 cases now before this court, the plaintiffs must
establish by a preponderance of the evidence that (1) the dece-
dent or living plaintiff having cancer was probably exposed to
fallout radiation significantly in excess of "background" radiation rates; (2) the injury is of a type consistent with those
known to be caused by ionizing radiation; and (3) that the person injured had resided in geographical proximity to the Nevada
Test Site for some if not all of the years of atmospheric testing between 1951 and 1962. If these factual connections are
established, other relevant factors will also be evaluated in determining the "substantial factor" issue.

Only 3 of the 24 cases failed the threshold test of satisfying the 3 basic
requirements outlined above. Only 10 of the remaining 21 cases, however,
met the substantial factor test.

The case of Melvin O. Orton is an example of a case in which the evidence
satisfied the threshold requirements but failed to meet the substantial factor

test. Melvin Orton was diagnosed as having stomach cancer in 1970 and died in 1971. In favor of a finding that the substantial factor test had been met was the fact that his latency period for developing stomach cancer correlated with estimates based on data from survivors of the nuclear attack on Hiroshima. In addition, there was a statistically significant increase of stomach cancer among Mormon women in southern Utah for the period of 1958–1966 (6 observed/0.6 expected, p=0.01.) There was, however, no material increase found in the incidence of stomach cancer in men for the periods of 1958–1966, 1972–1975, or among both sexes in the 1972–1980 period. After addressing several other factors, the judge found:

> Though several factual connections weigh strongly in the plain-
> tiff's favor in this case, the absence of identifiable statistical
> evidence of augmentation tips the scales against the plaintiffs,
> even if the fairly strong rebuttal testimony is ignored entirely.
> While exposure to fallout may well have been a factor contribut-
> ing to Melvin Orton's cancer, the evidence in the record does
> not demonstrate it to be a legally "substantial" one.

Four of the cases that did pass the substantial factors test involved children who had died of leukemia. In each case the biological and statistical evidence supporting the judge's conclusion of a causal connection was overwhelming. First, all four children were exposed to heavy fallout at least once. Second, the scientific record had firmly established a causal relationship between various forms of leukemia and exposure to ionizing radiation. Third, the latency periods were consistent with data gathered in Japan. Finally, empirical data showed a significant excess of leukemia cases in southern Utah; among southern Utah Mormons the data were: 19 observed/3.6 expected [p = 0.01] for 1958–1966; 12 observed/3.4 expected [p = 0.01] for 1972–1980, with a higher excess among men.

The cases cited above showed a heavy reliance on observational statistical data indicating an increased incidence of cancer or leukemia within the exposed population. When there was a significant increase within the plaintiff's group, the court held for the plaintiff. Without convincing statistical evidence, the court ruled against the plaintiff.

Judge Jenkins relied on a large body of scientific knowledge in reaching his decisions. It had already been established prior to the case that there was a correlation between exposure to ionizing radiation and leukemia. That knowledge was provided through examination of the surviving victims of atomic warfare and through years of scientific research. Unfortunately, not all mass tort plaintiffs have such a vast body of knowledge to look to in seeking compensation for injuries they believe were caused by the action of others. The *Agent Orange* litigation is a case in point.

Causation was the primary issue in the *Agent Orange* litigation. Unlike *Allen*, however, in which the judge concluded that causation was established by some plaintiffs, the ultimate decision in *Agent Orange* if the case had gone to trial is unknown. One of the primary differences between the cases was in the evidence on the correlation between exposure and disease. The only one of the plaintiffs' alleged injuries that was demonstrably correlated with exposure to Agent Orange was chloracne—a sometimes severe but not fatal skin disorder. In *Allen*, however, a substantial body of scientific evidence showed a high correlation between radiation exposure and the diseases of leukemia and thyroid cancer.

Establishing the relationship between a particular disease and exposure to a substance is not sufficient to make a finding for the plaintiffs in tort litigation. Evidence is required that shows an increased incidence of the particular disease among the plaintiffs that would support (along with other factors) a finding that disease x was more likely than not caused from exposure to substance y. In *Allen*, the court was able to cite evidence showing a dramatically increased incidence of leukemia and thyroid cancer in a number of population groups. In *Agent Orange*, by contrast, there was no apparent evidence of increased disease at the time of settlement.

In approving the final settlement in *Agent Orange* in January 1985, Judge Jack Weinstein issued an opinion to the effect that it was scientifically and legally unfeasible to connect the alleged ailments to Agent Orange exposure and he ordered that the distribution of \$200 million among 250,000 Vietnam veterans be made on the degree of disability, regardless of cause. In August 1986 the Second Circuit of the Court of Appeals ordered a stay in the implementation of Judge Weinstein's distribution plan, but, at the time of the completion of this report, it was not known whether the three-judge panel had serious objections to the plan or only wanted more time to review it.

Advances in science have been accompanied by new problems that traditional law addresses inadequately. That a person should be compensated for injuries caused by the negligent acts of another is a legal tenet, but mass torts present numerous roadblocks to the satisfaction of that moral standard, especially because they assume levels of certainty not present in most scientific data. By extrapolating from traditional tort analysis, however, courts appear to be formulating a variety of new solutions that seek to compensate victims as well as protect the rights of defendants. Both traditional tort analysis and these new formulations depend on statistical analyses and conclusions to inform critical issues such as causation.

3.4.7   Summary

The statistical analysis of environmental data is frequently complicated by such problems as complex cause-and-effect relationships, including long latency periods. Special statistical features of such data can include the following: errors are autocorrelated, distributions are skewed, data are unreliable, data are missing, data are inconsistent (see Hunter, 1982). The most perplexing problem is the lack of data in crucial regions of interest.

For example, in order to provide a sound scientific basis for establishing standards for hazardous substances, data are often needed on the health effects of these substances at low dose levels. Unfortunately, such data are frequently unavailable. Efforts have been made to develop mathematical models to describe dose-response relationships in these circumstances. Because data at the relevant low dose levels are unavailable, extrapolations must be relied on. The fundamental problem is that many models fit the available data; when they are extrapolated to the low-dose range, they usually give substantially different answers.

In their work as expert witnesses, statisticians often do not highlight pivotal assumptions. They need to try to step back from their work product and ask whether they are making such pivotal assumptions, discuss them with lawyers and substantive scientific experts, and thereby maximize the validity of these models. The courts, for their part, must try to understand when assumptions are being relied on that undermine the statistical and scientific conclusions that are reported by experts (for example, as is often the case with statistical analyses involving low-dose extrapolation).

In such situations, the courts must consider the balancing of errors and reflect prevailing norms of justice and values of society as they do in normal circumstances. The seductive simplicity (or dazzling complexity) of the models and the seemingly impressive sets of data being used in a case should not mislead the court. Such models and data are often given undue probative weight by the court.

4

Statistics, Law, and Expert Testimony

4.1   The Methodologies of Law and Statistics

The preceding two chapters reveal tensions between law and statistics that pose special problems for the judicial system and for those who must integrate statistical learning into the legal process. While neither statistics nor law assumes that decisions must rest on absolute certainty, we saw that courts seek certainty, not so much in their formal decision rules, as in the way they actually reach decisions in practice. In part this may be because our own system evolved from earlier forms that were premised on "certainty." Most conspicuously, trial by ordeal suggested that divine intervention would guarantee a correct answer to the factual question involved. This attitude was linked to notions of certainty shared by both science and the legal system, captured in the common use of the term *law* to describe both observed invariance and prescribed injunctions for behavior. Both science and law have undergone enormous changes in perception, moving toward more complex and conjectural understandings in both fields. But they have not moved in tandem. They operate sometimes in agreement and sometimes with different aims of prediction and control.

The earlier belief in absolute certainty is instructive. Legal systems play a certain role in legitimizing political regimes. In every society with a formal legal system, the adjudicative power rests its authority on the assumption that it will do justice. To the extent that this assumption is open to question, the legitimacy of the entire regime may be called into question. It is a probabilistic notion of justice that—though realistic, sensible, natural, and inevitable—creates unease.

Certainty, and even the appearance of certainty, are important in law. Mistakes on factual matters raise questions about the dependability of the legal system and threaten those who might be subject to it. The desire to reduce errors in adjudication, as we saw in the case studies, is part of the motive of the courts in seeking better use of statistical methods. Whenever factual determinations can be based on a well-developed, agreed-on body of knowledge, the courts have shown an inclination to avail themselves of this body of knowledge. Technically, such knowledge is made available to the courts by the testimony of expert witnesses, especially scientific experts. But statistical evidence typically involves the formal expression of uncertainty, and thus statistical experts do not bring the kind of certainty to which the courts aspire.

Like other experts, statisticians are typically introduced as witnesses for one side or the other in an adversarial proceeding. Only rarely are experts on opposing sides found in complete agreement. As a consequence, the introduction of statistical evidence does not necessarily simplify the courts' task. Statistical experts may raise rival criteria at odds with legal notions, bringing into the court intramural disciplinary disagreements, and the adversarial process often appears to lead to the undesirable outcome of different experts providing disparate views based on the same data. In this, statistical experts behave much as experts from other fields, when functioning as forensic specialists. Court experience with other types of experts thus can be one of the sources of lessons for using statistical expertise in the most constructive possible ways.

4.2   Major Differences Between Legal and Statistical Thinking

An understanding of the differences between inquiry and reasoning in law and those in science is essential for making statistical assessments more effective in the resolution of conflicts through the judicial process. The very goals of science and law differ. Science searches for truth and seeks to increase knowledge by formulating and testing theories. Law seeks justice by resolving individual conflicts, although this search often coincides with one for truth.

Compared with law, science advances more deductively, with an occasional bold leap to a general theory from which its deductions can be put to a test and the theory subsequently proved wrong or inadequate and replaced by a more general theory. The bolder a scientific theory, the more possibilities there are to prove it wrong. But these possibilities are the very opportunities of science, and the more a theory explains, the more science is advanced. Of course, within a scientific theory, reasoning from data proceeds inductively, as scientists generalize from samples to populations, even if they do not think formally in these terms.

Compared with science, law advances more inductively, with a test of the boundaries and an examination of relationships between particular cases before a general application is made. Thus, the judicial process is predominantly one aimed toward arriving at the "correct" answer in a concrete case; generalizations and rules, in the abstract, are a by-product. Thus, a judge cannot abdicate; the court is expected to provide a decision based on the evidence presented. The failure to answer is a dereliction of duty.

The emphasis on the individual case is reinforced by societal pressures. For most litigants, the individual case is a crucial event. For a severely injured accident victim, for example, or a defendant accused of a major felony, the trial and its outcome comprise one of the most important events of a lifetime. The decision on the adequacy of the evidence is of enormous moment. Procedures that may enhance justice over the range of cases may lead to unjust results in particular instances. Thus, rules of decision that are not tailored to individual cases, such as those that turn on statistical reasoning, are often viewed as suspect.

Closely coupled with this emphasis on individual cases is the mode of reasoning by example used in legal settings (Levi, 1962). Although scientists generate hypotheses in various ways, science knows no proof by example except when the examples constitute (or form a carefully selected sample of) all possible cases. A lawyer may build a case on many arguments, because they are more illustrations or examples than they are proofs. The failure of one need not necessarily mean the failure of others to substantiate the case. Indeed, the process requires that, among conflicting examples, the legal decision maker must choose as support for a decision the most relevant example and thereby reject the less relevant ones. In science, any one test of a consequence of a theory that proves wrong may invalidate the entire theory.

In some senses, the statistical approach to problems lies between these extremes. Statistical thinking is rooted in the probabilistic thinking modern law aspires to but sometimes resists. Inference about the individual instance is often based on multiple examples, as in predictions based on past observations. What is clearly not provable is often as important and notable as what is. Knowing when not to overstate knowledge and expertise is prized by statisticians as a professional virtue.

There is an analogue in law: the legal approach to a case recognizes the fallibility of its own processes by at times focusing more on the error to be avoided than on the truth to be found. This point is central to criminal law. It is expressed in the adage that it is better to acquit 10 guilty persons than to convict 1 who is innocent. In statistical terms this problem may be cast in terms of choosing between Type I and Type II errors. Statisticians often must make judgments based on the costs of the two types of error. Legal rules and presumptions may embody judgments abouts costs that must be recognized. From the Delaney amendment on drugs and cancer, in which any appearance of cancer in animals exposed to a substance may be sufficient evidence to prevent human use of that substance, to the "beyond a reasonable doubt" standard in criminal matters, the law may establish different thresholds for what is sufficient evidence in a case from those that statisticians would normally require in drawing conclusions. Clearly, the law must prevail and the statistician must adjust to the law's standards. Put another way, it is the utility function of the court that is appropriate, not the utility function of the statistician. In general, however, this is not a major source of conflict because adaptation is possible; the question the statistician is asked to answer is not the same as the one the court must decide.

Avoidance of error is a complicated criterion and is difficult to invoke.

With judicial systems such a criterion involves not only the actual avoidance of error, but also (even perhaps particularly) the avoidance of the *appearance* of error. It is not only important that justice be done, but also that justice be seen to be done. When statistical methods are used, there may be a particular danger that the rationale for judicial outcomes may suggest the appearance of error. While the objective of this panel is to enhance the contributions that statistical evidence makes to factually accurate decisions, we are also concerned that the "truth" of statistical evidence is actually understood. To ignore the problem of error and the appearance of error is to invite a popular impression that statistical methods are being used for mystification and obfuscation.

One consequence of the heavy judicial emphasis on the individual case is that it minimizes the ability of the law to achieve the long-run rationality that probabilistic statements might otherwise allow. If a factual proposition has a probability of being true equal to 60 percent, one might use such a proposition of fact to modify damages in individual cases. To some extent settlement processes are said (and have been found) to embody such discounting and spreading of intercase information, but legal norms often preclude or inhibit judicial judgments that take such forms (see the discussion of these issues in the Preliminary Memorandum and Order on Settlement, *In re "Agent Orange"*, 597 F.Supp. 740 (E.D.N.Y. 1984), *aff'd.*, 818 F.2d 145 (2d Cir. 1987)). Comparative negligence has been often suggested and is increasingly adopted, but it is, in theory, on the certain determination that the parties contributed in a particular proportion to the harm. It does not deal with those cases in which there is, for example, a 0.6 probability that A was negligent or that A's negligence harmed B. Moreover, the all-or-nothing rules continue to apply in many instances in which a fault basis for tort liability remains in effect as well as in other legal settings.

A major objective of the system of justice is that like cases be treated alike. Embodied within this principle is the idea that adversaries should face each other without being burdened by irrelevant disadvantages. The danger of disadvantage arising from superior resources has been a particular source of attention by critics of our system of justice. In a well-known analytic article, Galanter (1974) brought together in a systematic manner the many factors that help the "haves" to come out ahead. One of his arguments is that those who litigate repeatedly develop expertise and other efficiencies of scale and can work over time for rule changes that subsequently add to their advantage.

In exploring the use of statistics in the courts, one must be concerned with whether the increasing use of statistical analysis and data tends to equalize or to exacerbate differential advantage. Simplified uniform analytic rules might tend to equalize the situation of parties by making it unnecessary for the less-advantaged party to obtain high-priced experts. Or, if experts were necessary, the burden of obtaining their advice might be borne by the state. While impartial experts have not been readily accepted in the courts, their use seems to have produced favorable results in some settings (e.g., in utility rate determinations).

4.3 The Meeting of Two Cultures

We have identified the dominant difference between the judicial need for making decisions and the statistical-scientific desire for precision and proper caution. Scientific orthodoxy treats agnostic replies as costless; judges know better than that. Statisticians have recognized that their role is influenced by the need for answers more than have most professionals or scientists, but the limits in actual cases of data, time, and resources often prevent statisticians from unequivocally answering the central questions that the courts must resolve, even those questions that are in principle amenable to scientific answers. Moreover, the effort to present statistical information in the legal arena creates special problems.

(1) *The problem of intelligibility.* Both the law and statistics have specialized vocabularies and, like most argots, a subtle connotative as well as denotative system. Occasionally, the statistical expert and the legal decision maker totally fail to communicate with each other, but the more frequent problem is that the parties think they have communicated yet misinformation is conveyed. Both law and statistics employ everyday words in precise and sometimes counterintuitive senses. In statistics and law such terms as *significant, power, random, unbiased,* and *independent* have familiar meanings, but the meanings in statistics differ from those in law.

The following exchange, from the transcript of trial testimony in a case concerning whether to adjust the results of the 1980 census for underenumeration, illustrates this problem graphically. The case was tried early in 1984, and the opinion is pending (*Cuomo et al.* v. *Baldridge et al.*; S.D. New York). The principal defendant, the U.S. Bureau of the Census, called a large number of statistical witnesses, and the following exchange occurred between the judge and one of these witnesses:

> **Witness:** Another problem is that part of the output of the regression procedure is what are called standard errors. They measure the randomness that is left in your numbers after you are finished. If the assumptions behind the method are wrong, then you cannot rely on those standard errors. In other words, you do not know how much randomness is left in the —

> **Court:** You don't know what is standard and what is just error, basically?

> **Witness:** I think [that it is] a little bit [as if] you are flying in the dark if the assumptions are wrong.

Court: It is your standard error, I take it, that allows you to isolate the veracity of your other variables, I would assume?

Witness: Your Honor, could I use the board?

Court: Yes. I take it your standard error should be a fixed statistical number which you then subtract from your results and you get what is left, basically, which is supposed to measure the accuracy of what you are measuring?

Witness: I hate to argue with you, but it isn't quite like that.

Court: Don't argue. I am just asking.

Despite this exchange, the witness went on to give an in-depth critique of the complex statistical procedures used by two of the plaintiffs' experts, and the judge's further comments did not disclose whether he had misunderstood a basic statistical concept.

It is not merely problems of meaning that confront the courts in dealing with expert statistical testimony. There are important assumptions embedded in the deep structures of legal and statistical thought, for example about causation, which do not yield to easy analysis but do affect the relevance of testimony and require careful thought in both specific cases and the general situation.

(2) *The problem of translation.* The pressure placed on the statistical or scientific expert to use clear, crisp, and conclusionary language to influence the fact finder in a particular direction is strong. Minimizing technical language to that needed to be impressive is the aim of the lawyer. This places the expert on the horns of a dilemma. Describing technical matters in ordinary language involves imprecision, albeit imprecision that conveys more information (and possibly misinformation) to the average hearer. Furthermore, the acceptability of imprecision encourages pseudo-expert witnesses or unduly partisan experts to use language lacking precise meaning but seeming to justify confident conclusions.

In the famous Watergate trial (see *U.S.* v. *Haldeman, Ehrlichman, and Mitchell,* 559 F.2d 31, (D.C. 1976)), for example, the defendants submitted a public opinion poll in support of their motion for a change of venue. The affidavit of the expert whose organization conducted the poll described the *representativeness* of the poll in terms of *maximum variation* from the opinions of all registered voters. Neither term has a precise technical meaning, and the expert's statement is not easily interpretable. The trial judge discounted the value of the information from the poll and refused to grant a change in venue, a decision upheld by the appeals court.

The usual corrective for such problems is cross-examination. But, as we saw in *DiGiacomo,* this corrective may break down in the real world in which lawyers' skills and consultants skilled in coaching the lawyers are costly and are not uniformly distributed.

How much the expert needs to know of the legal matters is not clear. In most instances, the statistician will surely be more effective the better he or she is acquainted with the substantive legal matters, and in major cases informing the expert would almost certainly be a good investment for the litigant. Often this legal knowledge is crucial to the formulation of statistical problems.

(3) *The problem of acceptance of method.* Science and law differ in the acceptance of methods of analysis. In science in general and in statistics in particular, a method is evaluated according to well-established criteria. In the courts, theoretical justifications of a statistical method may be treated as if they are less important than the general acceptance of the method by statisticians and other scientists. In many cases, methods satisfying theoretical criteria are widely accepted by the scientific community, and there is no problem. But problems arise when scientists disagree on standards or criteria. Two now relatively common examples are disagreement about an appropriate regression model (described, e.g., in two of the case studies in Chapter 2) and the lack of generally accepted standards for many aspects of market research surveys.

(4) *The problem of adversarial approach.* Of the many points of tension between science and law, the aspect of law that is by far the most frustrating to scientists is the adversarial nature of court proceedings. Compromises are made in what evidence is introduced and solicited in the interests of partisan advocacy, and these militate against scientific inquiry.

Some have argued that a more inquisitorial process, such as that associated with the civil law tradition of continental Europe, might serve to enhance the truth-finding process. Courts can, however, take a greater role in controlling what evidence will be presented to them and what issues will be argued before them through the use of pretrial conferences. Rule 16 of the Federal Rules of Civil Procedure allows the court, at its discretion, to require lawyers for both sides to appear before it to consider, among other things, simplification of the issues, admissions of facts and documents, the number of expert witnesses, and possible reference to a court-appointed master. Following the conference, the court issues an order that subsequently controls the procedure of the trial. Other approaches to enhancing the capability of the fact finder are discussed in Chapter 5.

(5) *The problem of relative competence.* "In the valley of the blind the one-eyed man is king." Legally, the court can accept as experts virtually anyone who by virtue of special training or experience may aid the court. It is not efficient for courts to sift out levels of expertise at the point of entry. Good information may come from weak experts, and bad from the best, though that is not the outcome to bet on a priori. It is assumed that cross-examination will deal with both the competence of the expert and the persuasiveness of the argument. This approach requires competent

questioners and perceptive decision makers.

When scientists reach questionable judgments in their ordinary course of work, errors and limitations are likely to be pointed out through repeated opportunities that science allows for disinterested (and sometimes partisan) critiques to be submitted to the judgment of unknown future specialists. In a sense, both the initial expert and (if there be one) the original judge of the effort are graded by posterity.

Obviously courts cannot wait for posterity. But there are models that do not entail substantial waiting, such as peer review for grant money or hospital tissue committees, that might be adapted to help courts sort out more and less reliable information. Courts, however, have not easily found a place for "disinterested" participants, partly because their contentious procedures engulf disinterestedness.

Most of the problems that stem from the important differences between legal and statistical thinking also arise when courts are confronted with other kinds of expert testimony. But the statistician is probably more amenable to and at home with prior specification of decision rules and more willing to provide the conclusion from the evidence in accordance with externally specified rules and restrictions than are most experts.

4.4   Working Relationships Between Scientists and Lawyers

Quantitative Facts and Qualitative Values

The working relationships between lawyers and statisticians and other scientists have grown in number and depth with the increasing need for quantitative evidence in court cases and other legal proceedings. Oliver Wendell Holmes, Jr., foresaw this trend and found that society, particularly in legal settings, would need to address the tension that arose between new quantitative facts and established qualitative values. As Holmes (1899) stated (p.456):

> The growth of education is an increase in the knowledge of measure. To use words familiar to logic and to science, it is a substitution of quantitative for qualitative judgments. ... Well, in the law we only occasionally can reach an absolute final and quantitative determination, because the worth of the competing social ends which respectively solicit a judgment for the plaintiff or the defendant cannot be reduced to a number and accurately fixed. The worth, that is, the intensity of the competing desires, varies with the varying ideals of the time. ... But it is the essence of improvement that we should be as accurate as we can.

Today the careful weighing of scientific facts and social values is unavoidable. Almost every aspect of our lives is affected by laws and regulations that reflect both facts and values. For example, in regulating workplace exposure to carcinogens, the Occupational Safety and Health Administration (OSHA) must consider the scientific data on the risks associated with a chemical when balancing the benefits of the chemical against the hazards it presents. The task is difficult when high levels of uncertainty exist both in the data and their analysis and in the perception of values. The need for expert opinion arises when lawsuits challenge the fairness of the balancing process and question the statistical accuracy of the scientific information.

Concern with scientific accuracy is also part of the broader issue of quantitative accuracy that arises when data collection and statistical analysis are used in determining legal compliance or violation. Evidence intended to prove employment discrimination or participation in monopolistic practices is often statistical, with its relevance dependent on the quality of data collection and analysis. The balancing of quantitative facts and qualitative values by triers of fact is more difficult when great uncertainty surrounds the relevant quantitative data. The task of scientists and lawyers is to help the trier of fact balance these two sets of factors and thereby make sound decisions possible.

Who Is an Expert?

The Federal Rules of Evidence set out the role of the expert witness as assisting the trier of fact in understanding specialized issues that are outside the ken of the average person. Experts are given more leeway than lay witnesses to draw inferences from facts in the form of opinions (F.R.E., Rule 701 and 702). Attorneys must determine what type of expertise is needed and how it is to be used. Finding experts for any particular case may require consultation with academic and professional associations and institutions, review of professional journals, and discussions with other attorneys who have handled similar cases. After experts have been located and have agreed to provide advice and professional or scientific judgment, lawyers define the roles they will play in the litigation process. Experts may serve as consultants, as witnesses, or in both roles.

Persons acceptable as experts by the court may not hold lofty positions in the eyes of their peers. For instance, people without advanced degrees or with training that is primarily in a substantive field are often regarded for litigation purposes as statistical experts and routinely present statistical assessments as evidence since they satisfy the minimal tests that courts apply in qualifying experts. Finney (1982), commenting on his experience as a statistical expert witness, noted his dissatisfaction with this "equality" (p.433):

> It was galling to find that several degrees, 40 years of experience, and even the Presidency of this Society [the Royal Statistical

Society] gave me no greater standing as a statistical expert than
that of a witness whose errors of method were such as I would
condemn in a second-year student.

Although Finney was sure of his standing in the profession, his lawyer was
required to convince the trier of fact that he was more credible and that
his testimony should have been given greater weight than the testimony of
another.

The Expert as Teacher and Student

The expert serves as an educator of the lawyers who hired him or her
and of the triers of fact who must decide a case on the evidence before
them. The expert must also reverse roles and become a student of the legal
process. Even if a statistical expert has testified previously and an attorney
is familiar with an expert's field, some education is required.

Experts need at least a rudimentary lesson in the legal process to understand their position in it, beginning with the concepts of legal relevance
and admissibility. Even the most experienced witnesses should have their
testimony reviewed and be prepared for cross-examination. If a witness for-
gets a key element of an answer, an attorney must be able to detect the
omission and follow through with an appropriate question that will produce the desired information. All this requires statistical knowledge, and
the expert usually helps teach the attorney the relevant ideas and concepts.

Problems and Perspectives

Unfortunately, some of those in the scientific and legal communities occasionally regard each other with disdain. In part, such attitudes are the product of the judicial process. In *Introduction to English Law,* James (1979)
relates: "the position of an expert witness is not a happy one, for our 'adversary' system pits doctor against doctor, engineer against engineer, and that
circumstance leads lawyers to talk deprecatingly of 'liars, damned liars and
expert witnesses' in order of unreliability." Not only must experts testify in
conflict with the testimony of professional colleagues, but they must defend
their own procedures and methodologies against attack. And lawyers have
come to expect that there will always be some expert willing to testify for
their client in a way that will be considered helpful.

Disappointment can be part of the relationship between statisticians and
lawyers. On one hand, statisticians have had the experience of preparing
careful statistical analyses, only to have lawyers ignore them. On the other
hand, lawyers have retained statisticians in the belief that the results of certain statistical analyses would favor their clients' positions, only to discover
that the analyses may be ambiguous or damaging to their clients, or that
the statistician is unable to communicate effectively with nonstatisticians.
Although the American Bar Association's Code of Professional Responsibility suggests the disclosure to an adverse party of *legal authority* "in the

controlling jurisdiction known to him to be directly adverse to the position of his client and which is not disclosed by opposing counsel," there is no requirement to disclose adverse *factual evidence*. The standards of objectivity and full disclosure inherent in the scientific process are not paralleled in the legal process.

4.5 Psychological Problems With Statistical Testimony

Even when the use of expert witnesses to provide statistical evidence presents no special issue of law, it may raise important psychological problems. Chief among these is whether people in general, and judges or jurors in particular, can (1) understand such evidence and (2) accord it proper probative weight. While these same issues arise in connection with all expert evidence, statistical evidence and the testimony of statistical experts often pose special problems for triers of fact.

Subject Matter Versus Statistical Expertise

The choice of which data to look at or how best to model a particular process may require subject matter information that a statistician does not necessarily possess. It makes no sense for a statistician to testify about the calculation of a mean score of 22.7 or that the explanatory variables in a regression model were associated with 39 percent of the variance of the response variable unless the fact finder is also informed about the data for which the mean was calculated or the situation the regression equation sought to model. For this reason, cases involving statistical evidence are often "two-expert" cases, calling on experts in the substantive area under study and in the techniques of statistical analysis. The case studies of Chapter 2 provide examples of this phenomenon.

Consider for illustrative purposes a case in which women workers claim that they are underpaid relative to men of comparable training doing comparable work. The plaintiffs might require testimony both from someone skilled in job evaluation and from a statistician. The expert on job evaluation, selected because of familiarity with the occupations and industry in question, would evaluate the relative plausibility of different models for the industry's compensation scheme or the conceptual implications of available data. The statistician would analyze the data collected and describe to the fact finder the implications of the analysis. Since what can be done by way of evaluation depends on what data are collected, statistical expertise as well as subject matter familiarity would be needed in the data-gathering stages as well as in the courtroom. The job evaluation expert might testify first, followed by the statistician, who would explain the mathematical characteristics of the models specified, the way in which analysis proceeded, and the statistical results together with their implications. This might present special problems since the fact finder, whether judge or jury, would have to appreciate the ways in which implications drawn by the second witness are crucially dependent on the reasonableness of the actions and decisions described by the first witness.

In some instances, the lack of coordination in the presentation of testimony by two different experts called by the same party will produce considerable tension between them and with counsel. In the case of disagreement, the statistical witness may attempt unwisely to avoid criticizing what the first witness has done, even though criticism is warranted. Yet such reservations may be obvious on direct examination, and they may be laid bare by the opposing counsel on cross-examination.

In some instances a single expert is presented on all phases of a litigation research project, including the statistical phases. Such a person inevitably will have greater expertise in some areas than in others. Yet, as we have noted, the law does not recognize grades of expertise. If a witness has, through training or experience, acquired knowledge that promises to aid the fact finder, the witness will be allowed to testify as an expert even though substantially more qualified experts may be available. For example, a labor market economist who is a leading expert on patterns of employment in a field may have only a "cookbook" knowledge of various statistical techniques. Or a statistician may have only a superficial familiarity with the labor market. Nevertheless, in law, either may serve as an expert on the appropriateness of data collected and on statistical aspects of methods designed to make inferences regarding the existence of discriminatory behavior or its absence. The problem here is the one pointed out by Finney (1982). Even during the case, there is no clear mechanism for the fact finder to sort out the real level of expertise of the expert witnesses. In addition, if the true expertise of witnesses for both parties is limited, the resulting statistical assessments as evidence may not achieve their potential probative value, and the fact finder may consequently be misled.

Numerical Mystification: Weighing Statistical Evidence

The apparent precision of statistical evidence often stands in marked contrast to the uncertainties of other testimony. Many courts fear that if lay fact finders attempt to resolve disputed facts with the assistance of statistics they will be swayed by its seeming precision and numerical mystification. The danger is that such evidence will overshadow equally probative but admittedly unscientific and anecdotal nonstatistical evidence (see, e.g., Loh, 1979, or Tribe, 1971).

To return to a variant on our earlier example, consider a case involving an *individual claim* in which a woman attempts to demonstrate that her employer discriminatorily failed to promote her because of her sex. Suppose that the evidence presented by the plaintiff is in large part anecdotal but also includes some statistical tabulations and analyses, and that the defense, through a statistical expert, presents a "well-done" logistic regression analysis for estimating the probability of promotions for the members of a cohort of workers of both sexes, which has the estimated coefficient of sex as a predictor that is not significantly different from zero, at the .10 level of significance. The fact finder may partially understand these results and may conclude that they mean that the plaintiff was not discriminated against in regard to promotion because of her sex. The conclusion is unwarranted. While the data may provide good evidence that there is no systematic or cohort-wide discrimination, it is only to this extent that they suggest that the individual plaintiff was not discriminated against because of her sex. If the plaintiff had shown by anecdotal or other direct evidence that her supervisor passed over her for promotion because she was a woman, she would be entitled to recover regardless of the overall patterns of promotions for men and women. A fact finder told that there was, from a statistical viewpoint, no evidence of sexual discrimination might mistakenly perceive this as a scientific judgment that the anecdotal evidence suggesting discrimination was not worthy of belief.

Another situation in which there is a substantial possibility that statistical evidence will be overvalued is when statistical evidence bears on only one aspect of a case. Yet a fact finder who has invested substantial energy and emotion in trying to understand difficult statistical issues, or one who is overly impressed by statistical precision, may believe that the party who prevailed on such a hotly contested and difficult decision deserves to prevail in the entire suit.

Statistical evidence may be either overweighted or underweighted because statistical concepts are not properly understood. For example, most people do not know that the accuracy of inferences from sample characteristics to population characteristics varies with the size of the sample rather than the proportion of the population sampled (Tversky and Kahneman, 1971), and there is a general tendency, even among those who should know better, to attach excessive importance to inferences from relatively small samples (Kahneman and Tversky, 1973). This second bias may lead to the overweighting of statistical findings based on small samples, whereas the first may lead to undervaluing findings based on large samples from large populations. For example, it is true but not intuitively obvious that a survey of 1,000 people can tell us a great deal about the distribution of attitudes in a diverse city of 3 million. Thus, evidence from large samples of large populations may not be given the weight it deserves.

In the appellate opinion in the case of *U.S.* v. *Haldeman, Ehrlichman, and Mitchell* the majority commented in a footnote on the trial judge's discretion in assessing expert evidence in the form of results from a public opinion poll as follows: "Indeed, such discretion is peculiarly necessary when the expert evidence consists of the results of a public opinion poll—data that is open to a variety of errors," 559 F.2d 46 (D.C. 1976). They went on to note that the judge has the discretion to rely less heavily on a poll taken "in private by private pollsters and paid for by one side" than on a recorded comprehensive voir dire examination conducted by the judge in the presence of all parties. This may well have led to the undervaluing of evidence from a credible survey with 303 respondents. The dissenting appeals court judge, however, felt that the results of the public opinion poll should be given far greater weight, and was sufficiently compelling to mandate the reversal of the conviction and an order for a new trial.

Undervaluing statistical evidence may also occur because many people find mathematical and statistical concepts difficult to comprehend and have difficulty understanding the terms in which statistical results are expressed. Some judges may react to this problem by dismissing the statistical evidence altogether. Although we know there are vast individual differences in people's ability to follow mathematical arguments, it is not clear why these differences exist (Willerman, 1979), nor what the implications are for the use of statistical assessments.

An illustration of this problem can be found in the following exchange involving the plaintiffs' statistical expert extracted from the trial transcript from *Stasny* v. *Southern Bell Tel. & Tel. Co.* 458 F.Supp. 314 (W.D.N.C. 1978):

> **Counsel:** Dr. X, these various weights, are they weights that you determine or weights that the computer determines?
>
> **Witness:** These are weights that are determined by the computer because the regression equation is obtained through the program that's used.
>
> **Court:** How does this theory cope with the absolutely arbitrary decisions that an employer might make to pay one person $5 and another $10/hour for doing the same work?
>
> **Witness:** We look at the wages for all employees and these wages are converted to natural logs and then ...
>
> **Court:** What do you mean by natural laws? Not any natural laws about wages.
>
> **Witness:** What happens is that you take a wage ...
>
> **Court:** I have been hearing law all afternoon, natural law. I thought we were getting back to Rousseau.

Given this exchange it is not surprising to find that the judge swept away the regression analyses of both sides with the following statement in his opinion (p.323):

Regression analysis begins with the assumption that certain independent variables in fact determine the outcome of decisions to raise pay and promote. Such assumptions are intellectually questionable and not grounded in any solid evidence.

People also undervalue statistical information because they fail to realize how small the incremental gain is from using complete population information. This point is well illustrated by a much-discussed case in which sample statistics were used to estimate an unknown population value (see Bar-Hillel, 1984, Solomon, 1985, and Sprowls, 1957). The case revolved around a local ordinance that imposed a sales tax on local residents of a small town in California. Nonresidents were exempt. An accountant for Sears Roebuck & Co. discovered that over a period of some years the store had overpaid taxes due to an error in determining where the town boundaries lay. Sears filed for a refund of $27,000 for that time period and supported its application with evidence presented by statisticians hired by the store who randomly sampled 33 of the 826 sales days and estimated that the ratio of out-of-city to total sales to be 36.69 percent (*Sears, Roebuck & Co.* v. *City of Inglewood*, L.A. Sup. Ct. 1955). In terms of dollars, the estimate of overpaid taxes was $28,250, with a 95% confidence interval for the amount running from approximately $24,000 to $32,500. Thus the evidence tended to support at least a $24,000 tax refund and is quite consistent with the claim of a $27,000 tax refund. The court rejected these sampling results as evidence, objecting to the presentation of a "guess" where "facts" were available. The court forced the store to conduct a complete audit of the 826 days at a cost of $3,500. The resulting figure, $26,750.22, was paid to Sears by the city—just a bit short of the $27,000 claim. Although today statistical estimation is more likely to be accepted as a standard method of approach, it is still occasionally viewed with suspicion because of skepticism about whether it really works.

Statistical Versus Anecdotal Evidence

When statistical evidence conflicts with anecdotal evidence that bears on the same issue, highly probative statistical data may be rejected in favor of a less probative but more striking anecdotal instance. Nisbett and Ross (1980) offer as a thought experiment the example of a person who wants to buy a new car, has consulted *Consumer Reports*, and has learned from their compilation of the reports of readers that the Volvo has a better repair record than the Saab. Armed with this information and intending to buy a Volvo, the person attends a cocktail party at which he announces his intention to an acquaintance. The acquaintance tells him about an unhappy relative who bought a Volvo that presented nothing but problems. The single experience of the unhappy relative is far less probative and should have far less influence on the decision than the mass of statistical evidence supplied by *Consumer Reports*, unless there is a richness of detail in the single case that is absent in the magazine report. Yet, it is plausible, if not likely, that the consumer in Nisbett and Ross's thought experiment would think otherwise.

In an actual experiment, with the quality of one's education at stake, psychology majors were more moved by the way a fellow student described various professors than they were by course evaluation statistics (Nisbett and Ross, 1980). The tendency to overvalue single cases when anecdotal and statistical evidence compete may exist because anecdotal evidence is vivid and reaches us in a way that nonvivid statistical information cannot. Numerous psychology experiments have shown an effect of vividness (e.g., Reyes, Thompson, and Bower, 1980), although it has recently been suggested that any effects of vividness are mediated through salience (Taylor and Thompson, 1982). One implication of this research is that statistical evidence may have a disproportionately smaller impact on beliefs and inferences than vivid anecdotal reports. The conflict between this possibility and the possibility that statistical evidence may distract the fact finder from legally relevant anecdotal evidence is only apparent. Both possibilities may occur, perhaps within the context of a single case.

Lack of Familiarity with Statistics

The unfamiliar mathematical nature of statistical evidence may also enhance the likelihood that the fact finder will misread the implications of attacks on that evidence. Consider a sex discrimination suit in which the plaintiff's expert statistical witness presents a regression analysis, the results of which are supportive of an inference of plant-wide sex discrimination. The defendants present their own statistical expert who argues that the regression model used in the analysis of the plaintiff's expert excluded a key variable and cannot be safely relied on. This evidence does not mean that a properly specified model would not be consistent with an inference of sex discrimination, i.e., that the extent of misspecification is slight, yet the fact finder caught up in the battle over the adequacy of the plaintiff's model may think so and may treat the defendant's successful attack on the plaintiff's statistical model as outweighing other, possibly nonstatistical evidence that tends to support the plaintiff's claim of discrimination.

In short, statistical evidence is likely to be unfamiliar to most fact finders, is often difficult to comprehend, and carries with it an undue appearance of precision. Furthermore, people's responses to statistical evidence, like their responses to many situations, are likely to be inconsistent and highly context-dependent (Tversky and Kahneman, 1981; Tversky, 1981). The challenge for both lawyers and statisticians is to develop ways of presenting statistical evidence so that people who are not used to dealing with statistical concepts can comprehend them, appreciate their implications, and do so in a reliable and consistent manner.

5

Some Partial Solutions to the Problems Arising From Expert Statistical Testimony

5.1 Introduction

In the preceding chapter we contrasted the methodologies of law and statistics and noted how various problems arise when expert witnesses present statistical testimony. Here, we explore some possible solutions to the problems that statistical assessments pose for the legal process.

In examining court records a statistician will often be struck by the contrast between the ordinary professional standards of statistical analysis and reporting and those employed by experts in legal proceedings. Important qualifications are often lacking and alternative plausible models are often left unexplored. Although some omissions may on occasion reflect the professional limitations of the statistical expert, they are often more directly attributed to the legal process. The lawyer who recruits the statistical expert is an advocate whose role is not to reach the closest approximation to the truth, but to put forward the strongest case for the client. When a statistical expert produces results that undercut a client's interest a lawyer may ask the expert to present material in a selective fashion, or may seek out another statistician whose findings are more acceptable, or may simply not offer the expert's testimony. The statistician who is asked to present material in a selective fashion properly feels ethical qualms, and there may be a serious dissonance between the professional obligations of the statistical expert and those of the lawyers.

Statistical assessments are often presented as statistical reports that can be entered into the court record if the case goes to trial (Deming, 1965, p. 1893). Statistical reports also may be used as part of the discovery process that precedes the actual trial. If the expert is a potential witness, the report often serves as the basis of a lengthy deposition, during which the opponents' lawyers question the witness on the report and other matters that relate to the planned trial testimony. There are no well-accepted standards for the preparation, organization and documentation of statistical evidence similar to the standards for engineers serving as expert witnesses (see Appendix D). Thus considerable variability is likely to be found, even in relatively narrow areas of litigation.

Statisticians can adopt a variety of roles when working with attorneys in developing a case or as an expert witness. At the extremes are the role of *advocate* and the role of *impartial evaluator and educator.* Section 5.2 explores to what extent the statistician or other scientific expert does or should assume the role of advocate or impartial educator in deciding which analyses to perform and what form the expert testimony should take.

Following this discussion of the proper role of expert witnesses, we explore a series of issues that the courts confront when faced with expert statistical testimony, especially in the form of a battle of experts. Some of our proposed solutions require changes to the present system, while others simply bring to the courts' attention mechanisms already available but not widely used in connection with statistical testimony. In Section 5.3 we take up issues relating to pretrial matters, including the provision of adequate resources to both parties in litigation. In Sections 5.4 and 5.5 we consider specific devices available to the court for controlling battles of experts. We conclude the chapter with a discussion of the role of statistical education, both at trial and more broadly for lawyers and judges.

While these partial solutions may help the courts to overcome some of the problems encountered in the presentation of statistical assessments as evidence, how much they will contribute to the objective of truth finding is unclear. Whenever innovations and changes such as those proposed here are tried, they need to be accompanied, wherever possible, by careful experimental research so that we can evaluate their contribution and spot unexpected costs. This is a basic tenet of good scientific practice.

5.2   The Expert Witness: Advocate or Impartial Evaluator and Educator?

Scientific experts are now routinely called on to assist the fact finder in determining facts that are relevant to particular cases. For example, in criminal cases a forensic pathologist may be called on to report on the blood alcohol content of a deceased driver, or a psychologist may testify as to the mental illness of a criminal defendant or to whether a plaintiff suffered psychological trauma as the result of an auto accident. In civil litigation, scientific experts testify on a wide variety of substantive and legal matters.

Scientific experts commonly provide fact finders with information that differs in kind from the information they receive from ordinary witnesses. Often their testimony does not relate directly to the behavior of the parties involved in the case, but draws primarily on information of a general sort derived from scientific research. In such cases, the expert's contribution is often to provide the fact finder with information about how classes of objects or individuals behave. For example, an economist might testify that the research on capital punishment fails to reveal consistent deterrent effects but might be unwilling to venture an opinion on whether the execution of a person whose life is at stake will deter anyone. A biologist might testify about the general effects of alcohol on human performance and might even be willing to give an opinion that the reflexes of the defendant whose blood alcohol measured .20 percent were substantially impaired but might be unable to say whether drinking caused a particular accident. A clinical psychologist might testify about the general inability of researchers to forecast accurately the occurrence of violent behavior. On other occasions, as with the presentation of much statistical evidence, the expert will be talking directly about data relevant to the facts of the case at hand, but such testimony will often be against a background of more general knowledge not shared by the fact finder.

Any expert who is asked to testify confronts a variety of scientific and ethical questions. Loftus and Monahan (1980) give these examples: (1) Are findings that are being presented trustworthy, that is, do they possess internal validity? (2) Can one fairly generalize from the findings the expert presents or relies on to the situation at trial, that is, do the findings result from research that possesses adequate external validity? (3) When scientists disagree about the interpretation of prior research, does the expert have a duty to present both sides of the controversy? (4) How should the expert deal with the fact that any conclusion that might be reached can only be probabilistic in nature? That is, how does the expert report on the uncertainties associated with conclusions?

In answering questions like these, the expert needs guidance on what is an appropriate role to adopt when testifying as an expert witness in court. Focusing only on the extremes, we may say that the expert must decide whether to be an *advocate* or an *impartial evaluator and educator*. Should the expert accept the role of advocate, putting forward the strongest possible case for the employing attorney's client and being careful only to avoid outright falsehood (or tendentiousness so transparent as to be blatant), or should the expert seek to prepare a report with findings that, in principle, could be presented to either side in the dispute? The panel believes that it is desirable that the expert be as neutral as possible but is aware that recommendations to this effect must take account of the realities of the situations in which expert testimony is sought and presented.

Foremost among these realities is the fact that the expert is nearly always hired by attorneys for one side or the other, who are interested in testimony that supports their client's position. Under our system of justice, this is not improper, for it is the attorney's job to act as an advocate for the client. But it is not necessarily the job of the statistician to serve as an advocate.

A second reality is that there is a natural tendency to identify with the side for which one is testifying. The statistician who serves as an expert witness is working within an adversary system, the essence of which is that one side of the case is presented and subsequently challenged by the other. As Schofield (1956) noted almost 30 years ago, there is something in the very nature of this system, and in a court trial in particular, that "arouses the adrenals" (p. 2). During cross-examination, attorneys will try to portray witnesses as "ignorant, irresponsible, or biased" (Brodsky, 1977). Based on his own participation and observations of trials, Schofield (1956) came to believe that only a superhuman being could avoid becoming identified with one of the sides.

The view that statisticians may serve as advocates, presenting only evidence that helps the client, begins with the argument that the trial is an adversarial process in which each side has the right to make the best possible case. As a participant in this process, experts may limit their testimony to points that support the arguments of one side, leaving to the opposing counsel the task of presenting evidence and arguments favoring their position. Not only can the opposing attorneys cross-examine testifying experts, but they can also present expert witnesses to state their side of the case. With this opportunity for the exposition of conflicting viewpoints, some social scientists who are scrupulous about the need to reveal evidentiary weaknesses in scientific articles, have taken the position that evidence that does not support one's general opinion "has no function in the adversary game" (Wolfgang, 1974, p. 246). Rivlin (1973) went so far as to suggest that we acknowledge the development of a "forensic social science" and not pretend to be balanced, objective, free of personal biases, or acting as if we are offering all sides of the case so that people can judge for themselves. Following Rivlin's design, a social scientist would simply prepare a position paper for or against a particular proposition. The position would be clearly stated, and the evidence that supports the position would be mastered as effectively as possible. The job of critiquing the case that has been presented and of detailing the counterevidence would be left to a scholar working for the opposition. One advantage of this forensic social science approach is that it would reduce the hypocrisy of pseudo-objectivity and hidden biases that now pervade the so-called scientifically balanced approach.

While acknowledging the impossibility of total neutrality, however, proponents of the opposite view argue that the statistical expert will be most helpful to the legal process by distancing himself or herself from the attorney's objectives. The expert should acknowledge the one-sided source of information provided and should condition testimony on the assumption that adequate information has been presented. Although the expert should review planned testimony (and response to likely cross-examination) with the attorney in advance, the expert should decline to shape that testimony to adversarial ends. This view recognizes that complete neutrality is unobtainable, but it presumes that the closest feasible approach to neutrality is likely to be more useful to the court than a frank abandonment of it. This position has the merit, also, of minimizing the dissonance between professional ethics and legal requirements.

Experts may be asked implicitly or explicitly to act as advocates through their testimony. Advocacy can take many forms; it may involve putting a professional tone on a subjective opinion, or it may involve the manipulation of data and analyses to achieve a desired result. When data have been analyzed in a way likely to favor the employing party, the statistician should ask whether the alternative methods of analysis are likely to yield similar conclusions. Not only is this the professionally proper thing to do, but it is also likely that a well-counseled opposing attorney will ask such questions during cross-examination and will have an opposing expert ready to testify on the issue if the choice of method really does matter.

In arguing that statisticians and other experts should take the role of impartial educator regardless of who employs them, one might begin with the observation that all witnesses take an oath before they testify to tell "the truth, the whole truth, and nothing but the truth." By selectively leaving out analyses that are crucial to some particular question, the statistician may commit the professional sin of failing to ascertain the whole truth. By not presenting analyses that are unhelpful to the client, the statistician may be failing to perform according to the oath. The whole truth is not being told. For example, Van Matre and Clark (1976) argue that it is the lawyer who has the primary responsibility to present the facts in the light most favorable to the client. The statistician, they claim, is not an advocate. "He can best serve himself and his employer by being neutral. He should remain an independent agent" (p.5).

When an expert witness is viewed as an outspoken advocate, the expert's credibility as perceived by the jury or judge may be diminished. In a sense, this potential credibility problem serves to protect the witness from being pushed into an unwanted advocate's role. Deming (1965) noted the danger of a statistician acting as an advocate (p.1885):

> His career as an expert witness will shatter in shipwreck if he indicates concern over which side of the case the results seem to favor. As a statistician, I couldn't care less, is the right attitude in a legal case, or any other report.

This ideal neutrality of an expert witness, if it is an ideal, is, however, a difficult position to maintain, especially when the effect of the adversarial process on objective judgment is considered.

To avoid the advocate's role, Deming stressed the importance of distinguishing between statistical and substantive experts. He emphasized the need to identify clearly the divisions of responsibility between the substantive and statistical aspects of work during preparation and presentation. Deming stated (1965, p.1884):

> A clear statement of responsibilities will be a joy to the client's lawyer in a legal case, especially at the time of cross-examination. It will show the kind of question that the statistician is answerable for, and what belongs to the substantive experts.

Although following Deming's advice helps to limit the scope of cross-examination, separation of statistical and substantive issues often is impossible. Frequently, adequate statistical analyses require fairly detailed knowledge of certain subject matter. Statisticians must make assumptions of how the real world works to choose among differing methods of statistical analysis. For example, consider the statistician who must analyze the risk of increased incidence of cancer from exposure to a carcinogen. Assume that the only data available are from an animal bioassay. In performing the risk assessment, the statistician will be faced with numerous options and will know that each option will affect the outcome in favor of either the plaintiff or the defendant. The choices to be made will be based on substantive knowledge. Therefore, as a practical matter, it may be impossible for statisticians to defer to substantive experts in all instances (see Barton, 1983).

If the expert insists on neutrality in advance, the client's lawyer may well agree, expecting even a neutral analysis to strongly favor the client's position. When this happens, the expert, the client, and those who insist that ethical scientists must be neutral will all be satisfied. There remains, however, the possibility that a neutral portrayal of the evidence and the presentation of all data, although favorable to the client, may not be as persuasive as a somewhat biased presentation. The attorney who senses this may not give the expert a chance to tell the entire story, but the expert should insist on it. This is one of the reasons favoring the preparation of a written report. Furthermore, the expert who sees his role as an impartial educator may in the course of working for a client or responding to a rigorous cross-examination come to identify with the client's cause and lose sight of the kinds of disclosure and data characterization that true impartiality entails.

One of the difficulties that an expert must face in presenting "neutral" testimony is that expert witnesses frequently are viewed as "hired guns" who will bend their testimony according to the dictates of attorneys. Advertisements placed by consultants and experts in legal trade journals enhance this viewpoint. This image of expert witnesses is not new; Moenssens (1979, p.64) noted:

> Evidence of ... dissatisfaction with the partisan system was reported as early as 1858 when, in commenting on the natural inclination of a party to find, not the best scientist, but the "best witness," Justice Grier of the United States Supreme Court stated: "Experience has shown that opposite opinions of persons professing to be experts may be obtained to any amount."

One reason for the expert-for-hire image, however, is the difference between the ideal and actual roles of expert witnesses. Although experts may view their role as involving objective evaluation, attorneys often see the role of experts as advancing the positions of clients. Therefore, attorneys want witnesses with the demeanor of impartial, authoritative experts but with opinions clearly favorable to their clients. Indeed, experts may be chosen precisely because of their known professional biases. Courts should be aware that when this happens that the picture painted by the expert can be badly distorted.

The hired gun image of expert witnesses arises unfairly in cases for which there are legitimate areas of uncertainty. If all cases were black and white in terms of conceptual understanding, there would be little need for lawyers and the courts. On the conceptual color palette, however, there are many shades of gray. Legal arguments are based on which shade of gray is best. There is room for divergent opinions. The same is true when it comes to understanding how two expert witnesses arrive at differing opinions after examination of the same facts. The greater the uncertainty, the more room there is for divergence of opinion. Judge Bazelon (1977) addressed the main source of divergent opinions in noting (p.827):

> Experts usually disagree not so much about the objectively ver-
> ifiable facts, but about the inferences that can be drawn from
> those facts. And they disagree precisely because it is impossible
> to say with certainty which of the inferences are correct.

For these reasons it is impossible for a witness employed by a party to play completely the role of impartial educator. But it does not follow from this that no ethical demands may be placed on the expert who testifies at a party's behest. Even lawyers, the consummate advocates, have their behavior constrained by rules. *Partisanship* is not the last word in the adversary process. In the case of statistical experts, ethical considerations and professional standards properly place a number of constraints on the expert's behavior.

First, while an expert witness, like any witness, should not lie under oath, the obligation of the expert extends further, for the expert is given a special dispensation to present opinions. An expert should not give any opinion he does not personally believe, even if a creditable expert could reasonably hold that opinion, unless he makes it clear that the opinion is not one he shares. Fact finders are asked to accept an expert opinion in part because of the person who holds it. Even if a reasonable expert could hold an opinion, if the testifying expert does not in fact hold the opinion he offers, the fact finder is being misled.

Second, there is a requirement of candor. While an expert is ordinarily under no legal obligation to volunteer information, professional ethics may compel this. This will most often be the case when the expert believes that withholding information will change dramatically the picture that his statistical analyses, properly understood, convey. For example, suppose a statistician in a sex discrimination case finds that the estimated coefficient on the sex variable in a regression equation is in the direction consistent with an inference of discrimination. If, however, the estimated coefficient falls short of being statistically significant at some commonly used level such as .05, then the statistician should not draw conclusions from the direction of the estimated coefficient without mentioning the actual descriptive level of significance.

Third, experts should not allow themselves to be used by the attorney for behavior that would be unethical if it were that of an attorney. Thus, a statistician cannot destroy original data sources forwarded to him knowing that the attorney could not ethically destroy them. Similarly, a statistician should not engage or cooperate in actions by attorneys that are merely intended to harass or raise the expenses of the opposition.

Fourth, there are certain professional standards that a statistical expert must meet in preparing a work product, even though there is no general legal obligation to undertake studies or tests that might yield unwelcome results. For example, in reporting on sample survey results, professional standards dictate providing information on response rates and making available the actual questionnaire used. Similarly, in working with time series data, more broadly defined standards strongly suggest that some attention must be paid to the possibility that serial correlation accounts for results that might otherwise appear to be attributable to specific causal factors. In short, the interests of the client, including questions of cost, generally determine what questions are to be considered. But once this is determined, the expert is required to meet standards of professional competence and ethics for the conduct of such work. Unfortunately, there has not been sufficient attention given to the preparation of a formal statement of such standards. Therefore,

> *The panel recommends that professional organizations develop standards for expert witnesses in legal proceedings who use statistical assessments with respect to (1) procedures required to ensure reliability in connection with frequently used statistical techniques, (2) disclosure of methodology, and (3) disclosure of aspects of their work that may raise ethical considerations.*

Such standards should be developed by professional organizations, either individually or cooperatively, in fields such as statistics, biology, economics, engineering, epidemiology, psychology, sociology, and others whose members make use of statistical assessments in expert testimony.

One aspect of ethics on which there is not uniform agreement is contingency fees for expert witnesses. The law allows the use of contingency fees for lawyers, primarily because this practice makes it easier for people without substantial resources to finance their cases, and this factor is deemed to outweigh various ethical or professional considerations. The question is: Should the same social concern outweigh the ethical drawbacks to the use of contingency fees for experts?

Disciplinary Rule 7–109C of the *Lawyers' Code of Professional Responsibility*, adopted by the American Bar Association in 1969, states:

A lawyer shall not pay, offer to pay or acquiesce in the payment

of compensation to a witness contingent upon the content of
his testimony or the outcome of the case.

In *Person* v. *Association of the Bar of the City of New York*, 414 F.Supp.
144 (D.C. N.Y. 1976), 554 F.2d 534 (C.A. N.Y. 1977), an attorney representing plaintiffs in an antitrust case challenged the constitutionality of
such a prohibition of contingency fees. The district court upheld Person's
challenge. The court of appeals, however, reversed the decision and upheld the constitutionality of the ban. In doing so the court noted some
of the arguments advanced against the rule: (a) cross-examination would
reveal whatever financial stake a witness has in the outcome of litigation,
(b) experts often have ongoing business relations with the parties who retain them, and in such situations have an indirect stake in the outcome
of the litigation, and (c) some experts retained on a "fixed fee" basis do
not expect to receive payment unless the party for whom they testify is
supported. But the court ruled that these reasons were not sufficient to invalidate the rule. There remains ambiguity, however, on the implications of
the *Lawyers' Code of Professional Responsibility* for actual court practice.

According to at least one group of professionals proposing ethical guidelines for statistical practice (see Ad Hoc Committee on Professional Ethics,
1983), standards should prohibit statisticians from accepting contingency
fee arrangements. Several panel members endorse this view for experts expected to testify in court, and in doing so they note the importance of
not only avoiding unethical conduct but also avoiding the appearance of
impropriety. Other panel members are of the view that experts who accept
contingency fees should be allowed to testify since the rules of some courts
do not prohibit contingency fee arrangements. But they do see the importance of making the contingency fee arrangement part of the court record
so that the trier of fact can take that information into account in assessing
the expert's testimony.

We return to what may be thought of as the bottom line, the credibility
of the expert statistical witness.

There are various means by which the testimony of an expert witness is
held accountable by the legal system. The expert's qualifications may be
examined and challenged. The expert's reports and testimony are subject to
scrutiny and cross-examination. The evidence the expert presents is subject
to rebuttal by other experts. And, of course, the law imposes a stricture
on perjury. But courts look even beyond these means to hold the expert
ultimately responsible to professional standards.

Regardless of whether an expert exhibits an allegiance to one party or
an inclination to a particular point of view, the court may accept the credibility of testimony because the expert's knowledge and research methods
devolve from a professional scientific community. Rather than being looked
on by the court to present a view that is a consensus of statisticians or
other scientists, experts are looked on to present their own views based on

the principles and standards of their professional community. It is important that experts be cognizant that they represent their profession in this manner and that they conduct their research accordingly.

> *The panel recommends that statistical experts who consult or testify in litigation maintain a degree of professional autonomy similar to that associated with independent scientific research.*

Examples of such independence may include: (1) if the expert testifies, or if his results are used in testimony by others, he be free to do whatever analysis and have access to whatever data are required to address the problems the litigation poses in a professionally respectable fashion; (2) the expert be free to consult with colleagues who have not been retained by any party to the litigation; and (3) the expert receive an engagement letter that expressly provides for the above and other appropriate safeguards for independence that the expert deems necessary given the context of the case. Several members of the panel would add the further safeguard that (4) the compensation of the expert should not, either formally or informally, depend on the opinion the expert gives or the outcome of the case. The freedom to carry out extensive data gathering and analyses is often tempered by the resources of the client.

But these are really only minimal standards, and many argue that statistical experts, like all other experts, should hew to principles that transcend that which is minimally required. Thus they urge that the expert should insist on being allowed to present a picture that is fuller and less helpful to the client in order to be certain that everything he knows is revealed. In addition, the expert may well refuse to participate in a case because he does not believe that aiding the side that seeks to employ him, even if that side has a meritorious case, will enhance some end—social justice, for example—that the expert values. Except in the last instance, the expert whose personal ethical standards go beyond what is minimally required, should make clear in advance the principles that he will follow and how they might work to the client's detriment. Indeed, until the minimal standards become familiar, the expert would probably be wise to specify these as well.

5.3   Statistics and Pretrial Discovery

Discovery Generally

Approximately 90 percent of civil cases brought in the federal courts are resolved without a full trial and some 70 percent of criminal cases are terminated by a plea of guilty. Even when there is no full trial, however, the pretrial procedures will often be elaborate and will involve experts.

The scope of pretrial discovery of evidence in civil cases is extensive (*see* Appendix E). A party may seek to discover all matter "relevant to the subject matter in the pending action" if "reasonably calculated to lead to discovery of admissible evidence." For example, the parties may, by written interrogatories, seek specific factual data and contentions. They may depose experts and others. They can obtain documents and data from opponents and witnesses, whether in the form of computer tapes or otherwise. The court may decide that the cost of quantifying data from existing materials will be borne by one side or the other.

Efforts have been made in recent years to cut down on the cost, although not the scope, of discovery. The rules now (1) require certification by the lawyer that the procedures being used are "reasonable," (2) provide for discovery conferences between the attorneys and the courts, (3) authorize the court to impose costs and expenses incurred because of unreasonable use of discovery, and (4) encourage the courts to take more control over the pretrial stages of litigation. Yet the scope of discovery remains quite broad, and if the client can afford to pay the legal fees and other costs, almost any needed information, not specifically protected by law, that exists in the files of an opponent can be obtained.

Discovery of Experts' Identity and Their Work

Of particular concern to the statistician is Rule 26(b)(4) of the Federal Rules of Civil Procedure covering pretrial discovery from experts. This rule permits a party to request the names of experts an opponent intends to call at the trial and to require a statement of the "substance of the facts and opinions to which the expert is expected to testify and a summary of the grounds for each opinion." Experts "retained or specially employed by another party in anticipation of litigation or preparation for trial" but not expected to testify can be compelled, under court order, to give information before trial but only when it is impracticable for the party seeking discovery to obtain facts or opinions on the same subject by other means. In some instances, the material sought from the expert will be protected against discovery as the "work product" of the attorney, because it may reveal the attorney's legal strategies.

It is possible for parties to obtain court orders to protect against embarrassment or the revelation of trade secrets. In some instances, an order will permit the information to be obtained from an opponent subject to a condition of secrecy. Revealing information in violation of the order may be punishable as a contempt of court by fine and imprisonment. The expert should be fully advised regarding any limitation on revealing the data used in statistical analyses in connection with litigation.

An expert is expected to retain all essential notes and records, bearing in mind that they may be demanded by an opponent before trial, at a deposition, or on cross-examination at the trial. Deliberate destruction of such records for the purpose of covering up can create a disastrous claim of spoliation by the opponent and can prove embarrassing to the expert, the attorney, and the client. This issue creates special problems for the expert who in good faith uses computers, blackboards, and scratch sheets that are destroyed in the exercise of reasonable professional attempts at trial and error. These problems are compounded when statistical analyses are done using computer video display terminals, which produce no permanent record automatically. When in doubt, it is probably best for the expert to retain records of analyses in hard copy, details of computations, and notes. The good judgment of the expert must be relied on in deciding whether a failure to preserve preliminary analyses and intermediate work products is unethical.

There is usually an obligation to update information supplied in discovery. Thus, when answers to interrogatories are no longer accurate because, for example, the expert has discovered an error, found new data, or carried out additional analyses, new information must be provided. Witnesses are given an opportunity to correct their depositions, but it is best to be prepared to say it accurately the first time, since cross-examiners tend to pick on such inaccuracies.

In many instances, discovery matters will be supervised by magistrates of the respective district courts. Their power in these matters is usually that of a district judge, subject to the right of prompt appeal from the magistrate's order to a district judge. In complex cases, the district judge will tend to supervise discovery closely and may require conferences with and among the experts.

Because the collection of acceptable statistical data is often expensive and some agreement on the "facts," if not the "analysis," is desirable, the existence of statistical issues often mandate even greater pretrial judicial control than do other issues involving experts.

The *Manual of Complex Litigation, 2d* (1985) recommends that pretrial procedures be adopted to facilitate the presentation of statistical evidence at trial and to reduce disputes over the accuracy of the underlying data and compilations derived from such data. It does not, however, suggest what procedures to use. To the panel's knowledge, only a special committee of the New York Bar has prepared detailed protocols for handling large-scale data bases. The panel found these protocols statistically sound and consistent with both the recommendations in the *Manual* and the goals of the panel.

> *The panel recommends that, to facilitate understanding of statistical procedures and analyses, the legal profession should adopt procedures designed to (1) narrow statistical disputes prior to trial, particularly with respect to the accuracy and scope of the data and (2) disclose to the maximum extent feasible the methods of analysis to be used by the testifying experts. To foster these aims the panel supports the development and use of protocols such as those recommended by the Special Committee*

on Empirical Data in Legal Decision Making of the Association of the Bar of the City of New York (for details see Appendix F).

The attorney has an independent ethical obligation not to intentionally mislead the courts on the facts or the law. So, for example, if one or more samples or statistical analyses prove unsupportive of the client's position, it would be inappropriate to withhold them and only divulge "favorable" samples or analyses. While the rules of professional legal conduct do not require an attorney to reveal adverse facts, the panel's view is that, when alternative forms of data and analyses are known to attorneys, they are intentionally misleading the court, verging on deliberate misstatement, by revealing only those statistical data and analyses performed that are favorable to the client. There are, of course, times when statisticians will analyze the data using a variety of statistical models and methods that are possibly linked to different legal theories. In such situations the most acceptable practice, in the view of the panel, is for the statistical expert to reveal the history behind the development of the final statistical approach to an opponent when proper inquiry is made under the rules. From this perspective, it is not appropriate for the attorney to seek to avoid such revelation by consulting a series of experts without revealing to the experts ultimately retained the prior history of the involvement of other experts in the litigation.

> *In furtherance of the aim of full disclosure for experts, the panel recommends that, if a party gives statistical data to different experts for competing analyses, that fact be disclosed to the testifying expert, if any.*

Although the opinions of experts retained for litigation but not expected to be called as witnesses need not ordinarily be revealed to an opponent under Rule 26(b)(3)(B) of the Federal Rules of Civil Procedure, many members of the panel believe that the names of such nontestifying experts who have conducted statistical analyses should be revealed to opposing parties prior to trial. See the Agent Orange litigation, 105 F.R.D. 577 (E.D.N.Y. 1985), for a situation in which such revelation of the names of experts is important.

Provision of Statistical Resources

A partial solution to the problem of unequal data-gathering resources might be found through the use of discovery. The availability of statistical data bases and the disclosure of analytic techniques in advance of trial help to minimize the gap between those who have data-gathering resources and those who do not. Recommendations to this effect have been accepted in principle and drafted in detail for complex litigation. (See *Manual for Complex Litigation*, 2d, 1985, and draft recommendations of the Association of the Bar of the City of New York's Special Committee on Empirical

Data in Legal Decision Making, included here as Appendix F.) The panel believes that it is time to address the question of whether comparable access should be available whenever statistical bases are used. But such equal access is only an opening. If resources for gathering data are unequal, they will probably be equally unequal for the statistical analysis of data.

The problem of unequal or inadequate resources to pay for expert assistance has been addressed recently in the context of criminal cases. In *Ake* v. *Oklahoma*, 470 U.S. 68, 105 S.Ct. 1087 (1985), the U.S. Supreme Court held that an indigent state defendant is entitled to a state-provided psychiatrist to examine him and assist in the evaluation, preparation, and presentation of his defense once there is a preliminary showing that the defendants' sanity at the time of the crime is likely to be an important factor at trial. While it is premature to speculate on the possible implications of this case, the reasoning in the court's opinion could be used as authority to provide statistical assistance to an indigent defendant in a criminal case. In particular, the court noted:

> Congress has provided that indigent defendants shall receive the assistance of all experts "necessary for an adequate defense." Numerous state statutes guarantee reimbursement for expert services under a like standard.

The implications of this decision for civil litigation are remote and overall the problem of providing statistical expertise to poorer litigants remains a substantial one, despite useful advances in equalizing justice that have been made in recent years. In civil cases, the Equal Access to Justice Act provides for attorneys' fees and some expenses in actions by or against the government when the government's position is unreasonable. Funds may be available from sponsoring organizations such as environmental groups or from lawyers representing plaintiffs in class actions. Limited funds are also available from state, federal, or privately funded legal organizations for the poor, although these funds have decreased dramatically since 1980. Some money for experts is available from groups such as the Eastern District Litigation Fund, set up by the United States District Court for the Eastern District of New York to provide some funds for expenses incurred by attorneys appearing pro bono for indigent litigants who need expert testimony (Weinstein, 1986). Some aid may be given by the court appointment of a neutral expert under F.R.E. Rule 706, though the rule was not designed to aid the poor.

In general, however, the problem of poor litigants' obtaining adequate expert advice and assistance on statistical issues remains unresolved in most cases.

> *The panel recommends that a group be organized to supply expert statistical advice and assistance in selected cases in which the absence of such expertise might result in a denial of justice.*

The panel expects that experts working under the auspices of such a group would serve for modest fees or on a pro bono basis, with reimbursement for expenses. The panel envisions that such an effort would at least initially be focused on a single district and would use as its organizational model the Pro Bono Panel of the Eastern District of New York. This kind of expert statistical advice at the pretrial stage is particularly important and it should be coordinated with the *pro bono* work of attorneys.

The issue of access to resources goes well beyond the problems posed for poor litigants. Large corporations often have access to expertise that is unavailable to small corporations or individuals. The approach suggested here would not address the disproportionate resources available to opposing sides in civil litigation.

5.4 The Role of Court-Appointed Experts

Although judges have long had the common law power to appoint experts to serve the court, the adoption of the revised Federal Rules of Evidence provided an explicit procedure for such appointments. With the increasing complexity of statistical issues in dispute before the courts, many believe that the expanded use of court-appointed statistical experts would assist in the resolution of conflicting statistical testimony. The broad discretion for the court either to refrain from appointing or to appoint and use an expert is substantial.

The procedures for a judge to appoint an expert witness are set forth in F.R.E. Rule 706 (see the detailed statement in Appendix C). The detailed requirements of Rule 706 apply in civil and criminal cases. Although the rule does not so specify, it will ordinarily be invoked considerably before trial, since compliance with provisions in the rule requires that there must be time for: (1) a hearing on the order to show cause, (2) consent by the designated expert, (3) notification of the expert of his or her duties either in writing or at a conference, and (4) findings by the expert, which (5) must be communicated to the parties. Additional time may also be required if the judge exercises the option to request the parties to submit nominations or the parties exercise their right to subject the expert to deposition procedures. Usually the process can be set in motion at a pretrial conference pursuant to Rule 16 of the Federal Rules of Civil Procedure or Rule 17.1 of the Federal Rules of Criminal Procedure (Weinstein and Berger, 1982, Vol. 3, pp.706–12).

The judge has discretion to choose whether or not to appoint an expert the parties agree on. The judge may wish to follow the parties' agreement, since their agreement constitutes a guarantee against abuses of the rule. However, the judge may feel that appointment of a particular expert is desirable, independent of any wishes of the parties.

The expert must freely consent to serve the court—a reluctant expert is unlikely to advance the goals that led to the rule. The trial judge may choose to inform the expert of his duties orally (at a conference the parties attend) or in writing. The parties are permitted to take the deposition of a court-appointed expert as a matter of right. A party is also expressly permitted to cross-examine the court-appointed expert, even if the party calls the witness at the trial. Rule 706, if used to appoint a statistical expert, does not eliminate the problem that any statistician faces in a legal context: What professional guidelines to follow.

The compensation of the court-appointed expert is left substantially to the discretion of the judge and in general may be charged to the parties like any other litigation cost. The factors a judge may take into account include the nature of the case, why the need for a court-appointed expert arose, the status of the parties, and the decision and its consequences (Weinstein and Berger, 1982, Vol. 3 pp.706–22). The language about "just compensation" in 706 (b) serves primarily to ensure that the costs for the court-appointed expert will not be taxed against (and thereby reduce) an award of just compensation guaranteed by the constitution.

The final two provisions of Rule 706 (subdivisions (c) and (d)) are straightforward. Under 706 (c), the judge is granted discretion as to whether or not to inform the jury that the court appointed the expert. This provision gives a judge latitude to withhold the fact of court appointment, when the judge thinks the jury will be unduly influenced by that fact. Finally, 706 (d) delimits the purposes of Rule 706 by expressly providing that nothing in 706 should be read to limit the parties' rights to call their own experts. This provision is in the nature of a reassurance as to the purpose of the rule and a barrier against creative legal analysis that might read a limitation on the parties' rights, by implication.

After Rule 706 was formally proposed, Congress made only minor changes in its wording. It was not the subject of floor debate. The advisory committee that proposed the rule did note that there were some concerns, especially on the part of lawyers who primarily represented plaintiffs, about the "aura of infallibility" that might cloak a court-appointed expert. And in congressional testimony, the American Trial Lawyers Association expressed the fear that, in medical malpractice cases, judges would appoint locally prominent physicians—physicians unduly sympathetic to a local colleague who was being sued. But Rule 706 generally raised little controversy (Weinstein and Berger, 1982, vol. 3 at 706–2 – 706-4).

Since its passage in 1975, the rule has been little used. For example, the *Federal Rules of Evidence Digest* (Pike and Fischer, Inc., 1981, 1983) reports a total of 14 cases concerning the appointment of experts of all kinds under Rule 706(a). A computer search of reported federal cases, using the Westlaw system, revealed few additional cases. These reported opinions, as a group, do not provide much information about how and why a judge might appoint a statistical expert. In interviews with participants in 9 carefully selected cases, Saks and Van Duizend (1983) elicited much enthusiasm and support for the idea of using court-appointed experts. But none of the judges interviewed had ever appointed a court expert, nor had the lawyers and experts interviewed ever participated in a case involving the use of such experts.

One of the difficulties in trying to assess the potential value of the use of court-appointed experts is that their greatest value may occur prior to trial, especially if they are able to resolve conflicting analyses in reports by opposing statistical experts. But in such cases the likelihood of a pretrial settlement is high, and for such cases there are no published opinions or other easily accessible records. In particular, cases settled prior to trial would not show up in searches of opinions such as the one carried out by the panel using the Westlaw system. The case study of *Carter et al.* v. *Newsday* in Chapter 2 of this report illustrates possible roles for a court-appointed statistical expert prior to trial.

The panel has learned informally about other uses of court-appointed experts in state and local courts. For example, one of the consultants to the panel served in that role in the criminal case of *People* v. *Mayberry* (1975) in Multnomah County Court, Portland, Oregon. The defendant had challenged the jury as not being representative and the procedures for its selection as being improper. The officials who carried out the selection testified regarding the procedures they used. Following counsels' questions, the court-appointed expert was allowed to ask them questions. Next the expert took the stand and gave his opinion regarding the fairness of the procedures based on the evidence he had heard—the thrust of his testimony was that the procedures were basically fair. He was cross-examined by both sides. The judge subsequently denied the defendant's motion, and the case was never reported.

In its consideration of ways to resolve conflicting statistical testimony, the panel sought to gain an international perspective on the role of experts in legal proceedings. A summary of the panel's discussion on this topic is included here in Appendix G. Our tentative conclusion is that the continental legal systems gain strength from their reliance on the use of neutral experts. The closest American parallel available to the neutral expert is the court-appointed expert, and the European experience provides additional motivation for the expanded use of court-appointed experts in statistical matters.

Although we are mindful of the additional burdens the use of court-appointed experts places on the parties, in balance the panel believes that the benefits that would result from their expanded use, especially in complex litigation, far outweigh the costs.

> *The panel believes that judges have been unduly reluctant to appoint statistical experts to assist the court and it recommends the increased use of court-appointment procedures such as those provided by Rule 706 of the Federal Rules of Evidence.*

The appointment of statistical experts by a court is appropriately considered when the discovery process reveals conflicting statistical assessments and conclusions by the parties, or when the court believes that an appointed expert will enhance the fact finder's understanding of statistical issues in the case. Other factors that should be considered include the preferences of the parties, likely delay, and the costs of the procedure relative to what is at stake in the litigation.

5.5   Enhancing the Capability of the Fact Finder

Legal approaches to enhancing the capability of the fact finder to understand statistical assessments is a two-stage process involving the development and presentation of evidence. First, it is necessary to develop the best sources of information for a particular case. In one instance, a court-appointed witness might best aid the trier of fact, while in another case, a special master or a magistrate might do the job, e.g. a special master might hear the evidence from the parties' witnesses. Second, the presentation of evidence must be improved. The court should be flexible about how evidence can be presented, and the parties should be innovative in their presentations.

Development of Evidence

There are numerous approaches that lawyers and expert witnesses can use in developing evidence that will enhance the capability of the fact finder to understand the issues and facts. Obviously, the court can be of assistance in helping to focus the real disagreement of the parties in trying to get agreement on a common statistical data base and similar issues. Another way is to use court-appointed experts as discussed above. This can be done in the pretrial and trial stages.

A third method to develop evidence is by reference to a master, that is, by referring a list of complicated issues to a master who can assimilate the material and present it at trial to the judge or jury. The provisions governing the appointment and use of special masters are contained in Federal Rules of Civil Procedure 53. The findings of the master are to be based on evidence presented at a hearing conducted in essentially the same way as a trial, with subpoena powers enforceable through the court, and are to be received in evidence at the trial by means of a written report. The parties are provided access to the master's report prior to the trial and have limited rights to present objections to the court; otherwise, they are not afforded pretrial discovery with respect to the master's findings nor allowed to examine the master at the trial. Under Rule 53(e)(4) the parties can stipulate that the master's findings are to be final, subject only to questions of law. Even without the stipulation, the master's findings in nonjury cases are binding "unless clearly erroneous."

The appointment of masters is intended to be the exception and not the rule—see Rule 53(b). In the case of an action tried by jury, reference is to be made only when issues are unduly complicated. In a nonjury case, a reference to a master requires even more justification because the master's findings are imbued with a presumption of correctness. This use of a master essentially displaces the other evidence, and it will be followed by the court in a nonjury case, absent some clear error. For that reason, complexity alone does not justify the use of a master.

The panel is not aware of cases referring matters to masters because complicated statistical issues must be resolved. In employment discrimination cases, however, there is a special provision that permits reference of employment discrimination cases to a master if they are not tried within 120 days after issue has been joined (42 U.S.C. §2000e–5(f)(5)). A master does not necessarily need to be a specially trained person, but simply an objective fact finder who is free from some of the constraints of the ordinary trial. With the growing availability of well-qualified magistrates in the federal courts, the panel expects that there will be greater references to magistrates who will function in the same way as do masters (and whose appointments are not restricted by the provisions of Rule 53(b)).

There are two major problems with the use of masters and court-appointed experts: selection and compensation. For example, in some cases it may be possible to predict the outcome by knowing whom the court selects. At least the judge can influence the outcome by knowing something about the views of the individual so appointed. There is also the question of whether the court is justified in spending the parties' monies on masters and court-appointed experts, particularly if the resources of the parties to the case are not in balance. As was noted above, under Rule 706 for the use of court-appointed experts, the judge has the discretion to allocate the costs between the parties. But if one party cannot afford to pay, the expert is, in effect, being put on a contingency fee basis. The selection of court-appointed masters or experts presents additional difficulties. Typically, the court would like to have someone that is acceptable to both sides. In this situation, the court would call for a nomination list. If that does not work, the court can create a new list, go to some scientific body and get a list of names of people, or the court can go out and pick someone (c.f. the approach used in Germany described in Appendix G). The parties, by agreeing to a particular person, do not waive the right to attack that person's testimony during the trial, but as a practical matter agreement on an expert will waive objections based on arguments that go to general competence or extreme bias. Use of a magistrate eliminates some of these problems because the magistrate is essentially a junior judge.

Presentation of Evidence

Given the essential resources that a court has—the evidence, the courtroom experts' reports, etc.—one must ask how they may be deployed effectively to enhance truth finding and justice. There is a general impression, consistent with the behavior of most courts, that witnesses have to be presented sequentially, one by one; that the plaintiff goes first and presents all of the plaintiff's case without interruption except for cross-examination; that the examination of witnesses follows in a sequence of direct examination, cross-examination, redirect examination, etc.; and that testimony should ordinarily be made by response to specific questions rather than by an extended narration. This sequencing of evidence and arguments is traditional but it is not necessarily a consequence of formal court rules. Especially in a long trial, where the fact finder may have difficulty remembering the evidence and the issues, alternative approaches can and have been used.

F.R.E. Rule 611 allows the trial judge to exercise power over the presentation of evidence to make it more effective and efficient. Many judges have used that authority in innovative ways to modify the traditional sequencing of evidence. For statistical matters, there are a variety of approaches that might be attempted. When the reports of witnesses go together, the judge might allow their presentations to be combined and the witnesses to be questioned as a panel discussion rather than sequentially. More narrative testimony might be allowed, and the expert might be allowed to deviate from the facts of the case in order to give a brief mini-course on statistics as a preliminary to some testimony. Instead of the experts being presented in the midst of other evidence in each party's case, the judge might call for the experts for opposing sides at about the same time, one right after the other. Some courts, particularly in bench trials, will have both experts placed under oath and, in effect, permit them to engage in a dialogue. In such a format experts are able to say whether they agree or disagree on specific issues. The judge and counsel can interject questions. Such practices may improve the judge's understanding and reduce the tensions associated with the experts' adversarial role.

There are times when a consensus among experts can be achieved to narrow the issues. One panel member reports such a consensus in a statistical case involving allegations of a form of discrimination, in which both experts first testified. Each was in the courtroom when the other testified, and the lawyers conducted the presentation. Then the judge brought both experts back and conducted a joint examination to see if he understood when they were in agreement and when they were not. By that process, the judge was able to narrow the dispute quite dramatically to just a few areas of disagreement.

Another important point regarding the presentation of evidence relates to the role of the judge in making independent evaluations and assessments of data, rather than relying solely on the analyses presented by the expert witnesses. The possibility for independent analyses ranges from finding a mathematical error in one of the columns of a table to regression and other statistical studies. With the ready availability of personal computers and with easy-to-use statistical software, it may not be difficult for a judge or the judge's staff to try out statistical analyses that the parties have not attempted. Court-conducted statistical analyses, however, present problems of specification and calculation errors and the misapplication of statistical methods or concepts. In addition, the court may misdescribe the implications of results when, instead of relying on the words of the expert, it relies on its own interpretation of what a statistical test means. For these reasons, the panel would discourage such judicial activism.

Judicial Deliberation

It is important to understand that the process of litigation does not assume that every fact has to be proved as if it were being written on a blank slate. It is also permissible for a judge to use his or her own background, training, and experience to evaluate and understand the evidence that has been introduced. In certain cases, the judge may turn to law clerks and fellow judges in seeking views and information or use them as sounding boards during the process of deliberation on decisions. Such informal discussions are permitted and statistically sophisticated judges or clerks can aid those with less knowledge.

Another source for enhancing the capability of the fact finder is nonpersonal—treatises, publications, and the like. Those can be made available either by the parties who introduce them into evidence or through judicial notice. Judicial notice is a system in which the court may take notice of certain matters, even though they are factual, relating to a case about which there can be no reasonable or genuine dispute and are rather easily ascertained (see F.R.E. Rule 201). Certain general concepts, such as how long division is accomplished, are assumed under judicial notice. There is also the possibility of the judge's reaching out or of looking at some highly regarded textbook and perhaps, under the doctrine of judicial notice, taking judicial notice of certain principles.

Judges may also rely on texts and treatises, not to determine a fact through judicial notice, but in a nonadjudicative sense, for general education or to resolve certain matters that are part of a judge's rationale in reaching a decision but are not directly facts in the case itself.

One way for judges to get information about the validity of statistical evidence is to conduct their own research. The American Bar Association's (1972) *Code of Judicial Conduct*, Canon 3A(4) forbids judges from receiving *ex parte* information on cases in which they are involved. But Monahan and Walker (1985) found that while most states follow this canon, 12 have modified it to permit the judge to obtain expert advice without notifying the parties.

Statisticians and lawyers need to be aware that the more education a judge receives in statistics, the more temptation there is for him or her to assume the role of the expert—to go to the textbooks. The judge may not remember how to do a chi-square test, but he or she certainly can find a book to remind him of how to do it. If the judge is familiar with a statistical method the parties have not applied to data in evidence, and the judge wants to know what the application of the method shows, nothing prohibits him from doing his own ad hoc analysis. These techniques, we reiterate, present possible dangers.

> *The panel recommends that, in general, judges should not con-*
> *duct analytical statistical studies on their own. If a court is*
> *not satisfied with the statistical evidence before it, alternative*
> *means should be used to clarify matters, such as a request for*
> *additional submissions from the parties or even, in exceptional*
> *circumstances, a reopening of the case to receive additional ev-*
> *idence.*

Statistical analyses and reanalyses can be very time-consuming and it is the panel's view that, in general, it has not proved to be expeditious for courts to engage in such activities. Moreover, the appropriateness of even commonly used forms of statistical analysis is frequently a highly technical matter and the risk of misuse by a nonexpert is substantial. The chance of error may be enhanced when a court's work is not subjected to adversarial testing.

5.6   The Role of Statistical Education in the Presentation of Evidence

Once statistical evidence has been ruled admissible and the expert qualified, the next question is how best to present the evidence so that the fact finder will understand it and accord it proper probative weight. Both judges and jurors are likely to be unfamiliar with the language of statistics and unfamiliar with statistical modes of thought. Without special training, they are in a difficult position when it comes to evaluating statistical data and inferences drawn from the data.

A judge as fact finder in a trial involving statistical evidence has two important advantages over a jury. First, the judge has substantially greater ability to become educated about the statistical issues that are likely to arise at trial. The judge can read articles designed to introduce lawyers to statistics and can seek out law clerks with statistical training. Of course, the danger with judicial self-education in statistics is the same as the danger that exists when judges notice any sort of nonadjudicative fact. The facts noticed may not be indisputable, and the judge may fail to understand how what has been learned fits in with the particular circumstances of the case.

These problems can be alleviated if the judge reveals his or her assumptions and understandings to the parties as the case progresses so that any misunderstandings can be corrected. Judges are able to engage in dialogue with the parties during the course of the litigation. Thus, when they do not understand some point, they can seek an explanation. If they are unclear about the details of a statistical procedure, they can ask for more information or for a better explanation.

The jury as fact finder in a trial involving statistical evidence has additional obstacles to overcome, not the least of which is that jurors have difficulty understanding much of the information that they receive (Severance and Loftus, 1982). The problem of misunderstanding is likely to be acute when statistical information and analyses are offered. The literature on information processing offers clues on how to best proceed. Although the panel has not canvassed this literature systematically, it has extracted support for the following suggestions.

One possible approach is to educate jurors about statistics prior to or as the initial part of the presentation of statistical evidence. It is well established that people have an easier time comprehending and remembering information when they have prior knowledge about the general topic. There are numerous ways in which the legal system could capitalize on this established psychological finding. First, before any testimony was given, the court could instruct the jury on the meaning of statistical concepts and on how the statistical evidence was expected to fit into the case. If the matter were of sufficient import, a mini-course of several hours or even several days, devoted to the logic and concepts of statistics, might be justified. Even if only a subset of the jurors are helped by such presentations, the entire jury can benefit, for knowledgeable jurors can instruct the less knowledgeable in deliberations. There are, of course, obvious difficulties in attempting to instruct the jury before trial about a nonlegal matter such as statistics. For example, who would do the teaching? Only the rare judge would be qualified to do so. Perhaps a neutral expert could be used, or the statistical experts of both parties could share the job. In either situation, costs would be an important consideration.

A second possibility is to extend to juries the advantages that judges derive from their ability to engage in dialogue with attorneys and witnesses. In many jurisdictions, jurors can and do ask questions during court proceedings. Permitting and encouraging jurors to ask questions of statistical experts is, however, not without its problems. Such questioning would necessarily be limited, since chaos could result if 12 or even 6 people continually inquire about whatever puzzles them. Another problem with questioning by jurors is that it cannot be very spontaneous. Typically, jurors must put their questions in writing and submit them through the judge to ensure that information barred by the rules of evidence is not requested. Moreover, to minimize uncoordinated interruptions, juror questions are typically posed only at the conclusion of a witness's testimony or during a substantial break. These restrictions are probably wise. The deficiencies they entail can to some extent be countered by the judge. A good judge, sensitive to complexities that are likely to confuse, should be able to interrupt witnesses with questions designed to clarify what is said without disrupting the flow of evidence. So long as such questions are genuinely designed to clarify, even detailed inquiries should not run afoul of the structures against judicial partisanship.

A member of the panel related an experience involving the preparation of a report to be used by attorneys during the selection of juries in a Medicare fraud case. As is often the case in the rush to prepare for trial, the report was completed just before it was to be used. One table in the report listed 10 correlations, with a comment on how to interpret each correlation. For example, a correlation of -.13 between the verdict in a mock criminal case and the age of the jurors meant that older people were more conviction prone. A correlation of +.21 between verdict and sex meant that women were more conviction prone. A footnote at the bottom of the table instructed the attorneys to pay attention only to the size of the correlation and to ignore the sign since the "sign was affected by the way the data were coded." This footnote totally baffled the attorneys, who, not surprisingly, asked for clarification. With only five minutes available before jury selection was scheduled to commence, the task of clarification seemed almost hopeless. Sufficient time was simply not available for a detailed explanation. The problem suggested by this story is a general one and is applicable to actual courtroom presentations. When statistical analyses are presented in court, the "educators" do not always have the luxury of a series of 12 or 36 lecture hours to get their ideas across.

Nonetheless, lawyers and experts must approach the presentation of statistical evidence from the perspective of educator. They must find ways of presenting the statistical concepts to be used, the data to be analyzed, and the results of the statistical analyses in such a way that the material, or at least its importance, will be understood. As with a classroom lecture, or even an entire course, this requires organization, advance planning, and perhaps a full-scale rehearsal.

Statistical evidence is typically presented through the direct examination of a witness. Advice to lawyers on how to examine witnesses is plentiful and freely available (e.g., Wellman, 1962; Bailey and Rothblatt, 1971; Oliphant, 1978). There is advice on direct and cross-examination techniques with special reference to questioning friendly witnesses, hostile witnesses, and expert witnesses who might be of either persuasion. However, little scientific scrutiny has been given to the received wisdom of the trial bar. Since an exploration of different treatises will occasionally reveal contradictory advice, it cannot all be sound. Moreover, even generally sound advice might need to be modified if it is to be applied to expert witnesses who present statistical assessments and the results of statistical analyses.

Looking at some of the sources of advice, one finds not only such pearls of wisdom as "Be prepared" and "Don't be boring," with which no one could reasonably disagree, but also more useful suggestions such as "Reveal any negative information yourself."

One piece of advice that applies to a wide range of witnesses, but is especially crucial to the expert statistical witness, is to avoid jargon. Jargon is an insidious barrier to communication in the courtroom because professionals can grow so accustomed to the language of their specialty that they lose sight of the fact that they are talking a special language that jurors are unlikely to comprehend. While a statistical expert is probably well aware that terms like *beta coefficient* or *homoscedasticity* need to be explained to lay fact finders, the words *normal distribution* might be used by a statistician as if they were part of ordinary English. Similarly, describing R^2 as "the proportion of variance explained" will provide no explanation for people who think that a *variance* has something vaguely to do with zoning, and the familiar term *median* may call to a juror's mind strips of land that run down the center of major highways.

Transforming technical jargon and concepts into lay terms is not an easy task. In describing problems in preparing direct testimony as an expert, Barton (1983) comments (pp. 374–375):

> My major problem with the lawyers was a difference in opinion as to what constitutes a sufficiently simple explanation. I prepared a draft. ...I thought it was extremely simple and easy to understand. ... [O]ther statisticians ... agreed with me that I had done a good job of presenting things simply and non-mathematically. Our attorneys, on the other hand, thought it much too difficult for the intended audience and had the same opinion about subsequent, increasingly simplified drafts.

It is certainly true that not all complex statistical methods can be satisfactorily explained to statistical neophytes. At the same time, a great deal in the way of clarification can be accomplished by the judicious use of appropriately chosen examples. Few statistical experts have developed their expository talents in this direction.

Although simplifying testimony may present problems for expert witnesses, the benefits of having triers of fact understand testimony are clear. Experts do not go into judges' chambers or jury rooms to clarify tricky points. In a congressional hearing, Judge McGowan (1982) explained how one particular administrative law case looked to him as a judge on the Court of Appeals for the District of Columbia (pp. 930–931):

> I had the *Weyerhauser* case—the pulp and paper company— under the Clean Water Act. There were 180,000 pages of that record. All I had to do was decide whether it [the decision of the Environmental Protection Agency based on the record] was arbitrary and capricious. ...What was my job at this point? To be able to understand—and this was essentially chemical engineering—my job was to really master the differences between these differing operations of the different companies so

that I could make a reasoned disposition of the case. I would
have needed to spend 6 months on that. *With no expert help
available to me, no expert that I could call in and say, "What
about this? Let's put our feet up on the table, and you explain
it to me," I had to do it by myself* [emphasis added].

In addition to the general problem of jargon, it must be recognized that
statistical analysis, by its very nature, is likely to be abstract. Comprehension of abstract information is enhanced if references are illustrated
by concrete illustrations or metaphors. For example, in explaining why a
mean in certain circumstances is a less appropriate measure of central tendency than the median, an expert may wish to supplement a description
of how the two measures are calculated by an example that illustrates the
sensitivity of averages to extreme observations.

Another piece of advice that applies widely but is especially crucial to the
statistical expert is that testimonial material needs to be well organized.
There should be a coherent theme to the testimony of the statistician, as
there should be to the testimony of all witnesses, expert and nonexpert, and
it should be left to the lawyer to make clear how the statistician's testimony
fits into the story of the case as a whole. This requires attention at all stages
of the trial, not simply when the expert is testifying. The attorney's opening
statement should tell the fact finder what the statistical expert's testimony
is going to involve and how this testimony fits into the larger story of the
case. The attorney's closing statement should reiterate these themes. It
is especially important for the lawyer to tie statistical testimony to the
testimony of other witnesses, if at all possible. For example, one might ask
a plaintiff's statistical expert: "You have been advised of the testimony of
Witness A regarding the importance of seniority to promotion decisions at
the All American factory. Did you take this into account in developing your
model?" Or one might inquire of a defendant's witness: "Mr. Statistician
testified about the importance of including a measure of seniority in all
models of promotions at the All American factory. What is your view?"
Such explicit cross-references will give more meaning to a party's story as
a whole.

An important principle that should apply particularly to the presentation of statistical evidence is the avoidance of mystification, in this case the
mystification of probability and mathematical statistics. In questioning an
expert presenting statistical evidence, a lawyer should be clear about the
empirical, conceptual, and statistical assumptions that underlie the material presented and the conclusions reached. Some lawyers may not, however,
want to be clear about the way in which their statistical expert's conclusions rest on a series of assumptions of varying plausibility. They may wish
to gloss over dubious statistical assumptions, such as the assumed linear
relationship between education and income, or the assumptions of independence and normality of error terms in regression models. It is, of course,

when the plausibility of key assumptions is most questionable that lawyers may be most anxious to gloss over or obscure the way that their expert's conclusions depend on those assumptions, and when the courts should be more diligent in acquiring clarification. In the panel's view, this may require the active intervention of the judge, and it may even justify allowing one party to interfere somewhat with the other party's presentation of testimony. The judge has the authority, under F.R.E. Rule 705, to require an expert to provide the basis for an opinion prior to offering it. To the extent that a statistical analysis rests on various statistical assumptions, it is proper professional practice for the statistician to explain the foundations of the statistical analysis, and how the statistical results or opinions based on those results depend on these foundations. This is particularly important because fact finders who cannot judge the appropriateness of elaborate forms of statistical analysis may be relatively well situated to judge the reasonableness of underlying and crucial assumptions.

Statistics in Legal Education

The practical considerations described above underscore the need for familiarization with law by statistical experts and statistical education in law schools.

The panel has used as a point of departure in its discussion of statistical training for law students the Report of the American Statistical Association Subcommittee on Law of the Committee on Training in Statistics in Selected Professions (Kaye, 1984). Most of the panel members are strongly supportive of the development of courses in statistics for law students, and at least five panel members have taught such a course. The panel has, however, taken cognizance of the fact that the law school curriculum is (like many other curricula) already overcrowded. As one of our members has noted, that the complexities and extent of substantive law have increased to such an extent that the cry that students used to make against the value of the third year has been replaced in some quarters by the lament that there are more courses to take than one can accommodate. Many courses of great potential value to lawyers are not taught or are only sporadically taught in the nation's law schools. Moreover, there is in most law schools limited room for the offering of nonlaw courses, and it is not clear that a law school thinking about the best course to offer in its nonlaw slots should choose to offer statistics rather than, for example, economics or psychology as they pertain to litigation.

The law school tends to be a place where innovative courses, and we hope statistics fits this category, tend to follow faculty interests. Thus, if a faculty member wishes to offer a course in statistics or wishes to involve a statistician in offering such a course, or even wishes to discuss statistical concepts, modes of proof, and the like in a course that focuses on some areas of substantive law, statistics is likely to be taught provided that a sufficient number of students can be attracted to the course in question.

An alternative to courses on statistics is the "pervasive approach," which has some currency in the field of ethics. This simply means that the topic is taught in connection with case-specific material in all courses in which issues bearing on the topic arise. This approach has much to commend it. It means that many students will be exposed to some consideration of the subject and it exposes them to it in a context in which the importance of the topic and its career relevance are plain. In areas in which statistical issues are often intrinsic to the course material, such as courses in employment discrimination, torts, and evidence, teachers should be encouraged to talk about the statistical issues as they arise. Instead of regarding the task of illuminating the statistical aspects of a case as a digression, it should be regarded as an essential part of educating law students to be competent in the subject matter of the course, and time should be allotted accordingly.

What can be done through the pervasive method is, however, limited. Students in a substantive course will have markedly different backgrounds and markedly different interests in the fine points of statistics. In these circumstances, the instructor can at best seek to explain the basic logic of what is going on in the statistical aspects of the case in question. Often this can be done with relatively little mathematics, even if matters involving such complex topics as regression analysis are being discussed. Instructors, too, will need to know much more than their students about the statistical techniques that figure in the materials they are discussing if they are to instruct their students on the logic of what is going on. This means that the instructors themselves will need training in statistical methods. Even then, some form of joint instruction by legal expert and by statistical expert is likely to be the best approach, especially if the student is to learn about both the utility and the limitation of statistical methods.

To begin the process of providing statistical education for law students and for lawyers and judges:

> *The panel recommends that efforts be made to integrate instruction on basic statistical concepts into the law school curriculum and to provide instruction for practicing lawyers and judges on such matters. In law schools this can be done by allowing students to take for credit courses outside the law school, by developing courses on statistics for lawyers, and by discussing statistical issues and concepts in specific courses such as those dealing with antitrust law, discrimination, environmental law, evidence, and torts. For practicing attorneys and judges, such instruction may be provided by existing professional organizations, the Federal Judicial Center, programs for continuing legal education, and the like.*

The very breadth of coverage of the type of course proposed in the Kaye Subcommittee Report suggests an additional topic that should be a part of a law and statistics course. This is the use of and relations with statisticians as expert witnesses. Except in rare instances, lawyers facing statistical problems in practice will need expert advice. If a law and statistics course can aid students in communicating with experts and in intelligently using them, it may ultimately be of more value than a course that does a better job of teaching only basic statistical concepts. Unfortunately, there is to date little systematic knowledge about the ways in which lawyers and experts may most effectively work together. Clearly this is an area that calls for scholarly attention. One possibility is by adding a "clinical" component to a law and statistics course in which law students work with statistical graduate students to prepare and offer expert testimony. If these students could be trained to work together while in school, many of the difficulties of the sort illustrated elsewhere in this report might eventually be surmounted.

As we noted in Chapter 3, to contribute effectively in legal settings, statisticians need education in at least the rudiments of law. Education in a formal setting, such as a one-day seminar conducted by lawyers, statisticians, and other experienced professionals, would be of considerable value. An introduction to the role of expert witnesses, rules of evidence, litigation procedure, typical strategies and pitfalls, and some case studies could be included in such a program.

One final aspect of education involves the preparation of critiques of the statistical approaches adopted in actual cases.

> *The panel recommends that legal, statistics, and scientific journals publish, on a regular basis, critical statistical reviews of expert presentations and judicial opinions in cases involving important uses of statistics.*

Such statistical reviews would educate judges, lawyers, and statistical experts; promulgate higher professional standards; and improve the quality of evidence for decision making.

5.7 Implications for a Research Agenda

This report has studied the increased use of statistical assessments as evidence in the courts and the nature of the problems posed by this use. Through an examination of the differences in methodology between statistics and the law and a review of the uses of statistical assessments in a series of case studies and in selected areas of litigation, the panel has proposed some partial solutions to the problems arising from expert statistical testimony. In the process, the panel has developed a preliminary research agenda on issues at the interface of statistics and the legal process.

The research agenda outlined in this chapter is divided into three components: (1) research in statistics suggested by the use of statistics in a legal context, (2) research on the process whereby the courts and the legal process adapt to new areas of knowledge such as statistics (including research on legal innovations to strengthen the uses of statistics by the courts), and (3) statistical studies, transcending the capability of individual experts in particular cases, that would be of major assistance to the courts.

5.7.1   Implications for Research on Statistics

Many of the issues examined in the panel's review of statistical assessments as evidence in the courts have implications for basic research in statistical methodology and theory. As has been the experience in other substantive areas, the careful application of existing statistical concepts and techniques in a legal context by expert witnesses has revealed matters for which research has yet to provide a satisfying, much less complete, answer. While this situation often presents a dilemma to the expert witness who must provide answers to questions posed in court, it also provides new challenges to the statistical research community. The panel's review of selected areas of litigation in which statistical testimony is prominent has revealed several statistical issues and problems whose solutions would be of more general interest. We give a few illustrations here.

Courts often favor the statistical analysis of aggregate data in employment discrimination in order to avoid a legal inference of discrimination from isolated, accidental, or sporatic discriminatory acts. Yet, as Simpson's paradox shows, aggregation may lead to spurious findings of discrimination or nondiscrimination when component strata are proportionately different (e.g., see the case study of *EEOC* v. *Federal Reserve Bank of Richmond* in Chapter 2). In contrast, data are sometimes disaggregated to a point at which statistical significance at some prespecified level is difficult to achieve or, what is often equivalent, the ratio of an estimated parameter in a statistical model to its estimated standard error is quite small (e.g., see *Penk* v. *Oregon State Board of Higher Education*, 816 F.2d 458 (D.C. OR. 1986)). Methods exist to show how tendencies in separate tables that individually do not achieve statistical significance can collectively do so. But when such patterns are not clear, it may be quite difficult to discern the total picture of employment, which the courts seek, without a spurious finding of discrimination by aggregation of strata and an incorrect level of significance from a selection among multiple comparisons. In part, what is needed is a reexamination and restructuring of asymptotic statistical theories in which not only the sample size gets large but there is also an increasingly large number of nuisance parameters.

Related to the preceding problem is the role of statistical significance as a measure of disparity in a discrimination context or of the consequences of an act in an antitrust context. Statistical models, such as those used in regression analysis, have associated "error terms," whose assumed random structure is used as the basis of the calculation of standard errors and levels of statistical significance. But from where does this randomness come when the data being fitted by the statistical model represent the universe of interest, e.g. all employees of a company in a given year? Even if inferences from complete data on a finite population are not an issue, the use of the usual measures of variability and statistical significance may be inappropriate when they are associated with a model that has resulted from an examination of the data rather than from a substantive theory that yields a complete model specification. In this context the panel sees the need for the development of micro-level econometric models, for the activities of individual firms, which will withstand the rigors of statistical inquiry. A third problem is that the usual variance assumptions associated with standard statistical models are crude and ignore heteroscedasticity, the combination of random error with lack of fit, and so on. Such problems with variability may be especially crucial for assessing the uncertainty associated with predictions for particular combinations of explanatory variables.

A striking statistical problem occurs when courts sensibly constrain the use of variables in models that are to be used for inference. For example, courts have ruled that certain variables may not be used as explanatory variables in regression-like models of possible employment discrimination because these variables are "tainted," being the products of the alleged discrimination. But, if these variables are included with permitted variables, they often turn out to be important (and statistically significant) predictors of employment outcomes, such as promotions and wages. *In the absence of discrimination* these variables would logically be included in the regression model. Deleting a variable in a regression model changes the meaning of the estimated coefficients for all of the remaining explanatory variables. The mathematical statistics interpretation of estimated coefficients in properly specified multiple regression models is expressed in terms of "conditional expectations," and in properly specified log-linear or logit models is expressed in terms of products and ratios of "odds-ratios." How are the estimated coefficients in the constrained statistical models to be interpreted, especially when these models have a dynamic longitudinal structure? Only when careful technical interpretations of parameters and their estimates are available can statistics assess the appropriateness of the looser interpretive language used by those presenting statistical testimony in a court of law.

A final statistical problem, that of attenuation, arises both in antitrust and in employment discrimination litigation and is the result of the use of proxy explanatory variables, e.g. variables used in place of productivity measures in regression models to predict wages. When explanatory variables are measured with error, the standard method of least squares can produce biased estimates of the true regression coefficients. In the case of simple linear regression (i.e., one predictor), if the measurement error is uncorrelated with the regression error, then the least-squares coefficient is on average too small (e.g., see Draper and Smith, 1981: 122–125). In multiple linear regression, the effect of measurement error in one explanatory variable that is uncorrelated with the regression error is propagated and results in least-squares coefficients for some of the other explanatory variables that are too large—a form of compensation. Unfortunately, the attenuation problem is more complex when there are multiple explanatory variables subject to measurement error, and these errors are correlated with the regression error. Here the usual least-squares estimates are biased, but the direction of the bias is unclear. Reverse regression (see Section 3.2) has been proposed as a solution to a special aspect of this problem, but there is considerable technical debate over its value in this regard. New statistical methodology is required to provide techniques for measuring the direction of and bounds on the magnitude of the attenuation bias in both multiple regression and logistic regression analyses. Recent papers by Patefield (1981), Klepper and Leamer (1984), and Krasker and Pratt (1986) have made substantial progress on these problems, and the recent book by Fuller (1987) presents an integrated discussion of related measurement error problems.

Solutions for these and other statistical problems arising in the context of the uses of statistics in expert testimony will come from new methodological research in the statistical community and will be applicable to problems in other areas of substantive interest, not just to legal situations.

5.7.2   Implications for Research on the Adaptation of the Legal Process to Statistical Knowledge

The Federal Courts and System Research

Unlike most legal systems, our court system has operated largely without much self-knowledge. Until the comparatively recent establishment of the Federal Judicial Center and the intermittent existence of a research unit in the Department of Justice, the federal courts have had to be content with a rather simple auditing of case numbers and crude classifications. These have been used to estimate backlog in a rough manner and are often the basis of requests for allocation of new judgeships, but they are not usually useful for finer measurement. Efforts to refine assessment tools continue, but inherently different cases present complex and different characteristics so that such measurement is not easy. There have been fewer attempts to look ahead and to make forecasts on the impact of legislation and other structural changes in the workloads of the courts (see e.g., Boyum and Krislov, 1980).

In addressing the problem of the impact of the use of statistics on court, we have been struck at how difficult it is to establish the baseline of litigation burden that the burgeoning use of statistics might perturb and add to. The courts have not consciously sought to learn much about themselves. Perhaps this is because such knowledge has little immediate consequence since by and large concepts of justice and not court convenience dominate decisions as to how courts are expected to behave.

At both the federal and state court levels, there has been a growing awareness that there are many acceptable and just ways of handling matters. Some produce better results than others. To be sure, a great deal depends on and derives from the style and skill of the individual judge, but some findings should be generalizable to all or most. Furthermore, exposure to alternative modes of presentation and evaluation and the confidence derived from these experiences need to be monitored.

In these tasks of assessment the Federal Judicial Center has played a major role. It is constrained by its quite appropriate role as handmaiden to the courts and its agenda is fixed by the judiciary. What it seemingly loses in some aspects of critical independence, it perhaps gains back in access and credibility with judges. But its view is a partial one. Much the same can be said of the brief years of the Office for Improvement of Justice, which was located in the Department of Justice under President Carter. By design it did short-range work on subjects mainly of concern to the Department of Justice and the Carter Administration.

These organizations, especially the Federal Judicial Center, which has had time to develop, have done well at studying specific judicial problems and have helped stimulate scholarly study. While the center has done studies on the amount of time different types of cases require, e.g., antitrust cases compared with contracts or tort cases, it has not done any studies within areas, comparing cases with statistical evidence with those that do not have such evidence, as to burden of judicial time. Such studies would be of great value for the allocation of judicial resources.

There is also a need to develop long-range studies on aspects of the judiciary, information that is useful in many settings and is independent of current problems and even fads. Therefore, the panel encourages those federal agencies that currently monitor the courts to develop programs for evaluating court operations on a longer-range basis. The panel notes that there is particular need for measurement and assessment of internal procedures that have potential for serious disruption or overloading of the courts. A program for developing substantive information of this sort must begin with the government. Evaluation activities would probably work best with cooperation between several agencies or with a mixed community advisory system that planned well for practical use, applied research, and basic research as well. Given the proper data base, research of the type suggested below would be enhanced.

Problems of Statistics in Courts: Effects and Costs

While there is a fair body of case study and anecdotal material on statistics and courts (and this report adds to that literature), there are no systematic studies—attempts, for example, to match similar cases with and without statistics or genuine attempts to survey a subject area to determine the use or abuse of statistical evidence.

While there exists expert opinion of considerable plausibility, the following are all basically unknown and unestimated by even crude measures for cases with or without statistical presentations: (1) the range of cost for parties, (2) length of trial, (3) jury and judge comprehension, (4) litigation strategies, and (5) outcome, including settlement rates.

We do not have even case study judgments that might deal with the question of whether there is an improvement in the quality of decision or acceptance of decisions as a by-product. What is called for is an expanded effort to develop a social science perspective on the courts and how they respond to or adapt to new knowledge. In the area of statistical evidence, this perspective has yet to emerge, although fragments of it are available from diverse sources. In Appendix H, we have reviewed some of the commentary on this issue, but we recognize that much of this commentary is not well grounded in rigorous research. What is required is a systematic research effort. In the process, we should learn not only how courts use statistics, but also more generally how courts respond to scientific knowledge.

Alternative Structures and Comprehension of Statistics

In this chapter the panel has recommended several innovations designed to improve the comprehension of statistical evidence by judges and juries. Some of these recommendations involve alternative structures and others only minor modifications of existing procedures. The impact of the adoption of these recommendations is at best speculation and, as in any other area, innovations require careful evaluation. The cornerstone to such evaluation is careful experimentation, in the form of randomized controlled trials in the courts. Such experimentation should also be coupled with a program of experimental research involving simulation of trials using alternative modes of presentation and decision making. The panel urges that priority be given to the task of planning randomized experiments, since randomization in this area presents legal as well as other problems.

5.7.3   Implications for Statistical Studies to Assist the Courts

There are situations in which one can foresee that major litigation affecting many people is likely to require statistical studies that transcend the capability of individual experts in particular cases. Examples include studies relating to the causes or effects of Agent Orange, asbestos, chemical dumps, DES, formaldehyde, swine flu, thalidomide, and toxic shock syndrome.

In Chapter 3, we discussed aspects of the data problems associated with mass tort litigation in an environmental context and we reviewed the need in the case of *Allen* v. *U.S.*, 588 F.Supp. 247 (C.D. Utah 1984) for data on potential increased risk of various forms of cancer and leukemia in civilians exposed to fallout downwind from a government nuclear testing range. Similarly, for the Agent Orange litigation discussed in Chapter 3, the plaintiffs were unable to acquire adequate epidemiological data on the effects of exposure to dioxin, one of the components of Agent Orange. At the time of the 1984 settlement just prior to trial, a government-sponsored epidemiological investigation by the Centers for Disease Control (CDC) had not yet begun (see also Chapter 15 of Gough, 1986). In the summer of 1987, the CDC finally concluded that they could not even complete the study because it had been unable to find enough soldiers who were exposed to high levels of the herbicide on the basis of blood tests. Moreover, the CDC concluded that neither military records nor self-assessments of veterans are reliable guides to past exposure to dioxin (see Booth, 1987).

Similarly, there has been extensive litigation in connection with mass torts and/or product liability suits brought against manufacturers of drugs and related products that have been alleged to cause various illnesses, defects, and even death. Many cases brought against the manufacturers of Bendectin, DES, superabsorbent tampons, and the Dalkon Shield are still before the courts, but critical to those decisions already reached (both positive and negative) have been epidemiological and statistical studies that attempt to measure the health consequences of exposure. Not only are the health consequences of public concern (e.g., as in the deaths due to toxic shock syndrome), but the size of damage awards in individual cases and in class action and multidistrict litigation may be so large as to lead to the bankruptcy of the major companies (e.g., both Johns Manville, the manufacturer of aesbestos, and A.H. Robins, the manufacturer of the Dalkon Shield, have sought protection through bankruptcy filings).

As suspicion grows regarding the health consequences of exposure to drugs and other substances affecting large numbers of people, there is typically need for neutral, well-financed, and timely studies that can assist the courts during the litigation that inevitably will follow. In our review of *Gulf South Insulation*, described in Chapter 2, the environmental cases described in Chapter 3, and the various mass tort and product liability cases discussed at the panel meetings over a three-year period, the panel recognized that there was not a clear mechanism for initiating the required statistical studies in advance of litigation except in special instances.

> *The panel recommends that a mechanism be created whereby impartial bodies, such as the Centers for Disease Control, can consider conducting relevant studies in advance of, or during, particular litigation to assist the courts, other public bodies, and the public in evaluating the issues.*

Without neutral, well-financed, and timely studies of this kind, serious mistakes can be made such as those that authorize public access to unacceptably dangerous drugs and other substances or deny the public access to useful drugs and other substances when benefits outweigh risks.

Appendix A

Statistical Approaches, Probability Interpretations, and the Quantification of Standards of Proof

A.1 Relevance Versus Statistical Fluctuations

The term *statistics* is often used to mean data or information, that is, numerical quantities based on some type of observations. *Statistics* in this report is used in a more specific sense to refer to methods for planning scientific studies, collecting data, and then analyzing, presenting, and interpreting the data once they are collected. Much statistical methodology has as its purpose the understanding of patterns or forms of regularity in the presence of variability and errors in observed data:

> If life were stable, simple, and routinely repetitious, there would be little need for statistical thinking. But there would probably be no human beings to do statistical thinking, because sufficient stability and simplicity would not allow the genetic randomness that is a central mechanism of evolution. Life is not, in fact, stable or simple, but there are stable and simple aspects to it. From one point of view, the goal of science is the discovery and elucidation of these aspects, and statistics deals with some general methods of finding patterns that are hidden in a cloud of irrelevancies, of natural variability, and of error-prone observations or measurements (Kruskal, 1978b:1078).

> When the Lord created the world and people to live in it—an enterprise which, according to modern science, took a very long time—I could well imagine that He reasoned with Himself as follows: "If I make everything predictable, these human beings, whom I have endowed with pretty good brains, will undoubtedly learn to predict everything, and they will thereupon have no motive to do anything at all, because they will recognize that the future is totally determined and cannot be influenced by any human action. On the other hand, if I make everything unpredictable, they will gradually discover that there is no rational

basis for any decision whatsoever and, as in the first case, they will thereupon have no motive to do anything at all. Neither scheme would make sense. I must therefore create a mixture of the two. Let some things be predictable and let others be un-predictable. They will then, amongst many other things, have the very important task of finding out which is which" (Schumacker, *Small is Beautiful*, 1975).

This view of statistics has inherent in it the need for some form of inference from the observed data to a problem of interest. There are several schools of statistical inference, each of which sets forth an approach to statistical analysis, reporting, and interpretation. The two most visible such schools are (1) the proponents of the Bayesian or "subjective" approach and (2) the frequentist or "objective" approach. The key difference between them is in terms of how they deal with the interpretation of probability and of the inferential process.

A statistical analyst, whether a Bayesian or a frequentist, must ultimately confront the relevance of the patterns discerned from a body of data for the problem of interest. Whether in the law or in some other field of endeavor, statistical analysis and inference are of little use if they are not designed to inform judgments about the issue that generated the statistical inquiry. Thus perhaps a better title for this introductory section might have been "Discovering Relevance in the Presence of Statistical Fluctuations."

This appendix describes the two basic approaches to drawing inferences from statistical data and attempts to link the probabilistic interpretation of such inferences to the formalities of legal decision making.

As one turns from the use of statistics in both the data and the methodological senses, i.e., in the plural and the singular, in various scientific fields to its use in the law, there will clearly be occasions when statistics has little to offer. In a somewhat different context Bliley (1983) notes:

> Our tendency to rely on statistics is understandable. Statistics offer to our minds evidence which is relatively clear and easy to understand. By comparison, arguments about the rights of individuals, the natural authority of the family, and the legitimate powers of government are complex and do not provide us with answers quickly or easily. But we must remember that these are questions which are at the root of our deliberations. Until these questions are answered, statistics are of limited use. Statisticians could not have written the Declaration of Independence or the Constitution of the United States, and statisticians should not be depended upon to interpret them.

A.2 Views on Statistical Inference

Rule 401 of the Federal Rules of Evidence provides the following definition of relevance:

> "Relevant evidence" means evidence having any tendency to make the existence of any fact that is of consequence to the determination of the action more probable or less probable than it would be without the evidence.

From this rule one might infer that the court wishes and expects to have its judgments about facts at issue to be expressed in terms of probabilities. Such a situation is tailor-made for the application of Bayes' Theorem and the Bayesian form of statistical inference in connection with evidence. Thus some have characterized the Bayesian approach as *what the Court needs and often thinks it gets*. Rule 401 has traditionally been thought of, in much less sweeping terms, as being applicable only to the admission of evidence and not to its use in reaching judgments, even though the evidence is admitted to aid the fact finder in reaching judgments.

Our review of the use of statistical assessments as evidence in the courts suggests that, with some special exceptions, such as the use of blood group analyses in paternity cases, *what the court actually gets* is a frequentist or "classical" approach to statistical inference. Such an approach is difficult to reconcile with the language of Rule 401 (but see the discussion in Lempert, 1977, and Tiller, 1983). The key weapon in the frequentist's arsenal of statistical techniques is the test of significance whose result is often expressed in terms of a *p-value*. There is a tendency for jurists, lawyers, and even expert statistical witnesses to misinterpret p-values as if they were probabilities associated with facts at issue (see the discussion of this issue in the case study in Section 2.6).

In this section, we describe the two approaches to statistical inference: the Bayesian approach and the frequentist approach. Then we discuss the interpretation of p-values and their relationship or lack thereof to the tail values that are interpretable as probabilities in a Bayesian context.

The Basic Bayesian Approach

Suppose that the fact of interest is denoted by G. In a criminal case, G would be the extent that the accused is legally guilty, and for specificity we speak of the event G as guilt and of its complement $\bar{G}$ as innocence or nonguilt.

Following Lindley (1977) and Fienberg and Kadane (1983), we let H denote all of the evidence presented up to a certain point in the trial, and E denote new evidence. We would like to update our assessment of the probability of G given the evidence H, i.e., $P(G \mid H)$, now that the new evidence E is available. This is done via Bayes' Theorem, which states that:

$$P(G \mid E\&H) = \frac{P(G \mid H)P(E \mid G\&H)}{P(G \mid H)P(E \mid G\&H) + P(\bar{G} \mid H)P(E \mid \bar{G}\&H)}.$$

All of these probabilities represent subjective assessments of individual degrees of belief. As a distinguished Bayesian statistician once remarked: coins don't have probabilities, people do. It is also important to note that for the subjectivist there is a symmetry between unknown past facts and unknown future facts. An individual can have probabilities for either.

The well-known relationship of Bayes' Theorem is more easily expressed in terms of the odds on guilt, i.e., the ratio of the probability of guilt, G, to the probability of innocence (or nonguilt), $\bar{G}$:

$$\text{odds } (G \mid E\&H) = \frac{P(E \mid G\&H)}{P(E \mid \bar{G}\&H)} \times \text{odds } (G \mid H).$$

Lempert (1977, p.1023), notes that

> This formula describes the way knowledge of a new item of evidence (E) would influence a completely rational decision maker's evaluation of the odds that a defendant is guilty (G). Since the law assumes that a factfinder *should* be rational, this is a normative model; that is, the Bayesian equation describes the way the law's ideal juror evaluates new items of evidence.

In this sense Bayes' Theorem provides a normative approach to the issue of relevance. One might now conclude that when the likelihood ratio

$$\frac{P(E \mid G\&H)}{P(E \mid \bar{G}\&H)}$$

for an item of evidence differs from one, the evidence is relevant in the sense of Rule 401. Lempert (1977) refers to this as *logical relevance*.

Now, the way to incorporate assessments of the evidence in a trial is clear. The trier of fact (a judge or juror) begins the trial with an initial assessment of the probability of guilt, $P(G)$, and then updates this assessment using either form of Bayes' Theorem given above, with each piece of evidence. At the end of the trial, the posterior estimate of G given all of the evidence is used to reach a decision. In the case of a jury trial, the jurors may have different posterior assessments of G, and these will need to be combined or reconciled in some way. This Bayesian prescription is simple and alluring, yet its implementation in actual legal settings is rare. A problem often cited is the difficulty in calculating the likelihood ratio, although, in many legal problems for which a frequentist approach is used, the likelihood ratio determination is often straightforward. A much greater problem is the reluctance of parties in a legal case to express prior probabilities, $P(G)$ and $P(\bar{G})$, in the absence of evidence at the beginning of a trial.

Lempert (1977) describes ways in which Bayes' Theorem can also be used to help understand aspects of the law relating to the discretion that courts have to exclude relevant evidence when the jury is likely to give it undue weight as well the reluctance of the court to exclude highly probative evidence. He also argues (p.1025):

> There are aspects of, and justifications for, the relevance rules that have nothing to do with the rational evaluation of evidence. As with almost any other area of law, values that defy quantification must be attended to in analyzing relevance.

Tiller, in his revision of *Wigmore on Evidence* (1983), goes much further and argues, inappropriately it is suggested, against reliance on the Bayesian perspective, indicating that (p.1072):

> Its principal defect is its failure to adequately account for the fashion in which a fact-finder in fact uses a complex of assumptions, beliefs, theories, and received or self-developed perspectives in his evaluation of the degree to which an item of evidence adds force to the probability of some fact in issue.

Yet to many there is no inconsistency between adoption of the Bayesian approach and a recognition of the fact that a trier's assessment of probabilities may involve a highly subjective component.

Later in this appendix, there is a detailed discussion of both the relationship between these prior probabilities and such legal phrases as "innocent until proven guilty" and how the posterior odds should relate to findings in a case. The description here is intended only to give the flavor of the Bayesian approach and extensions are required to deal with facts at issue that are not immediately expressible as one of a series of alternatives such as guilt or innocence, e.g., amount of damages. The basic concepts, however, remain the same. For some detailed proposals for the use of the Bayesian approach in the evaluation of forensic evidence see Evett (1984, 1986, 1987) and Makov (1987). Berry and Geisser (1986) discuss the use of Bayesian inference in cases of disputed paternity.

The Basic Frequentist Approach

The cornerstone to the frequentist approach to statistics is that statistical analysis must be based on a frequency concept of probability. As such it adopts, as a basis for the assessment and construction of statistical procedures, the long-term behavior of the procedures under repeated sampling under identical circumstances. Thus the probability interpretation in the frequentist approach lies in the procedure used and not in the outcome observed in one of an infinite sequence of repetitions.

The frequentist approach to inference contains a variety of approaches and procedures for testing and estimation. One of the most commonly used statistical procedures in the frequentist approach is the significance test. Its general structure is as follows (Kruskal, 1978a: 944):

> A significance test starts with observations and with a hypothesis about the chance mechanism generating the observations. From the observations a *test statistic* is formed. Large values of the test statistic (or small values, or both, depending on circumstances) lead to strong skepticism about the hypothesis, whereas other values of the test statistic are held to be in conformance with the hypothesis. Choice of the test statistic usually depends upon the alternatives to the hypothesis under test.

The key concept is that if the hypothesis (often called the *null hypothesis*) is really true, then values of the test statistic more extreme than some critical value would occur with low frequency under repeated generation of observations "like those actually produced" and the subsequent recalculation of the test statistic. This frequency or probability is the level of significance of the test. In this context a significance test can be viewed as a procedure, agreed on beforehand, that will result in one of two conclusions (or actions or viewpoints): if the test statistic is more extreme than the critical value, one tends to act as if the null hypothesis is false; otherwise one tends to act in some different way, not necessarily as if the null hypothesis is true but at least as if its falsity is not proved.

Interpretation: Suppose the hypothesis is that the mean value of the test statistic for a population is equal to some standard. Then if one rejects the equality of the mean of the test statistic with the standard using a 5% level of significance, one cannot say that the probability is 0.95 that the mean of the statistic does not equal the standard. All one can say is that if the mean of the statistic and standard were equal, a difference smaller than that observed would occur at least 95% of the time in repeated sampling. As a practical matter, one does not suppose that the mean exactly equals the standard, to many decimal places, but rather that they might be near enough to each other that compared with sampling variation their difference seems small.

Associated with the frequentist technique of significance tests is the computation of that level of significance at which the observed statistics would just lead to the rejection of the null hypothesis. The resulting observed level of significance or p-value is then a measure of surprise; the smaller the p-value, the more surprising the result if the null hypothesis is true. As Kruskal (1978b) notes:

Usually a very rough knowledge of the degree of surprise suffices, and various simplifying conventions have come into use. For example, if the observed significance level lies between .05 and .01, some authors say that the sample is *statistically significant*, while if it is less than .01, they call it *highly statistically significant*. The adverb "statistically" is often omitted, and this is unfortunate, since statistical significance of a sample bears no necessary relationship to possible subject-matter significance of whatever true departure from the null hypothesis might obtain.

One often meets a statement of significance testing that confusedly presents a p-value as if it were the probability of the null hypothesis, much as in the Bayesian approach. For example, certain investigators examining evidence in connection with the assassination of President John F. Kennedy drew the following conclusions on the basis of a test of significance: "the odds are less than 1 in 20 that the impulses and echoes were not caused by a gunshot from the grassy knoll, and at least 20 to 1 that they were." As a National Research Council's *Report of the Committee on Ballistic Acoustics* (1982) notes:

Even if the only alternative to impulses from a gunshot were the hypothesis of randomly located impulses, a single observed result whose P value under the random location hypothesis is 5% does not imply a 95% probability that there was gunfire from the knoll (the P value or significance level in current statistical theory is the probability, assuming the hypothesis to be true, of observing data as or more extreme than what actually is observed). The situation is analogous to that in a card game where the significance level for the dealer to receive three aces is $P = 0.044$ but 3 aces going to the dealer on the first deal does not by itself indicate a 95.6% probability that the dealer is dishonest if there were no prior reason for suspecting him of cheating. The issue of the probability of gunshots is one of posterior probability.

Another example of this misinterpretation of p-values—this time in a legal setting—is given by Whitmore (1986), in describing statistical evidence in a case, *Canadian Reynolds Metals Company* v. *Confederation des Syndicats Nationaux* in Quebec Superior Court. He notes that one of the defendant's experts interpreted a p-value of 20% in a chi-squared goodness-of-fit test for normality to mean that there was an 80% chance of the hypothesis being wrong.

In addition to the misinterpretation of a p-value as the probability of the truth of the null hypothesis, there is also a companion confusion that occurs in the implication that the null hypothesis must be one of random occurrence or of chance alone. Chance or randomness is a property describing, in a formal way, the fluctuations from one observation to another. The null hypothesis and alternatives to it focus on specific characterizations of chance mechanisms. While these misinterpretations or confusions are widespread in many different fields, they also occur in the context of legal disputes with high frequency, either explicitly or implicitly. For example, the following quotations come from reports submitted to the court by expert statistical witnesses in connection with *Vuyanich* v. *Republic National Bank*, which is the subject of a case study in Section 2.2 of this report:

> Since this "Z" statistic is distributed normally, if its absolute value is greater than 1.96, we can conclude that there is less than a 5% chance that the Republic and availability proportions would have been as far apart as they are from chance alone. (Plaintiffs' expert)

> This question is answered at a specified significance level, which is the largest probability that the estimate will be accepted as true when in fact it is due to chance or sampling variability. (Defendant's expert)

A.3   Standards of Proof

Considerable legal commentary has focused on the meaning of the standards of proof enunciated in Anglo-American law. This section provides a brief review of that commentary especially as it relates to attempts at quantification and the links of standards to the Bayesian decision-making framework.

The Criminal Standard

A juror or judge in a criminal case is typically asked to determine whether the defendant is guilty "beyond a reasonable doubt." Although this standard has been used for almost two hundred years in Anglo-American law (see Underwood, 1977), it was restated again in re *Winship*, 397 U.S. 358 (1970), in which the Supreme Court opinion stated that the "Due Process Clause protects the accused against conviction except upon proof beyond a reasonable doubt of every fact necessary to constitute the crime with which he is charged" (p.364). Underwood (1977), citing Morano, notes that the reasonable doubt formulation was actually intended to caution against the use of an impossibly high standard.

How does this standard get interpreted from the Bayesian decision-making perspective? There is reasonable agreement among commentators that the meaning of the standard can vary with the crime as well as with other aspects of the trial. In fact, there seems to be little discussion of whether the standard should be interpreted by everyone in exactly the same manner. For these reasons, Fienberg and Kadane (1983) suggest that, for the jth juror (or judge) in a given case, the Bayesian approach need only assume the existence of a threshold probability, b_j, as yet unspecified. If juror j's probability that the defendant is guilty after seeing the evidence presented at the trial is written as $P_j(G \mid E)$, then, at a minimum, the injunction to find for guilt only if the defendant is guilty beyond a reasonable doubt can be represented by asking for a guilty vote from the jth juror (or verdict in the case of a judge), when, and only when $P_j(G \mid E) \geq b_j$. Legal commentary suggests that b_j should be well above $1/2$, perhaps quite close to 1.

In arguing against attempts to quantify standards of proof, Tribe (1971) states (p.1374):

> The [legal] system does *not* in fact authorize the imposition of criminal punishment when the trier recognizes a quantifiable doubt as to the defendant's guilt. Instead, the system dramatically—if imprecisely—insists upon as close an approximation to certainty as seems humanly attainable in the circumstances. The jury is charged that any "reasonable doubt," of whatever magnitude, must be resolved in favour of the accused. Such insistence on the greatest certainty that seems reasonably attainable can serve at the trial's end, like the presumption of innocence at the trial's start, to affirm the dignity of the accused and to display respect for his rights as a person—in this instance, by declining to put those rights in deliberate jeopardy and by refusing to sacrifice him to the interests of others.

But Tribe notes that the standard, if it were quantifiable, should not be interpreted to mean $P(G \mid E) = 1$. It is for this reason that the law uses "beyond a reasonable doubt" rather than "beyond any doubt."

The Bayesian paradigm has what is for some people the legally uncomfortable consequence that each juror is presumed to have some prior probability of guilt, $P_j(G)$ for juror j, before the evidence is heard. Whatever else "innocent until proven guilty" or "the presumption of innocence" may mean, it must imply that $P_j(G) < b_j$. Thus, in principle, a trial in which no evidence is presented would lead to the unanimous acquittal of the defendant.

The quantity $P_j(G)$ pertains to a particular trial. It can depend, however, on information about the nature of charges, as well as such external information as the percentage of defendants found to be guilty when charged with a similar crime. Again to quote from Tribe (1971:1370–1371):

> It may be that most jurors would suspect, if forced to think about it, that a substantial percentage of those tried for crime are guilty as charged. And that suspicion might find its way unconsciously into the behaviour of at least some jurors sitting

in judgment in criminal cases. But I very much doubt that this
fact alone reduces the "presumption of innocence" to a useless
fiction. The presumption retains force not as a *factual* judgment,
but as a *normative* one—as a judgment that society *ought* to
speak of accused men as innocent, and *treat* them as innocent,
until they have been properly convicted after all they have to
offer in their defense has been carefully weighed.

The doctrine of a "presumption of innocence" presents a special difficulty,
from a Bayesian viewpoint, only if this is taken to mean that $P_j(G) = 0$.
Then, no evidence E could ever persuade a juror that $P_j(G \mid E) > 0$.
Thus, Fienberg and Kadane (1983) conclude that the presumption must
mean something else, and settle on the least restrictive interpretation.

The Civil Standard

The standards of proof in a civil case are different from those in a criminal case, as is the status of the parties involved. A juror or judge is required
to find for the plaintiff if such a finding is supported by "a preponderance
of the evidence," "more probable than not," or a "balance of probabilities."
The first term is the most common phrase used in the United States, while
the latter ones are more common in England and Australia. As before, the
standard varies somewhat from trial to trial, and possibly from individual
to individual. What is clearly stated in most discussions is that this standard is lower than that for criminal cases. Thus the minimalist Bayesian
requirement is to assume for the jth juror (or judge) the existence of another threshold probability, d_j, also unspecified, such that

$$P_j(P \mid E) \geq d_j,$$

where d_j is some number satisfying

$$b_j > d_j > 1/2$$

and P is the event that the plaintiff's version of the issue in dispute is
correct (note that P is not quite the same as G in the criminal case).

The legal commentary suggests that d_j should be "close" to $1/2$, and it
is often stated that the legal theory of a civil case requires jurors to start
with the common prior probability

$$P_j(P) = 1/2.$$

Fienberg and Kadane (1983) note that while this may be a requirement in
some legal theories, it would be difficult at best to find a jury for whom
$P_j(P) = 1/2$ exactly for each juror. Since in the absence of evidence the
juror's decision should go to the defendant, Fienberg and Kadane argue
that the legal theories really presuppose $P_j(P) \leq 1/2$ rather than strict

equality. They also argue that, as a practical matter, jurors rarely hear a case without preconceptions, and the recent extensive use of juror selection techniques in civil cases shows the importance to the trial attorneys of trying to find jurors for civil cases whose preconceptions are favorable.

The classic cases of *Sargent* v. *Massachusetts Accident Co.* 307 Mass. 246, 29 N.E. 2d 825 (1940) and *Smith* v. *Rapid Transit Inc.* 317 Mass. 469, N.E. 2d 754 (1945) deal with the interpretation of the preponderance standard and are discussed at length by Finkelstein (1978).

Other Standards

In some situations, other standards of proof are invoked. For example, in deportation proceedings, federal courts require "clear, unequivocal, and convincing evidence," a standard that is usually interpreted as intermediate between preponderance and beyond a reasonable doubt. The Bayesian approach would thus postulate an intermediate threshold probability, c_j, for each juror such that

$$1 > b_j > c_j > d_j > 1/2.$$

Quantifying Standards

Among the attempts to quantify the standards of proof discussed above, the three most widely cited are the London School of Economics Jury Project, a series of studies on the United States by Simon, and an informal survey of judges reported on in the opinion of *United States* v. *Fatico*, 458 F.Supp. 388 (E.D.N.Y. 1978).

The London School of Economics Jury Project (1973) conducted the same mock trial of a rape case before 22 juries, varying only the instructions on the standard of proof. That study showed that of the individual jurors involved, 68 percent of the 44 jurors instructed on preponderance convicted the first of the two defendants while 41 percent convicted the second; 66 percent of the 142 jurors instructed on a reasonable doubt standard (not the one described above) convicted the first defendant and 32 percent the second, and 55 percent of the 71 jurors instructed in a sure and certain standard convicted the first and 18 percent convicted the second.

Simon and Mahan (1971) reported summary information on a series of three studies involving judges, jurors, and college students in connection with a mock trial and a mail survey. The comparison of the probability judgments of these three groups for the beyond a reasonable doubt and preponderance of evidence standards (in general) is summarized in Table A.1. A probability scale with 0.05 increments was used. For the preponderance standard, over half the judges responded with the judgment 0.55 (the smallest allowable value greater than 1/2) but only 4.3 percent of jurors and 4.6 percent of students did so. The distributions for the jurors and students were thus shifted toward higher probabilities. For the beyond a reasonable doubt standard, all three groups were similar, with over 30 percent in each putting the probability at 1.0. The lack of gradations in the range from 0.9 to 1.0 make interpretation of these more extreme judgments difficult.

In the *Fatico* case, there was some question regarding what the standard of proof should be, and the judge in his opinion reported on an informal survey of the judges in his district court regarding the probabilities that they associated with four different standards ranging from preponderance to beyond a reasonable doubt (see Table A.2). For these judges the rank order of thresholds is as predicted, with preponderance being associated by all with slightly more than 0.5. This is in agreement with the Simon and Mahan study. Nine of the ten judges, however, placed beyond a reasonable doubt between .75 and .90, with none suggesting the unacceptable (to a Bayesian) value of 1.0.

In both the Simon and Mahan study and the *Fatico* opinion, the data show considerable variation among probability judgments and (except for the somewhat anomalous values of 1.0 for beyond a reasonable doubt) they can be intepreted as being roughly consistent with the minimalist Bayesian position described above.

A.4   Pascalian Versus Baconian Probability

L. Jonathan Cohen, an English philosopher, has strongly criticized the assumption that the usual rules of probability, which follow from either the frequentist or the Bayesian approaches, are the kinds of probabilities that are involved in decision making by judges or juries (see Cohen, 1977). According to Cohen, the traditional form of mathematical probability, which Cohen labeled "Pascalian," suffers from six basic difficulties:

1 *The difficulty of conjunction.* If a case is such that the plaintiff is required to prove each of several issues "on the balance of probability," then they must all be established at a very high level if their conjunction is, through the use of the product rule, also to be established on the balance of probability.

2 *The difficulty of inference upon inference.* Where a proof in a civil case involves a sequence of dependent issues, courts normally insist that each tier prior to the final one should rest on proof beyond a reasonable doubt, but the usual rules of probability do not require this in order for the conjunction to be a certain level, such as on the balance of probabilities.

3 *The difficulty of negation.* Probability theory requires that an event and its negation have probabilities that add to 1, and this would lead to situations in which a plaintiff's case succeeds

TABLE A–1: Distributions of Probability Judgments
for Two Standards of Proof by Judges, Jurors, and Students
(Simon and Mahan, 1971)

Probability	Preponderance Standard			Beyond a Reasonable Doubt Standard		
	Judges	Jurors	Students	Judges	Jurors	Students
0.0–0.5	0.6%	2.9%	1.1%	–	7.2%	3.4%
0.50	0.9%	4.3%	4.6%	0.3%	8.7%	2.3%
0.55	55.1%	7.2%	1.1%	0.6%	2.9%	1.1%
0.60	20.7%	4.3%	10.3%	2.3%	5.8%	1.1%
0.65	4.2%	2.9%	3.4%	0.6%	1.4%	
0.70	4.5%	5.8%	19.5%	4.0%	2.9%	1.1%
0.75	5.1%	21.7%	12.6%	6.6%	2.9%	1.1%
0.80	1.8%	17.4%	14.9%	16.7%	11.6%	10.2%
0.85	1.2%	1.4%	4.6%	6.1%	2.9%	3.4%
0.90	1.8%	17.4%	16.1%	19.6%	13.0%	23.9%
0.95	1.2%	2.9%	5.7%	12.7%	4.3%	19.3%
1.00	3.0%	11.6%	5.7%	30.5%	36.2%	34.1%
Sample Size	334	69	87	347	69	88
Nonrespondents	17	–	1	4	–	–

TABLE A–2: Probabilities Associated with Different
Standards of Proof by Judges in Eastern
District of New York (United States v. Fatico)

Judge	Preponderance (%)	Clear and convincing (%)	Clear, unequivocal, and convincing (%)	Beyond a reasonable doubt (%)
1	50+	60–70	65–75	80
2	50+	67	70	76
3	50+	60	70	85
4	51	65	67	90
5	50+	Standard is elusive and unhelpful		90
6	50+	70+	70+	85
7	50+	70+	80+	95
8	50.1	75	75	85
9	50+	60	90	85
10	51	Cannot estimate numerically		

under the civil standard of "more probable than not" if the
probability of the evidence is only 0.501.

4 *The difficulty about proof beyond reasonable doubt.* This standard of proof is not capable of being assessed using mathematical probability.

5 *The difficulty about a criterion.* To suppose that jurors should
evaluate proofs in terms of a coherent betting policy is to ignore the fact that rational people will not bet on issues if the
outcome is not discoverable. The structure of forensic proof can
be better analyzed using a kind of probability that makes no
such requirements.

6 *The difficulty about corroboration and convergence.* Two items
of evidence converge if they are independent and together they
raise the probability of a judicial outcome more than either
would alone. Mathematical probability cannot account for this
phenomenon without taking into account the prior probability
of the judicial outcome. Such positive prior probabilities are
legally inadmissible.

Given that the use of the terms of standards of proof in the common law
tradition predate the development of a coherent theory of probability, it

should not be surprising to find that the informal use of probabilistic language might contradict the rules of the theory, especially since those using this informal language typically have little or no training in probability. Thus as Eggleston (1983) notes, "where the classical rules [of probability] appear to have been contradicted, it is as likely that this has happened through ignorance as that it is the consequence of a deliberate decision that they should not apply."

After describing his six difficulties, Cohen goes on to present what he calls a theory of "Baconian" probability in which the probabilities do not obey the usual rules, and Cohen concludes that the probabilities applied by the courts are generally Baconian rather than Pascalian. This conclusion is based on qualitative reasoning, since Cohen does not really develop any statistical theory of inference to his Baconian system.

Others have critiqued Cohen's Baconian system and his criticisms of the usual theory of probability (see, for example, Dawid, 1987, Fienberg and Schervish, 1986, Kaye, 1979, 1981, Kahneman and Tversky, 1978, and the commentary on Cohen's paper in *The Behavioral and Brain Sciences* in 1981). Eggleston (1983) provides an excellent rebuttal to Cohen primarily from a legal perspective. The primary technical shortcomings of Cohen's arguments stem from confusion between the probabilities of evidentiary events and probabilities associated with factual propositions such as guilt and innocence, confusion over the meaning of conditioning, a misrepresentation of what the Bayesian approach to various problems might be, and the fact that beneath several of his "difficulties" is his denial of the fundamental aspects of the Bayesian approach. It is little wonder that based on these difficulties he rejects the coherent Bayesian framework in favor of his own incoherent one.

Some members of the panel strongly endorse the Bayesian approach, and others the frequentist one. The panel as a whole saw little reason to abandon the usual rules of probability theory on the basis of Cohen's criticisms. Thus, without choosing between the Bayesian and frequentist schools, this report discusses the uses of statistical approaches and probability in legal settings that conform with the usual rules of probability. By not endorsing the full Bayesian decision-making approach, the panel has chosen to distinguish between issues of a statistical nature in litigation and statistical approaches to legal decision making, a distinction also made by legal commentators such as Tribe (1971). This report deals primarily with the former.

A.5   Annotated Bibliography on Selected Topics in Statistical Methodology

(i) Introductory Texts and General Purpose References

Freedman, D., Pisani, R., and Purves, R. (1978). *Statistics*. Norton: New York.

> A well-written introduction on how to think statistically. Emphasizes the importance of formal randomization devices—box models—to statistical inference. Covers aspects of simple linear regression, one-sample t-tests, and chi-square tests for 2×2 tables.

Mosteller, F., Fienberg, S.E., and Rourke, R.E.K. (1983). *Beginning Statistics with Data Analysis*. Addison-Wesley: Reading, MA.

> A nonmathematical introduction to statistical methodology and inference, through the extensive use of real examples. Includes a discussion on alternative methods for data collection. Covers exploratory data analysis, two-sample comparisons, chi-square tests, multiple regression analysis, the analysis of variance (ANOVA), and nonparametric statistics.

Mosteller, F., Rourke, R.E.K., and Thomas, G.B., Jr. (1970). *Probability with Statistical Applications*, 2nd ed. Addison-Wesley: Reading, MA.

> A classic introduction to basic ideas in probability and statistics. Rigorous but elementary derivation of most results with many examples. Includes introduction to regression and two-sample binomial tests. Referred to in Supreme Court decision in *Castaneda* v. *Partida*.

Box, G.E.P., Hunter, Wm.G., and Hunter, J.S. (1978). *Statistics for Experimenters*. Wiley: New York.

> Careful exposition on the experimental approach to statistical data collection and related method of analysis. Emphasizes experiments for comparing two or more treatments and for measuring effects of variables (factorial and fractional factorial designs and response surface methodology).

Everitt, B.S. and Dunn, G. (1983). *Advanced Methods of Data Exploration and Modelling.* Heinemann: London.

> Intermediate text on statistical methodology that includes brief introductions to various techniques in multivariate analysis, including: multidimensional scaling, cluster analysis, generalized linear models, regression and ANOVA, log-linear and logistic models, models for time-dependent data, and factor analysis.

Kruskal, Wm. H. and Tanur, J.M., *eds.* (1978). *International Encyclopedia of Statistics (2 volumes).* Macmillan: New York.

> Contains discursive articles on virtually all major statistical topics and areas of statistical methodology. Each article has an extended bibliography.

(ii) Regression Analysis

Chatterjee, S. and Price, B. (1977). *Regression Analysis by Example.* Wiley: New York.

> An easy-to-read yet concise introduction to multiple regression that stresses underlying assumptions, graphical methods for residual analysis, and the use of computer-based approaches to variable selection.

Draper, N.R. and Smith, H. (1981). *Applied Regression Analysis (2nd ed.).* Wiley: New York.

> Provides a basic course in multiple linear regression with derivations of most results. Includes a discussion of residual analysis, computer-based variable selection methods, and nonlinear regression.

Weisberg, S. (1980). *Applied Linear Regression.* Wiley: New York.

> A thorough and modern treatment of multiple linear regression, complete with mathematical derivations and an up-to-date review of approaches to residual analysis and related inference problems.

(iii) Econometrics

Kmenta, J. (1971). *Elements of Econometrics.* Macmillan: New York.

> One of the standard texts on statistical method in econometrics. Includes an introduction to statistical theory, an extended discussion of multiple regression analysis, and a variety of special topics such as errors in the variables, generalized linear regression, and simultaneous equation systems.

Pindyck, R.S. and Rubinfeld, D.L. (1982). *Econometric Models and Economic Forecasts*, 2nd ed. McGraw-Hill: New York.

> A detailed, example-filled introduction to multiple regression, econometric model building, econometric simulation, simultaneous equations, and time series analysis using autoregressive integrated moving average (ARIMA) models. Assumes a minimal mathematical background.

Wonnacott, R.J. and Wonnacott, T.H. (1979). *Econometrics*, 2nd ed. Wiley: New York.

> A basic introduction to econometrics divided into two parts. Part 1 assumes a minimal background and focuses primarily on multiple regression, time series analysis, and simultaneous equations. Part 2 presents more advanced discussions based on matrix algebra and vector geometry.

(iv) Categorical Data Analysis

Fienberg, S.E. (1980). *The Analysis of Cross-Classified Categorical Data*, 2nd ed. MIT Press: Cambridge, MA.

> A comprehensive introduction, for those with training in statistical methodology, to the analysis of categorical data using log-linear models and maximum likelihood estimation. Emphasis on methodology, with numerous examples and problems.

Fleiss, J.L. (1981). *Statistical Methods for Rates and Proportions*. Wiley: New York.

> An introduction to the analysis of categorical data with an emphasis on two-dimensional cross-classifications. Some discussion of combining evidence from several 2 × 2 tables.

Haberman, S.J. (1978). *Analysis of Qualitative Data, Vol. 1: Introductory Topics*. New York: Academic Press.
Haberman, S.J. (1979). *Analysis of Qualitative Data, Vol. 2: New Developments*. New York: Academic Press.

> A somewhat advanced, methodologically oriented, two-volume introduction to the analysis of categorical data via log-linear models, using maximum likelihood estimates computed via the Newton-Raphson algorithm. Vol. 1 examines complete cross-classifications, and Vol. 2 considers multinomial response models, logistic regression, incomplete tables, and related topics. Contains several examples.

Upton, G.J.G. (1978). *The Analysis of Cross-Tabulated Data.* New York: Wiley.

> A brief introduction to the analysis of contingency tables via log-linear models, and to measures of association. For those with some training in statistical methodology. Contains several examples.

(v) Survival Analysis

Cox, D.R. and Oakes, D. (1984). *Analysis of Survival Data.* Chapman Hall: New York.

> Succinct introduction to the analysis of survival data that moves swiftly from the basic concepts of failure times, censoring, and hazard functions through parametric, nonparametric, and proportional hazards models.

Kalbfleisch, J.D. and Prentice, R.L. (1980). *The Statistical Analysis of Failure Time Data.* Wiley: New York.

> Presents a unified approach to the analysis of survival data, primarily using the proportional hazards model. Contains a mix of applications and theoretical discussions.

(vi) Sampling

Cochran, Wm. G. (1963). *Sampling Techniques*, 2nd ed. Wiley: New York.

> A classic text on the design and analysis of sample surveys. Discusses basic approaches to sampling including clustering, stratification, and subsampling and includes several proofs of theoretical results.

Deming, W.E. (1960). *Sample Design in Business Research.* Wiley: New York.

> Contains an excellent introduction to concepts and issues in the use of sampling and to standards of statistical practice. Introduction includes an example of legal testimony related to sampling.

Kish, L. (1965). *Survey Sampling.* Wiley: New York.

> Discursive introduction to survey sampling of human populations, with special attention to methods used in large-scale survey work, such as area sampling and multistage sampling. Considerable discussion of practical problems.

Williams, B. (1978). *A Sampler on Sampling.* Wiley: New York.

Elementary introduction to concepts and principles of statistical sampling. Includes a brief chapter on how to design your own survey and criticize another survey. Focus is on understanding basic ideas.

(vii) Time Series

Abraham, B. and Ledolter, J. (1983). *Statistical Methods for Forecasting.* Wiley: New York.

An introduction to the use of statistical models and methods for short-term forecasts. Emphasis is on regression models, exponential smoothing, and ARIMA models.

Box, G.E.P. and Jenkins, G.M. (1976). *Time Series Analysis: Forecasting and Control.* Holden-Day: San Francisco.

A classic description of the use of time domain models for the analyses of time series analysis (ARIMA models). Somewhat mathematical descriptions. Includes thoughtful discussions of model building, forecasting, and diagnostic checking. Methods are applied to several different examples.

Chatfield, C. (1980). *The Analysis of Time Series: An Introduction,* 2nd ed. Chapman and Hall: New York.

Concise introduction to concepts of time series analysis, emphasizing the use of simple descriptive techniques as well as ARIMA models and spectral analysis. Includes theoretical discussion and extensive mathematical notation.

Nelson, C.R. (1973). *Applied Time Series Analysis for Managerial Forecasting.* Holden-Day: San Francisco.

An elementary introduction to the analysis of univariate time series using ARIMA models. Good examples and exercises.

Appendix B

Brief Historical Survey of the Legal Uses of Probability and Statistics Prior to 1970

No comprehensive study exists of the legal applications of mathematical probability and statistics. Such a study would have to grapple with the fact that three distinct periods are discernible. Prior to World War II, legal applications of probability and statistics were few in number and often viewed with suspicion. After the war, the increasing scientific, industrial, and social use of statistical methods resulted, in certain areas, in their gradual legal acceptance, particularly in the case of sampling. Beginning in the 1970s, however, for reasons that are not entirely clear, this cautious approach was abandoned, and the last decade has witnessed a sharp increase in use by attorneys and judges of statistical methods of data collection, analysis, and inference. The following brief survey is highly selective and limited to the first two of these periods.

The recognition of the probabilistic nature of legal inference can be traced back to antiquity. In recent years several scholars have pointed to a rudimentary form of probabilistic inference present in ancient Talmudic law (Hasofer, 1969; Sternberg, 1970: xl; Rabinovitch, 1973), although some of the strongest claims made must be viewed with caution; see, e.g., Zabell (1976). Explicit discussion of the uncertain nature of judicial proof may likewise be found in the writings of the Roman legal orators Cicero and Quintilian; see Garber and Zabell (1979) for references and discussion.

Thus it is hardly surprising that, when the probability calculus was initially developed in the second half of the seventeenth century, both Leibniz and Jacob Bernoulli immediately recognized its potential legal applications (Hacking, 1975; Schneider, 1981). Indeed, Leibniz's interest in probability stemmed directly from his knowledge of continental civil law, which had a highly developed but artificial classification for degrees of proof. To develop the subject, Leibniz planned (but never wrote) a work in which lawyers would be presented as models of probability logic in "contingent" questions. Bernoulli devoted a considerable fraction of the fourth part of his *Ars Conjectandi* (1713) to a probabilistic analysis of the cumulative force of circumstantial evidence (Hacking, 1975: Chapter 16; Shafer, 1978; Garber and Zabell, 1979), and his nephew, Nicholas Bernoulli, continued the program, in a 1709 essay, applying the new calculus of probabilities to problems such as the presumption of death, the value of annuities, marine insurance, the veracity of testimony, and the probability of innocence.

In France such attempts became fashionable, and during the eighteenth and nineteenth centuries the legal uses of mathematical probability were discussed by Voltaire, Condorcet, Laplace, Lacroix, Poisson, Cournot, Guibert, and Bienaymé (Gillispie, 1972; Gelfand and Solomon, 1973; Baker, 1975; Heyde and Seneta, 1977; Pearson, 1978).

These initial attempts were largely theoretical and, except for Poisson's studies of jury size, had little impact on or interest for the legal profession. But across the channel, beginning in the nineteenth century, a series of English evidence texts began to refer to the new mathematical theory in discussions of the nature of proof and circumstantial evidence. As the efforts to provide a coherent theoretical justification for the reliance in English law on circumstantial evidence were written shortly after Laplace had reshaped the "doctrine of chances" into a sophisticated mathematical tool of widespread applicability, the authors of these evidence texts naturally gave serious consideration to whether the numerical quantification of evidence might aid in its assessment.

Jeremy Bentham appears to have been the first jurist to seriously propose that witnesses and judges numerically estimate their degrees of persuasion. Bentham (1827:225) envisioned a kind of moral thermometer:

> The scale being understood to be composed of ten degrees—in the language applied by the French philosophers to thermometers, a decigrade scale—a man says, My persuasion is at 10 or 9, &c. affirmative, or at least 10, &c. negative ....

Bentham's proposal was greeted with something just short of ridicule, in part on the pragmatic grounds of its inherent ambiguity and potential misuse, and in part on the more fundamental ground that legal probabilities are incapable of numerical expression. Thomas Starkie (1833) was merely the most forceful when he wrote:

> The notions of those who have supposed that mere moral probabilities or relations could ever be represented by numbers or space, and thus be subjected to arithmetical analysis, cannot but be regarded as visionary and chimerical.

Starkie, himself the author of a famous text on evidence, posed a hypothetical strikingly similar to the famous *Collins* case of the 1960s (see the discussion of *People* v. *Collins* below) (Starkie, 1833:752):

> Let it, for instance, be supposed that A is robbed, and that the contents of his purse were one penny, two sixpences, three shillings, four half-crowns, five crowns, six half-sovereigns, and seven sovereigns, and that a person, apprehended in the same fair or market where the robbery takes place, found in possession of the same remarkable combination of coin can be iden-

tified, and that no circumstances operate against the prisoner except his possession of the same combination of coin.

One might question, as did Starkie, whether precise numerical probabilities can even be assigned to events such as these, or whether, as in *Collins*, the events in question are statistically independent (so that the probability of their joint occurrence could then be calculated by invoking the so-called product rule). But Starkie went even further, questioning whether this type of probabilistic evidence, by itself, could ever suffice to identify a person who had committed a crime (Starkie, 1833:752):

> Here, notwithstanding the very extraordinary coincidences as to the number of each individual kind of coin, although the circumstances raise a high probability of identity, yet it still is one of an indefinite and inconclusive nature . . . .

> To hold that any finite degree of probability shall constitute proof adequate to the conviction of a defender, would in reality be to assert, that out of some finite number of persons accused, an innocent man should be sacrificed for the sake of punishing the rest.

Indeed it would. Starkie in fact would appear to deny the inevitable element of fallibility in legal decision making, and thereby highlights a key dilemma that all legal systems must grapple with: the justification for state-imposed penalties when evidence is less than absolutely certain.

In the past some legal systems have attempted to cope with this problem by adopting the stance that their system effectively rules out uncertainty and fallibility: three examples are Talmudic, Imperial Chinese, and medieval canon law. The Talmud required the testimony of two eyewitnesses in a capital case, the Imperial Chinese system a written confession, and medieval canon law either two eyewitnesses or a confession. The Talmudic position is very clearly summarized by Maimonides (Rabinovitch, 1973:111):

> The 290th commandment is the prohibition to carry out punishment on a high probability, even close to a certainty . . . . No punishment [should] be carried out except where there are witnesses who testify that the matter is established in certainty beyond any doubt, and, moreover, it cannot be explained otherwise in any manner. If we do not punish on very strong probabilities, nothing can happen other than that a sinner be freed; but if punishment be done on probability and opinion it is possible that one day we might kill an innocent man—and it is better and more desirable to free a thousand sinners, than ever to kill one innocent.

Such criteria are unrealistic in any actually functioning system, and all three of the systems mentioned above, while giving lip service to their fail-safe mechanisms, employed devices for circumventing them in application. When strong circumstantial evidence pointed to the guilt of an accused, the Talmud permitted his confinement under harsh and life-threatening circumstances, while both Imperial Chinese and medieval canon law permitted the use of torture to extract the necessary confession. Thus, while all three systems laid claim to infallibility, these claims were in effect for public consumption, rather than descriptive of how they actually functioned.

The discussion of the possible applications of mathematical probability found in the early English evidence texts is wholly theoretical, and one must turn to American law for the first practical attempt to use statistics in the courtroom. In the famous Howland will case (*Robinson* v. *Mandell*, 20 Fed. Cas. 1027 (CCD Mass. 1868) No. 111, 959), the allegation was that two signatures on different pages of a will were so similar that one (which was contested) must have been traced from the other (which both parties agreed was genuine). In order to support this claim, counsel for the defense retained as an expert witness Benjamin Peirce, professor of mathematics at Harvard University and one of the first persons to contribute to the development of mathematical statistics in the United States. Peirce undertook to demonstrate by statistical means that the disputed signature was indeed a forgery; his method was to contrast the similarities between the disputed signature and the unquestioned original with the lesser degree of similarity to be found in 42 other signatures penned by Sylvia Ann Howland in her later years on other documents.

In addition to being an example, in many ways excellent, of the early use of formal statistical methods in a scientific and social setting, the Howland will case is an interesting early example of the perils and problems posed by the use of expert witnesses. In addition to Peirce, other witnesses who testified included Peirce's son (the philosopher Charles Sanders Peirce), the famed naturalist Louis Agassiz, and Oliver Wendell Holmes, Sr., Parkman professor of anatomy and physiology in the Medical School of Harvard University. Holmes's testimony was lucid and compelling until he was destroyed on cross-examination and forced to admit that he had only first examined the will the previous day. The elder Peirce, by contrast, was an assured and effective witness, who took on the role of advocate with relish, stating of a significance probability (Meier and Zabell, 1980:499):

> This number far transcends human experience. So vast an improbability is practically an impossibility. Such evanescent shadows of probability cannot belong to actual life. They are unimaginably less than those least things which the law cares not for.

Unfortunately for the record, Professor Peirce's demeanor and reputation as a mathematician must have been sufficiently intimidating to deter any serious mathematical rebuttal; he confessed a lack of any general expertise in judging handwriting but was not questioned on the numerical and mathematical aspects of his testimony.

Considered against the background of his era, Peirce's analysis was unusually clear and complete, even though—from a modern viewpoint—his findings were less compelling than he argued. But while Peirce's testimony was not deliberately misleading, the identification of an expert witness with the side he is testifying for, and the ability of mathematical evidence to paralyze critical examination, can both lead to what may be termed the problem of *numerical obscurantism*: the use of mathematical evidence in a deliberate attempt to overawe, confuse, or mislead the trier of fact. The infamous trial of Captain Alfred Dreyfus is a case in point. Dreyfus was alleged to have written a key document (Tribe, 1971):

> To identify the writing in the document as that of Dreyfus, the prosecution's witnesses reported a number of close matches between the lengths of certain words and letters in the document and the lengths of certain words and letters taken from Dreyfus' home. Obscure lexicographical and graphological "coincidences" within the document itself were said by the witnesses to indicate the high probability of its disguised character and of its use to convey coded information.

Several years later, a panel of mathematical experts appointed to review the evidence reported that, given the many word pairs available for selection, there was in fact nothing remarkable about the existence of the matches noted by the prosecution witnesses (Mode, 1963).

Both Howland and Dreyfus are early examples of the attempt to establish identity by applying mathematical probability. Attempts at establishing identity via the use of probability occur sporadically throughout early twentieth century American law, most notably in *People* v. *Risley* (214 N.Y. 75, 108 N.E. 200 (1915)). Several later cases of interest include *State* v. *Sneed*, 76 N.M. 349, 414 P.2d 858 (1966); *Miller* v. *State*, 240 Ark. 340, 399 S.W. 2d 268 (1966); *State* v. *Coolidge*, 109 N.H. 403, 260 A.2d 547 (1969) reversed on other grounds; and *Coolidge* v. *New Hampshire*, 403 U.S. 443 (1971). The key point of interest in *Risley* may be neither its rejection of the statistical evidence (which it said was "not based upon observed data, but was simply speculative, and an attempt to make inferences deduced from a general theory in no way connected with the matter under consideration"), nor its stated acceptance of actuarial calculations, but the distinction it drew between probabilistic prediction of future outcomes and the use of probability applied to unique past events.

The Howland and Risley cases were not without impact. Albert A. Osborn, an expert in the field of questioned documents, discussed both cases in his 1929 treatise *Questioned Documents* and cited with approval use of the so-called product rule for calculating joint probabilities, although he overlooked the necessity for the events in question to be statistically independent in order for the rule to be applicable. Similar discussions appeared in Wigmore's *Science of Judicial Proof* (1937) and McCormick's *Handbook of Evidence* (1954).

The most widely cited example of this form of identification evidence occurred in the case of *People* v. *Collins* (68 Cal. 2d 319, 438 P. 2d 33, 66 Cal. Rptr. 497 (1968) en banc). Finkelstein (1978) provides following summary (pp. 78–79):

> In *People* v. *Collins*, an elderly woman walking home in an alley in the San Pedro area of Los Angeles was assaulted from behind and robbed. The victim said that she managed to see a young woman with blond hair run from the scene. Another witness said that a Caucasian woman with dark-blond hair and a ponytail ran out of the alley and entered a yellow automobile driven by a black male with a mustache and beard. A few days later officers investigating the robbery arrested a couple on the strength of these descriptions and charged them with the crime. At their trial, the prosecution called an instructor of mathematics at a state college in an attempt to establish that, assuming the robbery was committed by a Caucasian blonde with a ponytail who left the scene in a yellow car accompanied by a black man with a beard and mustache, the probability was overwhelming that the accused were guilty because they answered to this unusual description. The prosecutor then had the witness assume the following individual probabilities of the relevant characteristics:
>
> | | |
> |---|---|
> | Yellow automobile | 1/10 |
> | Man with mustache | 1/4 |
> | Girl with ponytail | 1/10 |
> | Girl with blond hair | 1/3 |
> | Black man with beard | 1/10 |
> | Interracial couple in car | 1/1000 |
>
> Applying the product rule [previously described by the witness] to the assumed values, the prosecutor concluded that there would be but one chance in twelve million that a couple selected at random would possess the incriminating characteristics. The jury convicted. On appeal, the Supreme Court of California reversed, holding that the trial court should not have admitted the evidence pertaining to probability (citations omitted).

Note that the unhappy prosecutor in *Collins*, who calculated that there was only a 1 in 12 million chance of the Collins couple being innocent, was merely following the advice and example of eminent legal authorities.

What set the *Collins* case apart from the previously cited attempts to establish identity mathematically was that, unlike some cases in which the issue was decided on other, technical grounds (e.g., Howland), dismissed out of hand, or excluded for other reasons, the *Collins* decision took the attempt seriously. After pointing out several basic errors in the testimony itself (the lack of empirical support for the probabilities used, the unsupported and faulty assumption of independence, and the misinterpretation of the calculated significance probability), the Supreme Court of California decision goes on to discuss at length the relevance of such evidence had it *not* been marred by the prosecution's errors. The first thoughtful attempt at assessing the utility of mathematical probability in establishing identity, *Collins* spawned a law review literature that, if largely theoretical and without practical impact, may have had some role in raising the consciousness of the legal profession about the possibility of employing statistical methods of proof more generally.

Thus, in the domain of identification evidence, the courts have been reluctant, despite the encouragement of distinguished authorities, to admit probability calculations purporting to establish identity. In this instance the intuitive skepticism of the courts has served well as a buffer against overenthusiastic adoption of "sophisticated" methods that were actually inappropriate for the application urged.

An important exception to the judicial rejection of statistical evidence of identity is the assessment of paternity based on evidence of blood type. As nonstatistical evidence is inherently inconclusive in this domain, quantitative assessment of the statistical evidence is seen as more urgent. In addition, the statistical model on which the mathematical calculations are based has considerable support in the well-established applications of probability theory to the inheritance of genetic traits. The statistical analysis of paternity may be traced to important papers of the Polish mathematicians Steinhaus (1954) and Lukaszewicz (1955) and has seen increasing application since the development of the HLA system of antigenic identification (Ellman and Kaye, 1979).

The courts have also been reluctant, until recently, to accept statistical assessments in a far less controversial domain: the use of probability theory in scientific sampling. The rejection of sample survey evidence was usually justified with the claim that it violated the hearsay rule; Barksdale (1957) describes several cases in the 1920s and 1930s in which respondents in surveys were subpoenaed to testify in court. There was a gradual shift toward the acceptance of sample survey evidence in the early 1950s, especially in administrative settings, as in *U.S.* v. *United Shoe Machinery Corp.*, 110 F.Supp. 295 (D. Mass. 1953) (a market share case) and *Illinois Bell Telephone Co.*, 7 P.U.R. 3d 41, 606 Ill. Commerce Comm'n 493 (1955); see generally Zeisel (1960).

Beginning in the 1950s, with the increasingly common acceptance of sampling evidence, the number of cases in which this type of evidence appears sharply increased. Solomon (1971) reports that prior to 1950 there were only 8 cases in federal appellate courts involving disputed use of sample survey data as evidence in civil cases and none in criminal cases; during the 1950s this increased to 28 civil and 2 criminal cases. Nevertheless, as late as 1955, it is possible to find cases such as *Sears, Roebuck, & Co.* v. *City of Inglewood*, discussed in Chapter 4, in which an estimate of taxes overpaid, based on a sample of receipts, was ruled inadequate and a more costly complete audit required.

The courts were also initially reluctant to use the methods of statistical inference to assess evidence of jury discrimination. An important distinction must be made here between exclusion cases, in which no blacks, for example, are present on a sequence of grand or petit juries, and underrepresentation cases, in which some members of a group are represented, but the percentage is "substantially" lower than an appropriate population standard. The courts were at first much more inclined to attend to the statistical evidence in exclusion cases than in underrepresentation cases.

After articles by Finkelstein (1966) and Zeisel (1969) advocated and illustrated the relevant statistical techniques, references to computations of statistical significance first began to appear in footnotes to Supreme Court decisions, although the Court continued to insist, until *Castaneda* v. *Partida* 430 U.S. 482 (1977), that additional, nonstatistical evidence was necessary to prove the existence of discrimination. The use of statistical methods of proof in jury discrimination cases is of great historical interest because of their impact on the subsequent use of such methods in employment discrimination cases.

This selective review has focused primarily on a few paradigmatic instances of the direct use of statistical assessments as evidence and the use of statistical reasoning in judicial opinions. Often, however, statistical assessments will enter indirectly via expert testimony or court-submitted reports. For example, appellants in *Brown* v. *Board of Education*, 347 U.S. 483 (1954) appended to their briefs a report on the effects of segregation and the probable consequences of desegregation. The submitted report based several of its conclusions on statistical data (see, in particular, footnotes 10 and 11 of the decision). Another, more recent, example is the Supreme Court's repeated references to empirical data in its decisions on jury size; for a scathing review of the early cases, see Zeisel and Diamond (1974).

The enthusiastic judicial embrace of statistics in recent years tends to make one forget the limited, fragmentary, and suspicious approach exhibited by the same profession prior to 1960. But it is useful to remember that the science of statistics has itself undergone a tremendous expansion during the twentieth century, especially in the years after World War II. The recent and expanding resort to statistics by the courts may therefore be seen as merely the reflection and logical outcome of the now ubiquitous use of statistics in accounting, marketing, political science, psychology, economics, and throughout the social sciences generally.

Appendix C

The Federal Rules of Evidence

C.1 The Role of the Rules

The role of evidence at trial is conceptually a simple one. A judgment is reached by the fact finder based on evidence presented and only on that evidence. The rules of the court describe what evidence is "relevant" and admissible as well as grounds for the exclusion of relevant evidence. During the early 1970s the Federal Rules of Evidence were revised to codify and update court practice surrounding evidentiary issues. A majority of states have adopted these rules with minor variations. The revised Rules state general rules regarding the admissibility and the "relevance" of evidence and also focus on scientific evidence provided through expert testimony. Thus the revised Federal Rules of Evidence can be viewed as guidelines that can assist the court and the expert witness in a variety of ways.

Rule 102 indicates that the Rules are oriented toward truth ascertainment. Rules 401 to 403 define relevancy broadly to include any information that may affect the trier's assessment of the probability that a litigant's contentions are true. But these rules allow the court broad discretion to exclude evidence when prejudice outweighs probative force.

Rules 608 and 611–614 allow full cross-examination subject only to the court's power to protect the witness against harassment. Thus, the statistical expert on cross-examination may be subjected to a review of his background, motives, capability, and the basis for his conclusions.

It has been suggested by some that nonlawyer statistical experts be used to conduct cross-examination of experts in the same discipline (see, e.g., the discussions of this point in Saks and Van Duizend, 1983). Others argue that little is to be gained by this mode since, under current rules, the attorney conducting the cross-examination can be thoroughly briefed by the statistical expert he is relying on before and during the examination. To facilitate this more traditional approach, a substantial recess between direct and cross-examination may be afforded, on request, to permit consultation between attorney and expert. Of course, there may be instances in which one expert can elicit from another expert information of a technical nature and, if so, the court may allow this procedure. The court can, for example, encourage consultation among the experts both before and during the trial to avoid unnecessary disputes.

Rules 702 to 706 on opinions and expert testimony have considerably reduced barriers to full expert testimony. The expert will be permitted to testify if he or she "will assist" the trier in determining any fact in issue. While under the Frye doctrine (based upon the ruling in *Frye* v. *United States*, 293 F. 1013 (D.C. Cir. 1923)), the field of expertise of the witness must have some general scientific acceptance, this doctrine will almost never limit a statistical expert even if his or her particular statistical theories or methods of analysis are not generally accepted (Thomas, 1983). Qualification of an expert is determined by the judge and may be based on knowledge and skill, however acquired (Rule 703). It is unlikely that the court will exclude an expert because more qualified ones are available, but, of course, qualifications will be considered by the trier in deciding which expert to believe.

The expert may give testimony in the form of an opinion without disclosing the basis of the opinion unless the court requires otherwise (Rule 705). As a practical matter, the basis of the opinion is usually fully developed on direct examination so that the expert's testimony tends to be presented to the trier in the most effective and persuasive manner possible.

The materials relied on by the expert need not themselves be admissible as evidence so long as they are "of a type reasonably relied upon by experts in the particular field" (Rule 703) in forming such opinions—and the expert thus may provide this insight on what experts rely on to the judge. This rule permits a wide array of "hearsay," but if the data or analyses on which opinions are based are suspect or open to challenge on the grounds of unreliability, this fact should be, and often is, emphasized on cross-examination and argument to the jury.

The expert is not necessarily precluded from giving an opinion on the ultimate issue to be decided by the judge or jury—e.g., was the plaintiff's injury the result of exposure to the defendant's product (Rule 704). Generally, a less abstract opinion will be required—e.g., how likely was it that a person would be injured when exposed to a product under certain circumstances—leaving it to the judge or jury to draw the final inference.

Rules 803(17) and 803(18) allow the introduction into evidence of market reports, commercial publications, and learned treatises and articles. Rules 806 and 808 facilitate the introduction into evidence of business records and various government and other studies and reports. These exceptions are particularly useful both in presenting information to support an expert and in confronting an expert with opinions contrary to his or her own. Since it is difficult to prepare an expert for direct or cross-examination without some forewarning of what treatises and articles will be relied on, many federal courts require notice of their intended use before the trial begins.

The Federal Rules of Evidence have made it much easier to authenticate documents and to avoid the burdens of the best evidence rule requiring production of originals (Rule Articles IX and X). Thus computer printouts are readily admitted.

Court appointed nonparty experts are permitted in the court's discretion (Rule 706). This power is little used, since the adversarial presentation of information continues to operate with almost undiminished vigor. It may be desirable to utilize this power more fully in developing agreement on data bases for use in statistical analyses by the respective parties' experts. The prospective savings in money and the increased assurance in accuracy make this option particularly useful in statistics cases. The use of Rule 706 on court-appointed experts is discussed more fully in Chapter 5.

In short, the federal practice permits an expert to investigate and give an opinion with a minimum of hinderance.

C.2   Selected Rules

Rule 102. Purpose and Construction

These rules shall be construed to secure fairness in administration, elimination or unjustifiable expense and delay, and promotion of growth and development of the law of evidence to the end that the truth may be ascertained and proceedings justly determined.

Rule 201. Judicial Notice of Adjudicative Facts

(a) **Scope of Rule**. This rule governs only judicial notice of adjudicative facts.

(b) **Kinds of Facts**. A judicially noticed fact must be one not subject to reasonable dispute in that it is either (1) generally known within the territorial jurisdiction of the trial court or (2) capable of accurate and ready determination by resort to sources whose accuracy cannot reasonably be questioned.

(c) **When Discretionary**. A court may take judicial notice, whether requested or not.

(d) **When Mandatory**. A court shall take judicial notice if requested by a party and supplied with the necessary information.

(e) **Opportunity to be Heard**. A party is entitled upon timely request to an opportunity to be heard as to the propriety of taking judicial notice and the tenor of the matter noticed. In the absence of prior notification, the request may be made after judicial notice has been taken.

(f) **Time of Taking Notice**. Judicial notice may be taken at any stage of the proceeding.

(g) **Instructing Jury**. In a civil action or proceeding, the court shall instruct the jury to accept as conclusive any fact judicially noticed. In a criminal case, the court shall instruct the jury that it may, but is not required to, accept as conclusive any fact judicially noticed.

Rule 401. Definition of "Relevant Evidence"

"Relevant evidence" means evidence having any tendency to make the existence of any fact that is of consequence to the determination of the action more probable or less probable than it would be without the evidence.

Rule 402. Relevant Evidence Generally Admissible: Irrelevant Evidence Inadmissible

All relevant evidence is admissible, except as otherwise provided by the Constitution of the United States, by Act of Congress, by these rules, or by other rules prescribed by the Supreme Court pursuant to statutory authority. Evidence which is not relevant is not admissible.

Rule 403. Exclusion of Relevant Evidence on Grounds of Prejudice, Confusion, or Waste of Time

Although relevant, evidence may be excluded if its probative value is substantially outweighed by the danger of unfair prejudice, confusion of the issues, or misleading the jury, or by considerations of undue delay, waste of time, or needless presentation of cumulative evidence.

Rule 501. General Rule

Except as otherwise required by the Constitution of the United States or provided by Act of Congress or in rules prescribed by the Supreme Court pursuant to statutory authority, the privilege of a witness, person, government, State, or political subdivision thereof shall be governed by the principles of the common law as they may be interpreted by the courts of the United States in the light of reason and experience. However, in civil actions and proceedings, with respect to an element of a claim or defense as to which State law supplies the rule of decision, the privilege of a witness, person, government, State, or political subdivision thereof shall be determined in accordance with State law.

Rule 608. Evidence of Character and Conduct of Witness

(a) **Opinion and Reputation Evidence of Character**. The credibility of a witness may be attacked or supported by evidence in the form of opinion or reputation, but subject to these limitations: (1) the evidence may refer only to character for truthfulness or untruthfulness, and (2) evidence of truthful character is admissible only after the character of the witness for truthfulness has been attacked by opinion or reputation evidence or otherwise.

(b) **Specific Instances of Conduct**. Specific instances of the conduct of a witness, for the purpose of attacking or supporting his credibility, other than conviction of crime as provided in rule 609, may not be proved by extrinsic evidence. They may, however, in the discretion of the court, if probative of truthfulness or untruthfulness, be inquired into on cross-examination of the witness (1) concerning his character for truthfulness or untruthfulness, or (2) concerning the character for truthfulness or untruthfulness of another witness as to which character the witness being cross-examined has testified.

The giving of testimony, whether by an accused or by any other witness, does not operate as a waiver of his privilege against self-incrimination when examined with respect to matters which relate only to credibility.

Rule 611. Mode and Order of Interrogation and Presentation

(a) **Control by Court**. The court shall exercise reasonable control over the mode and order of interrogating witnesses and presenting evidence so as to (1) make the interrogation and presentation effective for the ascertainment of the truth, (2) avoid needless consumption of time, and (3) protect witnesses from harassment or undue embarrassment.

(b) **Scope of Cross-examination**. Cross-examination should be limited to the subject matter of the direct examination and matters affecting the credibility of the witness. The court may, in the exercise of discretion, permit inquiry into additional matters as if on direct examination.

(c) **Leading Questions**. Leading questions should not be used on the direct examination of a witness except as may be necessary to develop his testimony. Ordinarily leading questions should be permitted on cross-examination. When a party calls a hostile witness, an adverse party, or a witness identified with an adverse party, interrogation may be by leading questions.

Rule 612. Writing Used to Refresh Memory

Except as otherwise provided in criminal proceedings by section 3500 of title 18, United States Code, if a witness uses a writing to refresh his memory for the purpose of testifying, either—

(1) while testifying, or

(2) before testifying, if the court in its discretion determines it is necessary in the interests of justice, an adverse party is entitled to have the writing produced at the hearing, to inspect it, to cross-examine the witness thereon, and to introduce in evidence those portions which relate to the testimony of the witness. If it is claimed that the writing contains matters not related to the subject matter of the testimony the court shall examine the writing in camera, excise any portions not so related, and order delivery of the remainder to the party entitled thereto. Any portion withheld over objections shall be preserved and made available to the appellate court in the event of an appeal. If a writing is not produced or delivered pursuant to order under this rule, the court shall make any order justice requires, except that in criminal cases when the prosecution elects not to comply, the order shall be one striking the testimony or, if the court in its discretion determines that the interests of justice so require, declaring a mistrial.

Rule 613. Prior Statements of Witnesses

(a) **Examining Witness Concerning Prior Statement**. In examining a witness concerning a prior statement made by him, whether written or not, the statement need not be shown nor its contents disclosed to him at that time, but on request the same shall be shown or disclosed to opposing counsel.

(b) **Extrinsic Evidence of Prior Inconsistent Statement of Witness**. Extrinsic evidence of a prior inconsistent statement by a witness is not admissible unless the witness is afforded an opportunity to explain or deny the same and the opposite party is afforded an opportunity to interrogate him thereon, or the interests of justice otherwise require.

This provision does not apply to admissions of a party-opponent as defined in rule 801(d)(2).

Rule 614. Calling and Interrogation of Witnesses by Court

(a) **Calling by Court**. The court may, on its own motion or at the suggestion of a party, call witnesses, and all parties are entitled to cross-examine witnesses thus called.

(b) **Interrogation by Court**. The court may interrogate witnesses, whether called by itself or by a party.

(c) **Objections**. Objections to the calling of witnesses by the court or to interrogation by it may be made at the time or at the next available opportunity when the jury is not present.

Rule 615. Exclusion of Witnesses

At the request of a party the court shall order witnesses excluded so that they cannot hear the testimony of other witnesses, and it may make the order of its own motion. This rule does not authorize exclusion of (1) a party who is a natural person, or (2) an officer or employee of a party which is not a natural person designated as its representative by its attorney, or (3) a person whose presence is shown by a party to be essential to the presentation of his cause.

Rule 702. Testimony by Experts

If scientific, technical, or other specialized knowledge will assist the trier of fact to understand the evidence or to determine a fact in issue, a witness qualified as an expert by knowledge, skill, experience, training, or education, may testify thereto in the form of an opinion or otherwise.

Rule 703. Bases of Opinion Testimony By Experts

The facts or data in the particular case upon which an expert bases an opinion or inference may be those perceived by or made known to him at or before the hearing. If of a type reasonably relied upon by experts in the particular field in forming opinions or inferences upon the subject, the facts or data need not be admissible in evidence.

Rule 704. Opinion on Ultimate Issue

Testimony in the form of an opinion or inference otherwise admissible is not objectionable because it embraces an ultimate issue to be decided by the trier of fact.

Rule 705. Disclosure of Facts or Data Underlying Expert Opinion

The expert may testify in terms of opinion or inference and give his reasons therefor without prior disclosure of the underlying facts or data, unless the court requires otherwise. The expert may in any event be required to disclose the underlying facts or data on cross-examination.

Rule 706. Court Appointed Experts

(a) **Appointment**. The court may on its own motion or on the motion of any party enter an order to show cause why expert witnesses should not be appointed, and may request the parties to submit nominations. The court may appoint any expert witnesses agreed upon by the parties, and may appoint expert witnesses of its own selection. An expert witness shall not be appointed by the court unless he consents to act. A witness so appointed shall be informed of his duties by the court in writing, a copy of which shall be filed with the clerk, or at a conference in which the parties shall have opportunity to participate. A witness so appointed shall advise the parties of his findings, if any; his deposition may be taken by any party; and he may be called to testify by the court or any party. He shall be subject to cross-examination by each party, including a party calling him as a witness.

(b) **Compensation**. Expert witnesses so appointed are entitled to reasonable compensation in whatever sum the court may allow. The compensation thus fixed is payable from funds which may be provided by law in criminal cases and civil actions and proceedings involving just compensation under the fifth amendment. In other civil actions and proceedings the compensation shall be paid by the parties in such proportion and at such time as the court directs, and thereafter charged in like manner as other costs.

(c) **Disclosure of Appointment**. In the exercise of its discretion, the court may authorize disclosure to the jury of the fact that the court appointed the expert witness.

(d) **Parties' Experts of Own Selection**. Nothing in this rule limits the parties in calling expert witnesses of their own selection.

Rule 803. Hearsay Exceptions: Availability of Declarant Immaterial

The following are not excluded by the hearsay rule, even though the declarant is available as a witness:

(6) **Records of Regularly Conducted Activity**. A memorandum, report, record, or data compilation, in any form, of acts, events, conditions, opinions, or diagnoses, made at or near the time by, or from information transmitted by, a person with knowledge, if kept in the course of a regularly conducted business activity, and if it was the regular practice of that business activity to make the memorandum, report, record, or data compilation, all as shown by the testimony of the custodian or other qualified witness, unless the source of information or the method or circumstances of preparation indicate lack of trustworthiness. The term "business" as used in this paragraph includes business, institution, association, profession, occupation, and calling of every kind, whether or not conducted for profit.

(8) **Public Records and Reports**. Records, reports, statements, or data compilations, in any form, of public offices or agencies, setting forth (A) the activities of the office or agency, or (B) matters observed pursuant to duty imposed by law as to which matters there was a duty to report, excluding, however, in criminal cases matters observed by police officers and other law enforcement personnel, or (C) in civil actions and proceedings and against the Government in criminal cases, factual findings resulting from an investigation made pursuant to authority granted by law, unless the sources of information or other circumstances indicate lack of trustworthiness.

(17) **Market Reports, Commercial Publications**. Market quotations, tabulations, lists, directories, or other published compilations, generally used and relied upon by the public or by persons in particular occupations.

(18) **Learned Treatises**. To the extent called to the attention of an expert witness upon cross-examination or relied upon by him in direct examination, statements contained in published treatises, periodicals, or pamphlets on a subject of history, medicine, or other science or art, established as a reliable authority by the testimony or admission of the witness or by other expert testimony or by judicial notice. If admitted, the statements may be read into evidence but may not be received as exhibits.

Rule 901. Requirement of Authentication or Identification

(a) **General Provision**. The requirement of authentication or identification as a condition precedent to admissibility is satisfied by evidence sufficient to support a finding that the matter in question is what its proponent claims.

(b) **Illustrations**. By way of illustration only, and not by way of limitation, the following are examples of authentication or identification conforming with the requirements of this rule:

(1) **Testimony of Witness with Knowledge**. Testimony that a matter is what it is claimed to be.

(2) **Nonexpert Opinion on Handwriting**. Nonexpert opinion as to the genuineness of handwriting, based upon familiarity not acquired for purposes of the litigation.

(3) **Comparison by Trier or Expert Witness**. Comparison by the trier of fact or by expert witnesses with specimens which have been authenticated.

(4) **Distinctive Characteristics and the Like**. Appearance, contents, substance, internal patterns, or other distinctive characteristics, taken in conjunction with circumstances.

(5) **Voice Identification**. Identification of a voice, whether heard first-hand or through mechanical or electronic transmission or recording, by opinion based upon hearing the voice at any time under circumstances connecting it with the alleged speaker.

(6) **Telephone Conversations**. Telephone conversations, by evidence that a call was made to the number assigned at the time by the telephone company to a particular person or business, if (A) in the case of a person, circumstances, including self-identification, show the person answering to be the one called, or (B) in the case of a business, the call was made to a place of business and the conversation related to business reasonably transacted over the telephone.

(7) **Public Records or Reports**. Evidence that a writing authorized by law to be recorded or filed and in fact recorded or filed in a public office, or a purported public record, report, statement, or data compilation, in any form, is from the public office where items of this nature are kept.

(8) **Ancient Documents or Data Compilation**. Evidence that a document or data compilation, in any form, (A) is in such condition as to create no suspicion concerning its authenticity, (B) was in a place where it, if authentic, would likely be, and (C) has been in existence 20 years or more at the time it is offered.

(9) **Process or System**. Evidence describing a process or system used to produce a result and showing that the process or system produces an accurate result.

(10) **Methods Provided by Statute or Rule**. Any method of authentication or identification provided by Act of Congress or by other rules prescribed by the Supreme Court pursuant to statutory authority.

Rule 902. Self-Authentication

Extrinsic evidence of authenticity as a condition precedent to admissibility is not required with respect to the following:

(1) **Domestic Public Documents Under Seal**. A document bearing a seal purporting to be that of the United States, or of any State, district, Commonwealth, territory, or insular possession thereof, or the Panama

Canal Zone, or the Trust Territory of the Pacific Islands, or of a political subdivision, department, officer, of agency thereof, and a signature purporting to be an attestation or execution.

(2) **Domestic Public Documents Not Under Seal**. A document purporting to bear the signature in his official capacity of an officer or employee of any entity included in paragraph (1) hereof, having no seal, if a public officer having a seal and having official duties in the district or political subdivision of the officer or employee certifies under seal that the signer has the official capacity and that the signature is genuine.

(3) **Foreign Public Documents**. A document purporting to be executed or attested in his official capacity by a person authorized by the laws of a foreign country to make the execution or attestation, and accompanied by a final certification as to the genuineness of the signature and official position (A) of the executing or attesting person, or (B) of any foreign official whose certificate of genuineness of signature and official position relates to the execution or attestation or is in a chain of certificates of genuineness of signature and official position relating to the execution or attestation. A final certification may be made by a secretary of embassy or legation, consul general, consul, vice consul, or consular agent of the United States, or a diplomatic or consular official of the foreign country assigned or accredited to the United States. If reasonable opportunity has been given to all parties to investigate the authenticity and accuracy of official documents, the court may, for good cause shown, order that they be treated as presumptively authentic without final certification or permit them to be evidenced by an attested summary with or without final certification.

(4) **Certified Copies of Public Records**. A copy of an official record or report or entry therein, or of a document authorized by law to be recorded or filed and actually recorded or filed in a public office, including data compilations in any form, certified as correct by the custodian or other person authorized to make the certification, by certificate complying with paragraph (1), (2), or (3) of this rule or complying with any Act of Congress or rule prescribed by the Supreme Court pursuant to statutory authority.

(5) **Official Publications**. Books, pamphlets, or other publications purporting to be issued by public authority.

(6) **Newspapers and Periodicals**. Printed materials purporting to be newspapers or periodicals.

(7) **Trade Inscriptions and the Like**. Inscriptions, signs, tags, or labels purporting to have been affixed in the course of business and indicating ownership, control, or origin.

(8) **Acknowledged Documents**. Documents accompanied by a certificate of acknowledgment executed in the manner provided by law by a notary public or other officer authorized by law to take acknowledgments.

(9) **Commercial Paper and Related Documents**. Commercial paper, signatures thereon, and documents relating thereto to the extent provided by general commercial law.

(10) **Presumptions Under Acts of Congress**. Any signature, document or other matter declared by Act of Congress to be presumptively or prima facie genuine or authentic.

Rule 1002. Requirement of Original

To prove the content of a writing, recording, or photograph, the original writing, recording, or photograph is required, except as otherwise provided in these rules or by Act of Congress.

Rule 1003. Admissibility of Duplicates

A duplicate is admissible to the same extent as an original unless (1) a genuine question is raised as to the authenticity of the original or (2) in the circumstances it would be unfair to admit the duplicate in lieu of the original.

Appendix D

Expert Witnesses in Other Fields

When individuals from different fields of substantive knowledge have been called on to testify as expert witnesses in legal proceedings, there have been differing responses both by the courts and by their professional colleagues. Although the panel focused only on the role of statistical testimony, it found the following glimpses of the experienced experts from other fields to be informative.

D.1 Expert Testimony in Psychology

For many years, it has been routine for psychologists to be called on as expert witnesses to assist the jury in determining such facts as to whether a given person was mentally ill at the time a crime was committed, whether someone suffered psychological trauma as the result of an auto accident, or whether a defendant is competent to stand trial (these areas of expertise overlap with those of psychiatry, discussed below). But there is a new way in which psychologists have been called on to inform the triers of fact in a trial. It does not have to do with providing a clinical evaluation of individuals involved in legal cases, but rather with the offering of empirical information of a general sort derived from psychological research. In such cases, the contribution of the psychological expert consists of informing the jury or judge of empirical facts of which they may be unaware relating to the behavior of people in general, or at least to the behavior of large classes of people. The testimony does not speak directly to the behavior of a given person, such as a defendant or witness at the trial, as clinical testimony would, but indirectly includes such persons as specific instances of the general findings observed.

One member of the panel, for example, has testified on numerous occasions regarding the ability of people to perceive and recall complex events and to identify persons who they may have seen on a prior occasion (Loftus, 1979; Wells and Loftus, 1984). Such testimony grew in popularity during the 1970s, primarily because it presented lawyers with a means to deal with the problem of highly persuasive, but occasionally mistaken, eyewitnesses. Opposition to this form of testimony came primarily from some lawyers and judges. In particular, judges would often exclude the testimony for one of two legal reasons: (1) it invaded the province of the jury and (2) it was well within the common knowledge of the average juror and therefore not a proper subject matter for expert testimony.

One interesting consequence of this legal debate is that it sparked a new form of psychological research. The "common knowledge" exclusion led many researchers to want to evaluate the validity of the common understanding doctrine, that is, to find out exactly what ordinary citizens believe is true about the nature of perception and memory. Many such studies have now been completed and these generally show that there are areas in which citizens hold misconceptions about human information processing (see the article by Wells in Wells and Loftus, for a review). There is a belief among many that psychological expert testimony could profitably correct these misconceptions.

Despite the new research evidence, courts remained divided over whether to admit such expert testimony. In virtually all the cases in which a judge has prohibited the jury from hearing expert testimony, the higher courts have upheld the decision. They have found that the admission of the testimony is a matter of judicial discretion, and its exclusion is not an abuse of discretion. Two state court decisions departed from this stance: *State of Arizona* v. *Chapple*, 660 P.2d 1208 (Ariz. 1983) and *People of California* v. *McDonald*, 36 Crim. L. Rep. (BNA) 2201 (1984). In the first of these cases, defendant Dolan Chapple had been convicted of three counts of murder chiefly on the testimony of two witnesses who identified him over a year after the crimes. Chapple's lawyer tried to introduce expert psychological testimony on the accuracy of such identifications. The judge refused to permit the testimony on the grounds that it would pertain only to matters "within the common experience" of jurors. The Arizona Supreme Court disagreed, maintaining that expert testimony would have provided scientific data on such pertinent matters as the accuracy of delayed identification, the effect of stress on perception, and the relationship between witness confidence and accuracy. Chapple's conviction was reversed, and he was granted a new trial. In *MacDonald*, the California Supreme Court held that, under certain circumstances, trial courts would be in error if they exclude qualified expert testimony on eyewitness perception and memory.

In federal courts, two recent appellate rulings appear to support the admissibility of such psychological evidence. In *U.S.* v. *Smith*, 736 F.2d 1103 (6th Cir. 1984), the court held that expert testimony on the reliability of eyewitness identification met the "helpfulness" test of F.R.E. 702 and had therefore been improperly excluded. And more recently, in *U.S.* v. *Downing* (3rd Cir. 1985), the court remanded the case for a foundational hearing to determine if proffered evidence is relevant to the eyewitness testimony presented by the prosecution. The district court had originally refused to admit testimony of a psychologist offered by the defendant because the court believed that such testimony can never meet the "helpfulness" standard of F.R.E. 702. The defendant in this case was convicted solely on the basis of the testimony of 12 eyewitnesses who identified the defendant with varying degrees of confidence.

A recent attack on the use of psychological expert testimony on human perception and memory comes not from members of the legal field, but from psychologists themselves (McCloskey and Egeth, 1983). These psychologists have developed four major themes of attack. First, they argued that the empirical evidence documenting the need for expert testimony is weak at best. Second, even when it can be shown that jurors are fallible in the decisions they reach, they claim it has not been shown that psychological testimony can provide much beyond the intuitions of ordinary experience. Third, they say there is disagreement about the proper inferences to be drawn from the empirical data. Fourth, such testimony could in their view ultimately lead to a battle of experts that would make the profession look bad. Given this sorry state of affairs, they argue, experimental psychologists may do more harm than good by premature intrusion into court proceedings. The ensuing debate is still taking place.

D.2   Expert Testimony in Psychiatry

For many years, when a psychiatrist was called into court to testify in connection with mental disorders being suffered by someone accused of committing a crime, the witness inevitably appeared for the defense. Bazelon (1978) noted the lack of competent psychiatrists on both sides of a criminal case, and he encouraged involvement on the side of the prosecution with a request that psychiatrists "recognize and accede to the higher ethical framework of the adversarial system's search for justice" (Stone, 1984). The impact of this involvement is not what Bazelon had anticipated, and today the public and the courts have the image of the medical expert as "hired gun," so vividly portrayed in the press in some cases and in recent movies.

The trial of John Hinckley, Jr., who was accused of shooting President Ronald Reagan, presented an opportunity to overcome the negative image of the American forensic psychiatry community. Three psychiatrists testified as expert witnesses for the defense and two for the prosecution. Taken separately, each witness's testimony seemed plausible, but there were radical discrepancies between the defense and the prosecution psychiatrists' diagnoses. In the end, because the trial took place in federal district court, the prosecution had the burden of proving the defendant's sanity. In June 1982, the jury found Hinckley not guilty by reason of insanity.

The outcry was immediate. Congress made efforts to change the law on the insanity plea and the American Psychiatric Association (APA) reacted to the public and political outrage by proposing its own set of restrictions regarding psychiatric disorders and the insanity plea. As Stone (1984) describes the situation, a "basic theme of the APA's proposal was to get psychiatrists to practice psychiatry in the courtroom and not to try to practice law or morality. It was also hoped that if psychiatrists practiced psychiatry there might be less of a 'battle of experts' and more of the diagnostic reliability that psychiatrists have achieved with the APA's official *Diagnostic and Statistical Manual of Mental Disorders*, Third Edition."

In a review of a capital punishment case before the Supreme Court, *Barefoot* v. *Estelle*, 103 S.Ct. 3383 (1983), the APA filed an amicus curiae brief arguing that all testimony by psychiatrists on the likelihood of future violent conduct should be barred from U.S. courtrooms on constitutional grounds. Citing a review by Monahan (1981) and other studies, the APA claimed that two–thirds of the time psychologists and psychiatrists were inaccurate in their long-term predictions of violent behavior. The majority of the Court dismissed the APA's argument, noting that not all psychiatrists agreed with the APA's position—it was unwilling to totally exclude psychiatric testimony.

The debates over psychiatric expert testimony have raged for years, and Stone (1984) suggests there are four intellectual and ethical boundary problems that need to be addressed:

1 Does psychiatry have anything true to say to which the courts should listen?

2 There is the risk that a forensic psychiatrist will go too far and twist the rules of justice and fairness to help the patient.

3 There is the opposite risk that the forensic psychiatrist will deceive the patient in order to serve justice and fairness.

4 There is the danger that forensic psychiatrists will prostitute the profession, as they are alternatively seduced and assaulted by the power of the adversarial system.

Points (1) and (4) on this list are, not surprisingly, similar to McCloskey and Egeth's concerns about expert psychological testimony.

Stone (1984) concludes his discussion of the Hinckley trial with the following comment (p.96):

> Psychiatry is held hostage by the psychiatrists who testify in courts whatever their standards and whatever the test of insanity may be. They undertake an enterprise which has hazards for us all. The reputation and credibility of our profession is in their hands. And if I am correct about the iceberg, they know not what they do.

D.3 Standards for Expert Opinions in Engineering

Throughout Chapter 5, the panel makes reference to the desirability of the use of written reports on the part of statistical experts. While the panel stopped short of actually specifying the format and contents of such reports, the engineering community presents a model on which standards for statistical reports might be built.

The American Society for Testing and Materials (ASTM) promulgates standards in a variety of areas, dividing up what it deems to be its jurisdiction into areas that are then placed under the direct responsibility of committees. The ASTM Committee E–40 on Technical Aspects of Product Liability Litigation has produced a standard on the Evaluation of Technical Data (ANSI/ASTM E678–80), and the following standard (ANSI/ASTM E620–77) on reporting opinions in litigation.

Standard Practice for REPORTING OPINIONS OF TECHNICAL EXPERTS

1. Scope

1.1 This practice covers the written technical opinions which are rendered concerning the adequacy or inadequacy of a product that is involved in litigation, or for use by others in determining whether or not a claim for damages arising out of the use of a product should be initiated.

2. Significance

2.1 This practice establishes those elements of the expert's opinion report which will make the report self-teaching and focus on the technical aspects germane to the purpose for which the opinion is rendered.

3. Procedure

3.1 Any person who is requested to render an opinion within the scope of this practice shall report his opinions and conclusions in conformance with the format in Section 4.

4. Format for Report

4.1 *Introduction* — The introduction portion of the report shall contain the following:

4.1.1 Identifying number and the date the report was prepared,

4.1.2 Name, address, and affiliation of each person who has rendered an opinion contained in the report,

4.1.3 Name of the person or organization, or both, requesting the report (optional at the discretion of the expert),

4.1.4 Generic description of the item(s) examined together with specific data to uniquely identify the item(s) such as a serial number, marking, or some other means of adequately identifying the item(s) examined,

4.1.5 Date and location of each examination, and

4.1.6 Purpose for which the opinion is being rendered.

4.2 *Pertinent Facts* — The report shall contain all facts that are pertinent to the opinion rendered and shall be reported in accordance with the classifications set forth in 4.2.1 and 4.2.2.

4.2.1 Those facts which are based on the personal observations by the expert of the product or items in question or photographs thereof, and other products or items which are similar thereto.

4.2.2 All other facts based on the personal observations by the expert, and other facts and information that the expert relies upon in rendering his opinion. This section of the report should also include the description, model number, and calibration data of each piece of equipment used in the expert's examination. If the information about the equipment is too voluminous to include in this section, the information should be included in an appendix.

4.2.3 Whenever pertinent findings of fact are established through examination or testing, the person(s) rendering the opinion based on such findings shall have either supervised, conducted, participated in or observed such examination or testing, and failing to do any one of them shall list the name and business address of each person who supervised or conducted each examination or test establishing such findings of fact.

4.3 *Opinions and Conclusions:*

4.3.1 The report shall contain all of the technical opinions and conclusions rendered by the expert concerning the purpose for which he was engaged.

4.3.2 The report shall contain the logic and reasoning used by the expert in reaching each of the opinions and conclusions.

4.4 *Signature* — The report shall contain the signature of each person who has rendered a joint or separate opinion contained in the report. The signature(s) shall be at the end of the opinion. A professional seal should be used, if applicable. If an opinion rendered is that of two or more experts, a signature page may be used.

4.5 *Qualifications* — Information contained in this portion of the report should be pertinent to the opinion rendered.

4.5.1 The expert shall report his education and training which bear on his ability to render opinions of the nature contained in the report, including the applicable dates and names of the educational institutions.

4.5.2 The expert shall report his experience that bears on his ability to render opinions of the nature contained in the report, including the number of years in responsible charge, the dates, location, and name of employer.

4.5.3 The expert shall report his professional affiliations.

4.6 *Appendix* — An appendix may be used in connection with the report. The appendix may contain tables, graphs, charts, photos, drawings, test results or data, and other appropriate documents pertinent to the opinion.

Appendix E

Excerpt From Federal Rules of Civil Procedure

Rule 26. Provisions Governing Discovery

(a) **Discovery Methods.** Parties may obtain discovery by one or more of the following methods: depositions upon oral examination or written questions: written interrogatories; production of documents or things or permission to enter upon land or other property for inspection and other purposes; physical and mental examinations; and requests for admission.

(b) **Discovery Scope and Limits.** Unless otherwise limited by order of the court in accordance with these rules, the scope of discovery is as follows:

(1) *In General.* Parties may obtain discovery regarding any matter, not privileged, which is relevant to the subject matter involved in the pending action, whether it relates to the claim or defense of the party seeking discovery or to the claim or defense of any other party, including the existence, description, nature, custody, condition and location of any books, documents, or other tangible things and the identity and location of persons having knowledge of any discoverable matter. It is not ground for objection that the information sought will be inadmissible at the trial if the information sought appears reasonably calculated to lead to the discovery of admissible evidence.

The frequency or extent of use of the discovery methods set forth in subdivision (a) shall be limited by the court if it determines that: (i) the discovery sought is unreasonably cumulative or duplicative, or is obtainable from some other source that is more convenient, less burdensome, or less expensive; (ii) the party seeking discovery has had ample opportunity by discovery in the action to obtain the information sought; or (iii) the discovery is unduly burdensome or expensive, taking into account the needs of the case, the amount in controversy, limitations on the parties' resources, and the importance of the issues at stake in the litigation. The court may act upon its own initiative after reasonable notice or pursuant to a motion under subdivision (c).

(3) *Trial Preparation: Materials.* Subject to the provisions of subdivision (b)(4) of this rule, a party may obtain discovery of documents and tangible things otherwise discoverable under subdivision (b)(1) of this rule and prepared in anticipation of litigation or for trial by or for another party or by or for that other party's representative (including his attorney, consultant, surety, indemnitor, insurer, or agent) only upon a showing that the party seeking discovery has substantial need of the materials in the preparation

of his case and that he is unable without undue hardship to obtain the substantial equivalent of the materials by other means. In ordering discovery of such materials when the required showing has been made, the court shall protect against disclosure of the mental impressions, conclusions, opinions, or legal theories of an attorney or other representative of a party concerning the litigation.

A party may obtain without the required showing a statement concerning the action or its subject matter previously made by that party. Upon request a person not a party may obtain without the required showing a statement concerning the action or its subject matter previously made by that person. If the request is refused, the person may move for a court order. The provisions of Rule 37(a)(4) apply to the award of expenses incurred in relation to the motion. For purposes of this paragraph, a statement previously made is (A) a written statement signed or otherwise adopted or approved by the person making it, or (B) a stenographic, mechanical, electrical, or other recording, or a transcription thereof, which is a substantially verbatim recital of an oral statement by the person making it and contemporaneously recorded.

(4) *Trial Preparation: Experts.* Discovery of facts known and opinions held by experts, otherwise discoverable under the provisions of subdivision (b)(1) of this rule and acquired or developed in anticipation of litigation or for trial, may be obtained only as follows:

(A) (i) A party may through interrogatories require any other party to identify each person whom the other party expects to call as an expert witness at trial, to state the subject matter on which the expert is expected to testify, and to state the substance of the facts and opinions to which the expert is expected to testify and a summary of the grounds for each opinion. (ii) Upon motion, the court may order further discovery by other means, subject to such restrictions as to scope and such provisions, pursuant to subdivision (b)(4)(C) of this rule, concerning fees and expenses as the court may deem appropriate.

(B) A party may discover facts known or opinions held by an expert who has been retained or specially employed by another party in anticipation of litigation or preparation for trial and who is not expected to be called as a witness at trial, only as provided in Rule 35(b) or upon a showing of exceptional circumstances under which it is impracticable for the party seeking discovery to obtain facts or opinions on the same subject by other means.

(C) Unless manifest injustice would result, (i) the court shall require that the party seeking discovery pay the expert a reasonable fee for time spent in responding to discovery under subdivisions (b)(4)(A)(ii) and (b)(4)(B) of this rule; and (ii) with respect to discovery obtained under subdivision (b)(4)(A)(ii) of this rule the court may require, and with respect to discovery obtained under subdivision (b)(4)(B) of this rule the court shall require, the party seeking discovery to pay the other party a fair portion of the fees and expenses reasonably incurred by the latter party in obtaining facts and opinions from the expert.

(c) **Protective Orders**. Upon motion by a party or by the person from whom discovery is sought, and for good cause shown, the court in which the action is pending or alternatively, on matters relating to a deposition, the court in the district where the deposition is to be taken may make any order which justice requires to protect a party or person from annoyance, embarrassment, oppression, or undue burden or expense, including one or more of the following: (1) that the discovery not be had; (2) that the discovery may be had only on specified terms and conditions, including a designation of the time or place; (3) that the discovery may be had only by a method of discovery other than that selected by the party seeking discovery; (4) that certain matters not be inquired into, or that the scope of the discovery be limited to certain matters; (5) that discovery be conducted with no one present except persons designated by the court; (6) that a deposition after being sealed be opened only by order of the court; (7) that a trade secret or other confidential research, development, or commercial information not be disclosed or be disclosed only in a designated way; (8) that the parties simultaneously file specified documents or information enclosed in sealed envelopes to be opened as directed by the court.

If the motion for a protective order is denied in whole or in part, the court may, on such terms and conditions as are just, order that any party or person provide or permit discovery. The provisions of Rule 37(a)(4) apply to the award of expenses incurred in relation to the motion.

(d) **Sequence and Timing of Discovery**. Unless the court upon motion, for the convenience of parties and witnesses and in the interests of justice, orders otherwise, methods of discovery may be used in any sequence and the fact that a party is conducting discovery, whether by deposition or otherwise, shall not operate to delay any other party's discovery.

(e) **Supplementation of Responses**. A party who has responded to a request for discovery with a response that was complete when made is under no duty to supplement his response to include information thereafter acquired, except as follows:

(1) A party is under a duty seasonably to supplement his response with respect to any question directly addressed to (A) the identity and location of persons having knowledge of discoverable matters, and (B) the identity of each person expected to be called as an expert witness at trial, the subject matter on which he is expected to testify, and the substance of his testimony.

(2) A party is under a duty seasonably to amend a prior response if he obtains information upon the basis of which (A) he knows that the response was incorrect when made, or (B) he knows that the response though correct when made is no longer true and the circumstances are such that a failure to amend the response is in substance a knowing concealment.

(3) A duty to supplement responses may be imposed by order of the

court, agreement of the parties, or at any time prior to trial through new requests for supplementation of prior responses.

(f) **Discovery Conference**. At any time after commencement of an action the court may direct the attorneys for the parties to appear before it for a conference on the subject of discovery. The court shall do so upon motion by the attorney for any party if the motion includes:

(1) A statement of the issues as they then appear;

(2) A proposed plan and schedule of discovery;

(3) Any limitations proposed to be placed on discovery;

(4) Any other proposed orders with respect to discovery; and

(5) A statement showing that the attorney making the motion has made a reasonable effort to reach agreement with opposing attorneys on the matters set forth in the motion. Each party and his attorney are under a duty to participate in good faith in the framing of a discovery plan if a plan is proposed by the attorney for any party. Notice of the motion shall be served on all parties. Objections or additions to matters set forth in the motion shall be served not later than 10 days after service of the motion.

Following the discovery conference, the court shall enter an order tentatively identifying the issues for discovery purposes, establishing a plan and schedule for discovery, setting limitations on discovery, if any; and determining such other matters, including the allocation of expenses, as are necessary for the proper management of discovery in the action. An order may be altered or amended whenever justice so requires.

Subject to the right of a party who properly moves for a discovery conference to prompt convening of the conference, the court may combine the discovery conference with a pretrial conference authorized by Rule 16.

(g) **Signing of Discovery Requests, Responses, and Objections**. Every request for discovery or response or objection thereto made by a party represented by an attorney shall be signed by at least one attorney of record in his individual name, whose address shall be stated. A party who is not represented by an attorney shall sign the request, response, or objection and state his address. The signature of the attorney or party constitutes a certification that he has read the request, response, or objection, and that to the best of his knowledge, information, and belief formed after a reasonable inquiry it is: (1) consistent with these rules and warranted by existing law or a good faith argument for the extension, modification, or reversal of existing law; (2) not interposed for any improper purpose, such as to harass or to cause unnecessary delay or needless increase in the cost of litigation; and (3) not unreasonable or unduly burdensome or expensive, given the needs of the case, the discovery already had in the case, the amount in controversy, and the importance of the issues at stake in the litigation. If a request, response, or objection is not signed, it shall be stricken unless it is signed promptly after the omission is called to the attention of the party making the request, response or objection and a party shall not be obligated to take any action with respect to it until it is signed.

If a certification is made in violation of the rule, the court, upon motion or upon its own initiative, shall impose upon the person who made the certification, the party on whose behalf the request, response, or objection is made, or both, an appropriate sanction, which may include an order to pay the amount of the reasonable expenses incurred because of the violation, including a reasonable attorney's fee.

(As amended Dec. 27, 1946, eff. Mar. 19, 1948; Jan. 21, 1963, eff. July 1, 1963; Feb. 28, 1966, eff. July 1, 1966; Mar. 30, 1970, eff. July 1, 1970; Apr. 29, 1980, eff. Aug. 1, 1980; Apr. 28, 1983, eff. Aug. 1, 1983.)

Appendix F

Recommendations on Pretrial Proceedings in Cases With Voluminous Data

By THE SPECIAL COMMITTEE ON EMPIRICAL DATA IN
LEGAL DECISION MAKING

Introduction

The purpose of these recommendations is to address certain problems that have arisen in cases involving large-scale data bases that may be subjected to statistical analysis and in which statisticians (or persons in related disciplines with statistical training) may be called to testify as to the import of the data. The *Manual for Complex Litigation* (5th ed. 1982) (the "Manual") recommends that voluminous data and summaries thereof that are proposed to be offered at trial "should be made available to opposing counsel well in advance of the time they are to be offered, to permit all objections to be raised and if possible resolved prior to the offer." *Id.* §2.711. Similarly, the *Manual* recommends that "[t]he underlying data, method of interpretation employed, and conclusions reached" in polls and samples should be made available to the other parties "far in advance of trial, and, if possible, prior to the taking of the poll or sample." *Id.* §2.713. The Committee's recommendations here are aimed at establishing a set of "protocols" to implement recommendations of this sort with respect to the handling of large-scale data bases during pretrial proceedings and to expand upon those recommendations with respect to statistical analysis of that data.

The principal types of litigation in which statistical data have played a significant role involve race or sex discrimination, antitrust, environment, tax, rate-making, and a variety of other cases in which issues of fact are sought to be resolved with sampling studies. Objections to statistical presentations in such cases may be made at various levels.

First, it may be argued that the data base does not represent a correct set of facts for the problem at hand in that some of the data may be viewed as inappropriate, or even irrelevant, to the issues in the case. Or, the data base may be seen as incomplete in that some important items of information have been excluded. The issues raised by such arguments are matters for substantive expertise and judgment.

Second, the data may have simple errors of fact caused, for example, by incorrect transcription or other clerical errors. Or, it may be argued that the data have been collected by imperfect procedures, or from imperfect sources. Generally, the issues raised by such challenges relate to the degree to which the data are accurate.

Third, if the data represent a sample, they may be challenged as not sufficiently reliable or precise for the problem at hand. The answer will depend on whether the method of selection was biased in some fashion and whether a large enough sample was selected to restrict sampling error.

Fourth, in cases in which the data are used as input for statistical or other kinds of analysis, the appropriateness of the analysis and the usefulness of its answers may be challenged. Most types of analysis rest on important assumptions, and there may be questions about the reasonableness of those assumptions.

The way in which these questions about data and their uses arise may be illustrated by reference to class-action antidiscrimination litigation in which the data base consists of information on employee salaries and productivity factors, such as education and years of experience.

Questions of appropriateness or relevance include (1) whether the salary data include all compensation, (2) whether various proxies for productivity such as years of experience are good measures of productivity, (3) whether the inclusion of a factor such as performance evaluation is appropriate, and (4) whether the failure to include a factor such as special education is inappropriate.

Questions of accuracy include (1) whether there were errors in the collection and the coding of personnel data, and (2) whether the source of the data (*e.g.*, personnel records) was subject to greater error than more trustworthy sources. Questions of reliability arise if the study of employees is limited to a statistical sample. In that case the issues would be whether the method of selection was biased and whether the size of sample was sufficient to restrict sampling error.

Finally, if regression methods were used to analyze the data base, issues could be raised with respect to the form of the regression equation or the form in which the variables were entered into the equation.

Given the welter of arguments that statistical data usually provoke, the technicality of some of the issues, and the cost and difficulty of preparing such evidence or rebutting it, the Committee believes it desirable to make every effort in the pretrial stages to resolve disputes and narrow the issues for trial. Toward that end, we make recommendations concerning: (1) settlement of the data base; (2) reports by experts; (3) confidentiality; and (4) nontestifying experts. In framing procedures relating to these matters in the pretrial discovery phase, the Committee has attempted to strike a balance that recognizes the benefits of sharpening the issues by advance disclosure of asserted defects in a study and the objection that a party challenging a study should not have to educate an incompetent expert who proposes to introduce a defective study.

At the outset, we make three points concerning the scope and use of these protocols. First, the suggested procedures discussed below apply equally to studies based upon data from existing business records and from samples or polls made for the purposes of litigation. They do not necessarily apply to studies made by entities unconnected with the litigation, which may be published in learned journals or government reports. The use in evidence or citation of such material raise issues outside these protocols. Second, the procedures suggested here are not seen as rigid, but rather are intended as general guides to be used flexibly in light of the circumstances. Third, it would of course be desirable for parties to use a common data base whenever possible even if there is disagreement over the significance or interpretation of the statistics. The retention of an appropriate joint expert to collect data for both parties is a welcome technique that has been used in some cases. *See, e.g., Chance* v. *Board of Examiners*, 330 F.Supp. 203 (S.D.N.Y. 1971), *aff'd*, 458 F.2d 1167 (2d Cir. 1972).

However, the Committee recognizes such agreements frequently will not be forthcoming and consequently it is desirable to consider the best procedural techniques for resolving disputes over the data and their interpretation. To that end we have formulated the recommendations for pretrial procedures that are discussed below.

Disclosure of Data

FIRST RECOMMENDATION:

A party who proposes to offer data or data analyses at trial, shall make the following materials available to the other parties for inspection and copying: (a) any hard copy of the data and underlying records from which the data were collected; (b) any computer tapes, cards, disks, or other machine-readable source upon which the data are recorded; (c) full documentation of the physical and logical structure of any machine-readable source; (d) any computer programs used in generating the data (both in hard copy and machine-readable form); and (e) full documentation of such computer programs. These materials shall be made available as far in advance of the time required for any response as is practicable.

COMMENT: (a) This recommendation follows the spirit of the *Manual* recommendations approving the use of summaries, the results of samples and polls, and computer-maintained business records at trial, focusing upon their admissibility under various exceptions to the hearsay rule, and in particular the requirement of some showing of "trustworthiness" (*Id.* §§2.711, 2.713, 2.714, and 2.716). *See* Fed. R. Evid. 803(24). In maintaining the burden upon the proponent to show "trustworthiness," the *Manual* requires the proponent to disclose both underlying data and methodology far in advance to trial so that meaningful challenges to "trustworthiness" are possible.

(b) Advance disclosure of data avoids the situation in *Trout* v. *Hidalgo*, 517 F.Supp. 873, 877 n. 4 (D.D.C. 1981), in which data were first requested from the employer-defendant only five weeks before trial and "the deficiencies in the parties' statistical analysis can be traced directly" to "gaps" in these data. Production of both computer tapes and printout avoids the result in *Williams* v. *Owens-Illinois, Inc.*, 665 F.2d 918, 932–33 (9th Cir. 1982), in which discovery of computer tapes was denied because the underlying data had been produced. The Committee believes this result is undesired because there is no justification for time-consuming and wasteful replication of data entry and verification when a machine-readable version of a proposed data base already exists.

(c) Full documentation with respect to machine-readable data files is essential if the files are to be used by the other parties. In terms of current technology, the physical documentation should include the following: tape density, number of tracks, record format, logical record length, block size, and character set. The documentation of the structure of the data file should include a list of variable names with the location of each variable within the logical record, and a list of admissible codes with definitions of each code. For a fuller description of the type of technical information required see Appendix I.

(d) If the cost or difficulty of moving data or software would be substantial, the court (references to the court in these protocols should be deemed to include any magistrate) should consider requiring the party generating the data to permit access by the adverse party directly to the system in which the data are stored.

(e) Disclosure may be limited if there is good cause for confidentiality. *See Ninth Recommendation.*

SECOND RECOMMENDATION:

A party proposing to offer at trial data or data analyses should make available the personnel involved in the compilation of such data for informal conferences with the other parties to answer technical questions concerning the data and the methods of collection or compilation.

COMMENT: (a) This protocol is designed to encourage informal conferences between the parties, their experts, or persons representing their experts, to resolve questions as to the nature of the data collection or compilation used by the offering party. The purpose of such meetings would be to clarify technical details with respect to definitions of the data and methods of collection or compilation. Such conferences generally will be useful even before a formal expert's report is issued.

(b) In addition to informal conferences, the parties may by agreement wish to record and transcribe depositions in which technical questions are asked by experts rather than lawyers.

Method of Analysis

THIRD RECOMMENDATION:

A party proposing to offer an expert's analysis at trial should cause the expert to prepare a formal report disclosing fully the following: (a) the data base and its sources, (b) the methods of collecting the data, and (c) methods of analysis. Such a report should be made available to the other parties sufficiently in advance of trial to permit them to consult their experts, draft responding reports, and prepare cross-examination.

COMMENT: (a) This protocol is in line with the *Manual* comment that "[a]s soon as practical, each party should be required to disclose the name, qualifications, and content of the testimony of each expert witness proposed to be called at the trial. This should be done in a written offer of proof. ... Objections to the written offers of proof should be heard and tentative rulings announced in the pretrial proceedings." *Manual* §2.60.

(b) Annexed to this report as Appendice II is a set of recommendations for disclosure in data collection studies prepared for the Committee by Professor Gerald Glasser of New York University Graduate School of Business, a statistician member of the Committee. The Committee believes it would be useful if similar standards of disclosure were drafted for reports involving other commonly used stastistical [sic] techniques.

(c) To facilitate the resolution of disputes with respect to the "objective" parts of analysis, such as routine sorting or matrix manipulation, the court should recommend that the parties use generally available program packages in preference to "in-house" programs that are likely to create problems of validation. When nonstandard programs are used, full documentation as specified in paragraph (d) below is of particular importance.

(d) Full documentation with respect to a program that is not standard and widely available should include descriptions in English of the program's function, appropriate information for running the program, including specification of the hardware required plus input and/or output formats, and comments on the function of each group of commands. For further information see Appendix I.

FOURTH RECOMMENDATION:

A Court generally should permit depositions of an expert a party proposes to call at trial, such depositions to take place after that expert has submitted his initial report.

COMMENT: In the complex cases covered by these protocols, an expert's report submitted prior to trial will not usually answer all of the questions that a party challenging the report may need for cross-examination and rebuttal. Nor are interrogatories under Fed. R. Civ. P. 26(b)(4)(A)(i) likely to be a satisfactory substitute. Thus the court generally should exercise its discretion under Fed. R. Civ. P. 26(b)(4)(A)(ii) to permit an opposing party to depose the expert. *See Manual* §2.716(d). It shall not be a basis for adjourning the deposition that the expert has not received a responding report of an opposing expert or party.

Disclosure and Resolution of Objections

FIFTH RECOMMENDATION:

A party objecting to a data base or to an analysis of data proposed to be offered at trial must within a reasonable period so advise the offering party of its objections to the data base and, to the extent determined by the court, to the methods of analysis. The objecting party should detail the reasons for its objections and identify the sources of information on which it relies.

(A) If an objection that the data contain errors is based upon information contained in the objecting party's records, and to which the objecting party has substantially better access than the party proposing the analysis, the objecting party shall in addition provide the correct data in hard copy or machine-readable form.

(B) An objecting party generally should designate its objections to the data base and, to the extent directed by the court, to the methods of analysis, with sufficient particularity for the proponent to make an appropriate response. If the objecting party demonstrates that the proposed data base has a relatively high rate of errors, it need not designate every erroneous item.

Comment: (a) The objections covered by this protocol may range from simple clerical mistakes in data entry, as to which there could be little dispute, to much more complex issues of appropriateness of data selection, construction, or analysis as to which there may be sharp disagreement. Thus, the disclosure required of objecting parties may range from the designation of plainly incorrect items or entries to "judgmental" or "substantive" challenges to the data base.

(b) With respect to simple clerical errors, this recommendation is in line wth the *Manual's* recommendation that "[i]ssues concerning the admission of polls, samples, summaries, or computer runs should be resolved well in advance of trial. ... To the extent feasible and fair, deficiencies and errors in such summaries should be corrected." *Id.* §3.50. The comment to that recommendation warns against the "confusion and waste of trial time" occasioned by minor deficiencies in summaries and suggests that "the court should, if feasible, ordinarily require parties against whom summaries will be offered to disclose in advance of trial any challenges to the mathematical and clerical accuracy of the summaries." The requirement that incorrect entries be identified in the Committee's recommendations assumes that the party proposing to offer a data base has made a good faith effort to collect accurate data and is not using the disclosure device unfairly to impose a burden of verification on other parties.

(c) The Committee is agreed that objections to the accuracy and scope of the data base should be exposed and, to the extent possible, resolved prior to trial. Committee members disagree as to what further disclosure of objections should be required, and most particularly whether all objections to methods of analysis should be disclosed. Some Committee members believe that a full disclosure of objections would do the expert's work for him and eliminate the most forceful demonstration at trial of the weaknesses of his analysis. Other Committee members believe that the truth-determining process outweighs these considerations and would best be served by advance disclosure of all objections. In view of this disagreement the Committee takes no position on where to draw the line in individual cases beyond the disclosure of mathematical or clerical errors. In considering what more to require, the court should weigh the desirability of full disclosure of objections against any claim that the proponent of a study would unfairly use the disclosure device to have the opponent's expert do his work for him, or would shield an incompetent expert.

(d) In the event an objecting party intends to call an expert to rebut a proposed study, or to present an answering study, it should disclose the data base and submit an expert's report as provided in these recommendations.

(e) After receiving objections, the offering party should be given a reasonable time in which to submit an amended report, and the objecting party a reasonable opportunity to further respond. Generally there should be no need for more than a report and an amended report, with responses to each.

SIXTH RECOMMENDATION:

The parties shall resolve differences as to the appropriateness, accuracy, and reliability of the data to the extent possible by informal conference. In the event differences persist, either party may move for an order resolving such differences. The court should make every effort to resolve differences to the extent possible in advance of trial, particularly when a resolution would reduce the time and expense of pretrial preparation and narrow the issues for trial.

COMMENT: (a) Experience has shown that many serious conflicts in analysis of statistical data arise from differences at the starting point, namely the data. By resolving at least data base disputes first, much time and effort should be saved by the elmination [sic] of unnecessary or irrelevant analyses.

(b) The Committee recognizes that pretrial resolution of disputes is more likely with respect to simple clerical errors and the like than with more complex issues of appropriateness, reliability, or methods of analysis. Nevertheless, a court should be willing in advance of trial to deal with more difficult issues when doing so would reduce the burden of pretrial preparation and narrow the scope of trial. This type of activity by the court is consistent with the recent proposed amendment to Rule 16 of the Federal Rules of Civil Procedure, which provides for more extensive use of pretrial conferences to include the objectives of (1) early and continuing control by the court to avoid unnecessary protraction of the litigation; (2) discouragement of wasteful pretrial activity; and (3) more thorough preparation for trial.

(c) In the event analyses proposed to be offered by parties reach significantly different conclusions with respect to the same subject matter, the parties should pinpoint the specific reasons for such differences.

(d) Reference to magistrates and masters may be particularly helpful in resolving disputes over at least clerical issues with respect to the data.

Implemental of Recommendations

SEVENTH RECOMMENDATION:

A schedule for the submission of reports and data and responding reports and data should be established by the court after hearing the parties. Amendments to the schedule should be granted freely in the interests of justice if the party seeking the amendment demonstrates diligence in attempting to comply with the original schedule.

COMMENTS: (a) If the parties and the court are to benefit from this recommendation, it is essential that the parties be given sufficient time in which to explore the accuracy of the data base and to perform their analyses of it. We emphasize that the data must be available well in advance of the time required for any response. There can be no fixed rule for the time necessary, but in establishing a pretrial schedule the court should be aware that computer studies are extremely time-consuming. *See Manual* §2.70. In particular, transferring data from one type of system to another (*e.g.*, from an IBM system to a Control Data system) generally will not be simply a matter of pressing a button. The operation may be difficult, requiring some trial and error and extensive cooperation between experts.

(b) In establishing a schedule, among the factors to be considered are (1) the length of time required by the proponent to construct the study; (2) the complexity of verification of the underlying data; (3) the need for original programming as compared with the use of standardized programs; (4) the need for manual entry of data as opposed to data in machine readable form; and (5) the complexity of the analysis.

EIGHTH RECOMMENDATION:

Objections to the data, to the methods of analysis, or to any other matter, required to be raised but not raised in the pretrial proceedings, should be deemed waived unless the court for good cause shown relieves the objecting party of the waiver.

COMMENT: Exxon Corporation v. *XOIL Energy Resources*, 80 Civ. 3347 (VLB) (S.D.N.Y.) is an example of a case in which plaintiff sought and obtained a pretrial order requiring it to disclose fully and in advance the experts it was considering and the design proposal for a projected sample survey. In turn, defendants were required to disclose in advance any objections to the proposed experts and to the design of the study. Any objection not resolved by the parties would he presented to the court for resolution, and no new objection could be made at trial. A copy of the pretrial order establishing these procedures is annexed as Appendix III.

Confidentiality

NINTH RECOMMENDATION:

In the event a party desires to maintain confidentiality of certain data for which disclosure is sought, it may by agreement or by application to the court (a) redact and/or encode records, or (b) seek a protective order limiting access to the data. In the absence of special circumstances, the interest in confidentiality should be satisfied by a protective order limiting access to the data to the independent experts and trial counsel for opposing parties. Any person or firm permitted access to confidential data should be prepared to provide an undertaking controlling the making of copies, providing for limited access and security within its organization, and providing for the return of all confidential material when its retention is no longer needed for the litigation.

COMMENT: Good cause for confidentiality may exist if a party demonstrates that the data are proprietary and their disclosure would be injurious to business interests, or that they are confidential and their disclosure would be injurious to individuals. A claim of confidentiality by a data analysis firm retained by a party (usually with respect to some proprietary computer program) should be allowed only upon a clear showing of injury from disclosure. Where confidentiality is established, the material should still be produced, subject to a protective order. The Committee agrees with the position taken in the *Manual* that "When statistical analyses have been prepared by computer in anticipation of litigation, the data (inputs), the methods used to prepare the analyses, and all the results (outputs) are proper subjects for discovery." *Id.* §2.715.

Nontestifying Experts

TENTH RECOMMENDATION:

Facts known or opinions held by nontestifying experts are discoverable only on a showing of "exceptional circumstances." Fed. R. Civ. P. 26(b)(4)(B). Where statistical analyses are involved, exceptional circumstances should be deemed to arise if the testifying expert obtained significant informaton [sic] directly or indirectly from a nontestifying expert.

COMMENT: Cases within this protocol arise when a testifying expert uses and builds upon studies prepared by others. Thus a statistician may be called upon to make calculations with respect to data shaped by others. Those who supply input should not be shielded by having the information that is used by the testifying expert passed through the client or its lawyers.

Special Committee on Empirical Data in Legal Decision Making
Michael O. Finkelstein, *Chair*

Leona Beane	Laura Sager
Michael S. Davis	Myra Schubin
John P. Flannery II	A. Jared Silverman
Frank P. Grad	Mathias L. Spiegel
David Klingsberg	Jay Topkis
David Paget	Judith P. Vladeck
William C. Pelster	Jack B. Weinstein

ADJUNCT MEMBERS
David Baldus
Gerald Glasser
Jules Joskow

APPENDIX I
Glossary of Computer Terms

bit
— The smallest unit of information on a computer. A bit can take the value of 0 or 1.

byte
— The first level of organization of bits into units of information usable by the computer. In general, 8 bits are grouped into one byte.

tape
— A device for storage of data and programs by the computers. Tapes are generally the method for transferring data between computer systems. Tapes store information on a magnetic strip or tape which is then spun onto a reel for storage and handling.

label
— The identification markings on a tape. A tape can have 2 types of labels: an external label that is a physical identification marking on the outside of the tape, and an internal label that is machine dependent and readable only by computer and serves the purpose of identification for the computer.

track — The rows of bits which run the length of a tape and contain the information the tape has stored. While other systems exist, in general, a tape is written in 9 tracks—8 for data, and one for parity as a check for errors.

tape density — The number of characters stored per unit of space on the tape. Measured in bits per inch (BPI), tapes are generally written at 800, 1600, or 6250 BPI.

logical record — The amount of space required for a record or logically grouped set of data (e.g. information on an individual) or portion of this record to be written on a tape.

Blocks — The method by which records are grouped to form efficient units of storage. Blocks are the result of having stored records by one of the various conventions (record formats) into these storage units.

Record Format — The method by which records are written onto the unit of storage. Various schemes are currently in use, including fixed format (F), Variable format (D or V), Spanned format (S), and Undefined (U).

Character set — The method by which bits are combined to form machine readable characters. Two standards are in use: ASCII—The American Standard Code for Information Interchange, and, EBCDIC—Extended Binary Coded Decimal Interchange Code.

Variable list — The information that is contained on a given record. The variable list is the compendium of all the information that has been stored for each record or unit of study.

Variable format — The position or location by which the units of information (variables) as well as the character set by which the variables are stored on the record. The record format provides the scheme for translating the string of characters associated with a record into meaningful units of information—variables.

Variable codes   — A physical recording (code book) that provides a translation scheme for interpreting the characters for each variable on a record into logical and meaningful information for use by the individual who is processing the records. This document contains all possible values for a given variable, translates these values into their substantive meaning, and provides information about values coded when information about the unit of study is missing.

Program function   — The task or tasks which a program was written to perform. The documentation of the program function contains the limitations of the program.

Commands   — The instructions a programmer must give a program in order for the program to perform its task. The nature and meaning of these commands are dependent upon the nature of the program being used.

APPENDIX II
Recommended Standards on Disclosure of Procedures
Used For Statistical Studies to Collect Data Submitted
in Evidence in Legal Cases

[Prepared by Professor Gerald G. Glaser, New York University]

1. NATURE OF THE STATISTICAL INFORMATION
    1.1 Purpose of the Study
    1.2 Elements of the Data Base

2. THE STATISTICAL POPULATION AND SAMPLE SELECTION
    2.1 The Statistical Population
    2.2 The Frame
    2.3 Sampling Plan

3. SURVEY METHODS, OPERATIONS AND PROCEDURES
    3.1 Method of Data Collection
    3.2 Field Work
    3.3 Nonresponse
    3.4 Editing and Coding Procedures
    3.5 Processing and Computational Procedures

4. ACCURACY AND RELIABILITY OF STUDY RESULTS
4.1 Sampling Error
4.2 Nonsampling Errors

INTRODUCTION

Background. On many occasions, the results of a statistical study will be submitted as evidence in a legal or quasi-legal proceeding. These results may be intended to speak for themselves, or may be the basis for some substantive interpretation and conclusions, or may be input for subsequent technical statistical analysis.

In any of these circumstances, it is usually of great importance to understand how the results of a study were obtained. That is, it is necessary, for proper assessment of the evidential data, to know the procedures by which the study was conducted. This knowledge helps one to judge the proper and appropriate meaning of the results and, moreover, to understand the limitations of the information as well, thereby indicating what weight should be given to the results in the decision-making process.

A statistical study involves the collection, tabulation and presentation of information. Usually, but not necessarily, the information is quantitative, or numerical. Thus, the term "data" is often used. Also, interest is normally in aggregative results, rather than in individual case-by-case detail, such as in clinical research.

Statistical work often entails analysis and interpretation, as well as the collection, tabulation and presentation of data. This document, however, relates primarily to the latter activities which involve the compilation of a data base rather than to the subsequent analysis and interpretation of the data.

Scope and Objectives. This document specifies standards for the disclosure of procedures used for statistical studies to collect data submitted in evidence in legal cases. These standards are directed primarily to two questions:

(1) What is the minimum amount of information about the procedures used to collect, tabulate, and present the results that should be disclosed?

(2) What is the form in which such information should be reported? In general, these standards recommend disclosure of information relating to four matters: (a) the nature of the statistical results derived from the study; (b) the method of sampling employed in the study; (c) the procedures used in collecting, processing and tabulating the results; and (d) the accuracy and reliability of the results.

Information of this kind is generally essential to any understanding of the meaning of statistical results, to their proper interpretation, and to assessment of the limitations of the data.

The standards, as set forth, should be regarded as minimum standards of disclosure. That is, they suggest the minimum amount of detail about "what was done" that should be provided with any statistical study that is submitted in evidence. It may well be appropriate, at least in some circumstances, to include additional facts about a study, or to provide more detailed information than is proposed by the standards.

It is also important to remember that the recommendations included herewith are disclosure standards, not performance standards. No recommendations on appropriate methodology should be imputed to the language used.

Neither is it correct to give credence to any statistical study submitted in evidence merely because the recommended standards on disclosure are met. The standards merely suggest reporting of what was done. What was done may or may not be found acceptable by other professionals.

Standards on Format. In general, the disclosure standards herewith proposed require a well-organized and coherent report with a variety of different kinds of information. To facilitate review and understanding of the material, it is proposed that the information be organized, as are the standards themselves, in four main sections, relating to:

(1) The nature of the statistical results obtained by the study, including appropriate definitions;

(2) Specifications of the statistical population and the method of sampling employed in the study;

(3) Methods, operations and procedures used in the collection, processing and tabulation of the data; and,

(4) Reliability and accuracy of the results derived from the study.

Within each of these main sections, information reported should be further organized in parallel with the several subsections enumerated by the standards.

In the preparation of descriptive material, it is recommended that, to the extent it exists, standard statistical terminology be used. Specific suggestions are contained herewith.

1.1 Purpose of the Study. A report on a statistical study submitted in evidence in a legal proceeding should begin with a clear statement of what information the study is intended to provide.

In describing the objectives of a study, it is particularly important to indicate (a) the time frame to which it applies, and (b) the statistical population to which the results are being projected.

All studies have a time frame. That is, a study may be directed at real estate values during a period of years, or invoices processed over several months. Often, the purpose of the study dictates this time frame, but in any case it should be reported together with some rationale for its choice.

The statistical population for a study is the set of observations deemed relevant and pertinent for a given problem. (See Section 2.1.) It also is often dictated by the purpose of the study, but in any case it should be reported together with some rationale for its choice.

This preliminary statement on the purpose of the study should be accompanied by a summary description of the study that indicates in a general way what was done and by whom. Auspices of the study should also be indicated.

To the extent possible, a brief summary of the main results should also be provided in this subsection. Detailed results from the study may be submitted as an appendix to this report on study procedures, or as a separate document, as seems appropriate.

1.2 Elements of the Data Base. The tabulation of data in a statistical study normally involves, in some way, measuring presumably relevant characteristics of a series of elementary units. Together these two considerations, characteristics and units, define the dimensions of the data base produced by a statistical study. For example, the elementary unit might be a person, or a business establishment, or an invoice. A list of the characteristics might include age or sex or annual income, or responses given to certain attitudinal questions.

A report on a statistical study should define, precisely, the elementary unit chosen for the study. This definition should include any delimiters applied; for example, the elementary unit might be an employee with an annual rate of compensation equal to or in excess of $20,000 on the full-time payroll as of a certain date, etc.

The report should further enumerate the characteristics of interest in the study, and again provide precise definition of each. This will involve some explanation of how the data on the characteristics were obtained, because the proper meaning and interpretation of data cannot be divorced from the manner in which they are obtained.

If the study has required the use of auxiliary data, apart from that collected by the study itself (e.g., population estimates for geograhic areas), the report should state this fact, explain the need for such data, and describe the source of those data.

Second, the statement should make clear any restrictions set forth on the population. For example, a study might be restricted to persons 18 years of age or older, or to distributors in New York State, or to invoices carrying a date within a particular calendar year. Criteria should be completely enumerated.

Third, the report should list, clearly define, and describe each of the items of information collected for the elementary units. This should be done conceptually, and also operationally. For example, in a study to measure unemployment, it is important to define the intended meaning, and the means by which the characteristic is ascertained.

2.1 The Statistical Population. The complete set of observations that conceptually is deemed relevant and pertinent for a given problem is generally referred to as the statistical population, or sometimes more fully as the target (statistical) population. In most statistical studies, there are several items of information that are relevant and, hence, there are several populations of interest.

For example, in a study of distributors, the statistical populations might be represented by sales, costs and several other items of information about all distributors who ordered some product from the parent company during a specific three-month period. Or, in a study of hiring practices, the statistical populations might be represented by the several characteristics (sex, age, salary, and so forth) of all employees on payroll as of a specific date.

Sometimes the term statistical population may be used, nontechnically, to reference the relevant elementary units rather than the observations on those units that are of interest in a problem.

A report on a statistical study should provide a clear and detailed description of the statistical population(s) for which the study is intended to provide results.

This statement should include, first, a description of the elementary unit; that is, the basic unit in a study about which information has been obtained. For example, in some studies, the unit may be a household, or an individual person, or a business establishment. In other studies, the unit may be an invoice, or a manufactured part. A detailed definition is important.

2.2 The Frame. A frame is a list, file of index cards, map or some other form that identifies, directly or indirectly, all of the elementary units that are to be given some chance of appearing in a statistical study. Under statistical smpling [sic] procedures, the sample for a study is generally drawn from a frame. Units in the frame must be clearly identifiable, so that when a sample is selected, designated units may be located without ambiguity and information collected from them.

Thus, a frame provides a working definition of the statistical population in a study, and a means of access to the units actually selected for study.

For example, the frame in a particular problem might simply consist of a computer tape identifying subscribers to a newspaper or magazine, along with addresses. Or, in a survey of consumers the frame might be represented by telephone directories or city directories. A frame is sometimes in the form of a map, or series of maps.

A report on a statistical study must make clear whether a frame was employed and, if not, explain why not. If a frame or frames were used, the report should provide a clear and complete description of the nature of the listings, and the procedures by which the frame was compiled.

In practice, a frame may be an imperfect representation of a statistical population. That is, a frame may be subject to various imperfections such as incompleteness, or duplication, or both. Timeliness of the frame, or lack thereof, frequently causes imperfections.

The report on the study should attempt to address the questions of incompleteness and duplication, including to the extent possible, estimates of the degree of both phenomena. Further comment is required on the extent to which the imperfections in a frame relative to the statistical populations may cause inaccuracies in the results of a study. (See Section 4.2.)

A frame is as essential for an attempted complete study as it is for a sample study.

2.3 Sampling Plan. The term sample technically refers to data, or observations. A sample is part of a statistical population. One normally refers to sample data. The term may also be used, nontechnically, to reference the elementary units chosen in a study that provide the basic data.

In any case, a sample is presumably selected according to specific procedures. These procedures, or instructions, are referred to as the sampling plan or the sample design. The plan should include specifications for obtaining or constructing a frame, for defining the unit of sampling, and/or for designating units for inclusion in a study.

Sample data are never of interest for what they tell about the sample itself. By definition, a sample is intended to serve as a basis for generalizing about the statistical population from which it was selected.

While there are many different specific methods of sampling, which result in different kinds of samples, professional statisticians, in general, recognize two approaches: probability sampling and nonprobability sampling.

Probability sampling is characterized by two properties: (1) selection of units from a well-defined frame and (2) mechanical selection, in some random manner. This method of sampling results in the probability of selection of any individual unit, or combination of units, being ascertainable from the nature of the procedure. Probability sampling procedures are objective. They are usually highly structured, and can be replicated independently.

Nonprobability sampling is normally a highly subjective operation and relies either on expert judgment, or other criteria, to select particular units for the sample.

A report on a statistical study should fully describe the sampling plan or sample design, as defined above.

In the case of probability sampling, this description would relate to the method of selecting units from the frame for the study, the use of random numbers, and any technical features employed such as stratifying, clustering, and staging a sample.

If the study presented is based on nonprobability selection, the report should so indicate, and explain the rationale of the particular methods employed. Procedures should still be explained fully, including the criteria used to select the sample for the study.

3.1 Method of Data Collection. There are many different methods of data collection, or methods of measurement, that are used in statistical studies. The word "measurement" is used, in this context, in a very broad sense. It may relate to such activities as physical measurement, per se, or to observation, transcription, judgmental assessment, or inquiry.

Physical measurements that relate to dimensions such as distance, weight, volume, time, temperature, and so forth provide one type of example. These measurements may be on things, or on human beings. Observations, made by persons or by mechanical recording devices, is another general method of data collection. Transcription involves copying information from one source to another, perhaps for purposes of detailed examination or analysis. Judgmental assessment refers to quantification or assessment simply on the basis of expertise.

In addition, a large number of statistical studies involve asking questions of persons; that is, data are collected by inquiry. Such studies, or surveys as they are often called, may collect information about persons, or their behavior or attitudes or opinions or about business establishments. Such surveys may be conducted by personal interview, telephone interview, mail questionnaire, or some combination of these techniques.

The meaning and proper interpretation of data cannot be divorced from the method of measurement that gave rise to those data. Different methods of measurement usually produce different statistical results.

Hence, it is essential to include a detailed description of the particular method or methods of data collection in a report on a statistical study. Such description should fully answer questions on how the data were collected and how they were recorded, and by whom.

In surveys of human populations, it is particulary important to explain what contacts were made with the sample respondents selected for the survey, how such contacts were made, and who was responsible for making them. Further, if incentives of any kind were used in conducting the survey, they should be fully disclosed.

If multiple methods of data collection were employed, the report should describe each method and indicate the extent to which each was used.

The report on a statistical study should make available facsimiles of the data collection forms used in the study. This includes the questionnaire, schedule or other type of reporting and recording forms used in the study. Preferably, all such documents should appear as an appendix to the report.

3.2 Field Work. A report on a statistical study should describe the type of field workers employed in the study; that is, the type of personnel responsible for the collection of data "in the field."

It should clearly indicate the nature of the responsibilities assigned to these workers, any qualifications required of them, the degree of training given them, and the extent to which they were supervised. The method of compensating field workers (e.g., at an hourly rate) should also be stated.

To the extent sample respondents rather than survey personnel are asked to complete questionnaires or other kinds of reporting forms, the instructions given to respondents should be described.

The report should further describe the methods by which field work was appraised, including any checking procedures that were employed.

Instruction sheets or manuals that were given to field workers should appear as an appendix to the report.

3.3 Nonresponse. When a group of units is predesignated for a statistical study, some nonresponse will normally occur. That is, there will be some units for which the required information is not actually obtained, either in part or in full. Some nonresponse can be expected in an (attempted) complete census as well as in a sample study.

Nonresponse may be caused by various circumstances; for example, failure to find and to measure particular units selected for study, or other circumstances which prevent application of the method of data collection. In studies of human populations, refusals by persons will also be a factor.

Nonresponse may introduce error or bias into study results. This occurs when nonrespondents differ from respondents with respect to characteristics being measured by a study. In such cases, the results obtained differ from the results that would have been obtained if nonresponse could have been eliminated. This particular type of survey error is a nonsampling error called bias of nonresponse.

Good statistical practice aims to keep the amount of nonresponse in any survey relatively small. This is done by using refined procedures, and by applying concerted effort in the data collection phases of a study.

Hence, it is important for a report on a statistical study to describe, in detail, provisions it makes to minimize nonresponse. This may well include description of search procedures to locate units not readily available. It should also include description of follow-up or callback procedures that attempt to convert nonrespondents by collecting data for them.

In addition, the report should give a detailed accounting of the disposition of a designated sample. This should include, first, the number of units initially designated. Second, it should detail the number or percentage of units that fall into various categories, as follows:

(1) Units originally selected that were not contacted in the course of the study, broken down into main subcategories by reason for failure to contact: [sic]

(2) Units selected that were contacted, but for which data could not be collected, broken down into main subcategories by reason for the nonmeasurement;

(3) Units selected, and measured at least in part that were eliminated from the sample at the coding or editing stages because of incompleteness, illegibilities, or inconsistencies in the data; and

(4) Units selected and measured, and included in the data base created by the statistical study.

Almost every statistical study is designed to collect several different items of information from each unit selected for the study. The degree of nonresponse may vary from one item to another. For example, sex and age data may be available for an individual, but information on his or her education may be incomplete. In general, the information on frequency of nonresponse should refer to the main items of information obtained in the study. However, in some cases, these results may have to be reported separately for several main items of information because of considerable variation in the nonresponse among the items.

A report on a statistical study should be careful not to imply that frequency or rate of response is the sole indicator of the accuracy of survey results. The ultimate question in judging the effects of nonresponse is whether respondents differ from nonrespondents with respect to the characteristics of interest in a study, and if so, what the impact on reported results is likely to be.

Thus, in the final analysis it is important for a report on a statistical study to assess and to state the effect nonresponse is likely to have on survey results. Any statement on this matter should be identified as being based either on opinion or on factual research, as the case may be. (See Section 4.2.)

3.4 Editing and Coding Procedures. Virtually every statistical study requires a phase of operations involving the editing and coding of data before processing and tabulating them. In general, suth operations are intended to check a set of data, as collected, for completeness and accuracy and then to decide whether or not the data are usable. This is an important phase of a study, and a report on a statistical study should describe editing and coding procedures fully. Moreover, some indication of the extent of application of these procedures should be given.

The description should relate to areas such as the following: (1) ways in which data collected from a unit are checked for completeness; (2) rules for using a data set which is incomplete; (3) checks on the basic data for consistency and accuracy; (4) how inconsistencies are reconciled; (5) rules for judging a data set as not usable and eliminating it from the sample; and (6) rules for revising data which is judged incomplete, inconsistent, or inaccurate.

While most editing and coding procedures may, to a large extent, be arbitrary, a report should provide whatever rationale or research basis exists for using them.

3.5 Processing and Computational Procedures. A report on a statistical study should describe how aggregative or summary results are tabulated from the raw, basic data records.

This description should indicate whether data records have been weighted, or otherwise adjusted, in this processing phase. If so, the reasons for such weighting or adjustments should be explained. Also, the basis for the weighting, and its impact, should be discussed in detail.

If computations are of a complex nature, appropriate explanation and formulas should be included in the description.

The extent to which verification and quality control checks were used in data processing operations should be indicated.

4.1 Sampling Error. Sampling error is the difference between (a) the result obtained from a sample study and (b) the result that would be obtained by attempting a complete study over all units in the frame from which the sample was selected, in the same manner and with the same care. The first result (a) is real. The second result (b) is hypothetical. Thus, sampling error can never be measured exactly. However, when a survey is based on probability sampling, the probabilities or risks of sampling errors of various sizes can be calculated. This requires the application of appropriate statistical formulas.

Assessments of sampling error are very often expressed in terms of a *standard error*. This is a universally accepted measure of the margin of error in a survey result that is attributable to sampling. It can be interpreted, with the aid of probability theory, to provide probabilities of sampling errors of various magnitudes. For example, under certain circumstances which are met in many, if not most statistical studies, probability theory enables the following interpretations:

> The probability that a sample estimate is subject to sampling error, in either direction, by more than one standard error is about 32 percent.
>
> The probability that a sample estimate is subject to sampling error, in either direction, by more than two standard errors is only about 5 percent.
>
> The probability that a sample estimate is subject to sampling error, in either direction, by more than three standard errors is virtually nil.

In any statistical study, each estimate will have its own standard error. These various standard error values may differ significantly.

Standard errors are meaningful only for results derived from probability samples. Somewhat different computational formulas apply for different kinds of statistical estimates, and for different kinds of probability samples. The exact interpretation of the standard error in terms of probabilities may also vary somewhat. These are matters to be decided based on statistical expertise.

A report on a statistical study must give, or provide a basis for properly calculating, standard errors of all estimates developed from the study. Comment about the proper interpretation of the standard errors should also be included.

The report should also include tabulations of sample size, overall and by relevant subcategories. Sample size, however, is one, but only one, of the determinants of the magnitude of the sampling error in study results. Many other features of a sampling plan influence sampling error.

A standard error does not reflect the extent to which a sample result is subject to nonsampling errors. Hence, it does not indicate, in itself, the extent to which a result is accurate, and certainly suggests nothing about its usefulness. A full assessment of the accuracy of the results from a statistical study must take into account the possibility of nonsampling errors, as discussed in the next subsection.

The use of probability concepts to calculate standard errors and thereby assess sampling errors is not appropriate with nonprobability sampling methods. A report on a study conducted by such means should specifically state that sampling errors can be inferred only on the basis of judgment, and not by the mechanical application of any standard statistical formulas. This, however, does not relieve a user of a nonprobability sample from reporting on sampling error.

4.2 Nonsampling Errors. Nonsampling error is any one of several different types of error, apart from sampling error, that may affect survey results. Nonsampling error is also referred to as procedural bias, or merely as bias.

The overall accuracy of results from a statistical study depend on the extent to which both sampling error and nonsampling errors are present in study results, The standard error, as discusses in the last section, reflects only sampling error.

Nonsampling errors are the result of imperfect study procedures (which may be necessary from a practical point of view) or of imperfect workmanship in carrying out study procedures. Nonsampling errors are not attributable to the sampling process used in a study. They would presumably occur even if a "complete" study were attempted in the same manner and with the same care as a sample study.

There are three main categories of nonsampling error. First, there may be nonsampling error if the frame used for the study is incomplete, or suffers from duplication. To the extent units excluded from the frame, or duplicated in the frame, are atypical in the characteristics being measured in a study, results from the study may be in error.

Second, there may be nonsampling error if the required information is not collected from all units designated for the sample. This is the problem of nonresponse. If nonrespondents differ from respondents with respect to characteristics being measured in a study, results from the study will be in error. This error is usually referred to as bias of nonresponse.

Third, the data items collected for various units included in a study may be in error. This is often referred to as response error. Use of the term error in this connection, however, implies that a standard of measurement has been defined against which to assess actual responses or recordings. Response error may occur because of clerical error, or data errors at the source, processing mistakes, or human misreporting, or machine failure.

Nonsampling errors will occur to some degree in any statistical study. They are minimized by carefully designed and well-tested procedures, by concerted and diligent effort in conducting a study, and by the use of controls and checking procedures.

A report on a statistical study should describe what procedures, controls and checks were employed to minimize nonsampling errors.

The report should also attempt to access the magnitude of nonsampling errors.

Often, such assessment may be done by reference to methodological research studies. If so, that research should be fully referenced, and amply described.

In addition, many statistical studies are followed by an after-the-fact audit, by those who conducted the study or by an independent party. Such an audit aims to assess the extent to which there were deviations from stated procedures, and what the effect on study results might be from those deviations. If such an audit was conducted, it should be reported in full.

APPENDIX III
United States District Court Southern District of New York

The Court, at the request of Plaintiff having held pre-trial conferences to consider certain proposals made by Plaintiff with regard to the conduct of a survey to be offered in evidence, and related matters, and having heard counsel for the parties in connection therewith:

NOW, THEREFORE, upon consent of the parties, the following pretrial order is entered:

1. This pre-trial order is in addition to and not in lieu of any other pre-trial order or orders herein and is limited to those matters specifically set forth herein.

2. The parties shall follow the following procedures with regard to a survey to be conducted by plaintiff in this action.

A. Plaintiff shall draft a written description outlining the issues and objectives to be examined in the survey in light of the factual and legal issues in this civil action. A copy thereof shall be submitted to the defendants. Defendants' objections or suggestions, concerning this draft, if any, shall be served in writing upon plaintiff. The parties shall meet in an attempt to resolve any differences between them. Plaintiff shall, thereafter, prepare a final written description and serve a copy on defendants. Any objections to such final description shall be brought before the Court for resolution.

B. Plaintiff shall thereafter prepare a list of not less than 3 recognized survey experts any one of whom it proposes to engage for this purpose and will serve a copy of that list on defendants with a statement outlining the qualifications of each, which list shall also indicate whether or not there has been any prior business relationship between plaintiff and each proposed expert. Adequate opportunity for examination of the proposed experts' qualifications shall be afforded to defendants and plaintiff agrees to provide defendants with further information, if available, concerning the qualifications of said experts, upon request.

(i) If defendants have any objections to the qualifications of any of the proposed experts, except with regard to the expert's relationship to plaintiff, if any, they shall advise plaintiff in writing specifying the nature thereof. Plaintiff shall designate as its survey expert one of such experts to whom defendants have made no objections other than a possible subsequent objection based upon prior business relationships between plaintiff and said expert. If defendants object to all proposed experts, the parties shall meet to attempt to resolve their differences. If no resolution is achieved, plaintiff shall nevertheless select one listed expert.

(ii) Following plaintiff's selection of an expert, plaintiff shall supply to defendants a statement covering the preceding five years disclosing (a) the number of projects undertaken by the expert for plaintiff, (b) the subject matter of each such project, (c) the total amount of fees received by the expert from plaintiff, and (d) whether there is any on-going or retainer arrangement between the expert and plaintiff. At defendants' request plaintiff will produce the selected expert for a deposition relating to the experts' qualifications and prior business relations with plaintiff. The defendants shall notify plaintiff in writing of their objections, if any, to the selected expert based upon his relationship with plaintiff.

(iii) If plaintiff believes that defendants' objections to its selection of an expert are groundless or insubstantial, whether as to the expert's general qualifications or prior relationship to the plaintiff, plaintiff may take them to the Court for a ruling.

(iv) In any event, defendants shall be free to raise any of their objections to the qualifications of the selected expert at such time as the survey may he offered in evidence or at any time, provided, however, that no objections not raised initially may be raised thereafter unless the basis for such an objection arises subsequently, or is discovered by defendants subsequently and could not reasonably have been discovered at the time defendants' objections, if any, were originally to have been interposed.

C. The expert so selected shall, in light of the written description, report what information and/or materials, if any, the expert believes are needed or desirable in order to design or conduct the survey, and the reasons therefor. Counsel for the parties shall then discuss whether discovery is necessary to provide such information or materials to the expert, and shall attempt to agree upon the nature or scope of any proposed discovery. Absent such agreement, counsel shall apply to the Court for rulings. Any such discovery conducted by agreement or under Court order shall be subject to all objections and shall in all respects be governed by the Federal Rules of Civil Procedure.

D. The designated expert shall propose a design for a projectable survey in light of the issues set out in the written description. That design proposal, which shall conform to accepted practices in such matters, shall be reduced to writing and shall comprise a specification of the steps, methods and procedures to be followed, including, among others an adequate description of:

(1) The definition of the universe to be surveyed and the reasons therefor:

(2) The method of selecting the sample, the size of the sample, and the computation of the sampling error;

(3) Design and specimen of respondent screeners and question-

naires which shall include a request to interviewees for authorization to disclose the name and address of the interviewees;

(4) The method of selection of supervisors and interviewers and instructions to supervisors and interviewers;

(5) Method of conducting the survey;

(6) The monitoring and validation procedures to be used and by whom or where such procedures will be conducted;

(7) The editing, tabulating and coding procedures to be used;

(8) The pre-test and/or pilot survey procedures to be used, if any.

E. A copy of the expert's proposal shall be served on defendants. Defendants shall have the right to ask for and receive further details relating to any aspect of the design and proposed conduct of the survey. At defendants' request plaintiff shall produce its expert and its employees with knowledge of facts relevant to the design and conduct of the proposed survey for deposition relating thereto. Defendants shall prepare and serve on plaintiff in writing all objections, if any, which they may have to any part of the proposal. Plaintiff shall transmit such objections to the expert for consideration and for modification of the proposal if deemed appropriate by the expert. A final proposal shall be prepared and served on defendants. The parties with their own experts shall meet to attempt to resolve any differences still remaining after the expert's consideration of defendants' objections and proposed modifications of the proposal first submitted. Any objections of defendants not resolved by the parties or accepted in whole or in part by the expert shall be presented to the Court for determination. Defendants shall not thereafter raise any new objections to the design of the survey, but shall be free to renew objections previously made at the time the survey is offered in evidence.

F. The expert shall have sole responsibility for the actual conduct of the survey and the parties shall not participate in the selection of subcontractors, if any, employed by the expert to conduct the survey or any part thereof.

G. The survey shall then be conducted in accordance with the expert's proposal as modified by the parties or in accordance with the Court's rulings. Following completion of the survey, a final written report of the survey results shall be prepared by the expert which, together with copies of all prior informal, preliminary and draft reports, computations, printouts, coding sheets, records of contacts or attempts, questionnaires completed in whole or in part, and all other documents used in the design and conduct of the survey within the expert's custody, possession or control, which shall include the names and addresses of all persons interviewed who shall have authorized such disclosure (as provided in 2(D) (3) above) (collectively referred to as the "Documents") shall be served upon defendants and a copy of said final report shall be filed with the Court.

H. After receipt of said report and documents, the parties shall have the right, as provided by the Federal Rules of Civil Procedure, to depose any persons who participated in, or were in any manner associated with the conduct of the survey, except for counsel. Plaintiff shall cooperate with defendants in attempting to ascertain the name and address of person designated for deposition by defendants. Within 60 days of the completion of said discovery, defendants shall serve upon plaintiff in writing any objections they may have to the manner in which the survey was conducted. If plaintiff shall thereafter cause the survey or parts thereof to be supplemented, corrected or re-run and a new additional Documents referred to in Paragraph 2(G), *supra* and file with the Court any resulting new or revised written report, defendants shall be entitled to conduct such additional discovery as they may deem necessary in respect thereof in accordance with the discovery procedures above set forth and shall serve any further objections on plaintiff in writing. No further round of corrections and objections will be undertaken without leave of the Court.

3. Plaintiff shall be deemed to have waived its work product privilege with regard to the reports and the Documents referred to in Paragraphs 2(G) and (H) above, (including any drafts or non-identical copies thereof) and as to all communications with the persons identified therein. Either party may offer the same at the trial of this action subject to any available objections under the Federal Rule [sic] of Evidence not specifically waived hereunder.

4. Defendants shall be free to renew at trial, or prior to trial, any of their objections made in accordance with the procedure set forth herein including any objections the Court may have overruled or any changes made as a result of the Court's rulings. Those aspects of the survey proposal not objected to and brought before the Court for resolution by the defendants as hereinabove provided, shall be deemed to have been agreed to by the defendants. Defendants shall make all objections relative to the conduct of the survey based on facts then known to them at the time specified in Paragraph 2(H) so that plaintiff will at the time be adequately apprised thereof. Upon the discovery of any additional facts which defendants believe bear on the weight or admissability [sic] of the survey they shall notify plaintiff thereof of newly discovered facts. Nothing herein shall be deemed (a) a waiver of defendants' right to object to or contest at any time the manner in which the survey was conducted and any conclusions drawn from or asserted by any party based upon the survey results; (b) a waiver of defendants' right to object to the admissibility of the survey report and Documents on any grounds preserved hereunder; (c) a consent to the evidentiary weight, if any, to be given to the survey report and results; or (d) a waiver of any parties' right to review on appeal any rulings made by the Court in accordance with the procedures provided by hereunder.

5. Nothing herein shall preclude defendants or plaintiff from retaining other experts, conducting other tests or polls or adducing any other or

additional evidence at the trial on the merits, and these procedures shall apply only to the survey to be conducted by plaintiff as hereinabove set forth.

6. Discovery in this action other than that provided for herein, shall be suspended (except upon motion to the Court) pending completion of the survey. Adequate time for the conduct and completion before trial of all remaining discovery shall be afforded the parties after completion of the survey and the procedures provided for herein.

7. The normal and reasonable cost of designing and conducting the survey herein provided shall be borne by plaintiff. No part of such costs to the parties (other than discovery) of participating in any of the procedures provided regardless of the outcome of said survey or the final determination of this action shall be assessed. This provision shall not, however, constitute a waiver of the right of any party to seek to tax as costs, any other or additional expenses relating to the procedures provided for herein which the Court may find were incurred as a result of unwarranted or burdensome conduct by the other party.

Appendix G

A Comparative Perspective on the Role of Experts in Legal Proceedings

The American legal system is based in large part on what legal scholars refer to as the common law tradition, which is treated as beginning in 1066 A.D. with the Norman conquest of England. This tradition is in force today not only in the United States but also in many parts of the former British Empire, such as Great Britain, Canada, Australia, and New Zealand. The role of the expert witness and the attitudes toward the acceptance of statistical assessments as evidence in the courts are quite similar in these jurisdictions and, at various places in this report, the panel has occasion to refer to such similarities and to describe the use of statistics in actual cases from these countries. At an early stage in the panel's deliberations, we recognized that we did not possess expertise on alternative legal systems, especially those from the civil law tradition, in force in most of Western Europe and Latin America (e.g., see Merryman, 1969). Thus two experts in the civil law tradition were invited to meet with the panel, and to describe the differences in how the two traditions utilize the expertise of professionals such as statisticians. This summary of the panel's discussion on the topic draws heavily on Langbein (1985), and, while quite incomplete as a treatment of the role of experts in the civil law tradition, it does offer some additional motivation for the panel's recommendations regarding the utilization of court-appointed experts in Section 5.4.

G.1   Overview of a Continental System

There are two fundamental differences between continental and Anglo-American civil procedure, and these differences lead in turn to many others. First, in the continental system, the court rather than the parties' lawyers takes the main responsibility for gathering and sifting evidence, although the lawyers exercise a watchful eye over the court's work. Second, there is no sharp distinction between pretrial and trial, between discovery for trial and evidence at trial; trial is not a single continuous event. Rather, the court gathers and evaluates evidence over a series of hearings, as many as the circumstances require.

For example, in the West German system, the plaintiff's lawyer initiates a lawsuit with a complaint. Like its American counterpart, the German complaint narrates the key facts, sets forth a legal theory, and asks for a remedy in damages or specific relief. Unlike an American complaint, however, the German document proposes means of proof for its main factual contentions. The major documents in the plaintiff's possession that support his claim are scheduled and often appended; other documents (for example, hospital files or government records such as police accident reports or agency files) are indicated; witnesses who are thought to know something helpful to the plaintiff's position are identified. The defendant's answer follows the same pattern.

The judge to whom the case is entrusted examines these pleadings and appended documents, and routinely sends for relevant public records. These materials form the initial part of the official dossier, the court file. All subsequent submissions of counsel, and all subsequent evidence-gathering, will be entered in the dossier, which is open to counsel's inspection continuously.

When the judge first has a sense of the dispute from these materials, he schedules a hearing and often invites or summons the parties as well as their lawyers to this and subsequent hearings. If the pleadings have identified witnesses whose testimony seems central, the judge may summon them to the initial hearing as well.

The course of the hearing depends greatly on the circumstances of the case. Sometimes the court will be able to resolve the case by discussing it with the lawyers and parties and suggesting avenues of compromise. If the case remains contentious and witness testimony needs to be taken, the court will have learned enough about the case to determine a sequence for examining witnesses. The judge serves as the examiner-in-chief. At the conclusion of his interrogation of each witness, counsel for either party may pose additional questions, but counsel are not prominent as examiners. Witness testimony is seldom recorded verbatim; rather, the judge pauses from time to time to dictate a summary of the testimony into the dossier.

The lawyers sometimes suggest improvements in the wording of these summaries, in order to preserve or to emphasize nuances that are important to one side or the other. Since the proceedings in a complicated case may require several hearings extending across many months, these summaries of concluded testimony—by encapsulating succinctly the results of previous hearings—allow the court to refresh itself rapidly for subsequent hearings. The summaries also constitute the building blocks from which the court will ultimately fashion the findings of fact for its written judgment.

If an issue of technical difficulty arises on which the court or counsel wish to obtain the views of an expert, the court—in consultation with counsel—will select the expert and define the expert's role.

After the court takes witness testimony or receives some other infusion of evidence, counsel have the opportunity to comment on the proofs orally or in writing. Counsel use these submissions in order to suggest further proofs or to advance legal theories. Thus nonadversarial proof-taking alternates with adversarial dialogue across as many hearings as are necessary.

The process merges the investigatory function of our pretrial discovery and the evidence-presenting function of our trial. This is a key source of the efficiency of continental procedure. A witness is ordinarily examined once. This is in contrast to the American practice of partisan interview and preparation, pretrial deposition, preparation for trial, and examination and cross-examination at trial.

When the court has developed the facts and it has the views of the parties and their lawyers, it decides the case by means of a written judgment that must contain full findings of fact and make reasoned application of the law.

G.2   The Role of Experts in the West German System

In the continental tradition, experts are selected and commissioned by the court, although with great attention to safeguarding party interests. In the German system, experts are not even called witnesses. They are thought of as "judges' aides" (Jessnitzer, 1978). Expertise is frequently sought. The literature emphasizes the value attached to having expert assistance available to the courts in an age in which litigation involves facts of ever-greater technical difficulty. The essential insight of continental civil procedure is that credible expertise must be neutral expertise. Thus, the responsibility for selecting and informing experts is placed on the courts, although with important protections for party interests. The court may decide to seek expertise on its own motion, or at the request of one of the parties. The code of civil procedure in Germany allows the court to request nominations from the parties—indeed, the code requires the court to use an expert on whom the parties agree—but neither practice is typical. In general, the court takes the initiative in nominating and selecting the expert. Cappelletti and Perillo (1965) describe a similar role and a similar selection procedure for experts in the civil procedure of Italy.

The only respect in which the German code of civil procedure purports to narrow the court's discretion to choose the expert is a provision whose significance is less than obvious: "If experts are officially designated for certain fields of expertise, other persons should be chosen only when special circumstances require" (*Zivilprozessordnung*, Section 404(2)). Officially designated experts are found on various lists compiled by official licensing bodies, and quasi-public bodies designated by state governments.

Langbein (1985) notes that the most important factor predisposing a German judge to select an expert is favorable experience with that expert in an earlier case. Experts thus build reputations with the bench. Someone who renders a careful, succinct, and well-substantiated report and who responds effectively to the subsequent questions of the court and the parties will be remembered when another case arises in this specialty.

If enough potential experts are identified to allow for choice, the court will ordinarily consult party preferences. In such circumstances a litigant may ask the court to exclude an expert whose views proved contrary to his interests in previous litigation or whom he otherwise fears. The court will try to oblige the parties' tastes when another qualified expert can be substituted. Nevertheless, a litigant can formally challenge an expert's appointment only on the narrow grounds for which a litigant could seek to recuse a judge.

The court that selects the expert instructs him, in the sense of propounding the facts that he is to assume or to investigate, and in framing the questions that the court wishes the expert to address. In formulating the expert's task, as in most other important steps in the conduct of the case, the court welcomes adversary suggestions. If a view of premises is required—for example, in an accident case or a building construction dispute—counsel for both sides attend.

The expert is ordinarily instructed to prepare a written opinion. When the court receives the report, it is circulated to the litigants. The litigants commonly file written comments, to which the expert is asked to reply. The court on its own motion may also request the expert to amplify his views. If the expert's report remains in contention, the court will schedule a hearing at which the dissatisfied litigant can confront and interrogate the expert.

The code of civil procedure reserves to the court the power to order a further report by another expert in the event that the court should deem the first report unsatisfactory. A litigant who is dissatisfied with the expertise in a case may encourage the court to invoke its power to name a second expert. The code of criminal procedure has a more explicit standard for such cases, which is worth noticing because the literature suggests that the courts have similar instincts in civil procedure. The court may refuse a litigant's motion to engage a further expert in a criminal case. The code says (*Strafprozessordnung*, Section 244 (4)):

> If the contrary of the fact concerned has already been proved through the former expert opinion; this does not apply if the expertise of the former expert is doubted, if his report is based upon inaccurate factual presuppositions, if the report contains contradictions, or if the new expert has available means of research that appear superior to those of a former expert.

When, therefore, a litigant can persuade the court that an expert's report has been sloppy or partial, or that it rests upon a view of the field that is not generally shared, the court will commission further expertise.

Parties may also engage their own experts, much as we are used to seeing done in the Anglo-American procedural world, in order to rebut the court-appointed expert. The court will discount the views of a party-selected expert on account of his lack of neutrality, but cases occur in which he nevertheless proves to be effective. Ordinarily, German courts will not in such circumstances base judgments directly on the views of the party-selected expert; rather, the court will treat the rebuttal as ground for engaging a further expert (called an *Oberexperte*, literally an "upper" or "superior" expert), whose opinion will take account of the rebuttal.

G.3   Differing Roles for American and Continental Experts

The basic difference between the American and the European procedures is that experts are not witnesses in the European system; rather they are auxiliaries of the judge (see Cappelletti and Perillo, 1965). They are part and parcel of the court. Their role arises when the judge wants to have an assistant who has knowledge that the judge does not possess, but the judge still remains the master of the experts and is not bound by expert opinion. The American system is based on a quite different philosophy involving the initiative of the parties and the lawyers, with each party choosing its own experts.

An expert can help to clarify the facts; or the expert can draw conclusions and inferences. Thus, the expert can do two things: establish the facts, and help the court understand the rules and principles, ideas, or techniques that are not within the ordinary knowledge of the court. As far as findings of fact are concerned, the panel's view is that the confrontational aspects of the American system are healthy, because then the expert witness is *really* a witness about the facts. But when it comes to the scientific rules, principles, and techniques, the panel's view is that confrontation seems to be, to some extent, out of place. The one aspect of the American system that comes close to the "impartial" role of the expert in the continental system is Rule 706 of the Federal Rules of Evidence, which allows for court-appointed expert witnesses (see Chapter 4).

Appendix H

Assessing the Impact of Statistical Evidence, A Social Science Perspective

Neil Vidmar
University of Western Ontario
and
Duke University

Purpose and Scope of this Paper

In commissioning this paper, the panel asked for a review of social science literature bearing on how statistical evidence in litigation affects the court process. This paper includes the literature review, a discussion of how courts appear to adapt to statistical evidence, and suggestions for research. The Index to Legal Periodicals from 1980 to the present was perused. Similar scanning of the Social Science Source Index for the same period was also undertaken. A number of texts and reports provided secondary sources. Finally, a number of colleagues provided unpublished reports and papers.

The review indicated that the material having a direct bearing on the use and impact of statistical evidence is very sparse. What does exist, however, offers some tantalizing insights and identifies a large number of problem areas in which social science research is needed. I have tried to shape the resulting paper to complement the panel's report, as was intended. The report is organized around a number of substantive areas that are self-explanatory.

Statistics in the Courts

The panel's report attempts to document the increasing use of statistical data in the courts. A search of Lexis, the computer-based legal information retrieval system, revealed that between 1960 and September 1982 the term *statistics* or *statistical* appeared in 4 percent of the reported federal district court opinions. Disaggregation of these data according to specific statistical terms showed that the influx of complex statistics, such as regression, is very recent. Rubinfeld's (1985) search of federal decisions from 1969 to July 1984 yielded 84 references to regression analyses. Both of these analyses suggest that, while the frequency of complex statistics in legal proceedings is a relatively recent phenomenon, it is probably on the increase.

Although suggestive of general trends, these figures may greatly underestimate the use of statistical data in the legal system. For example, since

1981 over half the decisions in the federal circuits have been unpublished decisions and therefore would not be catalogued in the Lexis system (see Stienstra, 1985: 40). Whether the unpublished opinions have the same, lesser, or greater likelihood of containing statistical analyses is an empirical question for which confident a priori predictions cannot be made. The data, of course, also do not reveal anything about the number of settled cases. Far more cases are settled than actually reach the point of adjudication, but little information is available on whether the presence of statistical evidence affects settlement and how.

There are some data bearing on the frequency of scientific evidence in trial courts, but it does not speak specifically to the issue of statistical data. Schroeder (reported in Saks and Van Duizend, 1983) conducted a survey of 5,550 judges and lawyers, of whom 1,363 responded (i.e., a 25 percent response rate). The survey indicated that of those polled 23 percent said that they encountered scientific evidence in at least half of their criminal cases; 24 percent believed that in at least half the cases in which it was not used it could have been; and 86 percent said they would like to see such evidence used more frequently. These figures are contradicted by other data, however, and lead to an inference that there was a sampling bias in the study. Parker (cited in Saks and Van Duizend, 1983: 8) concluded that fewer than 2 percent of criminal cases in one local sample benefited from a laboratory analysis of any kind. In another study, Parker and Peterson (cited in Saks and Van Duizend, 1983: 8) found that in a sample of 3,303 felony cases only 4 involved the submission of laboratory evidence. In a study of capital trials in Illinois, Lassers (1967) found that only 25 percent of them included scientific testimony. Jacoby (1985) has recently documented the increasing use of survey research in U.S. courts, particularly with respect to trademark infringements.

The most systematic data on scientific evidence in criminal cases is reported in Kalven and Zeisel's (1966) study of over 3,000 jury trials. They found that in 25 percent of all cases the prosecution introduced at least one expert witness but the defense brought in an expert in only 6 percent of cases. However, the study is more than two decades old and developments in the intervening years may make it dated. Myers (1979) studied 201 felony jury trials that occurred in one Indiana county between January 1974 and June 1976. She found that in 68 percent of trials there was no expert witness, in 27 percent there was a single expert, and in 5 percent there were two or more experts. Saks and Van Duizend (1983) conducted interviews with judges and lawyers involved in a small, nonrandom sample of trials in which scientific evidence was used. Their informants suggested that scientific evidence is very often not called when it could be and, even when it is, it is not used very effectively. Scientific evidence may be used less frequently in criminal than in civil cases, at least in part because the financial resources to obtain it are not available in criminal cases. Another reason for the failure to use scientific evidence is that lawyers often do not understand its potential usefulness in their case or, if they do, do not know where to find experts. In addition, in criminal cases defense lawyers may not call experts because they are perceived as prosecution witnesses, and in fact such witnesses may be reluctant to testify for the defense. Saks and Van Duizend (1983: 52–54) also identify some factors arising outside the legal system that may impede the use of experts.

These sources exhaust what is known empirically about the use of statistical data in the courts. It is meagre knowledge. However, other more speculative and theoretical articles put these findings into a broader perspective and suggest that the growth curve of statistical evidence may be far from having reached asymtote.

Chayes (1976) analytically distinguished between private law cases and public law cases. His analysis helps us to understand why statistics may be used with increasing frequency in civil cases and why federal trial courts may be faced with more statistical evidence than state courts. Chayes suggested that over recent decades the federal courts have increasingly dealt with public as opposed to private law. Public law cases include such obvious examples as school desegregation, employment discrimination, and prisoners or inmates' rights; they also include other cases in which the government is a party in the proceedings, such as antitrust, securities, bankruptcy, consumer fraud, housing discrimination, electoral reapportionment, and environmental management suits. The dominating characteristic of public law cases is that they do not arise from disputes between private parties about private rights; rather, the object of the litigation is the vindication of constitutional or statutory policies. Chayes does not discuss specifically the use of statistical evidence, but closer examination suggests that in public law cases such evidence is often essential to the proof and to the remedy stages of litigation. Chayes reported that statistics on the federal courts show that in 1940 53 percent of cases were federal questions or involved the United States as a party but in 1974 that figure had risen to between 72 and 81 percent. This trend may help to explain the increasing use of statistical evidence in terms of the substantive nature of the cases that now appear in federal courts.

There is also reason to believe that in criminal, as well as civil cases, the increasing impact of statistical evidence may just now be beginning to manifest itself. In the criminal law area, however, the statistical evidence is less likely to be derived directly from substantive law than from the tools and technologies used by experts testifying about substantive matters, for example, the probabilistic nature of much forensic evidence. Gianelli (1980) argues that there is an ever increasing use of scientific evidence in criminal trials. This view is supported by Imwinkelreid (1983). The increasing use of forensic technologies may be ascribed to the facts that (a) the Warren Court's "due process" revolution led prosecutors to search for new forms of evidence and (b) there has been a very rapid advancement in technologies that can be applied to forensic issues.

Three additional developments portend increased use of statistical evidence. The first is the erosion of the *Frye* test for the admission of scientific evidence. In the mid–1970s *Frye* was the controlling law in at least 45 states (Gianelli, 1980; Imwinkelreid, 1983, 1984). To be admissible under *Frye*, the basis on which the scientific testimony was drawn had to be demonstrated to be generally accepted within the scientific community. However, in the late 1970s and 1980s, the *Frye* rule began to be replaced in many jurisdictions by rules modeled after the Federal Rules of Evidence. Under these latter rules the trier of fact is given the burden of assessing the reliability and validity of the techniques and data that underlie the expert's opinion; this, of course, often raises some complex statistical arguments. The second development is the discovery that the high levels of reliability traditionally accorded much forensic evidence are not justified (see Imwinkelreid, 1981, 1983; Moenssens, 1984; Saxe, Dougherty, and Cross, 1985). For example, an issue of the 1983 *Journal of Forensic Sciences* reported results from a study of 105 laboratories in 49 states that concluded that the laboratories produced a large number of false positives and false negatives; moreover, on quantitative analyses of samples the coefficient of variation was as high as 133 percent. The third development is the trend toward increased use of social science evidence in criminal trials (see Monahan and Walker, 1985; Saks and Baron, 1980). Examples of such evidence are predictions of dangerousness; psychological syndrome evidence such as battered women, battered child, and rape trauma syndromes; identification profiles of hijackers, illegal aliens, or drug couriers; and evidence bearing on witness unreliability. Unlike traditional psychiatric assessments, which largely rely on direct assessments of a particular individual, this type of evidence is based on probability estimates derived from the study of characteristics of a known (or alleged) population. The problem with this form of social science evidence is the same as with the technologies of more traditional forensic evidence: namely, arguable validity and low rates of reliability that yield large numbers of false positive or false negative classifications.

The longer-run consequence of these developments is likely to be increased challenges of forensic experts, either through cross-examination or through counter-experts called by the opposing side (see Decker, 1982; Loftus, 1986). A central part of this clash of expert opinions will unquestionably involve statistical arguments about such things as base rates, significance tests, and regression techniques. Making sense of the conflicting opinions will fall on the judge and the jury.

Litigation Strategy

Litigation strategy is a broad concept. It includes such things as what evidence is called by whom and when, its extent and complexity, counter-responses by the opposing party, and choice of resolution forum. Litigation strategy is a central determinant of the impact that a case has on the legal system. Litigation strategy affects settlement attempts, the length and complexity of trials, the cost of litigation, coping responses on the part of fact finders, and the appeal process. It is therefore important to ask what influence statistical evidence has on litigation strategy.

The number of studies bearing overtly on litigation strategies are relatively few in number but extremely rich in suggestive information. As a consequence they are reviewed below in some detail. In overview one might say that the use of statistical evidence depends on a number of factors, among them case type, evidentiary admissiblity, access to experts, ideology, lawyer sophistication, and financial resources. Use of statistical evidence evokes counter-strategies. The use and presentation of the evidence, moreover, appears to vary substantially, depending on whether the case is tried before a judge or a jury.

One of the best studies of litigation strategy, conducted by Sanders, Rankin-Widgeon, Kalmuss, and Chesler (1982), examined the use of social science experts in school desegregation cases. The authors interviewed lawyers, judges, and social scientists involved in 17 school desegregation cases and focused on the violation stage of the litigation. Sanders et al. drew on Chayes' (1976) distinction between private law and public law litigation. They noted that plaintiffs view such cases from the perspective of public law and government policy: segregation derives from socially determined patterns that overshadow individual intentions or specific acts. Defendants—the school boards and their lawyers—view them from a private law perspective that attempts to refute the plaintiff's claims by denying any specific intention to discriminate.

In the 17 cases in the sample, plaintiffs used 14 different experts while the defendants used only 5. Moreover, the defendants' experts usually appeared later in the litigation process. The nature of the evidence also differed. The plaintiff's expert testimony typically addressed two different sets of issues: the educational and psychological effects of segregation and the nature, causes, and effects of residential segregation. The defendants' experts never testified about educational and psychological effects.

Sanders et al. suggest that a number of factors account for these differences. First, the defendants had an evidentiary problem. Courts have tended to dismiss defense evidence purporting to show that desegregation might have harmful effects on minority group children as an attack on the basic holding of *Brown* v. *Board of Education*. Second, plaintiffs had more ready access to experts than did defendants. Generally, social scientists had an ideological bias that favored the plaintiffs and made them reluctant to testify for defendants. The plaintiff's lawyers were usually experienced litigators, whereas fewer than 20 percent of defense lawyers had previous experience in desegregation cases. Defense lawyers were usually chosen simply because they represented the school board on other matters. Third, the two sides had differing conceptions of the case, the plaintiffs favoring a public law model and the defendants favoring a private law model. Social science evidence is consistent with a public law model because it speaks to behavior that is inherently observable only in relative terms. Such evidence tactically favors the plaintiffs' case because "it establishes the context within which apparently neutral acts lead to further discrimination" (Sanders et al., 1982: 418). Defendants call their own experts primarily to counter plaintiff witnesses or to cloud the issues, not because the experts are considered central to their position. Finally, there are ideological differences. Plaintiff lawyers tend to see the cause of racial inequality in terms of institutional discrimination, whereas defendant lawyers prefer to see the cause in individual actions. This ideology may blind defense lawyers to alternative strategies. Indeed, Sanders et al. point out that defense lawyers in an Atlanta case, *Armour* v. *Nix* (1979), were successful with a strategy that came very close to a public law model, yet defense lawyers have seldom tried to build their case around such a model.

Sanders et al. also attempted to assess the impact of expert testimony. They used three different sources to make these assessments: what judges said in interviews; what judges wrote in their opinions; and what could be inferred from the remedies. They concluded that expert testimony does have impact. A number of judges indicated that they had been persuaded to consider, some even came to accept, a public law view of the case. The conclusions of Sanders et al. are generally consistent with the conclusions of other authors who have studied school desegregation cases (see e.g., *Law and Contemporary Problems*, 1975).

Another important study was conducted by Bermant et al. (1981) under the auspices of the Federal Judicial Center. Its purpose was to assess a number of issues associated with protracted civil trials, including questions about litigation strategy. The authors interviewed participants in 17 civil trials that terminated in federal district courts between 1977 and 1979. The sample was intended to be representative of the 159 cases during that period that took 20 or more court days to be tried and included both bench and jury trials. Archival data from a larger sample of other cases were also analyzed. The researchers did not specifically tease out statistical or social science data for analysis, but 16 of the 17 cases were characterized by evidence that was specialized or otherwise difficult for a nonexpert to comprehend.

The ideology issue documented by Sanders et al. (1982) reappeared in this study, particularly in the jury trials, but it sometimes occurred in a different way. In antitrust cases, for example, plaintiffs' lawyers tended to stress the importance of corporate intent and deemphasize the importance of scientific and engineering facts; consequently, they were less likely to acknowledge the difficulty of evidentiary facts. Judges, it should be noted, tended to agree with the defendants that the issues were complex.

Bermant et al. (1981) also asked whether the evidence influenced the management of litigation before trial. There are a number of expediting procedures available to judges, such as requirement of pretrial briefs or stipulation of facts. The use of these expediting procedures was dependent on the cooperativeness of the parties and on the willingness of the judge to become involved before trial. No single picture emerged of pretrial preparation, although there was fairly widespread pretrial agreement on admission of documents and depositions. Appointment of neutral experts under Federal Rule 706 occurred in only 2 of the 17 cases, despite the fact that equally complex technical matters were at issue in most of the other cases.

A third matter bearing on litigation strategy involved the choice of a jury or a judge as the trier of fact when the case was eligible for jury trial. The decisions appear to have been made on tactical grounds. The deciding factor named most often by the lawyers was the identity of the judge and their perception of the judge's biases. Several lawyers stated that they preferred jury trials when their cases were weak. Another contributing factor was the anticipation of appellate review. Some lawyers asserted that the chance of overturning an unfavorable decision on appeal was greater in jury trials. To examine the validity of this last assertion, Bermant et al. traced the appellate histories on 18,528 jury-eligible civil cases terminating between July 1976 and December 1978 in which jury trials would be permitted. Of these, 24 percent of bench trials were appealed, compared with 22 percent of jury trials. The "success rate" of appeals based on the percentage of the trials that were reversed or remanded was also examined. The success rate for bench trials was 5 percent, and for jury trials it was 4 percent. There was some considerable variation in the above figures when they were disaggregated by individual circuits, and it is not clear whether this variation reflects differences in case types or some other factor. On the whole, however, jury and bench trials do not significantly differ on either rate of appeal or success of appeal.

The Bermant et al. study also concluded that there were many more differences between bench and jury trials than just the trier of fact. One important difference was the density of trial activity, with jury trials averaging 13.5 days per month and bench trials averaging 6.9 days per month. Bench trials took many more calendar days from commencement to final termination. Another difference was the extent of colloquy between judge or jury and the witnesses and lawyers. Particularly important were the findings of differences regarding the amount of evidence called and the organization of the evidence and arguments. In jury trials, lawyers tended to simplify the case as much as possible so as to bring it within what they regarded as the comprehension and attention span of the jury. In several jury cases, difficult scientific and technical facts were ignored; instead emphasis was placed on commercial issues. Finally, there were some interesting findings about the conduct of the jury trial: most of the special or extraordinary organizational efforts undertaken in certain trials derived not from the needs or abilities of the jurors but rather from other factors inherent in the cases.

Saks and Van Duizend (1983) interviewed the lawyers, judges, and experts involved in nine cases in which scientific or technical evidence was a major issue in the trial. The cases were not randomly selected, but, in contrast to the two studies just discussed, the authors focused predominantly on criminal trials and on state as opposed to federal cases. Saks and Van Duizend also placed more emphasis on the prefiling and pretrial stages of the litigation process. The decisions to retain experts and to select particular ones are often crucial components of litigation strategy, yet in the sample of criminal cases studied these decisions appeared to be haphazard. Despite a rule of thumb that experts should be chosen early in the case, the decision was often made much later. Lawyers decided intuitively whether an expert was needed and did not appear to have any systematic strategies across cases. Moreover, the lawyers did not clearly distinguish between types of experts (e.g., ballistics experts and firearms identification experts), although in fact these experts provide very different types of evidence. Experts tended to be contacted through informal networks. Defense lawyers were less likely to call experts than prosecutors, primarily because they tended to view forensic experts solely as prosecution witnesses. There was some suggestion that defense lawyers may indeed have difficulty getting forensic or medical experts to testify, because such experts do not want to contradict their colleagues who are working for the prosecution. Another important consideration was cost: defense lawyers often had limited financial resources (see also Decker, 1982).

Saks and Van Duizend also asked about the impact of scientific evidence on pretrial discovery. They report that 37 states and the District of Columbia follow the federal rule permitting discovery of expert evidence in civil trials. The cases studied indicated that there was a high degree of information sharing between parties. However, Saks and Van Duizend also documented the fact that lawyers develop both "clean" and "dirty" experts. The former are those who are given information that is largely favorable to the client's case, that is, "safe" information. The latter are given all the information that the lawyer thinks is relevant to the case and are used solely in an advisory capacity to help devise trial strategy. By using the two-expert system lawyers shield harmful information from their adversaries and still obtain complete expert advice. Such a two-expert system can, of course, be used only when there are adequate resources. With less well-off conditions, lawyers cut costs by making only selective use of experts. Another much-discussed aspect of expert testimony is the "shopping" for favorable experts and "controlling" the expert by withholding information. Saks and Van Duizend found some evidence that these practices did occur frequently as part of trial strategy. Despite the fact that experts who testify should be tested for their qualifications, Saks and Van Duizend found that only rarely were objections raised about the qualifications of the expert or the scope of the testimony, suggesting the possibility that the qualification of experts may be too routine in many trials.

Austin's (1985) case study of the trial and retrial of an antitrust case in

Cleveland also provides some additional insights into litigation strategies. After the first trial resulted in a hung jury, the defense team modified its trial tactics with particular emphasis on responses to the plaintiff's main expert, an economist. Compared with the first trial, defense counsel increased the frequency of technical objections on evidentiary points and increased the intensity and vigor of cross-examination of witnesses. These tactics were apparently successful.

In summary, the literature, though sparse, provides some intriguing hints about litigation strategy, case characteristics, and the use of statistical evidence. It also hints at inadequate coping strategies by some of the parties to the dispute and by the courts. More in-depth field studies of the type reported in this section would go a long way toward illuminating why and when statistical evidence is or is not used.

The Quality of Expert Evidence

In addition to asking about the quantity of statistical evidence in the legal system, we should also ask about its quality. Is it accurate, derived from generally acceptable procedures, free of bias, and complete? Quality, of course, is partly a function of the competence of the individual expert or experts, but the matter is much more complicated. The adversary system is predicated on an ideal model wherein each side to a suit presents the best and most favorable evidence supporting its position. Through the accumulated facts presented by both sides and the process of cross-examination, which is intended to expose unreliable evidence, the decision maker will be presented with the best possible body of evidence on which to render a verdict (see e.g., Thibaut and Walker, 1975; Damaska, 1975). This ideal is seldom met, however. In the real world the adversary process often results in the bending or distorting of facts, omission of facts, and failures to rebut facts. The preceding section on litigation strategy exposes some of the problems arising from the adversary system. Additional problems are discussed in this section.

In the literature one can find numerous references and anecdotes bearing on the quality of evidence (see e.g., Saks and Baron, 1980; also see the panel report's case studies and comments). For example, Marvell (1980: 29) has noted that in *Larry P.* v. *Riles* (1972) there was a serious problem in the data presented to the court. The judge in that case issued a preliminary injunction prohibiting the use of IQ tests when placing students in special classes for the educable mentally retarded because the tests were biased against blacks. The judge reasoned that IQ tests were very important because of Rosenthal and Jacobsen's (1968) study, *Pygmalion in the Classroom*. However, attempts to replicate the study by other researchers produced different results. At the time of the *Riles* decision these contradictory studies were well known in the scientific community, but the plaintiff presented only one side of the issue, the defense offered no effective rebuttal, and the judge was unaware of the conflicting findings.

Eleanor Wolf (1976, 1977) studied the social science evidence that was tendered in the Detroit school segregation case that took place in the early 1970s. She examined evidence given at the hearing to establish whether a violation of the law had occurred and at the hearing to devise a remedy after the violation was established. In the violation hearing, social science experts testified about several issues: the extent, nature, and causes of racial separation in urban neighborhoods; the economic, social, and psychological factors asserted to be related to various aspects of learning; and allegations and refutations of segregative practices within the school system. At the remedy hearing they testified about the expected effects of the proportion of race and social class mixture and about the expected effects of residential behavior patterns, as well as other matters.

Wolf's study is an indictment of the quality of social science evidence presented in the Detroit litigation. She found that it was tendered almost exclusively by the plaintiffs rather than the defendant school board (see Sanders et al., 1982, discussed earlier). She systematically documented the fact that the evidence dealt with a restricted range of issues, was narrow in perspective, and often was predicated on inadequately verified hypotheses. Wolf's argument is that this other evidence was, or should have been, known by the social scientists who testified. The distorted presentation accrued from different sources. First, as already noted, the defendants did not call evidence that could have challenged the oversimplification of the data and the analyses. Second, the lawyers for the plaintiff, in accord with their adversarial role, were in pursuit of legal advantage rather than sociological relevance. Third, the experts were primarily from social action agencies rather than from academic disciplines; customarily, such experts are primarily concerned with persuasion and conversion rather than accuracy of reporting. At the remedy hearings there were several proposals to effect desegregation that involved still more evidence by social scientists (Wolf, 1976, 1977). As in the violation stage of the suit, the plaintiff's experts made errors of omission; and, even though the defendant did call expert witnesses at this stage, certain erroneous aspects of the plaintiff's expert witnesses were never corrected.

Fisher, McGowan, and Greenwood (1983) systematically analyzed the econometric evidence in the *U.S.* v. *IBM* (1969) antitrust case. They developed an argument that the government lawyers and their witnesses "... began with a plainly erroneous view of the facts .... It moved forward with an economic theory that made progressively less sense as it developed and changed in the course of the case .... The result was a tremendous waste of time and resources" (p.346). Fisher et al. ascribe much of the difficulty to the government's trial lawyers and the fact that, once started, the need to continue the case, despite contrary evidence, became paramount. The authors concluded that adversarial blindness in such cases is likely to deter lawyers from seeking or heeding "economists who take as their task a serious review of why the trial lawyers' case lacks economic coherence" (p.348).

Simon and Zusman (1983) conducted an investigation of psychiatric evaluations that also helps to illuminate some of the effects of the adversarial system on evidence quality. In 1972 a mine dam in Buffalo Creek, West Virginia, collapsed. The resulting flood killed over 100 people and destroyed several communities. The mining company admitted liability and paid for physical injury, but lawyers for a large group of plaintiffs claimed additional damages for psychological pain and suffering. As a result of the ensuing litigation, each of 42 residents was examined by different psychiatrists, some working for the plaintiff and some for the defendant. Seizing on this "natural experiment" of paired evaluations, Simon and Zusman analyzed the psychiatric evidence. The striking finding was that the plaintiffs' psychiatrists found a great deal of flood-related, long-term psychological damage, whereas defense psychiatrists, while admitting psychological damage, tended to evaluate it as being of temporary duration. There could be a number of possible explanations for these differences: the two sets of psychiatrists intentionally or unwittingly distorted their diagnoses; they were asked different questions by the respective lawyers (such as "Are they sick?" versus "Are they well?"), which might have affected the way they approached the evaluations of the victims; the lawyers for the respective sides selected psychiatrists who had professional biases that produced diagnoses of long- or short-term effects. Although no definitive answer can be given, the most plausible explanation seems to be that each side selected different types of psychiatrists. However, Simon and Zusman placed greater emphasis on the propensities of the lawyers to selecte experts who hold particular biases as the cause of the differences.

The studies reported in this section raise important questions about the quality of evidence and about the factors that affect quality. From what we have also learned about litigation strategies, we can surmise that often, possibly in the majority of cases, bad evidence will not be contradicted through counter-witnesses or cross-examination. The next section of this paper considers the ability of legal fact finders to comprehend and weigh the meaning of complex statistical data. Much of that research, however, is predicated on the assumption that the evidence is of good quality. The complexities multiply if the evidence on which fact finders must rely is bad. The evidence from the studies described above suggests that the difficulty with evidence quality derives from the adversarial system. It is, of course, a problem with all evidence but, as the panel's report has noted, statistical evidence is beyond the ordinary experience of legal fact finders, judge or jury, and makes evaluation more difficult.

The Competence of Decision Makers

Central to almost all discussions of the impact of statistical evidence on the legal system is the question of the ability of those charged with the decision making to understand it and use it appropriately. Most of the literature on this issue has focused on the jury rather than the judge.

The Jury and Complex Evidence, Including Statistics

The jury is a central player in the American legal system. Are 12 lay citizens capable of understanding, then evaluating, complex statistical evidence? Particular criticism has centered on the civil jury and controversy over whether there is a "complexity exception" to the Seventh Amendment's right to a jury trial in civil matters (see e.g., Sperlich, 1982; Lempert, 1981; Kirst, 1982). Proponents of a complexity exception argue that in some trials the evidence is just too complicated for jurors to understand. Implicitly or explicitly evidence complexity is understood to include statistical evidence. A second argument is that, even if the jurors could understand individual pieces of evidence in some trials, the sheer quantity of complex evidence and the length of some trials would tend to confuse and dull their minds. The third argument is that, because better educated jurors are more likely to be excused from service in long, complex trials, the result is that the collective intelligence of the juries in these cases is lower than in shorter, less complex trials.

In criminal law there has not been a comparable problem with regard to a jury trial. Nevertheless, the competence of the jury has been questioned. First, it has been argued that since the early 1970s there appears to have been a proliferation of the use of expert evidence in criminal trials, most of it involving statistical data or statistical assumptions. For example, it is claimed that there is an increased use of evidence involving such things as polygraphs, voiceprints, spectrography, evidence of psychological syndromes, and other evidence that is based on statistical probabilities. Second, with the erosion of the *Frye* rule, the jury is called on to actually assess the merits of the statistical data and procedures on which the evidence is based.

Assessing Competence: An Analytical Framework

The assessment of jury competence is not a simple matter. It involves three basic questions: Can the jury comprehend the substance of statistical evidence? Does the expert testimony have undue weight in the jury's decision-making process? Is the jury better, equal to, or worse than a judge? Each of these questions involve other questions and issues.

COMPREHENSION

Comprehension includes what is to be comprehended and other factors that bear on what is to be comprehended. The literature indicates that comprehension can be approached from a number of perspectives. Moreover, statistical evidence should not be treated as a uniform entity. Attempts to conceptualize problems involved in the comprehension of statistics should take cognizance of the fact that there are different types of statistics.

In the Federal Judicial Center's study of protracted civil trials, Bermant et al. (1981) were concerned with the legal system generally, including court administration, but some of their distinctions are useful to thinking about the issue of comprehension. Those authors distinguish between protraction of trials and complexity. Protraction has two different meanings. The first meaning is when the duration of the trial is so long that it places significant burdens on the resources of the judicial system. The second meaning is that a trial is prolonged beyond necessity, regardless of its duration. Complexity has three meanings: managerial, factual, and legal. Managerial complexity refers to such things as the number of parties or geographical distances between their home bases. Factual complexity increases with the amount of evidence produced, with the technical depth or difficulty of the evidence, and with markedly different theories pursued by two contending parties. Legal complexity involves multiple, overlapping, or ambiguous legal issues. These various components are conceptually but probably not empirically independent. For example, Bermant et al. (1981) found a positive relationship between civil trial complexity and protraction: more complex trials took longer. Factual complexity may influence managerial complexity in that there is a high likelihood of more witnesses or other evidence that places more demand on court resources. Factual complexity is usually related to legal complexity. More factually complex evidence is likely to involve competing doctrines of law in the verdict(s) requested, in special interrogatories, or in a broader scope and more complex form of instructions to the jury. The importance of the Bermant et al. discussion is to suggest that the assessments of the effects of statistical data are not easily separable from other factors in the trial.

In his case study of an antitrust suit, Austin (1985) distinguished between primary and economic facts. The primary facts involved three broad categories: historical facts, technological facts, and behavioral facts. These primary facts are dominant in tort and contract litigation. However, in antitrust litigation the jury must also assimilate economic facts. Economic facts involve judgments or interpretations as to the economic effect or the significance of primary facts. Usually economic facts involve some facet of market structure and performance whose essence is primarily statistical in nature. As discussed below, juries exhibit differential comprehension of these two types of facts.

Imwinkelreid (1981) distinguished between three types of scientific evidence, depending on the type of instrument that is used to gather the data. Some instruments produce numerical test results such as gas chromatographs or neutron activation analysis. Other instruments involve nonnumerical visual displays such as color tests, polygraphy, fingerprints, or sound spectrography. Others involve what is labelled software techniques, such as a psychiatrist's diagnosis of mental illness or a pathologist's characterization of a wound as homicidal. Imwinkelreid's analysis has a limited focus for our present purposes in that it ignores things like econometric analyses and it is not easy to classify many social science instruments within those three categories. Yet it raises interesting issues. In each instance the basic thrust of the evidence is statistical in nature. For each technique we can ask three questions: How valid is the analyst's interpretive standard? Is there an adequate comparative data base to allow evaluation of the statistical significance of the numbers? Has the expert collected all the factual data to have a reliable basis for an opinion? Juries (and judges) may be able to comprehend different kinds of statistical data at different levels. Some may be less technologically based or intuitively comprehensible than others.

WEIGHT GIVEN TO EXPERT TESTIMONY

Comprehension is only part of competence. Regardless of the ability of the jurors to comprehend the evidence, it is possible that expert testimony could cause them to suspend critical judgment. A number of courts have in fact stated that the jury may be misled (Imwinkelreid, 1983: 110): a California court referred to "a misleading aura of certainty which often envelops a new scientific process"; in the District of Columbia court of appeals it was said that jurors often ascribe a "mystic infallibility" to scientific evidence; the Maryland court of appeals stated that jurors routinely overestimate the certainty and objectivity of scientific evidence.

Analytically, then, there are several components to the issue of expert testimony. A distinction should be made between the credibility afforded to the instruments (and techniques and data base) from which the expert draws the opinion(s) and the credibility of the expert in the eyes of the jury. Imwinkelreid's (1981) distinction is relevant to the instrument component. It is possible that jurors give more or less credibility to statistical assessments depending on whether they are derived from numerical, visual, or "software techniques" instruments. Second, the expert's credibility may derive not only from apparent academic or other accomplishments but by what Rosenthal (1983) refers to as the expert's "paramessage," that is, the verbal and nonverbal information that is peripheral to the subject matter of the communication. In short, jurors or judges may pay attention to the source of the message rather than the content of the message.

A further distinction involves the weight that the evidence is given in relation to other evidence and the use of that evidence. This distinction is important when the evidence is ancillary to the main issues of the trial and a decision must be made as to whether its probative value outweighs any prejudicial effects. Does the evidence distract the jury and cause it to wander away from the legally relevant issues? Is it used to corroborate other testimony (e.g., to indirectly address the credibility of a witness) or to bolster other testimony (e.g., to directly address the credibility of a witness)? The former usage is acceptable, whereas the latter is not.

How these components of expert testimony affect the jury—if they do—could be through several paths. For example, the jurors may simply ignore the content of the statistical or scientific evidence in deference to the expert and the instruments, that is, perhaps not even attempt to comprehend it. Alternatively, they may defer to the expert or techniques only after they have made an attempt to comprehend the evidence. In addition, the evidence may be weighted inappropriately.

THE JURY IN COMPARISON WITH THE JUDGE

Jury performance with respect to statistical or scientific evidence can be assessed not only in absolute terms but also in relative terms. How much better or worse is the jury compared with the main alternative to a jury, a judge deciding the case alone? If there is no appreciable difference between judge and jury, then the debate over jury competence must shift to other grounds, such as the perceived fairness of the jury over judge or burdens on the administration of justice (see the report of the Ad Hoc Committee on The Use of Jury Trials in Complex Litigation, 1984).

Any attempt to compare judge and jury must also take cognizance of naturally confounded factors in real-world environments. Judges and juries may get different types of cases. Indeed, there is some suggestion that lawyers may seek juries when they have weak cases or when the judge is perceived to be biased (see Austin, 1985; Bermant et al., 1981). In addition, there is evidence that lawyers have different strategies in the presentation of expert testimony, depending on whether the case is tried to judge or jury (Austin, 1985; Bermant et al., 1981). Case management is also difficult in that jury trials take place over a brief and concentrated period of time, whereas bench trials are subject to delays and adjournments (see Bermant et al., 1981). Of course, all these differences may bear on the ultimate issue of competence, either directly or indirectly, but these factors are important to keep in mind when drawing inferences.

CHANGES IN PROCEDURES

Even if the jury is found to be not always competent, either at an absolute level or compared with judges, it is still important to consider whether changes in trial procedures could enhance jury performance. A growing body of literature suggests that jury comprehension with respect to legal terminology and concepts can be substantially improved by modifying the language by which these ideas are conveyed (see Hans and Vidmar, 1986: Ch. 8). It is possible that similar improvements could be made in the ways that statistical data are presented.

Empirical Literature on Competence

EDUCATIONAL DESELECTION IN COMPLEX TRIALS

Some authors (see Sperlich, 1982; Nordenberg and Luneburg, 1982, for reviews) have argued that the process of jury selection weeds out more educated jurors in complex civil trials, even though these are the very persons who may be the best prepared to evaluate and assess statistical or other special evidence. The result is that from the very beginning the jury is intellectually handicapped. The argument is predicated on three empirical assumptions: trials with complex evidence tend to be long; when trials are anticipated to be long, better educated jurors find ways of avoiding jury duty; better educated jurors are more competent jurors than less educated persons.

With respect to the first assumption, Bermant et al. (1981) did find a correlation between case complexity and the length of federal civil trials terminating between 1977 and 1979. However, the correlation was not large and in fact the proportion of long trials, as defined by two different criterion measures, constituted a very small fraction of total civil cases. An empirical inquiry conducted by the Federal Judicial Center bears on the second assumption. Cecil (1982) compared the demographic characteristics of jurors serving in protracted federal civil cases (defined as lasting 20 days or longer) with those serving in trials of average duration; the study found no differences with respect to age or race but did find that jurors in long trials were more likely to be unemployed or retired, female, unmarried, and less likely to have a college education. However, Cecil pointed out that the differences, while statistically significant, were "nevertheless quite small" and that the policy implications, therefore, remain uncertain. There is no evidence bearing directly on the third assertion, namely, that more educated jurors can more readily comprehend complex statistical evidence. Research by a number of researchers has found that higher levels of education resulted in superior comprehension of jury instructions (Charrow and Charrow, 1979; Marshall, 1980; but see Bridgeman and Marlowe, 1979). The implications of these various data sets are unclear for the specific issue of complex statistical evidence. If the evidence is so complex that even the best educated lawyers and judges have difficulty comprehending it, any small differences in intelligence between jurors in complex versus other trials becomes superfluous.

COMPREHENSION OF STATISTICAL EVIDENCE

Thompson (1984, 1985; Thompson and Schumann, 1987) has begun a program of research that bears on the ability of jurors to understand statistical evidence. In many criminal trials, jurors are faced with the task of deciding whether a characteristic associated with a defendant matches that of key evidence found at the scene of the crime. Such matches might be between hair, blood, semen, or fingerprints, or they might be between tests of fibers on ballistic markings. Testimony about these matters revolves around incidence rates and the reliabilities of the tests that are performed. Concerns about this type of evidence are that (a) jurors will misestimate the value of the testimony, (b) the incidence rates may be inappropriate in a particular case, and (c) jurors may fail to take into account the inaccuracy of laboratory tests.

In a series of simulation experiments Thompson has presented incidence rate information in a trial context and manipulated such variables as the explanation offered about the meaning of conditional probabilities and the extent to which the evidence is independent or partly redundant with other evidence. The results show that high percentages of the jurors made inferential errors and that whether the errors favored the prosecution or the defense was highly dependent on the form in which the testimony was presented. To date Thompson's research has investigated only individual decision making and not decision making arising from deliberative processes, which could correct individual misconceptions and errors. Nevertheless, it raises intriguing questions about jury competence and is consistent with broader bodies of research about human decision making (see, e.g., Nisbett and Ross, 1980). Moreover, the research presents a paradigm that can be widely applied to other problems in the comprehension of statistical evidence.

Austin (1985) studied two civil juries that heard the same antitrust case, the second trial occurring after the first jury became deadlocked. A central part of the case involved testimony from several experts about complex economic data. Austin interviewed a number of the jurors involved in these trials. The interviews involved in-depth examination of jury comprehension, but the author did not systematically report the data. For analytical purposes Austin distinguished between primary facts and economic facts. He concluded that the jurors basically had a good grasp of primary facts but little comprehension of the economic facts.

Selvin and Picus (1987) observed a complex trial involving exposure to asbestos and subsequently interviewed the jurors. They uncovered the fact that jurors failed to properly understand certain critical pieces of evidence. There was also a suggestion that evaluation of the merits of expert testimony was based not only on its substance but also on the expert's personality and behavior. Jurors also had difficulty remembering the judge's instructions and considered extralegal factors in their determination of liability and punitive damages.

In their study of protracted civil trials, Bermant et al. (1981) questioned the judges and lawyers about juries. Almost without exception, their informants who acknowledged the existence of difficult issues in the trial also explicitly mentioned that the jury had made the correct decision or that the juries had no difficulties applying the appropriate legal standards to the facts. The informants were also asked about additional jury cases in which they had been involved: juries were unanimously viewed as diligent in their task and, with slightly less than unanimity, the informants said jury deliberation processes had validity.

A substantial body of literature bearing on the general competence of juries and on their ability to understand judicial instructions exists (see Hans and Vidmar, 1986, for a review). The studies suggest that, on the whole, juries arrive at decisions that are consistent with those a judge would have made even though there are problems with understanding laws. None of these studies, however, bears on the comprehension of statistical evidence. Thompson's research shows how the issue might be investigated.

RESPONSES TO EXPERT EVIDENCE

Evidence provided by expert witnesses is usually seen as involving two questions: To what extent is it probative for the issues in question? To what extent does it have prejudicial effects on the trier of fact? The merit of expert testimony, then, is some weighing of the answers to these two questions.

Our analytical perspective suggests that understanding of the impact of expert testimony on the jury requires us to address a number of other questions. Do jurors evaluate the evidence critically or do they defer to the expert's status? To what extent and how often? If juries do sometimes defer to the expert's status, do they do so only when they do not understand the substantive heart of the testimony? Are different types of expert testimony treated differently by the jury and, if so, on what grounds? Is expert testimony given more weight than the weight given to other evidence? Kalven and Zeisel (1966), Myers (1979), and Bridgeman and Marlowe (1979) conducted field studies that attempted to determine how jurors responded to expert evidence in criminal trials. The conclusion of these researchers was that jurors are not overwhelmed by expert testimony. However, none of the studies teased out statistical testimony as opposed to other, possibly simpler, testimony by experts.

In addition to these general surveys of juror responses to experts, there are a number of field surveys and laboratory simulation experiments that have attempted to assess the responses of jurors to specific types of expert testimony. Some of the simulation studies have attempted to contrast the impact of the expert testimony with circumstantial evidence alone or with an eyewitness identification, while others have compared different types of expert testimony. The particular types of expert testimony that have been studied are as follows: economic testimony (Austin, 1985); ballistics and handwriting experts (Cavoukian, 1980; Loftus, 1980); polygraph testimony (Barnett, 1973; Brekke, 1985; Carlson, Passano, and Jannuzo, 1977; Cavoukian and Heslegrave, 1980; Forkosch, 1939; Koffler, 1957; Loftus, 1980; Markwart and Lynch, 1979; Peters, 1982); voiceprint identification (Greene, 1975; Rosenthal, 1983); psychiatric testimony (Brekke, 1985; Ellsworth et al., 1984; Simon, 1967); hypnotically induced recall (Greene,

Wilson, and Loftus, 1986); and psychological testimony bearing on the reliability of eyewitness identification (Cavoukian, 1980; Fox and Walters, 1986; Hosch, 1980; Hosch, Beck, and McIntyre, 1980; Loftus, 1980; Wells, Lindsay, and Tousignant, 1979).

The main conclusion that the authors of almost all of these studies draw is that jurors do not give undue weight or credibility to expert evidence. There are many methodological problems that plague individual studies, but in the collective they indicate jurors seem to have healthy skepticisms about expert evidence. The primary difficulty in the present context, however, is that none of the studies has addressed the issue of complex, difficult to comprehend, statistical evidence (although see Austin, 1985).

SUBSTANTIVE AND PROCEDURAL MODIFICATIONS

A number of judges (e.g., see *In re Financial Securities Litigation*, 1979; *In re Japanese Electronic Products*, 1980), practitioners (Ad Hoc Committee on Jury Trials in Complex Litigation, 1984), and scholars (e.g., Austin, 1985; Saks and Van Duizend, 1983; Sperlich, 1982) have argued that, even if juries can be shown to perform less than optimally in complex or difficult cases, the best solution is not abolition of the jury system but, rather, the introduction of substantive or procedural modifications that will remove barriers to understanding or assist juries in their fact finding or both. Such modifications, it is claimed, will preserve the merits of the jury system, yet produce better decision making.

The list of suggested changes is lengthy. A sampling of that list is all that is necessary here to provide an overview. Huttner (1979) has suggested that a partial solution is to redraft laws to eliminate some of the more esoteric bases of lawsuits, thereby eliminating some complexity problems. Others have argued for "blue ribbon" or special juries that would try complex or difficult cases (Nordenberg and Luneberg, 1982; Note, 1980). It has also been argued that more restrictive laws on jury exemptions and rules pertaining to the waiver of jury duty would probably increase the educational level of juries (see Nordenberg and Luneberg, 1982). Some have pointed their fingers at liberal joinder and discovery rules that unnecessarily complicate the trial process (Sperlich, 1982). Some have noted that better organization and management of the trial could reduce complexity (Austin, 1985; Sperlich, 1982). Special verdicts have been recommended for civil cases as an aid to appellate review of jury decisions (see Sperlich, 1982). It has been recommended that neutral experts be called by the court instead of, or in addition to, adversarial experts in order to produce a more balanced picture of the facts (see e.g., Rubinfeld, 1985; Saks and Van Duizend, 1983). Others argue for adversarial experts to educate the jury (Loftus, 1985). Still others have suggested that decision making in complicated cases be divided between the jury and special masters; the masters would decide the complex statistical or factual matters, leaving the jury to integrate the master's findings with other evidence to arrive at a verdict.

In addition to simplifying and eliminating the argot from legal discourse and jury instructions (see Charrow and Charrow, 1979; Elwork, Sales, and Alfini, 1980; Severance and Loftus, 1984), it has been suggested that juries should receive better orientation, including preliminary instructions, better exhibits, better access to transcripts; it has been further suggested that they should be allowed to ask questions and take notes (see Sperlich, 1982).

There is relatively little data bearing on these various propositions, either about the extent to which they have already been tried by innovative courts or the potential effectiveness of such changes as would be suggested by experimental research. Bermant et al. (1981) found that in complex cases judges almost always presented the jury with a preliminary charge. Moreover, in no case was the jury asked only for a single general verdict. In several cases the juries were asked only to provide several general verdicts, but one jury was presented with a book containing dozens of special interrogatories arranged in a branching, hierarchical order. The judges varied in their willingness to allow jurors to take notes. Bermant et al. (1981), as noted earlier, also found that lawyers changed the amount and form of evidence when it was to be presented to a jury rather than a judge. (Usually this is to simplify understanding, but sometimes adversarial tactics led to attempts to increase complexity to confuse the jury.) Most lawyers and their experts used visual aids.

Recently, a federal court (Sand and Reiss, 1985) and a state court (Heuer and Penrod, no date, a, no date, b) have experimented with some procedural innovations intended to improve jury functioning. The innovations have included juror note-taking, limited question asking, the use of preliminary instructions, and written judicial instructions. The scope and duration of the innovations were too limited to draw confident conclusions about their effects. However, the tentative findings suggest that some of the innovations produced modest improvements in juror performance, and they did not cause significant negative effects. More research of this kind is needed.

The Judge and Complex Evidence

While the literature on the ability of juries to deal with statistical evidence is sparse and incomplete, literature on judge competence is almost nonexistent. There are assertions that judges are comparatively superior to juries. It is argued that their training in fact finding, their legal experience and background, and their general levels of education make for relatively superior fact-finding ability. Moreover, unlike juries the judge has the opportunity to engage in colloquy with witnesses, to delay the trial and the verdict over extended periods so that study can be given to difficult issues, and, even to obtain ex parte advice and information. Furthermore, it is also argued that judges generally render written rationales for their verdicts, which at least make their fact finding amenable to scrutiny and reversal in appellate courts. Commentators have argued, however, that legal training does not prepare judges to understand complex statistical evidence. Few lawyers have an undergraduate background that prepares them for statistical analyses, and law schools, with a few minor exceptions, do not teach statistical courses. One pundit has noted that "Lawyers are highly literate but barely numerate" (Yarmolinsky, 1980: 44). In the absence of such skills it is possible that the collective ability of 12 jurors is equal or superior to that of the judge. Furthermore, Bermant et al.'s (1981) finding that lawyers present more complex evidence when the fact finder is a judge suggests that judges are given more difficult evidence to begin with. Some of these varying perspectives on judges and juries are discussed in Sperlich (1982).

In discussing competence we must not become totally absorbed in the relative merits of judge and jury because there are many types of cases involving statistical evidence that are eligible only for trial by judge. We must therefore be concerned with the absolute as well as the relative ability of judges, and we must consider procedural innovations that might assist the judge in bench trials. The analytic framework used to think about the issue of jury competence can be used to think about judge competence as well.

COMPREHENSION OF STATISTICAL EVIDENCE

The only real evidence bearing on general comprehension levels of judges comes from case studies. There are some fairly well-documented cases of the misuse of statistics. The difficulty with these case studies is, first, that we have no idea of how representative they are and, second, in many instances the apparent misuse of statistics may not be that the judge misunderstands them. Rather it may be that the judge is making the decision on grounds other than the statistical data or because the adversarial context prevents the judge from access to all of the relevant facts.

A prime example that documents basic judicial misunderstanding of statistical and other social science evidence involves the issue of the constitutionality of juries of fewer than 12 members (*Williams* v. *Florida*, 1970; *Colgrove* v. *Battin*, 1973; *Ballew* v. *Georgia*, 1978). The Supreme Court's misapprehension of the social science evidence in these cases is examined in Zeisel and Diamond (1974), Saks (1977), Lempert (1975), and Tanke and Tanke (1979). Grofman and Scarrow (1980) have discussed a series of cases on electoral representation involving weighted voting systems that also demonstrate serious judicial misunderstanding of statistics. In another example Besharov (1983) has shown that the Supreme Court articulated a new judicial standard bearing on parental rights that appeared to be based on an erroneous interpretation of statistics. Other examples are discussed in Loh (1984), Monahan and Walker (1985), Horowitz (1977), and in the case studies reported in the panel's report.

Aside from demonstrating that sometimes judges understand and sometimes they do not, these case studies tell us little about the average trial judge. Many of the cases in the literature discuss appelate court decisions written by some of the most intellectually capable members of the judiciary. In other instances the trial judges may have been selected for their presumed ability to cope with statistical evidence. On one hand, there may be a selection factor operating in the assignments of judges to cases, with better judges getting more difficult cases. This possibility must be taken into consideration in estimating the association between statistical evidence and competence. On the other hand, the selection process must be imperfect, particularly in those instances in which the proffering of statistical evidence becomes known only after the judge is assigned to the case. It would be very useful, therefore, to assess the competence of average trial judges in dealing with statistical data. Yet, as Sperlich (1982) among others has observed, it is unlikely that courts will cooperate in field research intended to assess their competence. It might be possible, however, to conduct simulation studies similar to those undertaken by Thompson and his colleagues, described earlier. Judges' responses could be compared with those of potential jurors and also evaluated on an absolute level. In the past, judges have agreed to participate in brief simulation studies (e.g., Simon and Mahan, 1971; Ebbesen and Konecni, 1982a; Partridge and Eldridge, 1974).

RESPONSES TO EXPERT EVIDENCE

To what extent might judges give undue weight to scientific evidence? Schroeder's survey (cited in Gianelli, 1980) of lawyers and judges found that 75 percent of respondents believed that judges accorded scientific evidence more credibility than other evidence, whereas only 70 percent believed that juries did so. Schroeder's research should not be given much weight itself, due to its methodological weaknesses, but it is consistent with opinion and research findings that often judges are quite susceptible to the extralegal and other decision-making biases that jurors are accused of having (see e.g., Diamond and Zeisel, 1976; Gibson, 1980; Ebbesen and Konecni, 1982a, 1982b). There are, moreover, studies showing that judges do defer almost exclusively to the opinions of experts on matters involving mental competence and insanity (see Roesch and Golding, 1980).

Impact on Case Outcome

The production of statistical evidence for use in litigation is often expensive. It is important, therefore, to ask about the frequency and nature of desirable outcomes for the litigants who use it. Is it cost effective? This question is particularly pertinent when a litigant has limited financial resources and allocation decisions must be made.

Assessing effectiveness is, however, a very complicated matter. There are, for example, instances in which the many legal questions hinge on facts or data that are essentially statistical in nature (e.g., trademark infringement or antitrust cases) and the litigants have little choice but to use statistical evidence if they want to win. In other instances, however, the calling of statistical evidence is discretionary. As the school desegregation studies by Wolf (1977) and Sanders et al. (1982) make clear, defendants often choose not to produce their own statistical evidence. The Saks and Van Duizend (1983) research indicates that the infrequent use of statistical evidence in criminal trials is partly based on economics, partly based on availability of experts, and partly based on lawyer awareness of its potential usefulness. There is the further problem of measuring the quantity and quality of the evidence even in those cases in which something statistical is almost required. A further issue is its impact on settlement as opposed to trial: a strong showing of statistical evidence in pretrial stages may foster settlement. An additional complication is that courts change: statistical evidence that has little acceptance today may be widely accepted tomorrow.

Even holding the issues of complexity in abeyance, there is little information bearing on the usefulness of statistical evidence. The studies by Wolf (1977) and Sanders et al. (1982) suggest that it did carry the day in some of the school desegregation cases, both at the violation stage of the trial and at the remedy stage. Abt (1982) asserts that in antitrust litigation experience has shown that the side that is willing to spend the most money on econometric research is usually best able to prove its point. Statistical evidence was more or less rejected, however, in a number of death penalty cases (e.g., see Ellsworth, in press; Gross, 1985).

Lambert (1981) has produced a rather compelling documentation of the selective use of social science data in *Larry P. v. Riles* (1972), the case on I.Q. tests, race, and school placement. Although Lambert is not unbiased, as she was a witness for the defense, her analysis of the competing testimony and the subsequent decision leads to the conclusion that the California judge's decision selectively reported on the evidence and "often testimony based on beliefs and impressions rather than on empirical findings was the basis for the conclusion." Edited casebooks by Monahan and Walker (1985) and Loh (1984), as well as the book edited by Saks and Baron (1980), contain other instances in which social science and statistical evidence was introduced into legal cases, with varying success.

While the question of impact on case outcomes is extremely complicated, some useful research on the topic could be undertaken. For example, are there kinds of cases in which statistical evidence has greater utility than others? What factors go into lawyers' decisions to tender or not tender statistical evidence? How much do cost considerations play a part? Does statistical evidence promote settlement and does it do so at a rate higher than cases in which it is not used?

Impact on the Courts

The basic question about the impact of statistical evidence on the courts is its effect on the administration of the courts. We include in administration such things as case flow, judge time, and financial cost. To appropriately answer the question, researchers must consider pretrial activity, including settlement rates, as well as trial time. Researchers should also be concerned with court procedural responses to any problems arising from statistical evidence.

A number of sources suggest that complex statistical evidence, particularly in civil cases, often results in considerable pretrial activity. Indeed, it is suggested that much of the argumentation should take place at this stage rather than at trial (see e.g., Finkelstein, 1980; Johnson, 1980; Bermant et al., 1981; Manual for Complex Litigation, 1982; see also Monahan and Walker, 1985).

The only empirical work that I uncovered on this topic was that undertaken by the Federal Judicial Center (Bermant et al., 1981). The authors of that report concede that their research is tentative, but their efforts at least begin to provide an outline of the problem and the issues. Those researchers examined the records bearing on all federal civil trials terminating between 1977 and 1979. One important finding was that, while duration and complexity of trials are conceptually independent, they were empirically strongly and positively related to one another. Of the 32,023 civil trials in the three-year sample, fewer than 1 percent lasted 100 hours or more. However, these long trials constituted almost 12 percent of the trial time required by the courts. Duration was also related to type of case. Long trials were more likely to arise in civil rights, antitrust, securities, and diversity contract actions. Measures of complexity showed that the most complex trials involved antitrust, civil rights, product liability, and personal injury arising from airplane accidents. The data also allowed a rough analysis of pretrial discovery activity as a function of case type. Among those cases involving the most extensive pretrial discovery findings were personal injury, product liability, and securities and commodities suits. Antitrust and civil rights cases also involved extensive pretrial activity, but not to the extent of the former types of cases.

Research on the administrative burdens posed by statistical evidence in criminal trials is also needed. We also need survey research to assess the scope and variety of responses that different courts have made when faced with statistical data. Do they attempt to shift activity to the pretrial discovery stages? What is its effect on the overall case load of the courts? Are procedural responses effective in reducing the burdens on the courts? Is the burden increasing or has it remained relatively static?

Impact on Statisticians and Scientists

One of the biggest problems that the statistician or social scientist faces is becoming ensnared in the adversarial process. The expert may not be allowed to give the full story or may be forced to give a distorted story.

There can be major effects on his or her self-esteem and professional integrity. There is the natural conflict between the neutral role of the scientist and the adversarial role placed on statisticians and scientists in the litigation process.

Rossi (1980) has described his experience as an expert for the Federal Trade Commission in three deceptive advertising cases. In one instance, the opposing lawyer asked Rossi a question in cross-examination that missed the point, but came close to an issue that might be helpful to the lawyer, that in fact might cut the ground from under much of Rossi's testimony. Rossi replied: "I can't answer that question, but I know the question that you should ask." The judge and the government lawyer were very upset because of this violation of the adversary process. This gaffe is probably not unusual for experts who are getting their first taste of the adversarial system, with an expectation that it should operate like a scientific fact-finding forum. One effect of such conflict may be that social scientists and statisticians who see their professional integrity being jeopardized may decline further involvement in litigation.

Another problem arising from the adversarial system involves the fact that a minority scientific opinion may appear to have more credence than it actually has within the scientific community. Peters (1980) points out the hypothetical situation in which 99 scientists may believe in the truth of a fact or opinion and 1 may hold a minority opinion. At trial, however, there will probably be only two experts testifying: one side will call one of the 99 scientists and the other side will call the minority of 1. The resultant picture is likely to be a distortion of scientific opinion. This hypothetical example has a basis in actual experience. For example, consider the issue of death qualified juries, i.e., those prepared to convict when the death penalty is involved. There is a substantial body of research indicating that such juries tend to be conviction prone, and the overwhelming majority of social scientists familiar with the research endorse its conclusions (see Ellsworth, in press). However, in several trials around the United States a particular social scientist who takes the opposite view has been called as a prosecution witness. The introduction of a contrary opinion is, of course, appropriate under the adversarial system and keeps the other witnesses honest. The difficulty was that due to inadequate financial resources and inadequate preparation on the part of defense counsel, the trial judge was left with an impression that the scientific community is about evenly split on the matter of death qualification and conviction proneness (V. Hans, personal communication, February, 1985).

On the other side of the coin, Simon and Zusman's (1983) research on psychiatric evidence in the Buffalo Creek mine disaster case, discussed earlier, raises the possible influences of the adversarial system in causing experts to bias their testimony in a direction favorable to the side that calls them. Fisher et al.'s (1983) study of government experts in the *United States* v. *IBM* antitrust case raises a similar point. These authors suggest that the danger of compromising professional integrity is often gradual as the expert becomes immersed in the case (p.351):

> Witnesses, working closely with trial lawyers, may gradually take on their point of view; they may want to win and thus be drawn into acting as law partners rather than as independent experts. The danger lies not in being tempted to step across some well-defined line but in remaining certain where the line is.

Finally, it should be observed that the scientific community may ostracize colleagues who take a view that is inconsistent with prevailing community values. There are anecdotal reports that social scientists who testified on behalf of the defendants in school desegregation cases believed that, although they testified with full integrity, their action was unfavorably received by their colleagues. Kalmuss, Chesler, and Sanders (1982) reported that 74 percent of all expert witnesses who testified for the defense claimed that their action resulted in adverse consequences for their professional careers.

More research on the distorting effects of the adversarial system on scientific findings and on the experts may prove highly profitable. Adverse effects of the adversarial system on scientists and statisticians and on the quality of their testimony is continually documented in anecdotal reports. What is needed are more systematic studies like that of Simon and Zusman.

Impact on the Law

What impact has statistical evidence had on the law itself, as distinct from individual cases? Framed another way, the question is: To what uses have appelate court judges put statistical evidence as they shape and frame the meaning of law? That statistical evidence has had some impact seems likely, but the problem is assessing when and how much. Simply counting the references to statistical evidence can be very misleading. There has been controversy over the impact of social science evidence on court decisions that illustrates the difficulties involved. In *Ballew* v. *Georgia* (1978), the case that ruled that criminal juries smaller than six members are unconstitutional, statistical evidence bearing on the effects of jury size formed the core of the Court's written reasoning and, by and large, the Court demonstrated competent understanding of the evidence. Yet the decision in *Ballew* was only partially consistent with that of the evidence, because the Court had a different agenda than what was stated in the reasoning (see Tanke and Tanke, 1979).

In *The Courts and Social Policy*, Donald Horowitz (1977) argues that there has been an increasing tendency for courts to downplay the search for truth between the parties in the particular dispute and to search instead for the right legal policy, using the lawsuit merely as a vehicle for enunciating that policy. In part the courts have been forced into this position by the kinds of lawsuits that are generated. Some of the change, however, is probably due to a change in the courts' views of their own functions. In many instances cases that could have been decided on narrow, private legal grounds have been interpreted more broadly to enunciate legal policies. A concomitant of this trend is that, in seeking to define policy, the courts have become more and more reliant on statistical and social science evidence because such evidence helps to define the scope and nature of the problem.

Horowitz's thesis is supported by a number of other authors. Miller and Baron (1975), for example, also conclude that the Supreme Court tends to ignore narrow adjudicative facts and focus on larger policy problems. Studying *Roe* v. *Wade* (1973) and other abortion cases, they conclude that the decisions of the Court in these cases were concerned with issues of social policy rather than the specific case at hand.

Michelson (1980) has detected a difference in the use of social science data from the famous footnote 11 in *Brown* v. *Board of Education* (1954) to the almost equally famous footnote 17 in *Castaneda* v. *Partida* (1977). In his view there has been a shift from statistics as an adjunct to a conceptually nonstatistical case as in *Brown*, to statistics as the only way to picture what is wrong, such as in the *Castaneda* jury discrimination case. He suggests that this is due to the Court's becoming aware that problems such as discrimination in jury lists are not observable in the sense that a criminal act or an automobile accident might be observed. With a claim of discrimination in jury lists it is not contended that a particular name is omitted but rather that a class of names relating to races or ethnicity is omitted.

Post (1980) has suggested that the court has different functions from case to case and the way that the court perceives its functions will dictate its receptivity to statistical information. One function of courts is to serve as a legitimizer of moral values; another is as a "scientific policy maker," which views values in an empirical, analytic way. For example, the psychiatrist's judgment of insanity is scientific in nature but the courts always reserve the determination of insanity to the jury, because the determination involves moral values. Post observes that in *Washington* v. *Davis* (1976) the Supreme Court sharply distinguished constitutional from statutory analysis by saying that only purposeful discrimination violates the Constitution. Purposeful discrimination is a vague, nonobjective, and nonstatistical concept. What does it mean and how is it to be distinguished from the discriminatory effect that statistics are capable of disclosing? The Court offered no guidelines. Looking at it one way, perhaps the Court wanted to reduce the number of constitutional violations that can be found. But looking at it another way, "the Court may have been disturbed that the moral judgment of discrimination was becoming almost entirely dependent on social science statistics" (p.175). That is, in the same way that insanity is a moral notion, so is discrimination. Post distinguishes this example from instances in which the purpose of the court is not so much to legitimate moral decisions as to accomplish certain policy ends. He observes that in the past tort doctrines were filled with discussions of moral questions, but such thinking has declined. Rather, today issues such as product liability, traffic regulation, and pollution control, "do not appear to be matters of rights and duties so much as systems of relationships in need of rational ordering for the achievement of social ends. Here the courts will be far more receptive to the introduction and use of statistical evidence." Post also observes that the legitimation function of courts is not primary in Title VII cases because the court is merely effecting the policy of a congressional statute; it may decide that Congress has already made the basic moral decisions. In these cases, then, the courts simply address technical questions of compliance. Post observes that "in contrast to their approach to constitutional suits, in Title VII suits the courts have remained extraordinarily open to the use of social scientific data to resolve disputes" (p.175).

An unpublished study of Supreme Court decisions by Victor Rosenblum (personal communication, April 9, 1984) indicated that the use of statistics was not confined to particular members of the court or to ideological blocks. Members of the court used them when it fitted their particular ideological positions. We can certainly find many examples of both acceptance and rejection of statistics by a particular member of the court. Former Chief Justice Burger, for example, has often regarded statistics as irrelevant. Yet in *Bivens* v. *Six Unknown Federal Narcotics Agents* (1971, p. 416) Burger used Oakes's (1970) study of the exclusionary rule as a basis for calling for the rule to be repealed (Wasby, 1980). Disagreement over the appropriateness of statistics is apparent in a number of other important cases. In the Bakke case, Justice Powell pointed out the difficulties courts would encounter if they had to classify various deprived minority groups: "The kind of variable sociological and political analyses necessary to produce such rankings simply does not lie within the judicial competence—even if they were otherwise politically feasible and socially desirable" (Rosen, 1980). Rosen observed that when justices are confronted with conflicting statistics they are not hesitant to reject them: Judge Wright's response in *Hobsen* v. *Hansen* (327 F.Supp. 844, at 859) (1971) is one example; another is Justice Brennan's reaction in *Craig* v. *Boren* (429 U.S. 190 at 204) (1976): "It is unrealistic to expect either members of the judiciary or state officials to be well-versed in the rigors of experimental or statistical technique. But this merely illustrates that proving broad sociological propositions by statistics is a dubious business, and one that inevitably is in tension with the normative philosophy that underlies the Equal Protection Clause." In that case Justice Rehnquist complained that Justice Brennan misused statistics (Wasby, 1980). In *Ballew* v. *Georgia* Justice Powell condemned Justice Blackmun's use of "numerology" to resolve a legal issue.

On the whole, the sparse literature suggests that courts' use of statistical evidence in the formulation and shaping of laws is selective and its actual effects are obscured by unstated agendas. The literature also indicates that there have been significant shifts in the tasks with which courts are faced and in judicial thinking that make the processing and use of statistical evidence more likely.

Court Adaptation to the Challenge of Statistical Evidence

One of the tasks of this paper is to discuss how courts have adapted to the challenges of statistical evidence and to speculate about the dynamics underlying that adaptation. Some aspects relating to the task have been indirectly covered in the earlier sections of this paper and directly covered in the panel's report.

Complex statistical evidence is being introduced in American courts with increased frequency. It ranges across a wide spectrum of cases involving both civil and criminal matters. A basic contributor to this trend appears to be social forces within American society that have caused a shift toward public as opposed to private law (Chayes, 1976), a tendency manifested in legislative enactments, in the framing of legal issues by particular interest groups (see Miller and Baron, 1975), and in appellate courts' willingness to engage in public policy making (Horowitz, 1977). Paralleling this trend, technological developments in statistics and in the social and physical sciences over the past several decades readily lend themselves to application in litigation proceedings. Not only do these technological developments respond to law, but they also help to create and shape the formulation of the legal issues. For example, developments in the forensic sciences have forced changes in procedural rules relating to the qualification of experts and determination of the bases of their conclusions (e.g., Imwinkelreid, 1983, 1984). Stepping back and viewing the legal system from a sociological level, the willingness of courts to use statistical evidence may also reflect attempts to maintain authority and legitimacy (see Friedman, 1975). In an increasingly secular, pluralistic, and technological society, the source of legal authority is derived not from custom or mere faith in a set of rules but rather from its perceived instrumentality. Willingness to accept scientific and statistical evidence helps to maintain the perception of instrumentality. There are undoubtedly some other levels of analysis that bear on these issues but the essential point to be made is that various indicators lead to the inference that the trend toward statistical evidence as a key component of certain kinds of litigation has not reached its apex. To the extent that courts have difficulty with statistical evidence, they are faced with a problem that will not only not go away, but will probably increase in magnitude.

A second inference from the literature review is that the courts have not adapted very well to the challenges posed by statistical evidence (see the panel's report and Miller and Baron, 1975; Saks and Van Duizend, 1983; Saks and Baron, 1980; Horowitz, 1977). Courts have engaged in inappropriate analogizing and they have misread statistical data. Sometimes they have even drawn conclusions about evidence that are the very opposite of what should have been drawn. They have made decisions with far-reaching consequences based on evidence that did not present the whole picture or, worse, was largely erroneous. In other instances, crucial evidence was not placed before the adjudicator. In others, evidence was brought into the legal process much later than it should have been, with the result that there was suboptimal decision making, procedural delay, or discouragement of settlement. Some commentators have suggested that the courts have often been ignorant of or avoided statistical evidence that could have aided them in reaching a desired outcome. Arguably, there are instances in which the courts have failed to recognize that they have a problem despite criticism by legal commentators and experts outside the legal system.

The essential question, then, is why have alternative mechanisms not been used, why the failure to adapt? One possibility is that adaptive responses will eventually develop, but there is often a substantial lag between innovations, in this case the introduction of complex statistical evidence, and response. In short, the legal system needs time. Whatever the validity of this proposition, it begs identification of elements that resist change and leaves adaptation to evolutionary trial and error rather than to a rational problem-solving approach. Because our knowledge about the courts and complex statistical evidence is in a rudimentary state, we cannot hope to identify all the dimensions of the problem of adaptation or even offer clear eludication of those that we do perceive. Nevertheless, an attempt to sketch some possible causes, none of which is mutually exclusive of the others, can at least provide matter for debate and inquiry.

One cause of courts' failures to adapt more readily probably lies in the way most judges and lawyers are taught to conceive of problems and reason from them. American legal training is tradition-bound and many vestiges of classical common law perspectives persist in contemporary thinking (see Friedman, 1975, 1986; Galanter, 1983; Haney, 1980; Lempert and Sanders, 1986). Law is conceived as a closed system of normative rules and procedures, and problem solving emanates deductively from that system. Law training, for example, emphasizes that cases can be resolved by analogizing from past cases, that factual evidence must bear on individual cases, and that a generalist judge can grasp the subtleties and nuances of all the evidence. The difficulty with statistical evidence is that it is of a different order. Its inferential basis is different; it is usually concerned with group probabilities rather than individual cases; its technical complexity is such that only a specialist can grasp its subtleties and nuances. In short, statistical evidence poses problems for which traditional legal training was not designed.

Monahan and Walker (1985) have set forth a critique of courts' use of social science that also speaks to modes of legal reasoning. They develop the thesis that courts have conceptualized and treated social science research as adjudicative facts even when the research is actually being used to formulate a rule of law. They argue that such evidence should rather be treated as a form of authority in the same way that prior cases are treated as precedent by the common law. They argue that social science research bears more of a resemblance to law than to fact because it has an attribute of generality that transcends specific persons, situations, and time, and because it addresses future contingencies that are not yet known. They further suggest that if social science were treated as authority rather than fact courts would have less difficulty devising intellectual and procedural ways of coping with it. The evidence could be presented in briefs rather than by oral testimony and independent judicial investigation of the research would be encouraged. Two consequences of this alternative approach would be that it would subject the research and the court decisions to independent review and evaluation; and higher courts would not be dependent on lower courts for an evalution of the quality of the research.

Monahan and Walker's conceptualization of the issues is innovative because it shifts the frames of reference. Their approach is addressed largely to instances in which evidence is used to formulate rules of law rather than to decide specific issues between parties, but, as we have seen, much complex statistical evidence is used for the former purpose. A central insight from Monahan and Walker's article is that some of the difficulties courts have with statistical evidence arises from the way it is conceptualized. By using a law rather than a fact analogy, courts would be encouraged to develop alternative notions about its meaning and find better procedural means of coping with it.

The high regard that is accorded the adversarial process in American legal culture is another contributing factor. As an idealized model for producing evidence and arguments, the adversarial system has much to recommend it (e.g., see Thibaut and Walker, 1975, 1978). However, the ideal and the results of actual practice are often at variance with one another (see Frankel, 1975; Damaska, 1975) and the flaws may be exacerbated when statistical evidence is involved. Two main tenets of the adversarial mode of procedure are that (a) the maximal amount of information and arguments bearing on the case will be placed before the adjudicator because of the self-interested motivation of the competing parties and (b) the best means of assessing the merits of a case is to have the adjudicator assume a passive, umpiring role. With respect to the first tenet, statistical evidence is often expensive to produce, thereby handicapping a party with few resources (Gianelli, 1980; Saks and Van Duizend, 1983). The production of the evidence has often been one-sided (e.g., Wolf, 1976, 1977), even when amicus curiae briefs form a substantial part of the submissions before the court (Miller and Baron, 1975). Cross-examination proves to be ineffective when one side does not have a clear grasp of what the problem is, let alone the ability to challenge the expert on arcane technical matters that only an expert can grasp (Wolf, 1976, 1977; Saks and Van Duizend, 1983). The second tenet presumes that the adjudicator will not only get all the evidence, but also have the capacity to comprehend it. Again, the highly technical nature of statistical evidence may defy comprehension to a decision maker not trained in that field unless there is outside assistance. However, influenced by the knowledge that the adversarial system has worked relatively well in coping with myriad other problems, judges are reluctant to face the possibility of a radically more difficult form of evidence for which they need outside help.

A further concomitant of allegiance to the adversarial system is that it also invokes other values and pressures. In some instances, for example, judges may recognize that they have a problem with the nature of the evidence or its comprehension but may be unwilling to invoke the assistance of a procedural mechanism if it is opposed by the parties and will cause them to challenge the fairness of the hearing (see Bermant et al., 1981; and Saks and Van Duizend, 1983).

Finally, a major cause of failure to innovate may be more mundane: financial cost. While rules of procedure provide the court with options, e.g., the use of neutral experts, they are often expensive. Funds are scant in existing judicial budgets for these additional accoutrements. A judge could force the parties to bear the cost, but he or she might be reluctant to do so if an imbalance of resources between them already exists. Indeed, the prospect of these additional costs might cause a party with relatively few resources to abandon its claim or at least to compromise it. While one can sympathize with these financial concerns, the failure to find appropriate funds for experimentation might prove short-sighted. For example, early evaluation of evidence by a neutral expert might encourage early settlement, thereby relieving the courts of the more costly burden of extended litigation.

Research Needs: A Summary Perspective

Our knowledge about the impact of statistical evidence on the legal system is meagre, despite indications that it is appearing with increasing frequency in the courts and that it poses substantial intellectual, procedural, and administrative burdens. In this literature review I have tried to highlight certain studies and also to provide some tentative schemas for thinking about particular substantive aspects of problems. Space limitations precluded methodological critiques of most studies that are described in the body of this paper. Many of them contain methodological flaws that deserve closer scrutiny, but to undertake this task here would interfere with the goal of presenting a broad picture of what we know and ought to know.

The review indicates that we need to learn much more about the impact of statistical evidence at the trial stages of litigation, and it also points to the need to intensely focus on the pretrial stages as well. For example, what influence does statistical evidence have on settlement rates? How and when does it shape litigation strategies and with what consequences? This review uncovered the disturbing fact that, in some cases involving far-reaching societal consequences, the evidence placed before the courts is biased, incomplete, or flawed. How frequently does this occur, what are its causes, and what remedies for it can be devised? We also have scant evidence bearing on the intellectual competence of decision makers, even for relatively simple statistical data. Any studies on competence should consider judges as well as juries. We need better assessment of the magnitude of the administrative burdens placed on the court by statistical evidence, particularly because it can aid in cost-benefit analyses when considering the need to innovate. Studies about how appellate courts actually use or fail to properly consider statistical data also require examination. I have also attempted to speculate as to some of the reasons courts have resisted innovative approaches to the problems posed by complex evidence. A much more comprehensive analysis should be undertaken, accompanied by field studies to empirically verify hypotheses.

REFERENCES

Abt, C. (1982). Comment in *The Use/Nonuse/Misuse of Applied Social Research in the Courts* (M.J. Saks and C.H. Baron, eds.). Abt Books: Cambridge, Mass.

Ad Hoc Committee on the Use of Jury Trials in Complex Litigation (1984). Report. *Federation of Insurance Counsel Quarterly*, **34**, 321–344.

Austin, A. (1985). *Complex Litigation Confronts the Jury System: A Case Study*. University Publications of America, Inc.: Frederick, MD.

Ballew v. *Georgia*, 413 U.S. 149 (1978).

Barnett, F. (1973). How does a jury view polygraph examination results? *Polygraph*, **2**. American Polygraph Association: Linthicum Heights.

Bermant, G., Cecil, J., Chaset, A., Lind, A., and Lombard, P. (1981). Protracted Civil Trials: View From the Bench and the Bar. Federal Judicial Center Report, Washington, D.C.

Besharov, D.J. (1983). Wrong statistics cited but opinion still stands. *The National Law Journal*, June 6, 13–14.

Bivens v. *Six Unknown Federal Narcotics Agents*, 403 U.S. 388 (1971).

Brekke, N. (1985). Expert Scientific Testimony in Rape Trials. Unpublished Ph.D. dissertation, University of Minnesota.

Bridgeman, D.L. and Marlowe, D. (1979). Jury decision making: An empirical study based on actual felony trials. *Journal of Applied Psychology*, **64**, 91–98.

Brown v. *Board of Education*, 347 U.S. 483 (1954).

Carlson, S., Passano, M., and Januzzo, J. (1977). The effect of lie detector evidence on jury deliberations: An empirical study. *Journal of Police Science and Administration*, **5**, 148–154.

Castaneda v. *Partida*, 97 S.Ct. 1272 (1977).

Cavoukian, A. (1980). The Influence of Eyewitness Identification Evidence. Unpublished doctoral thesis, University of Toronto.

Cavoukian, A. and Heslegrave, R.J. (1980). The admissibility of polygraph evidence in court. *Law and Human Behavior*, **4**, 117–131.

Cecil, J. (1982). Demographic Characteristics of Jurors in Protracted Civil Trials. Unpublished report. The Federal Judicial Center, Washington, D.C.

Charrow, R. and Charrow, V. (1979). Making legal language understandable: A psycholinguistic study of jury instructions. *Columbia Law Review*, **79**, 1306–1374.

Chayes, A. (1976). The role of the judge in public law litigation. *Harvard Law Review*, **89**, 1281–1316.

Colgrove v. *Battin*, 413 U.S. 149 (1973).

Craig v. *Boren*, 429 U.S. 190 (1976).

Damaska, M. (1975). Presentation of evidence and fact finding precision. *University of Pennsylvania Law Review*, **123**, 1083–1106.

Decker, J.F. (1982). Expert services in the defense of criminal cases: The constitutional and statutory rights of indigents. *University of Cincinnati Law Review*, **51**, 574–615.

Diamond, S.S. and Zeisel, H. (1976). Sentencing councils: A study of sentence disparity and its reduction. *University of Chicago Law Review*, **43**, 109–149.

Ebbesen, E. and Konecni, V. (1982a). An analysis of the bail system. In *The Criminal Justice System* (V. Konecni and E. Ebbesen, eds.). W.H. Freeman: San Francisco.

Ebbesen, E. and Konecni, V. (1982b). An analysis of the sentencing system. In *The Criminal Justice System* (V. Konecni and E. Ebbesen, eds.). W.H. Freeman: San Francisco.

Ellsworth, P. (in press). Unpleasant facts: The Supreme Court's response to empirical research on capital punishment. In *The Death Penalty and the Criminal Justice System* (K.C. Haas and J. Inciardi, eds.). Sage Publications: Beverly Hills, Calif.

Ellsworth, P., Bukaty, R., Cowan, C., and Thompson, W. (1984). The death-qualified jury and the defense of insanity. *Law and Human Behavior*, **8**, 81–93.

Elwork, A., Sales, B., and Alfini, J.J. (1980). *Writing Understandable Jury Instructions*. Michie/Bobbs-Merrill: Charlottesville, Va.

Finkelstein, M.O. (1980). The judicial reception of multiple regression studies in race and sex discrimination cases. *Columbia Law Review*, **80**, 737–754.

Fisher, F., McGowan, J., and Greenwood, J. (1983). Economics, economists and antitrust policy. In *Folded, Spindled and Mutilated: Economic Analysis and U.S. v. IBM*. The MIT Press: Cambridge, Mass.

Forkosch, M.D. (1939). Lie detector and the counts. *New York University Law Quarterly Review*, **16**, 202–235.

Fox, S.G. and Walters, H.A. (1986). The impact of general versus specific expert testimony and eyewitness confidence upon mock juror judgments. *Law and Human Behavior*, **10**, 215–228.

Frankel, M. (1975). The search for truth: An empirical view. *University of Pennsylvania Law Review*, **123**, 1031–1059.

Friedman, L. (1975). *The Legal System: A Social Science Perspective*. Russell Sage Foundation: New York.

Friedman, L. (1986). The law and society movement. *Stanford Law Review*, **38**, 763–780.

Galanter, M. (1983). Reading the landscape of disputes: What we know and don't know (and think we know) about our allegedly contentious and litigous society. *UCLA Law Review*, **31**, 4–71.

Gianelli, P.C. (1980). Scientific evidence. *Columbia Law Review*, **80**, 1239–1240.

Gibson, J. (1980). Environmental constraints on the behavior of judges: A representational model of judicial decision making. *Law and Society Review*, **14**, 343–370.

Greene, E., Wilson, L., and Loftus, E. (1986). Impact of Hypnotic Testimony on the Jury. Paper presented at the American Psychology and Law Society, Tucson, 1986.

Greene, H. (1975). Voiceprint identification: The case in favor of admissibility. *The American Criminal Law Review*, **13**, 171.

Grofman, B. and Scarrow, H. (1980). Mathematics, social science, and the law. In *The Use/Nonuse/Misuse of Applied Social Research in the Courts* (M.J. Saks and C.H. Baron, eds.). Abt Books: Cambridge, Mass.

Gross, S. (1985). Race and death: The judicial evaluation of evidence of discrimination in capital sentencing. *U.C. Davis Law Review*, **18**.

Haney, C. (1980). Psychology and legal change. *Law and Human Behavior*, **4**, 147–199.

Hans, V. and Vidmar, N. (1986). *Judging the Jury*. Plenum Press: New York.

Heuer, L. and Penrod, S. (no date, a). Increasing Jurors' Participation in Trials: A Field Experiment with Jury Note Taking and Question Asking. Department of Psychology, University of Wisconsin, Madison.

Heuer, L. and Penrod, S. (no date, b). Instructing Juries: A Field Experiment with Written and Preliminary Instructions. Department of Psychology, University of Wisconsin, Madison.

Horowitz, D. (1977). *The Courts and Social Policy*. The Brooklings Institution: Washington, D.C.

Hosch, H. (1980). Commentary: A comparison of three studies of the influence of expert testimony on jurors. *Law and Human Behavior*, **4**, 297–302.

Hosch, H., Beck, E., and McIntyre, P. (1980). Influence of expert testimony regarding eyewitness accuracy on jury decisions. *Law and Human Behavior*, **4**, 287–296.

Huttner, C. (1979). Unfit for jury determination: Complex civil litigation. *Boston College Law Review*, **20**, 511.

Imwinkelreid, E.J. (1981). A new era in the evaluation of scientific evidence. *William and Mary Law Review*, **23**, 261–290.

Imwinkelreid, E.J. (1983). A new era in the evolution of scientific evidence—A primer on evaluating the weight of scientific evidence. *William and Mary Law Review,* **23**, 261–290.

Imwinkelreid, E.J. (1984). Judge versus jury: Who should decide questions of preliminary facts conditioning the admissibility of scientific evidence. *William and Mary Law Review,* **25**, 577–618.

Jacoby, J. (1985). Survey and field experimental evidence. In *The Psychology of Evidence and Trial Procedure* (S. Kassin and L. Wrightsman, eds.). Sage Publications, Inc.: Beverley Hills, Calif.

Johnson, S. (1980). Misuses of applied social research. In *The Use/Nonuse/Misuse of Applied Social Research in the Courts* (M.J. Saks and C.H. Baron, eds.). Abt Books: Cambridge, Mass.

Kalmuss, D., Chesler, M., and Sanders, J. (1982). Political conflict in applied scholarship: Expert witnesses in school desegregation research. *Social Problems,* **30**, 168–192.

Kalven, H., Jr., and Zeisel, H. (1966). *The American Jury.* Little, Brown and Co.: Boston.

Kirst, R. (1982). The jury's historic domain in complex cases. *Washington Law Review* **58**, 1–38.

Koffler, J.H. (1957). The lie detector—a critical appraisal of the technique as a potential undermining factor in the judicial process. *New York Law Forum,* **3**, 123, 138–146.

Lambert, N. (1981). Psychological evidence in Larry P. v. Wilson Riles. *American Psychologist,* **36**, 937–952.

Larry P. v. *Riles,* 343 F.Supp. 1306 (N.D. California 1972).

Lassers, J. (1967). Proof of guilt in capital cases: Unscience. *Journal of Criminal Law, Criminology, and Police Science,* **1967**, 310–315.

Lempert, R. (1975). Uncovering "nondiscernable" differences: Empirical research and the jury size cases. *Michigan Law Review,* **73**, 643–708.

Lempert, R. (1981). Civil juries and complex cases: Let's not rush to judgment. *Michigan Law Review,* **80**, 68–132.

Lempert, R. and Sanders, J. (1986). *An Invitation to Law and Social Science.* Longman: New York.

Loftus, E. (1980). Impact of expert psychological testimony on the unreliability of eyewitness identification. *Journal of Applied Psychology,* **65**, 9–15.

Loftus, E. (1985). Psychological aspects of courtroom testimony. *Annals New York Academy of Sciences,* **347**, 27–37.

Loftus, E. (1986). Ten years in the life of an expert witness. *Law and Human Behavior,* **10**, 241–264.

Loh, W. (1984). *Social Research in the Judicial Process.* Russell Sage: New York.

Manual for Complex Litigation (1982). Fifth Ed. West Publishing: St. Paul, Minn.

Markwart, A. and Lynch, B. (1979). The effect of polygraph evidence on mock jury decision-making. *Journal of Police Science and Administration,* **7**, 324.

Marshall, J. (1980). *Law and Psychology in Conflict,* 2nd ed. Doubleday-Anchor: New York.

Marvell, T. (1980). Misuses of applied social research. In *The Use/Nonuse/Misuse of Applied Social Research in the Courts* (M.J. Saks and C.H. Baron, eds.). Abt Books: Cambridge, Mass.

Michelson, S. (1980). History and state of the art of applied social research in courts. In *The Use/Nonuse/Misuse of Applied Social Research in the Courts* (M.J. Saks and C.H. Baron, eds.). Abt Books: Cambridge, Mass.

Miller, A.S. and Baron, J.A. (1975). The Supreme Court, the adversary system, and the flow of information to the justices: A preliminary inquiry. *Virginia Law Review,* **61**, 1187–1245.

Moenssens, A. (1984). Admissibility of scientific evidence: An alternative to the *Frye* rule. *William and Mary Law Review,* **25**, 545–575.

Monahan, J. and Walker, L. (1985). *Social Science in Law.* Foundation Press: Mineola, N.Y.

Myers, M. (1979). Rule departures and making law: Juries and their verdicts. *Law & Society Review,* **13**, 781–797.

Nisbett, R. and Ross, L. (1980). *Human Inference: Strategies and Shortcomings of Social Judgment.* Prentice-Hall: Englewood Cliffs, N.J.

Nordenberg, M. and Luneberg, W. (1982). Decisionmaking in complex federal civil cases: Two alternatives to the traditional jury. *Judicature*, **65**, 420–431.

Note (1980). The case for special juries in complex civil litigation. *Yale Law Journal*, **89**, 1155.

Oakes, D. (1970). Studying the exclusionary rule in search and seizure. *University of Chicago Law Review*, **37**, 655–757.

Partridge, A. and Eldridge, W. (1974). *The Second Circuit Sentencing Study*. The Federal Judicial Center: Washington, D.C.

Peters, G. (1980). Overcoming barriers to the use of applied social research in the courts. In *The Use/Nonuse/Misuse of Applied Social Research in the Courts* (M.J. Saks and C.H. Baron, eds.). Abt Books: Cambridge, Mass.

Peters, R. (1982). A survey of polygraph evidence in criminal trials. *American Bar Association Journal*, **68**, 162–165.

Post, R. (1980). Legal concepts and applied social research concepts: Translation problems. In *The Use/Nonuse/Misuse of Applied Social Research in the Courts* (M.J. Saks and C.H. Baron, eds.). Abt Books: Cambridge, Mass.

Roesch, R. and Golding, S. (1980). *Competency to Stand Trial*. University of Illinois Press: Urbana, Ill.

Rosen, P. (1980). History and state of the art. In *The Use/Nonuse/Misuse of Applied Social Research in the Courts* (M.J. Saks and C.H. Baron, eds.). Abt Books: Cambridge, Mass.

Rosenthal, R. (1983). Nature of jury response to the expert witness. *Journal of Forensic Sciences*, **28**, 528–531.

Rosenthal, R. and Jacobsen, L. (1968). *Pygmalion in the Classroom*. Holt, Rinehart, & Winston: New York.

Rossi, P. (1980). Market research data in deceptive advertising cases. In *The Use/Nonuse/Misuse of Applied Social Research in the Courts* (M.J. Saks and C.H. Baron, eds.). Abt Books: Cambridge, Mass.

Rubinfeld, D.L. (1985). Econometrics in the courtroom. *Columbia Law Review*, **85**, 1048.

Saks, M. (1977). *Jury Verdicts: The Role of Group Size and Social Decision Rule*. D.C. Heath: Lexington, Mass.

Saks, M.J. and Baron, C.H. (Eds.). (1980). *The Use, Nonuse, Misuse of Applied Social Research in the Courts.* The Council for Applied Social Research. Abt Books: Cambridge, Mass.

Saks, M.J. and Van Duizend, R. (1983). *The Use of Scientific Evidence in Litigation.* National Center for State Courts: Williamsburg, Va.

Sand, L. and Reiss, S. (1985). A report on seven experiments conducted by district court judges in the Second Circuit. *New York University Law Review,* **60**, 423–497.

Sanders, J., Rankin-Widgeon, B., Kalmuss, D., and Chesler, M. (1982). The relevance of "irrelevant" testimony: Why lawyers use social science experts in school desegregation cases. *Law & Society Review,* **16**, 403–428.

Saxe, L., Dougherty, D., and Cross, T. (1985). The validity of polygraph testing: Scientific analysis and public controversy. *American Psychologist,* **40**, 355–366.

Selvin, M. and Picus, L. (1987). *The Debate Over Jury Performance.* The Rand Institute for Civil Justice: Santa Monica, Calif.

Severance, L.J. and Loftus, E. (1984). Improving the ability of jurors to comprehend and apply criminal jury instructions. *Law and Society Review,* **17**, 153–198.

Simon, J. and Zusman, J. (1983). The effect of contextual factors on psychiatrists' perception of illness: A case study. *Journal of Health and Social Behavior,* **24**, 186–198.

Simon, R.J. (1967). *The Jury and the Defense of Insanity.* Little, Brown & Co.: Boston.

Simon, R.J. and Mahan, L. (1971). Quantifying burdens of proof: a view from the bench, the jury, and the classroom. *Law and Society Review,* **5**, 319–330.

Sperlich, P. (1982). The case for preserving trial by jury in complex civil litigation. *Judicature,* **65**, 394–415.

Stienstra, D. (1985). *Unpublished Dispositions: Problems of Access and Use in the Courts of Appeals.* Federal Judicial Center: Washington, D.C.

Tanke, E.T. and Tanke, T.J. (1979). Getting off the slippery slope: Social science in the judical process. *American Psychologist,* **34**, 1130–1138.

Thibaut, J. and Walker, L. (1975). *Procedural Justice: A Psychological Analysis.* Erlbaum: Hillsdale, N.J.

Thibaut, J. and Walker, L. (1978). A theory of procedure. *California Law Review,* **66**, 541–566.

Thompson, W.C. (1984). Judgmental Bias in Reactions to Mathematical Evidence. Paper presented at the American Psychology and Law Meetings, Tucson, Ariz.

Thompson, W.C. (1985). Fallacious Interpretations of Statistical Evidence in Criminal Trials. Paper presented at American Psychological Association Annual Convention, 1985.

Thompson, W.C. and Schumann, E.L. (1987). Interpretation of statistical evidence in criminal trials: The prosecutor's fallacy and the defense attorney's fallacy. *Law and Human Behavior,* **11**, 167–188.

Wasby, S. (1980). History and state of the art. In *The Use/Nonuse/Misuse of Applied Social Research in the Courts* (M.J. Saks and C.H. Baron, eds.). Abt Books: Cambridge, Mass.

Wells, G., Lindsay, R., and Tousignant, J. (1979). Effects of expert psychological advice on human performance in judging the validity of eyewitness testimony. *Law and Human Behavior,* **4**, 275–285.

Williams v. *Florida,* 399 U.S. 78 (1970).

Wolf, E.P. (1976). Social science and the courts: The Detroit Schools Case. *The Public Interest,* **42**, (Winter) 102–120.

Wolf, E.P. (1977). Northern school desegregation and residential choice. *The Supreme Court Review,* **64**, 63–85.

Yarmolinsky, A. (1980). Comments. In *The Use/Nonuse/Misuse of Applied Social Research in the Courts* (M.J. Saks and C.H. Baron, eds.). Abt Books: Cambridge, Mass.

Zeisel, H. and Diamond, S.S. (1974). Convincing empirical evidence on the six member jury. *University of Chicago Law Review,* **41**, 281–295.

Appendix I

Biographies of Panel Members and Staff

STEPHEN E. FIENBERG (Cochair) is Maurice Falk professor of statistics and social science and Dean of the College of Humanities and Social Sciences at Carnegie Mellon University. He received a B.Sc. in mathematics and statistics from the University of Toronto in 1964 and an M.A. and a Ph.D. in statistics from Harvard University in 1965 and 1968, respectively. He previously taught at the University of Chicago and the University of Minnesota. His principal research has been on the development of statistical methodology, especially in connection with the analysis of cross-classified categorical data, and on the application of statistics in various areas. He has served as coordinating and applications editor of the *Journal of the American Statistical Association* and is coeditor of *Statistics and the Law*. He was the chairman of the Committee on National Statistics from 1981 to 1987.

SAMUEL KRISLOV (Cochair) is professor and chairman of the Department of Political Science at the University of Minnesota. He received a B.A. in 1951 and an M.A. in 1952 from New York University and a Ph.D. from Princeton University in 1955. He has served on the faculty at the University of Oklahoma and Michigan State University and as a visiting professor at Columbia University, Tel Aviv University, and the University of Wisconsin. He is a former president of the Law and Society Association and has served as editor of *Law and Society Review*. He is the author of numerous articles and books, which include *The Supreme Court and the Political Process* and *Compliance and the Law* (coauthor). He served as chairman of the Committee on Research on Law Enforcement and the Administration of Justice from 1975 to 1980.

GORDON J. APPLE is an attorney and former National Research Council fellow. He received a B.A. in economics in 1977 from the University of Wisconsin, and a J.D. in 1982 from the University of Wisconsin Law School. His primary interests are legal and scientific issues surrounding proof of harm and causation from exposure to hazardous substances. He is the coauthor of "Scientific Data and Environmental Regulation" (in *Statistics and the Law*).

THOMAS J. CAMPBELL is associate professor at the Stanford Law School. He received a B.A. and an M.A. in 1973 from the University of Chicago, a J.D. from Harvard Law School in 1976, and a Ph.D. in economics from the University of Chicago in 1980. He is a former director of the Bureau of Competition of the Federal Trade Commission and has testified before numerous congressional committees. His primary interests are comparable worth, antitrust, and corporate and international law. He is the author of many articles, including "Regression Analysis in Title VII Cases: Minimum Standards, Comparable Worth, and Other Issues Where Law and Statistics Meet."

MICHAEL O. FINKELSTEIN is a practicing attorney and partner in the law firm of Lord Day & Lord, Barrett Smith, in New York City and also a consultant in cases involving statistical presentations. He received an A.B. and an LL.B. from Harvard University in 1955 and 1958, respectively, and was admitted to the New York Bar in 1959. He teaches quantitative methods in law at Columbia University School of Law and is the author of *Quantitative Methods in Law*. He is the former chair of the Special Committee on Empirical Data of the Association of the Bar of the City of New York and currently serves on the Task Force on Proportionality Review in Death Sentence Cases of the National Center for State Courts.

JAMES J. HECKMAN is professor of economics at the University of Chicago. He received an A.B. from Colorado College in 1955, and an M.A. and Ph.D. in economics in 1968 and 1971, respectively, from Princeton University. He is an associate editor of the *Journal of Econometrics*, and a former fellow at the Center for Advanced Study in the Behavioral Sciences at Stanford.

WILLIAM G. HUNTER was professor of statistics and industrial engineering at the University of Wisconsin. He received a B.S.E. in 1959 from Princeton University and an M.S.E. in 1960 from the University of Illinois and an M.S. and a Ph.D. in statistics from the University of Wisconsin in 1961 and 1963, respectively. His primary research interests are design of experiments, model building, quality improvement, engineering statistics, statistical inference, environmental statistics, and data analysis. He was coauthor of *Statistics for Experimenters*. Professor Hunter died in December 1986 after this report was completed.

ALBYN C. JONES is assistant professor in the Department of Mathematics at Reed College. He received a B.A. in mathematics from the University of California, Los Angeles in 1977, an M.Phil. in 1980 and a Ph.D. in 1986 in statistics from Yale University. He was a research associate with the Committee on National Statistics. His research interests are in statistical computing, data analysis, large data sets, and policy analysis.

JOHN H. LANGBEIN is Max Pam professor of American and foreign law at the University of Chicago Law School. He received an A.B. from Columbia University in 1964, an LL.B. from Harvard University in 1968, and LL.B. and Ph.D. degrees from Cambridge University, England, in 1969 and 1971, respectively. A specialist in comparative law (as well as in American trust, succession, and pension law), he has written extensively about the legal procedural system in West Germany. His *Comparative Criminal Procedure: Germany* (1977) appears in the American Casebook Series.

RICHARD O. LEMPERT is professor of law and sociology at the University of Michigan. He received an A.B. from Oberlin College in 1964, a J.D. from the University of Michigan Law School in 1968, and a Ph.D. in sociology in 1971 from the University of Michigan. He is vice chair of the Committee on Research on Law Enforcement and the Administration of Justice. He has served as editor of the *Law and Society Review* and as a member of the executive committee of the Law and Society Association. He is coauthor of *A Modern Approach to Evidence* and *An Invitation to Law and Social Sciences.*

ELIZABETH F. LOFTUS is professor of psychology and adjunct professor of law at the University of Washington, Seattle. She received a B.A. in 1966 from the University of California, Los Angeles, and an M.S. and a Ph.D. in psychology from Stanford University in 1967 and 1970, respectively. Her major fields of interest are human memory and law and psychology. She is the author of *Eyewitness Testimony*, which won a National Media Award from the American Psychological Foundation in 1980.

PAUL MEIER is Ralph and Mary Otis Isham distinguished service professor of statistics and chairman of the Department of Statistics at the University of Chicago. He received a B.S. in 1945 from Oberlin College and an M.A. in 1947 and a Ph.D. in 1951 in mathematics from Princeton University. His many areas of statistical expertise include statistical methods for medical investigations, especially evaluation of medical therapies through clinical trials. He also has considerable experience as an expert witness in numerous court cases. He is a former member of the Committee on National Statistics.

LEE R. PAULSON was staff associate for the Committee on National Statistics. She received a B.S. in agriculture from the University of Maryland. She is interested in various computer applications, particularly uses for microcomputer and mainframe interaction.

SAM C. POINTER, JR., is a U.S. district judge for the Northern District of Alabama. He received an A.B. from Vanderbilt University in 1955, a J.D. from the University of Alabama in 1957, and an LL.M. from New York University in 1958 and was admitted to the Alabama Bar in 1957. He is on the Temporary Emergency Courts of Appeals and a member of the Judicial Panel on Multi-district Litigation. He also served on the board of editors for the *Manual for Complex Litigation.*

DANIEL L. RUBINFELD is professor of law and economics at the University of California, Berkeley. He received an A.B. degree in mathematics from Princeton University in 1967, an M.S. degree in 1968 and a Ph.D degree in economics in 1972 from M.I.T. His research interests include state and local public economics, the economic analysis of law, and applied econometric methods, especially as applied to the study of law and legal process. He currently serves on the editorial boards of *Public Finance Quarterly, Law and Society Review*, and *Evaluation Review.*

RICHARD D. SCHWARTZ is Ernest I. White professor of law at the College of Law and professor of sociology and social science at the Maxwell School of Syracuse University. He received a B.A. in 1947 and a Ph.D. in sociology in 1952 from Yale University. He is the former dean and provost of the Faculty of Law and Jurisprudence at the State University of New York, Buffalo. He is interested particularly in the sociology of law, criminal law and society, and administrative regulation and is a member of the Committee on Research on Law Enforcement and the Administration of Justice.

MIRON L. STRAF is director of the Committee on National Statistics. He has taught at the University of California, Berkeley, and the London School of Economics and Political Science. He received a B.A. and an M.A. in mathematics from Carnegie-Mellon University in 1964 and 1965, respectively, and a Ph.D. in statistics from the University of Chicago in 1969. He is a fellow of the American Statistical Association and of the Royal Statistical Society. His interests and research are in statistical theory and a variety of applications of statistics, including environmental management, epidemiology of skin cancer and of mental retardation, apportionment of funds by statistical formulae, linguistics, and the use of statistical assessments in the courts.

NEIL VIDMAR is professor of psychology and professor of law at the University of Western Ontario, London, Ontario. He received an A.B. in 1962 from MacMurray College and an M.A. and a Ph.D. from the University of Illinois in 1965 and 1967, respectively. He serves on the editorial boards of *Law and Human Behavior*, the *Journal of Applied Social Psychology*, and *Law and Society Review*. His research has been in the interaction of social science and law, English and Canadian grievance and dispute behavior, procedural justice and dispute resolution procedures, and social/psychological implications of surveillance and disclosure.

JACK B. WEINSTEIN is the chief judge for the United States District Court for the Eastern District of New York. He received a B.A. in 1943 from Brooklyn College and an LL.B. in 1948 from Columbia University School of Law. As a professor and adjunct professor of law, he has taught at Columbia University School of Law and other law schools. In addition to numerous publications, he is the coauthor of *Weinstein's Evidence, United States Rules, Cases and Materials on Evidence, Elements of Civil Procedure, and Basic Problems of State and Federal Evidence.*

SANDY ZABELL is associate professor of statistics at Northwestern University. He received an A.B. in 1968 from Columbia University and an A.M. and Ph.D. in 1971 and 1974, respectively, from Harvard University. His research interests are mathematical probability (large deviations and conditional expectations); Bayesian statistics (exchangeability and its generalizations); and history, philosophy, and legal applications of probability and statistics.

References

Abraham, B. and Ledolter, J. (1983). *Statistical Methods for Forecasting*. Wiley: New York.

Ad Hoc Committee on Professional Ethics (1983). Ethical guidelines for statistical practice. *American Statistician*, **37**, 5–6.

Adams, R.M., Smelser, N.J., and Treiman, D. (eds.) (1982). *Behavioral and Social Science Research: A National Resource*, Parts I and II. National Academy Press: Washington, D.C.

Aickin, M. and Kaye, D. (1983). Some mathematical and legal considerations in using seriological tests to prove paternity. *Proceedings of the American Association of Blood Banks International Conference on Inclusion Probabilities in Parentage Testing*.

Aitken, C.G.G. and Robertson, J. (1987). A contribution to the discussion of probabilities and human hair comparisons. *Journal of Forensic Sciences*, **32**, 684–689.

American Bar Association (1972). *Code of Judicial Conduct*.

American Bar Association (1983). *Model Rules for Professional Conduct*.

Armitage, P. (1985). Multistage models of carcinogenesis. *Environmental Health Sciences*, **63**, 195–201.

Bailey, F.L. and Rothblatt, H.B. (1971). *Successful Techniques for Criminal Trials*. Lawyer's Cooperative Publishing Co.: Rochester, NY.

Baker, K.M. (1975). *Condorcet, From Natural Philosophy to Social Mathematics*. University of Chicago Press: Chicago, Ill.

Baldus, D.C. and Cole, J.W.L. (1980). *Statistical Proof of Discrimination*. Shepard's: Colorado Springs, CO.

Bar-Hillel, M. (1984). Probabilistic analysis in legal fact finding. *Acta Psychologica*, **56**, 267–284.

Barksdale, H. (1957). *The Use of Survey Research Findings as Legal Evidence*. Printers' Ink Books: Pleasantville, NY.

Barnes, D.W. (1983). *Statistics as Proof: Fundamentals of Quantitative Evidence*. Little, Brown: Boston.

Barnett, P.D. and Ogle, R.R., Jr. (1982). Probabilities and human hair comparison. *Journal of Forensic Sciences*, **27**, 272–278.

Barton, A. (1983). My experience as an expert witness. *American Statistician*, **37**, 374–376.

Bartsh, T.C., Boddy, F.M., King, B.F., and Thompson, P.N. (1978). *A Class-Action Suit That Worked: The Consumer Refund in the Antibiotic Antitrust Litigation.* Lexington Books: Lexington, MA.

Bazelon, D.L. (1977). Coping with technology through the legal process. *Cornell Law Review*, **62**, 817–832.

Bazelon, D.L. (1978). The role of the psychiatrist in the criminal justice system. *American Academy of Psychiatry and Law*, **6**, 139–146.

Bentham, J. (1827). *Rationale of Judicial Evidence, Specially Applied to English Practice* (J.S. Mill, ed.). Hunt and Clarke: London.

Bernoulli, J. (1713). *Ars Conjectandi.* Basle.

Bernoulli, N. (1709). *Specimina Artis Conjectandi Ad Quaestiones Juris Applicatae.* Basle.

Berry, D.A. and Geisser, S. (1986). Inferences in cases of disputed paternity. In *Statistics and the Law* (M.H. DeGroot, S.E. Fienberg, and J.B. Kadane, eds.). Wiley: New York, 353–382.

Bishop, Y.M.M., Fienberg, S.E., and Holland, P.W. (1975). *Discrete Multivariate Analysis: Theory and Practice.* M.I.T. Press: Cambridge, MA.

Black, B. (1988). Evolving legal standards for admissibility of scientific evidence. *Science*, **239**, 1508–1512.

Bliley, T.J. (1983). Remarks reported in *U.S. Children and Their Families: Current Conditions and Recent Trends.* Select Committee on Children, Youth, and Families, U.S. House of Representatives 98th Congress, First Session. Washington: U.S. Government Printing Office, 63–64.

Booth, Wm. (1987). Agent Orange study hits brick wall (News and Comment). *Science*, **237**, 1285–1286.

Box, G.E.P., Hunter, Wm.G., and Hunter, J.S. (1978). *Statistics for Experimenters.* Wiley: New York.

Box, G.E.P. and Jenkins, G.M. (1976). *Time Series Analysis: Forecasting and Control.* Holden-Day: San Francisco.

Boyum, K.O. and Krislov, S. (1980). *Forecasting the Impact of Legislation on the Courts.* National Academy Press: Washington.

Brodsky, S.L. (1977). The mental health professional on the witness stand: A survival guide. In *Psychology in the Legal Process* (B.D. Sales, ed.). Spectrum: New York.

Campbell, T.J. (1984). Regression analysis in Title VII cases: minimum standards, comparable worth, and other issues where law and statistics meet. *Stanford Law Review,* **36**, 1299–.

Cappelletti, M. and Perillo, J.M. (1965). *Civil Procedure in Italy.* Martinus Nijhoff: The Hague, Netherlands.

Chatfield, C. (1980). *The Analysis of Time Series: An Introduction,* 2nd ed. Chapman and Hall: New York.

Chatterjee, S. and Price, B. (1977). *Regression Analysis by Example.* Wiley: New York.

Chayes, A. (1976). The role of the judge in public law litigation. *Harvard Law Review,* **89**, 1281–1316.

Chernoff, H. and Moses, L.E. (1959). *Elementary Decision Theory.* Wiley: New York.

Cochran, Wm.G. (1963). *Sampling Techniques,* 2nd ed. Wiley: New York.

Cohen, L.J. (1977). *The Probable and the Provable.* Clarendon Press.

Cohen, L.J. (1981). Can human irrationality be experimentally demonstrated (with various commentaries). *The Behavioral and Brain Sciences,* **317**, 331–359.

Conway, D.A. and Roberts, H.V. (1983). Reverse regression, fairness, and employment discrimination. *Journal of Business and Economic Statistics,* **1**, 75–85.

Conway, D.A. and Roberts, H.V. (1984). Rejoinder to comments on 'Reverse regression, fairness, and employment discrimination.' *Journal of Business and Economic Statistics,* **2**, 126–139.

Conway, D.A. and Roberts, H.V. (1986). Regression analyses in employment discrimination cases. In *Statistics and the Law* (M.H. DeGroot, S.E. Fienberg, and J.B. Kadane, eds.). Wiley: New York, 107–168.

Coulam, R. and Fienberg, S.E. (1986). The use of court-appointed experts: a case study. In *Statistics and the Law* (M.H. DeGroot, S.E. Fienberg, and J.B. Kadane, eds.). Wiley: New York, 305–332.

Cox, D.R. and Oakes, D. (1984). *Analysis of Survival Data.* Chapman Hall: New York.

Dawid, A.P. (1987). The difficulty about conjunction. *The Statistician,* **36**, 91–97.

Decker, J.F. (1982). Expert services in the defense of criminal cases: The constitutional and statutory rights of indigents. *University of Cincinnati Law Review,* **51**, 574–615.

Deming, W.E. (1954). On the presentation of the results of sample surveys as legal evidence. *Journal of the American Statistical Association,* **49**, 814–825.

Deming, W.E. (1960). *Sample Design in Business Research.* Wiley: New York.

Deming, W.E. (1965). Principles of professional statistical practice. *Annals of Mathematical Statistics,* **36**, 1883–1900.

Dempster, A.P. (1984). Alternative models for inferring employment discrimination from statistical data. In *W.G. Cochran's Impact on Statistics* (P.S.R.S. Rao and J. Sedransk, eds.). Wiley: New York.

Department of Justice Merger Guidelines (1984). Federal Register v. 49 no. 127, pp. 26823–37. June 29, 1984.

Draper, N.R. and Smith, H. (1981). *Applied Regression Analysis (2nd ed.).* Wiley: New York.

Eggleston, R. (1983). *Evidence, Proof and Probability* (2nd ed.). Weidenfeld and Nicolson: London.

Ellman, I.M. and Kaye, D. (1979). Probabilities and proof: Can HLA and blood group testing prove paternity? *NYU Law Review,* **54**, 1131–1162.

Evans, D.S. (ed.) (1983). *Breaking Up Bell: Essays on Industrial Organization and Regulation.* North Holland: New York.

Everitt, B.S. and Dunn, G. (1983). *Advanced Methods of Data Exploration and Modelling.* Heinemann: London.

Evett, I.W. (1984). A quantitative theory for interpreting transfer evidence in criminal cases. *Journal of the Royal Statistical Society Series C*, **33**, 25–32.

Evett, I.W. (1986). A Bayesian approach to the problem of interpreting glass eidence in forensic science casework. *Journal of the Forensic Science Society*, **26**, 3–18.

Evett, I.W. (1987). Bayesian inference and forensic science: Problems and perspectives. *The Statistician*, **36**, 99–105.

Federal Rules of Civil Procedure (1982). Compiled by Thomas A. Coyne. Federal Practice Series. Boardman.

Federal Rules of Criminal Procedure, 2nd ed. (1980). Edited by Michele G. Hermann. Boardman.

Federal Rules of Evidence for United States Courts and Magistrates (1983). West Publishing Co.: St. Paul, MN.

Federal Rules of Evidence Digest (1981, 1983). Pike and Fischer, Inc. (ed.).

Ferber, M.A. and Green, C.A. (1984). What kind of fairness is fair? A comment on Conway and Roberts. *Journal of Business and Economic Statistics*, **2**, 111–113.

Fienberg, S.E. (1980). *The Analysis of Cross-classified Categorical Data* (2nd ed.). MIT Press: Cambridge, MA.

Fienberg, S. E. (1982). The increasing sophistication of statistical assessments as evidence in discrimination litigation—a comment on Kaye. *Journal of the American Statistical Association*, **77**, 784–787.

Fienberg, S.E. and Kadane, J.B. (1983). The presentation of Bayesian statistical analyses in legal proceedings. *The Statistician*, **32**, 88–98.

Fienberg, S.E. and Schervish, M.J. (1986). The relevance of Bayesian inference for the presentation of statistical evidence and for legal decisionmaking. *Boston University Law Review*, **66**, 771–798.

Fienberg, S.E. and Straf, M. (1982). Statistical assessments as evidence. *Journal of the Royal Statistical Society* (A), **145**, 410–421.

Finkelstein, M.O. (1966). The application of statistical decision theory to the jury discrimination cases. *Harvard Law Review*, **80**, 338–376.

Finkelstein, M.O. (1978). *Quantitative Methods in Law: Studies in the Application of Mathematical Probability and Statistics to Legal Problems.* The Free Press: New York.

Finkelstein, M.O. (1980). The judicial reception of multiple regression studies in race and sex discrimination cases. *Columbia Law Review,* **80**, 737–754.

Finkelstein, M. and Fairley, W. (1970). A Bayesian approach to identification evidence. *Harvard Law Review,* **83**, 235–314.

Finkelstein, M.O. and Levenbach, H. (1983). Regression estimates of damages in price-fixing cases. *Law and Contemporary Problems,* **46** (No. 4), 145–169.

Finney, D.J. (1982). Discussion of papers on statistics and the law. *Journal of the Royal Statistical Society* (A), **145**, 432–433.

Fisher, F., McGowan, J.J., and Greenwood, J.E. (1983). *Folded, Spindled, and Mutilated: Economic Analysis and U.S. vs IBM.* MIT Press: Cambridge, MA.

Fleiss, J.L. (1981). *Statistical Methods for Rates and Proportions.* Wiley: New York.

Freedman, D.A. and Lane, D. (1983). Significant testing in a nonstochastic setting. In *A Festschrift for Erich L. Lehmann in Honor of His Sixty-Fifth Birthday* (P. Bickel, K. Doksum, J.H. Hodges, Jr., eds.). Wadsworth: Belmont, CA, 184–208.

Freedman, D., Pisani, R., and Purves, R. (1978). *Statistics.* Norton: New York.

Fuller, W.A. (1987). *Measurement Error Models.* Wiley: New York.

Galanter, M. (1974). Why the "haves" come out ahead. *Law & Society Review,* **9**, 95–160.

Garber, D. and Zabell, S. (1979). On the emergence of probability. *Archive for History of Exact Sciences,* **21**, 33–53.

Gaudette, B.D. (1976). Probabilities and human pubic hair comparisons. *Journal of Forensic Sciences,* **21**, 514–517.

Gaudette, B.D. (1978). Some further thoughts on probabilities and human hair comparisons. *Journal of Forensic Sciences,* **23**, 758–763.

Gaudette, B.D. (1982). A supplementary discussion of probabilities and human hair comparisons. *Journal of Forensic Sciences*, **27**, 279–289.

Gaudette, B.D. and Keeping, E.S. (1974). An attempt at determining probabilities in human scalp comparison. *Journal of Forensic Sciences*, **19**, 599–606.

Geisel, M.S. and Masson, J.L. (1986). Capital market analysis in antitrust litigation. In *Statistics and the Law*, (M.H. DeGroot, S.E. Fienberg, and J.B. Kadane, eds.). Wiley: New York, 289–303.

Gelfand, A. and Solomon, H. (1973). A study of Poisson's models for jury verdicts in criminal and civil trials. *Journal of the American Statistical Association*, **68**, 271–278.

Gelpe, M.R. and Tarlock, A.D. (1974). The uses of scientific information in environmental decisionmaking. *Southern California Law Review*, **48**, 371–427.

Gianelli, P.C. (1980). The admissibility of novel scientific evidence: Frye v. United States, a half-century later. *Columbia Law Review*, **80**, 1197.

Gianelli, P.C. (1980). Scientific evidence. *Columbia Law Review*, **80**, 1239–1240.

Gillispie, C.C. (1972). Probability and politics: Laplace, Condorcet, and Turgot. *Proceedings of the American Philosophical Society*, **116**, 1–20.

Goldberger, A.S. (1984a). Redirecting reverse regression. *Journal of Business and Economic Statistics*, **2**, 114–116.

Goldberger, A.S. (1984b). Reverse regression and salary discrimination. *Journal of Human Resources*, **19**, 293–319.

Gough, M. (1986). *Dioxin, Agent Orange. The Facts.* Plenum: New York.

Grad, F. (1984). Remedies for injuries caused by hazardous waste: the report and recommendations of the superfund study group. ALI-ABA Course of Study – Environmental Law. Environmental Law Institute/Smithsonian Institution, Washington, D.C.

Greene, Wm. H. (1984). Reverse regression: the algebra of discrimination. *Journal of Business and Economic Statistics*, **2**, 117–120.

Greenfield, J. (ed.) (1984). *The Use of Economists in Antitrust Litigation.* American Bar Association: Chicago.

Grofman, B. (1980). The slippery slope. Jury size and jury verdict requirements—legal and social science approaches. *Law and Policy Quarterly*, **2**, 285–304.

Haberman, S.J. (1978). *Analysis of Qualitative Data, Vol. 1: Introductory Topics.* Academic Press: New York.

Haberman, S.J. (1979). *Analysis of Qualitative Data, Vol. 2: New Developments.* Academic Press: New York.

Hacking, I. (1975). *The Emergence of Probability.* Cambridge Univ. Press: Cambridge, England.

Hand, L. (1902). Historical and practical considerations regarding expert testimony. *Harvard Law Review*, **15**, 40–58.

Hasofer, A.M. (1969). Some aspects of Talmudic probabilistic thought. *Proceedings of the Association of Orthodox Jewish Scientists*, **2**, 63–80.

Heyde, C.C. and Seneta, E. (1977). *I.J. Bienayme: Statistical Theory Anticipated.* Springer-Verlag: New York.

Holmes, O.W., Jr. (1897). The path of the law. *Harvard Law Review*, **10**, No. 8, 457–478.

Holmes, O.W., Jr. (1899). Law in science and science in law. *Harvard Law Review*, **12**, 443–463.

Horowitz, D. (1977). *The Courts and Social Policy.* The Brooklings Institution: Washington, D.C.

Hunter, Wm.G. (1982). Environmental statistics. In *Encyclopedia of Statistical Science*, Vol. 2 (S. Kotz and N.L. Johnson, eds.). Wiley: New York, 517–523.

James, P.A. (1979). *Introduction to English Law*, (10th ed.). Butterworth: London.

Jessnitzer, K. (1978). *Der Gerichtliche Sachverstaendige: Ein Handbuch fuer die Praxis* (7th ed.). Carl Heymanns Verlag KG: Cologne.

Kahneman, D. and Tversky, A. (1973). On the psychology of prediction. *Psychological Review*, **80**, 237–251.

Kahneman, D. and Tversky, A. (1978). On the interpretation of intuitive probability: a reply to Jonathan Cohen. *Cognition*, **7**, 409–.

Kalbfleisch, J.D. and Prentice, R.L. (1980). *The Statistical Analysis of Failure Time Data.* Wiley: New York.

Kaye, D. (1979). The paradox of the gatecrasher and other stories. *Arizona State Law Journal*, 101–109.

Kaye, D. (1981). Paradoxes, Gedanken experiments and the burden of proof: a response to Dr. Cohen's reply. *Arizona State Law Journal*, **635**, 642–643.

Kaye, D. (1982). Statistical evidence of discrimination (with discussion). *Journal of the American Statistical Association*, **77**, 773–792.

Kaye, D. (ed.) (1984). *Report of the Subcommittee on Law*, Committee on Training in Statistics, American Statistical Association (forthcoming).

King, B.F. (1977). Auditing claims in a large-scale class action refund— the Antibiotic Drug Case. *The Antitrust Bulletin*, **22** (Spring), 67–93.

King, B.F. (1986). Statistics in antitrust litigation. In *Statistics and the Law*, (M.H. DeGroot, S.E. Fienberg, and J.B. Kadane, eds.). Wiley: New York, 49–78.

Kish, L. (1965). *Survey Sampling.* Wiley: New York.

Klepper, S. and Leamer, E.E. (1984). Consistent sets of estimates for regressions with errors in all variables. *Econometrica*, **52**, 163–183.

Kmenta, J. (1971). *Elements of Econometrics.* Macmillan: New York.

Krasker, Wm. S. and Pratt, J.W. (1986). Bounding the effects of proxy variables on regression coefficients. *Econometrica*, **54**, 641–655.

Kruskal, Wm. H. (1978a). Tests of significance. In *International Encyclopedia of Statistics*, Vol. II, (Wm. H. Kruskal and J.M. Tanur, eds.). The Free Press: New York, 944–958.

Kruskal, Wm. H. (1978b). Statistics: the field. In *International Encyclopedia of Statistics*, Vol. II, (Wm. H. Kruskal and J.M. Tanur, eds.). The Free Press: New York, 1071–1092.

Kruskal, Wm.H. and Tanur, J.M., *eds.* (1978). *International Encyclopedia of Statistics (2 volumes).* Macmillan: New York.

L.S.E. Jury Project (1973). Juries and the rules of evidence (W.R. Cornish, A.P. Sealy, D.A. Thomas, and D.G. Harper, Directors). *Criminal Law Review*, April, 208–223.

Langbein, J.H. (1985). The German advantage in civil procedure. Unpublished manuscript.

Lempert, R.O. (1977). Modeling relevance. *Michigan Law Review*, **75**, 1021–1057.

Levi, E.H. (1962). *Introduction to Legal Reasoning* (Rev. ed.). University of Chicago Press: Chicago.

Levin, B. and Robbins, H. (1983). Urn models for regression analysis, with applications to employment discrimination studies. *Law and Contemporary Problems*, **46** (No. 4), 247–267.

Lindley, D.V. (1977). Probability and the law. *The Statistician*, **26**, 203–212.

Loftus, E.F. (1979). *Eyewitness Testimony*. Harvard University Press: Cambridge.

Loftus, E.F. and Monahan, J. (1980). Trial by data: psychological research as legal evidence. *American Psychologist*, **35**, 270–283.

Loh, W.J. (1979). Some uses and limits of statistics and social science in the judicial process. In *Social Psychology and Discretionary Law* (L.E. Abt and I.R. Stuart, eds.). Van Nostrand: New York.

Lukaszewicz, J. (1955). O dochodzeniu ojcostwa (On establishing paternity. *Zastosowania Matematyki*, **2**, 349–379 [includes English summary].

Makov, U.E. (1987). A Bayesian treatment of the 'missing suspect' problem in forensic science. *The Statistician*, **36**, 251–258.

Manual for Complex Litigation. 2d. (1985). Federal Judicial Center, Washington, D.C.

McCabe, G.P., Jr. (1980). The interpretation of regression analysis results in sex and race discrimination problems. *American Statistician*, **34**, 212–215.

McCloskey, M. and Egeth, H. (1983). Eyewitness identification. What can a psychologist tell a jury? *American Psychologist*, **38**, 550–563.

McCormick, C.T. (1954). *Handbook of the Law of Evidence* (1st ed.). West Publishing Co.: St. Paul, MN.

McGowan, C. (1982). Testimony in Hearings before the Subcommittee on Administrative Law and Governmental Relations of the Committee on the Judiciary on H.R. 746 Regulatory Procedures Act of 1981. U.S. Government Printing Office: Washington, DC.

Meier, P., Sacks, J., and Zabell, S.L. (1984). What happened in Hazelwood: statistics employment discrimination, and the 80% rule. *American Bar Foundation Research Journal*, No. 1, 139–186.

Meier, P. and Zabell, S. (1980). Benjamin Peirce and the Howland will. *Journal of the American Statistical Association*, **75**, 497–506.

Merryman, J.H. (1969). *The Civil Law Tradition*. Stanford Univ. Press: Stanford, CA.

Michelson, S. (1986). Comments on 'Regression analyses in employment discrimination cases' by Conway and Roberts. In *Statistics and the Law* (M.H. DeGroot, S.E. Fienberg, and J.B. Kadane, eds.). Wiley: New York, 169–181.

Michelson, S. and Blattenberger, G. (1984). Reverse regression and employment discrimination. *Journal of Business and Economic Statistics*, **2**, 121–122.

Miller, A.S. and Baron, J.A. (1975). The Supreme Court, the adversary system, and the flow of information to the Justices: A preliminary inquiry. *Virginia Law Review*, **61**, 1187–1245.

Miller, J.J. (1984). Some observations, a suggestion, and some comments on the Conway-Roberts article. *Journal of Business and Economic Statistics*, **2**, 123–125.

Miller, L.S. (1987). Procedural bias in forensic science examinations of human hair. *Law and Human Behavior*, **11**, 157–163.

Miller, R.G., Jr. (1981). *Simultaneous Statistical Inference* (2nd edition). Springer-Verlag: New York.

Mode, E.B. (1963). Probability and criminalistics. *Journal of the American Statistical Association*, **58**, 628–640.

Moellenberg, D. (1984). Splitting hairs in criminal trials: admissibility of hair comparison probability estimates. *Arizona State law Journal*, 521–538.

Moenssens, A.A. (1979). The "impartial" medical expert: a new look at an old issue. *Medical Trial Technique Quarterly*, , 63–76.

Monahan, J. (1981). *The Clinical Prediction of Violent Behavior*. Public Health Service, Washington, D.C.

Monahan, J. and Walker, L. (1985). *Social Science in Law: Case and Materials*. Foundation Press: Mineola, N.Y.

Morris, F.C., Jr. (1977). *Current Trends in the Use (and Misuse) of Statistics in Employment Discrimination Litigation*. Equal Employment Advisory Council, Washington, D.C.

Morris, F.C., Jr. (1978). *Current Trends in the Use (and Misuse) of Statistics in Employment Discrimination Litigation* (2nd ed.). Equal Employment Advisory Council, Washington, D.C.

Mosteller, F., Fienberg, S.E., and Rourke, R.E.K. (1983). *Beginning Statistics with Data Analysis*. Addison-Wesley: Reading, MA.

Mosteller, F., Rourke, R.E.K., and Thomas, G.B., Jr. (1970). *Probability with Statistical Applications*, 2nd ed. Addison-Wesley: Reading, MA.

National Research Council (1979). *On the Theory and Practice of Voice Identification*. Committee on Evaluation of Sound Spectrograms, Assembly of Behavioral and Social Sciences. Washington, D.C.: National Academy of Sciences.

National Research Council (1982). *Report of the Committee on Ballistic Acoustics*. National Academy Press: Washington.

National Research Council (1983). *Risk Assessment in the Federal Government: Managing the Process*. National Academy Press: Washington.

Nelson, C.R. (1973). *Applied Time Series Analysis for Managerial Forecasting*. Holden-Day: San Francisco.

Nisbett, R. and Ross, L. (1980). *Human Inference: Strategies and Shortcomings of Social Judgment*. Prentice-Hall: Englewood Cliffs, N.J.

Obadal, A. (1983). In "Environmental Health Letter," Dec. 1, 1983, page 3.

Oliphant, R.E., *ed.* (1978). *Trial Techniques with Irving Younger*. National Practice Institute: Minneapolis, MN.

Osborn, A.S. (1929). *Questioned Documents* (2nd ed.). Boyd Printing Co.: Albany, NY.

Patefield, Wm. M. (1981). Multivariate linear relationships: maximum likelihood estimation and regression bounds. *Journal of the Royal Statistical Society* (B), 342–352.

Pearson, K. (1978). *The History of Statistics in the 17th and 18th Centuries* (E.S. Pearson, ed.). Macmillan Publishing Co., Inc.: New York.

Pike and Fischer, Inc., *ed.*. (1981). *Federal Rules of Evidence Digest.* Callaghan: Wilmette, Ill.

Pindyck, R.S. and Rubinfeld, D.L. (1982). *Econometric Models and Economic Forecasts*, 2nd ed. McGraw-Hill: New York.

Poisson, S.D. (1837). *Recherches sur la Probabilite des Jugements en Matiere Criminelle et en Matiere Civile, Precedees des Regles Generales du Calcul des Probabilites.* Bachelier: Paris.

Prosser, W.L. (1971). *Law of Torts.* West Publishing Co.: St. Paul, MN.

Rabinovitch, N. (1973). *Probability and Statistical Inference in Ancient and Medieval Jewish Literature.* University of Toronto Press: Toronto.

Reyes, R.M., Thompson, W.C., and Bower, G.H. (1980). Judgmental biases resulting from differing availabilities of arguments. *Journal of Personality and Social Psychology*, **39**, 2–12.

Rivlin, A. (1973). Forensic social science. *Harvard Educational Review*, **43**, 61–75.

Rubinfeld, D.L. (1985). Econometrics in the courtroom. *Columbia Law Review*, **85**, 1048–1097.

Rubinfeld, D.L. and Steiner, P.O. (1983). Quantitative methods in antitrust litigation. *Law and Contemporary Problems*, **46** (No. 4), 67–141.

Saks, M.J. and Baron, C.H. (Eds.). (1980). *The Use, Nonuse, Misuse of Applied Social Research in the Courts.* The Council for Applied Social Research by Abt Books: Cambridge, Mass.

Saks, M.J. and Van Duizend, R. (1983). *The Use of Scientific Evidence in Litigation.* National Center for State Courts: Williamsburg, VA.

Sanders, J., Rankin-Widgeon, B., Kalmuss, D., and Chesler, M. (1982). The relevance of "irrelevant" testimony: why lawyers use social science experts in school desegregation cases. *Law & Society Review*, **16**, 403–428.

Schneider, I. (1981). Leibniz on the probable. In *Mathematical Perspectives: Essays on Mathematics and Its Historical Development* (J.W. Dauben, ed.). Academic Press: New York.

Schofield, W. (1956). Psychology, law and the expert witness. *American Psychologist*, **11**, 1–7.

Schumacher, E.F. (1975). Small is beautiful: economics as if people mattered. Harper & Row: New York.

Severance, L.J. and Loftus, E.F. (1982). Improving the ability of jurors to comprehend and apply criminal jury instructions. *Law and Society Review*, **17**, 153–197.

Shafer, G. (1978). Non additive probabilities in the work of Bernoulli and Lambert. *Archive for History of Exact Sciences*, **12**, 97–141.

Shoben, E.W. (1978). Differential pass-fail rates in employment testing: statistical proof under Title VII. *Harvard Law Review*, **91**, 793–813.

Simon, R.J. and Mahan, L. (1971). Quantifying burdens of proof: a view from the bench, the jury, and the classroom. *Law and Society Review*, **5**, 319–330.

Simpson, E.H. (1951). The interpretation of interaction in contingency tables. *Journal of the Royal Statistical Society, Series B*, **13**, 238–241.

Smith, A.B., Jr., and Abram, T.G. (1981). Quantitative analysis and proof of employment discrimination. *University of Illinois Law Review*, **1981**, 33–74.

Solomon, H. (1971). Statistics in legal settings in federal agencies. In *Federal Statistics: Report of the President's Commission* (Vol. II). Government Printing Office: Washington, D.C.

Solomon, H. (1985). Confidence intervals in legal settings. In *Statistics and the Law* (M.H. DeGroot, S.E. Fienberg, and J.B. Kadane, eds.). Wiley: New York, 455–473.

Sprowls, R.C. (1957). The admissibility of sample data into a court of law: A case history. *UCLA Law Review*, **4**, 233–250.

Starkie, T. (1833). *A Practical Treatise of the Law of Evidence* (2nd ed.). J. and W.T. Clarke: London.

Steinhaus, H. (1954). The establishment of paternity. Wroclawskie Towarzystwa Naukowe. *Prace Wroclawskiego Towarzystwa Naukowego*, Ser. A, No. 32, 5.

Sternberg, S. (ed.) (1970). *Studies in Hebrew Astronomy and Mathematics* (by Solomon Gondz). Ktov Publishing House: New York.

Stone, A.A. (1984). *Law, Psychiatry, and Morality.* American Psychiatric Press: Washington, D.C.

Sugrue, T.J. and Fairley, Wm. B. (1983). A case of unexamined assumptions: the use and misuse of the statistical analysis of Castaneda/Hazelwood in discrimination litigation. *Boston College Law Review*, **24**, 925–960.

Tawshunsky, A. (1983). Admissibility of mathematical evidence in criminal trials. *American Criminal Law Review*, **21**, 55–79.

Taylor, S.E. and Thompson, S.C. (1982). Stalking the elusive vividness effect. *Psychological Review*, **89**, 155–181.

Thomas, Wm. A., *ed.* (1983). *Symposium on Science and the Rules of Evidence, Federal Rules Decisions*, **99**, 188–234.

Tiller, P. (1983). *Wigmore, Evidence in Trials at Common Law*, Volume IA. Little, Brown: Boston.

Tribe, L. (1971). Trial by mathematics: precision and ritual in the legal process. *Harvard Law Review*, **84**, 1329–1393.

Tversky, A. (1981). L.J. Cohen, again: On the evaluation of inductive intuitions. *Behavioral and Brain Sciences*, **4**, 354–356.

Tversky, A. and Kahneman, D. (1971). The belief in the "law of small numbers." *Psychological Bulletin*, **75**, 27–36.

Tversky, A. and Kahneman, D. (1981). The framing of decisions and the psychology of choice. *Science*, **211**, 453–458.

Underwood, B.D. (1977). The thumb on the scales of justice: burdens of persuasion in criminal cases. *Yale Law Journal*, **86**, 1299–1348.

Upton, G.J.G. (1978). *The Analysis of Cross-Tabulated Data.* Wiley: New York.

Van Matre, J.G. and Clark, Wm. N. (1976). The statistician as expert witness. *American Statistician*, **30**, 2–5.

Vidmar, N. and Ellsworth, P. (1974). Public opinion and the death penalty. *Stanford Law Review*, **26**, 1245–1270.

Weinstein, J.B. (1986). Litigation and statistics: Obtaining assistance without abuse. *Toxic Law Reporter*, **12-24-86**, 812–821.

Weinstein, J.B. and Berger, M.A. (1982). *Weinstein's Evidence*, **3**. Matthew Bender: New York.

Weisberg, S. (1980). *Applied Linear Regression*. Wiley: New York.

Wellman, F.L. (1962). *The Art of Cross-Examination* (4th ed.). Collier Books: New York (originally published in 1903).

Wells, G.L. and Loftus, E.F. (eds.) (1984). *Eyewitness Testimony: Psychological Perspectives*. Cambridge University Press: London.

Whitmore, G.A. (1986). Reynolds v. C.S.N.: Evaluating equipment damage. In *Statistics and the Law* (M.H. DeGroot, S.E. Fienberg, and J.B. Kadane, eds.). Wiley: New York, 197–219.

Wigmore, J.H. (1937). *Science of Judicial Proof* (3rd ed.) Boston.

Willerman, L. (1979). *The Psychology of Individual and Group Differences*. W.H. Freeman: San Francisco.

Williams, B. (1978). *A Sampler on Sampling*. Wiley: New York.

Wolfgang, M.E. (1974). The social scientist in court. *Journal of Criminal Law and Criminology*, **65**, 239–247.

Wonnacott, R.J. and Wonnacott, T.H. (1979). *Econometrics*, 2nd ed. Wiley: New York.

Zabell, S. (1976). Book review of *Probability and Statistical Inference in Ancient and Medieval Literature* by N.L. Rabinovitch. *Journal of the American Statistical Association*, **71**, 996–998.

Zeisel, H. (1960). The uniqueness of survey evidence. *Cornell Law Quarterly*, **45**, 322–346.

Zeisel, H. (1969). Dr. Spock and the case of the vanishing women jurors. *University of Chicago Law Review*, **37**, 1–18.

Zeisel, H. and Diamond, S.S. (1974). 'Convincing empirical evidence' on the six member jury. *University of Chicago Law Review*, **41**, 281–295.

Index of Cases

Author Index

Subject Index